**Also by Andreas C**

C000054824

WHO SHALL GOVERN CYPRUS – Brussels or Nicosia?

An in-depth analysis of the political, social and economic consequences of Cyprus' relationship with the European Union. A book for serious debate.

ANDARTES

A NOVEL
Based upon Historical Events

By
ANDREAS C CHRYSAFIS

Published by Evandia Publishing

First Published in Great Britain by
EVANDIA PUBLISHING
151 Putney High Street
London SW15 ITA

ISBN: 1–904578–01–2

A catalogue record of this book
is available from the British Library

EVANDIA PUBLISHING (UK) LTD Reg. No. 4226650

www.evandia.com

Printed and bound in Great Britain for Evandia

Dedication

In memory of those brave young lads
Innocent boys and girls in their bloom . . .
Whose lives perished . . . in brutal hangings
Or souls snuffed in battle . . .
In forgotten graves they do now lay
Forsake not their deed . . . for they chose to die
So you may be free . . .

CHAPTER ONE

IT WAS A strange day in August . . . The sweltering heat of the mid-afternoon sun appeared to be the hottest it had ever been . . .! The blinding, piercing rays parched everything in sight, and a surreal atmosphere prevailed within the shabby neighbourhood. Nobody dared to venture into the open and face the stifling heat. Exhausted and dehydrated, people shut themselves indoors and waited for this peculiar day to pass.

Undeterred, an army of black flies tirelessly buzzed over a stinking rubbish heap in search of food, and they were not disappointed; among the decomposed rubbish, a lifeless mangled-feathered rooster provided them with a feast. The stench of the dead bird floated in the stale air and drifted across the crammed enclave suffocating people's nostrils.

Suddenly, an emaciated dog took the courage, gnashed his teeth and ferociously began to chase an alley-cat for daring to approach too close to his own patch. Barking as loudly as his weak lungs could manage, the dog tried to take revenge against the intruder. Instantly, the scrawny cat dashed in circles, in fear of its life, and sprinted up a small lemon tree leaving the fierce dog beneath jumping up to reach his local arch-enemy. The cat knew that she was temporarily safe up the tree and remained unmoved preening herself until the dog lost interest. Realising it was impossible to snatch the petrified cat off the tree the dog put his tail between his legs and dejectedly sloped away. With a pounding heart and pricked ears, the cat cautiously climbed down and quickly dived inside a rubbish bin in search of scraps.

The congested shacks of the sluggish neighbourhood sprawled across a large, arid ditch that formed a small community of poverty-stricken households. The ugly shelters were put together by their occupants with makeshift building materials: rusty corrugated sheets of metal with cardboard boxes and rags as fillers for protection against wind and rain. Between them lay a mass of overgrown, dried-up thorn bushes that grew to massive heights. At the far end of the enclave a refuse tip was growing bigger and bigger each day.

The schools were in summer recess and only the young ones were brave enough to defy the unbearable heat of the day. Under the shade of a timeless, ancient, gnarled and twisted olive tree, a group of six young girls with ribbons and wilted flowers in their hair were

1

sprawled on the ground killing time playing their favourite games and gossiping, pretending they were grown-up. They marked their territory by placing small rocks on the ground to show the boundaries of their pretend homes.

At a fair distance away, a group of four boys kept to themselves under the shade of their invention: a tent made up of layers of newspapers and boxes. Now and then, a boy would creep over to the girls' territory and destroy their pretend homes. Quickly, he would run off like a bullet to find safety among his three friends, who cheered him on for his bravery. In retaliation, the girls would chase after him, screaming and shouting at the top of their lungs.

It was a welcome excuse for the girls to mingle, briefly at least, with the boys, knowing that they were forbidden to play with them. Mindfully, the girls knew a mother's eyes would always be prying to ensure they behaved like young ladies should. It was a pity, because they so much wanted to integrate their own activities with the boys and search for hidden treasure in the rubbish heap. Their screams and high-pitched voices forever echoed across the enclave, disturbing the blissful silence that dominated the area.

Occasionally, a grown-up would be awoken from his afternoon nap and chase after the noisy youngsters. Once he caught the culprit, he would give him a couple of slaps on the head and warn the others of worse to come. Half-asleep, he would return to his home, moaning and cursing them between his teeth.

The air was dry and stale, choking the drowsy atmosphere. Now and again, a car would drive by over the sand-dune causeway leaving a cloud of fine dust behind. The steep dirt road ended at a big white mansion, perched at the very top of the hill overlooking the entire neighbourhood.

Around the mound, tall bamboo canes, palm trees, massive eucalyptus trees and thickets of acacias entwined with rhododendrons, had overtaken every bit of the dry terrain. They provided welcome shade and refuge for sparrows and other birds that flocked in their hundreds.

Somewhere in the distance, a radio was playing and a woman's melodic singing drifted into the air like a dream; one could hear it, but not quite make it out! Periodically, a mother's voice would scream out her child's name, and once she got a response she would continue her chores knowing all was safe and there was no need to worry. Then, the strange silence would prevail once again.

The emaciated, black dog was busy poking his head into an empty can, foraging for food when, suddenly, his attention was

2

directed towards another dog approaching cautiously in his direction. He stopped and stared at the intruder, waggled his tail and waited . . .! The dainty new visitor appeared reluctant to get closer, and had her long floppy ears drooped low to the ground. They flapped about nervously. Eventually, the timid dog plucked up courage and went alongside the black dog. Instantly the other stopped his scavenging to investigate the new visitor. There was a brief sniffing exchanged between them, and the scrawny dog started to sniff the other dog's rear. With a miraculous quick agile manoeuvre, the dog found himself over the back of the bitch in heat, and immediately started to copulate in spasmodic movements. Submissively, the bitch let out a small, wheezing howl, and allowed the dog to have his way with her.

Like hawks, the boys did not miss what was going on and began yelling to shoo the dogs away. Once the girls realised what was happening, they too started to yell in disgust for the dogs to stop mating.

They joined the boys who had already started to throw rocks at the dogs. The girls rushed back to their lair, dismantled their make-believe homes and filled their hands with rocks. In a group effort, they flung the rocks against their victims who could not disengage from each other. They howled in agony whenever a rock found its target, but somehow, the dogs could not separate . . .! They appeared to be permanently joined at their genitalia. In desperation, the trapped animals tried to pull away from each other, but without success. Dejected and unable to disjoin, they shambled slowly away to miss the volley of missiles. The children were determined to put a stop to the dogs' behaviour and persisted for a long time with their attack against the enemy. Stuck together, with heads facing in opposite directions, the dogs eventually dislodged from each other with yelps of relief and ran off in different directions.

Pleased with themselves, the children gave out cries of jubilation and clapped their hands as a sign of success. One diminutive young girl, with long braids hanging over her shoulders, could not stomach what she had just seen and seemed quite disturbed.

'Disgusting . . .! Disgusting . . .!' she kept repeating, over and over to herself.

One of the boys in torn shorts, and with no shirt over his dust-covered torso, went up to her and stood directly in front of her.

'That's what happens to girls . . .!' He bellowed out, and started teasing her.

'Michalaki, don't lie . . .! It's not true . . .!' the timid-looking girl yelled out, refusing to believe him.

3

'You'll find out when you grow up . . .!' insisted the same chubby boy, and moved his hips to imitate the dogs copulating. In spontaneous laughter the other boys joined the rumpus, and mockingly started to tease her, moving their own hips in a copulating motion.

Embarrassed and confused, the girl started to bawl her eyes out, and thick tears quickly flooded her skinny face. Unable to take the constant teasing, she lowered her head and took off to find comfort in her mother's arms. She cried all the way home in loud sobs that were still audible from inside her rundown shack.

An argument erupted between the two groups, and the girls decided to break contact with the boys and walked away, giving them the silent treatment by not responding to any of their comments. Soon, they both settled down in their own worlds of childhood fantasies.

Bored and frustrated, they tried to make their days eventful and seeing the dogs had given them ample ammunition for excitement. Ranging between the ages of seven to ten years old, they had their whole lives ahead of them to dream and make plans for the future. For them, their present predicament of living in poverty did not come into play, nor did they complain; as long as their families were together. Knowing no other lifestyle these conditions were as normal as a passing day. They felt no shame for being poor, because they knew that once they grew up their lifestyle would change for the better. For the moment they were happy to be young and free, for tomorrow was another day and they could not imagine that far ahead.

The children remained within their own imaginings, waiting for the passage of the sun so their neighbourhood could come back to life once again. The one thing they hated most . . . was having to wash before supper or before going to bed. They could not come to terms that cleaning oneself was necessary, especially after having a wonderful time during the day. Some of them expected to receive a regular evening spanking, while others might be luckier and get away with it if their mothers were visiting a neighbour for a gossip. Often, those afternoon sessions went on for hours over a cup of Turkish coffee, and their children loved every minute of it. The local women would stand on someone's doorstep chatting away, until they were persuaded to take the weight off their feet and find comfort indoors.

By the time their mothers returned home, the children would sneak to bed hoping to avoid washing themselves. They would pretend they were asleep, but instead would prick their ears and listen to what their parents were saying. They would talk to each other in whispers but their favourite pastime in bed was eavesdropping on their parents' discussion, particularly if it concerned them. Their worst nightmare was listening to them quarrelling till late at night, and hearing their father slamming the door behind him. Often, their mother would burst into tears, and sit alone on a chair pondering what was happening to her family.

Distressed and scared, the children would get out of bed, come up to their mother and try to console her grief and anguish. But they knew that tomorrow everything would be back to normal again.

*   *   *

An overloaded two-wheeled rickety wagon, drawn by a panting black horse, was seen in the far distance slowly approaching the slum neighbourhood. It left a streak of choking dust behind that gently settled upon the dry shrubs alongside the dusty road. Incongruously laden with household goods, timber, mattresses and a number of boxes, the load tilted dangerously to one side. At the very top of the pile, two bare-chested boys were enjoying the journey perched among the mattresses. At the rear of the wobbly wagon, an exhausted looking woman positioned herself between the furnishings with her legs dangling, unable to find space for them on the deck of the shaky wagon. Over her head was a white scarf which practically covered her face offering protection against the piercing sun's rays. Slightly over-weight she sat there unmoved, holding firmly onto the side-rails to stabilise herself against the constant erratic movements of the wagon.

Seated at the front, a weather-beaten man, also wearing a scarf, carefully guided the horse to gently move forward. There was permanent anxiety on his rugged face that clearly displayed his concern that a sudden move might cause the heavy load to collapse and come tumbling down. Gradually, the man brought his wagon to a stop, directly overlooking the children playing below. His eyes scouted round the enclave as if he were looking for something.

Unsure of his whereabouts, he decided to ask the children.

'Is this area called *Loukkos*?' he asked at the top of his voice, expecting the children to hear him.

The boys looked at him hesitantly and he called out again, this time much louder. 'Is this *Loukkos*?'

'Yes, this is *Loukkos*!' answered the boys in unison and quickly hurried to where the wagon had stopped, curious to find out about the newcomers.

5

'Where does the landowner live?' he asked again, when the boys came close.

'In that big white mansion, on the hill!' answered a curly haired boy, and pointed the direction to the man.

'He must be home, because the doctor's car drove by, earlier on.' interjected another.

'His wife is not that well!' explained another . 'She's having a baby.'

In the meantime, the girls began to climb up the small embankment, not wanting to miss out on the unexpected excitement of seeing new faces. They called off their silent treatment of the boys, and decided to declare a truce hoping the boys would not object and would allow them to join the group again. To show their good intentions, they wrapped ribbons around their wrists as a sign of peace and raised their hands up in the air, so the boys could see them and accept their peace treaty. As the enemy showed no resistance, they gathered around the loaded wagon and mingled with the boys, who became quite jovial about this whole new scenario.

Immediately, the two boys perched on top of the load carefully climbed down and joined the rest of the youngsters.

'You stay put until we come back . . .!' the man ordered his sons, and took off with his wife to see the landowner.

The couple appeared tired and exhausted from the journey and their worn-out garments were completely dust-covered from top to bottom. There was a serious expression on their faces and their dried-up chapped lips clearly showed signs of dehydration. In a slow trek, they both challenged the steep hill, until they disappeared beyond the bend.

The barefooted youngsters congregated around the wagon and began to examine it with curiosity, in case something of interest might catch their eyes. Cautiously, the girls surrounded the horse and they began stroking it gently and feeling the roughness of its sweaty hide. Totally obedient, the horse allowed them to continue their inspection of him from his mane to his hooves. Thirsty, the horse kept moving his head about in agitation, and a stream of saliva dribbled onto the scorched earth below. An army of large flies flocked about his wet, protruding lips, attempting to suck every available bit of moisture. Their constant nibbling irritated their victim, who kept moving his head about trying to shake them off— but without much success.

One of the girls, dressed in a long white dress, felt sorry for the horse and came to his rescue. She picked a scrap of paper off the ground and started to shoo away the persistent flies.

6

'Get some water someone . . .!' she ordered the others and puckered her pretty face.

Immediately one of the girls ran off towards the enclave's communal water tap and returned with a half-filled pail of water, spilling most of it on her way back. Gently, she placed the bucket on the ground under the horse's head and stood aside, beckoning the horse to drink up. It did not take much convincing because, once the horse realised there was water in front of him, he lowered his head and drank the bucket empty.

'Be careful not to spook him.' the eldest of the two newcomers warned, fearful lest the horse might get spooked and lose its load.

'My father had a horse,' replied the same girl, sure of herself and paying no attention to him. 'I used to feed our horse all the time . . . I know all about horses! This one looks very tame!' she added, and stared at the new boy who was standing next to her.

'Where was that?' asked the new boy.

'At Kantara village . . .'

'I have been there once . . .!' interjected the boy with torn shorts.

'Michalaki . . .! You are always a boaster and a liar you have never left *Loukkos.*' insisted the same girl with indifference, and turned her attention to the new boy. 'Where do you come from?' she asked, being curious to find out more about the newcomers.

'From a village near Kerynia but . . .

'I have been there too . . .!' the same chubby boy shouted at the top of his voice, and interrupted the new kid.

'*Loukkos* . . .! *Loukkos* . . .! *Loukkos* . . .!' Everyone chanted aloud. They screamed and ran in circles around Michalaki, who didn't seem to mind and laughed the incident away.

In no time at all, the youngsters gave the impression that they had known each other for years, and talked like friends rather than strangers. Destiny had brought them together and their lives were about to intermingle within this god-forsaken area full of destitute souls. The two new boys listened with great interest to everything about their new surroundings. But the best part about this enclave was that it was within walking distance of the seafront and they could go swimming daily. This was a great change from the last place they had stayed at, which was in a lifeless, arid place without trees but rocks and gravel.

The eldest of the new boys introduced himself as Alexis, and his younger brother's name was Marcos, who just started his third year at school. The local youngsters wasted no time and accepted the new boys into their group. Friendship was very important for them at that tender age, and they depended on each other for support and companionship, as a means of escaping their miserable surroundings. Growing up was difficult at the best of times, but for them even more so, having to cope with the daily struggle of poverty.

They congregated together at the top of the embankment waiting for their parents' return, while young Marcos was getting agitated and bored. He was invited to visit the boys' hide-out at the bottom of the slope and check out the refuse site, but appeared reluctant, fearing his dad's wrath. He needed the moral support of his older brother and begged him to join them, but Alexis was adamantly against leaving the wagon unattended.

'Just for a little while . . .!' he implored.

'You know very well what will happen!'

One of the boys, with thick, black, curly hair and dark skin, about the same age as Alexis, tried to convince him to change his mind. He pleaded with him but without success. When he spoke, Alexis detected a slight accent in his speech and realised he was not Greek.

'We won't be long . . . come and see our hide-out . . .!' pleaded the boy, anxious to have him join them.

Before Alexis could answer him, his young brother took off with the rest. With a few long leaps, they found themselves sliding down the sandy slope of the embankment, leaving a cloud of dust behind. The girls also decided to go back to their own private patch, under the shade of their large olive tree and away from the scorching heat.

Young Alexis was left behind, standing alone on the embankment, watching the others take off amid laughter and jubilant noises, but he could not bring himself to leave the wagon unattended. He was quite aware what might happen to him if something went wrong. Being the eldest of the two, he always got the blame for everything. If Marco broke something, he received the punishment on his behalf—'you should have looked after the young one,'—was the phrase used most often by his mother. If he took something from his brother—'let the young one have that first,'—another one of those frequent phrases used by his parents. He could never win . . . The responsibility fell upon his shoulders to ensure all was well.

He approached the frothing horse, and began to stroke his head gently. He then started speaking to him words of endearment and feeling sorry for the animal having to bear the scorching heat of the day and also carry such a heavy load. 'I am glad I am not a horse' he thought to himself, and examined the glazed eyes of the horse that stared past him.

His thoughts were interrupted by hearing someone approaching from below the embankment. It was the dark-haired boy, the one with a slight accent.

'Why don't you come?' asked the boy, eager to make friends with him.

'If father realises we left the wagon he will kill me!' answered Alexis.

'Are you going to live here?' the boy asked again and came alongside him.

'Maybe. My father can't find a job anywhere . . .' Alexis answered, and looked to see if his parents were on their way back. 'What are you, are you a Turk or Armenian?' he asked, curious about the boy's accent.

'I am Turk, my name is Ahmet. I was born in Ammohostos!' explained the boy then sat crossed-legged on the ground. Alexis sat next to him and both watched the other boys playing in the far distance.

'Where is that?'

'Not far, I'll take you there if you like . . .! We can explore the harbour! There are huge ships that come close to the street, one can touch them,' Ahmet explained, trying to convince his new friend.

Impressed, Alexis nodded his head in amazement. The boys made small talk, chatted away and a bond began to develop between the two. They appeared to understand each other and felt at ease talking with one another.

Wearing only shorts, their sun-tanned bodies and legs were raked with dust. Alexis was not as dark in complexion as Ahmet, but rather fairer, with brown hair and wide brown eyes. He also had a slim physique where Ahmet appeared to be more robust and more masculine. What made Ahmet stand out among other children was his wonderful smile and his set of white teeth that seemed to sparkle whenever he opened his mouth. He spoke in a soft manner and seemed to have a caring disposition towards others, but above all else, he did not give the impression that he was in any way selfish. Alexis liked him and felt that he made a pal unexpectedly. Gaining a new friend would make the transition of settling there much easier, and this Turkish boy seemed quite willing to be of help.

'I hope you will stay here . . .! There are not many rich people in the area except for the landowner but, he is not so bad! He is a kind man, and he always rewards us with candy or ice-cream whenever we wash his car . . .!' Ahmet persisted, trying to convince his new friend how good this part of the town was.

'In our last neighbourhood there were too many rich snobs . . . they threw us out!' explained Alexis, and let his innocent eyes inspect the area. 'It looks nice here . . .!' he said, and nodded his head approvingly.

Those words were music to Ahmet's ears and he clapped his hands very loudly with joy. He was a very inquisitive lad and wanted to know all about his newly found friend. Alexis obliged, convinced that today his life had taken a turn for the better.

They both started to dig their toes into the finely powdered dust, forcing it to form a small, popping cloud; the harder they pressed, the greater the height the dust floated in the air over their bare feet. Sitting on the ground, they waited for Alexis' parents to return and tell them of their decision.

'I have another younger sister, my aunt will bring her later!' Alexis informed his new pal as a matter of fact.

'Me too, she lives with my aunt . . .! They have adopted her because we cannot afford another mouth to feed. They live within the Walls of Ammohostos. There is a great bazaar to check-out,' Alexis' new friend said convincingly.

At that moment, the boys noticed Alexis' parents walking towards them. They got off the ground, and both ran to meet them, anxious to find out their fate.

'Are we going to stay?' Alexis burst out, the moment he approached his parents.

'Yes . . .!' his father said dryly.

Alexis thought his father had aged rapidly lately. His hair had turned much greyer and even his bushy moustache had changed colour to match his hair. At least he was not balding, but his hair was receding over his temples. He looked at his father's tired face covered in sweat and felt sorry for him, recognising the hardships this man had gone through to bring the family up. The grey trousers he was wearing were worn out and sown with so many different coloured patches it was impossible to distinguish their original colour. Today, he wore his white, short-sleeve shirt, a present from his mother-in-law, so he could impress the landowner.

His mother also appeared to be getting older. She was putting on weight and starting to feel heavy and slow. But one thing that never changed was her warm compassionate character and gentleness. She never complained about anything as long as her family was close to her, and never once demanded the impossible from Alexis' father. Always supportive, she was her husband's right hand, no matter what difficulties they encountered. Alexis loved them both dearly, and could not wait to grow up and help them in every way possible to overcome the awful poverty that seemed to follow them everywhere.

'Where is your brother?' asked his father, realising Marcos was nowhere to be seen.

'Over there . . .! Playing . . .!' answered Alexis and began to call Marcos to come before his father got angry.

Marcos instantly showed up with blood smudges all over his face, followed by the other boys. There was a guilty expression on his face and he avoided making direct eye contact with his parents because he knew the outcome.

'What happened to you?' his father asked angrily and grabbed him firmly by the ear, inspecting his face. Marcos did not make a sound nor did he object to his father's painful grip; he'd rather put up with a lesser pain than face his father's spanking.

'He was wrestling, but it was a friendly fight . . .' one of the boys started to explain.

'Okay! That's enough! We have plenty of work to do,' Marco's father interrupted and slapped him gently on the head.

The woman grabbed her son, held his head with both hands and gazed at his face and small, bleeding wound. Satisfied it was not serious she slapped him once on the cheek, as a warning.

'Go and pee and dab the wound . . .!' she said angrily to Marcos, who knew precisely what he had to do, this not being the first time he had got into a similar situation.

'But I don't want to go!' he objected with irritation.

'You just try . . . it will come out you will see!' his mother insisted angrily.

Embarrassed for getting a lecture in front of the other children, Marcos stomped across the dirt road without uttering a single word. He picked up a discarded tin off the parched ground and walked away from them. He pulled his pants down, squeezed his bladder and half filled the rusty can with his urine.

'You know what to do . . .!' his mother shouted after him.

Marcos furiously put his fingers into the can and reluctantly began to wipe his wound with his warm urine.

'. . . Especially the wound . . .!' his mother yelled at him again, and paid no further attention to him.

'Let's go and find a good spot . . .!' the man said to his wife and both walked down the slope of the embankment. They searched the compound and settled for an area at the bottom of the hill close to a cluster of bushes and palm trees.

'This is perfect . . .!' said the man, quite satisfied there was some shade.

His wife agreed and both returned to the stationary wagon from where the youngsters refused to move an inch in anticipation of the activity that was about to take place. The man picked up the reins of his horse, and on foot carefully guided the horse towards a nearby sloping section of the embankment that was not so steep. He slowly steered the horse down the gradual slope with all the children trailing behind in complete silence worried that the heavy load might tip over. Once at the bottom, he directed the horse to their chosen plot of land and began to make a clearing.

Without hesitation, the children volunteered and started removing loose rocks from the immediate area.

After a while, Alexis' father noticed that all the youngsters were sneaking small, smooth rocks into their pockets and discarding others aside. He pointed this out to his wife, who had also observed this strange behaviour. He decided to put his mind at rest and called one of the boys.

'What is your name son?' he asked a blonde boy with long legs.

'Spyros.' the lad answered and stood at attention.

'Tell me Spyros . . . what are those rocks in your pockets for?' he asked, curious to learn their purpose. 'I hope it's not for breaking windows!'

'No sir . . .!' answered the boy firmly '. . . they are bum-rocks.'

'Bum-rocks . . .?

'Yes . . .!'

'You mean bum-wipers . . .!'

'Yes, bum-wipers, you don't want to go into the toilet here . . .!'

'Why . . .?'

'You can die in there . . .!' the boy whispered and shook his head about.

'It's that bad . . . eh?' the man said and smiled at the self-assured boy.

'. . . We always use those bushes!' the boy whispered again pointing towards a cluster of thick shrubs. He walked off and carried on with his task alongside the rest of the children.

They unloaded the wagon and put all their belongings aside at a fair distance from the clearing. The man outlined the area of their home and started to dig holes in the hard soil. It was a very difficult undertaking, considering the dry earth was full of hard rocks and small boulders. By the time he finished digging the necessary holes his face, forehead and the upper part of his exposed hirsute body was covered in sweat. His armpits released a strong odour of rank sweat and the children kept their distance from him, unable to cope with such a stench. Periodically, he splashed himself with water from a clay pitcher his wife brought over, but that was never enough to cool him down. Determined, he carried on working without a rest, eager to finish before nightfall so the children could sleep indoors rather than spend the night out in the open. He was fortunate these eager youngsters were prepared to give him a helping hand. They were quite helpful in scouting the area for any kind of material that could be of any use. Like busy little beavers, they kept going back and forth, bringing discarded boxes, wood and all sorts of things that might be useful as building materials.

The constant banging of nails and general commotion soon attracted the attention of the other neighbours. The first one to arrive was a jolly looking fellow in his mid-fifties, with hardly any hair on his head and slightly overweight.

'Welcome to the neighbourhood!' he called out and greeted the newcomers from a fair distance away. Lethargically, he approached the site, and looked around briefly, nodding his balding head with approval and staring at the cheerful local youngsters, who were chattering ceaselessly.

'They call me Vasili . . . I am the local trouble-shooter here . . .! In my official capacity . . . I offer my services!' he boasted to the newcomers and removed his shirt, exposing his potbelly . . . ready to do battle with the nails and sheets of corrugated metal that were scattered around the yard.

As soon as he came close, the man extended his arm out and they exchanged a warm handshake.

'Thank you, Vasili . . .! We could do with some help . . .!' said the man, pleased that someone was offering them assistance. 'They call me Yiorkis . . . and this is my wife Soteria, and our two children,' he quickly added, introducing himself and his family.

'Don't worry, we'll have this place up in no time at all,' said Vasili with confidence and turned around towards the chubby little boy.

'Michalaki, you go and tell Andrea, Stavro, Moutta and Harilao to come here om the double!' the man ordered, in his deep, harsh voice.

'What if they are asleep, *papa*?' the boy asked.

'You wake them up . . .! Do exactly what you do to me!' he commanded and gave his son an endearing kick on his rounded behind.

The boy took to his heels with no further ado. He cannoned towards the enclave and disappeared among the huts.

'Where do you folks come from?' Vasili asked, while waiting for the extra workforce to arrive.

'Ayios Amvrosios . . . near Kerynia.'

'Ah . . .! The famous land of golden apricots . . .!' Vasili exclaimed enviously. 'I have been there once . . .! It's a beautiful village overlooking the sea, mountains . . . nice place . . .!'

'Yes, but no work! We had a coffee house there but lost it to the money lenders.'

'Them blood suckers they're everywhere . . .! There should be a law against them scoundrels! They suck the life out of poor peasants and prosper on other people's misery.'

Yiorkis agreed with him and spat out a large glob of phlegm on the ground in disgust, remembering what happened to him when dealing with such unscrupulous people in his ancestral village.

Michalaki was seen leading a group of reluctant men to lend a hand to their new neighbours at the expense of their afternoon nap. They had personally experienced a similar situation in the past, and knew precisely what it feels like to be homeless. One good deed deserves another, and they were more than ready to do their share with no demands. It was the least they could do to help their fellow-man in need.

Soon, the whole area became alive with men and women assisting each other in putting up the hut. The youngsters' jubilant yelling and shouting woke everyone in the locality and soon other people joined, including women and children, anxious to be of help.

'Just keep the water coming Kyra-Soteria and we will do the rest.' Vasili kept shouting at the top of his voice so he could be heard above the commotion. He appointed himself the foreman of the project—and he wasn't doing a bad job either.

By nightfall, the men put up a structure of two rooms and an adjacent side room, which acted as a small kitchen. They covered the sides and roof with sheets of corrugated metal over a wooden frame. After a lengthy argument, the men managed to agree on the appropriate angle of the roof-pitch for the rain to run off. When the building was finished everybody, including the children, stood back and admired their handy-work. Tired and exhausted, some of the men sprawled wearily on the ground, relieved they had finally completed their work before the evening fell upon them.

'I told you not to worry . . .!' Vasili kept repeating proudly, and praising himself for his achievement. Yiorkis could not thank him enough.

'We shall never forget your kindness we are indebted to you all . . .!' he kept saying to all the men and women who worked so hard.

Kyra-Soteria, with the help of other women, got busy organising her household goods and putting them in place. She unpacked the boxes and got all the plates, pots and pans out, and carefully put them in the right order in her makeshift kitchen. Her sister and her husband had also arrived, bringing with them Soteria's young daughter, Maro.

Maro was a tiny, bouncing girl, with an olive complexion highlighting her alert, striking black eyes. Wearing her favourite flowery yellow dress and long, braided, black ponytail, she instantly jumped on her dad and wouldn't let go of him. He cuddled her and held her in his arms for a long time until his wife separated them.

'We have exhausted our bodies . . . it is now time to exhaust our stomachs!' Yiorkis announced with gratitude and invited everyone to share a meal.

There were no objections . . .! On the contrary, they got excited at the prospect of such a gathering. They welcomed any excuse to liven up their monotonous lives—for one evening at least . . . The women got busy with the preparation of food while Kyra-Soteria's overweight sister slit with an expert movement, the throats of two hens and one troublesome rooster. She dumped them in a large pot full of scalding hot water for a brief moment, sat on a low stool, and then began to pluck their feathers one-by-one.

The men started a large wood fire in the open in anticipation of making *souvla* with fresh chicken morsels, and other meats, that soon accumulated for the occasion. Never empty-handed, the locals kept going back and forth, bringing cuts of meat and other foods to ensure the evening was a success and to celebrate the arrival of their new neighbours.

Ahmet's mother, a weak pale-looking woman, brought a pot of a Turkish speciality dish of lamb stew with aubergines and plenty of garlic. She joined the other women, and seemed quite happy with the lively festivities and never stopped talking in her broken Greek.

She had lost her husband two years earlier and she never got over his death. She lived in a constant morbid depression, wishing she could join him in eternity. Many times, the women found her sitting alone, crying her eyes out in absolute despair. Concerned about her, her neighbours did their utmost to console her, but they were confronted with an impossible task—she wished to die so she could be free forever . . .! Now that she smiled again, the women were encouraged and joked with her all evening in anticipation that maybe the worst was over and she was on her way to overcome her grief. These newcomers brought a new spark to life, and she felt good watching her son making friends with this Greek boy. She observed that he was a likable young lad, and she mingled contentedly with the chatty women. For a brief moment, she even forgot her state of mind and became excited about the whole affair.

The gathering turned festive and no-one could wait for the feast to begin. The children, hungry and tired, stayed put and were not prepared to miss out on this unexpected good fortune. They knew that tonight no-one would get spanked or go to bed early, but

15

instead, they would stuff themselves with food until they could no longer move.

Nightfall came and ozone pleasantly drifted in with the gentle breeze from the nearby seashore. A full moon glowed majestically in the vast clear sky, which was covered in a myriad of twinkling stars scattered throughout the immense hemisphere. Now and again, a bright shooting star shot across the vastness and disappeared into the distance, to the excitement of the children who lay flat on the ground, watching the starry sky and trying to anticipate the next shooting star. While feasting their eyes in the darkness, the whiff of the grilled morsels of meats on the open fire titillated their taste-buds and they could not wait to get their teeth into it. With rumbling stomachs, they continually complained to the adults to hurry things up so they could dig their teeth into the grilled meat off the spit. The persistent ones often got a slap as a warning to the others.

When the women had finally finished their never-ending preparations, they joined a few tables together and covered the resulting long table with an assortment of foods and salads for the feast to begin. Some distance away from the adults, they spread out straw mats on the ground and organised the children's food as a priority so they would stop their grumbling.

Happily, about a dozen children, girls and boys, grouped together, and began their long awaited task of devouring the food. In high spirits, like a flock of ravenous sparrows, their voices chirped away constantly.

The simple supper developed into a feast of neighbourly bonding, with plenty of *zivania* and wine. The men and women were jubilant and often erupted into spontaneous laughter. Their jovial voices echoed into the night with excitement and happiness seldom experienced within this enclave. Tonight, they succumbed to the joys of life rather than dwelling on their fate . . . They made merry by eating, drinking and bonding as one family and, as a result, they temporarily threw away the cast-iron ball and chain weighing their lives down.

One of the younger men went and got his accordion and volunteered to entertain everyone with his skilful playing. With fingers like lightning, he pressed the keys hard and moved his swift fingers agilely to force tangos and other popular tunes to fill the evening air. The sound of music quickly spread across the neighbourhood and soon other locals arrived to join the merry throng. When his accordion released, from deep inside its bowels, a well-known tune, all the men, women and children joined in and sang the words. Nobody, not even God, could stop them singing the night away. Their lusty singing amplified across the enclave making the women grab their men and force them to dance with them.

The men danced with passion while the children urged them on by clapping their hands in unison to the rhythm of the tune. Already inebriated, the men drank even more, and did not give a damn about anything. Tonight's activity came to them as a blessing, and they cherished every minute of it, for it might never repeat itself. This unexpected gathering was a golden opportunity never to be missed and they made sure to give it their best! Everyone was living for tonight, and kept singing at the top of their voices:

'To hell with tomorrow . . . to hell with tomorrow . . . for it may never come . . .!'

Vasili appeared to be the most energetic of all the men. He let his protruding flabby potbelly out of his loose shirt and never stopped dancing all night. It seemed that his behind was full of razor-sharp needles and he dare not sit down in case they pricked him to the bone. Instead, he danced and sang with the worst voice that God could possibly give to a man. His round face was covered in sweat, but that did not stop him, and he kept demanding a dry towel from his wife to wipe his face. His son Michalaki, who was the spitting image of his father, often joined him, and together they dominated the dancing area alongside the crowded table. They constantly shoved others aside for extra dancing space. If no space was available, they danced on their own—father and son—in the open field away from everyone. Under the brilliance of millions of stars and guided by the brightness of a majestic moon, they moved about like dark silhouettes, dancing with their own moon shadows, oblivious of all the others. Only the endless, piercing sound of crickets and cicadas seemed to get the better of them.

By the time the food was finished, nobody cared any more what they were drinking—*zivania, ouzo,* or wine; everything tasted the same . . .! The men gulped their drinks and became so intoxicated that some of them could not stand on their own two feet. They flopped onto the nearest chair and remained there unmoved. Not even a mighty wrestler could pull them off their seats. They moved their heads with difficulty and rolled their eyes trying to make sense what was going on around them. Some men who had drunk more than they could handle began to snore much to the embarrassment of their wives who kept prodding them to wake up. But they stubbornly refused to budge from this place, in case they missed out on something.

17

Yiorkis also drank with joy and was in great spirits. He picked up a carving knife and took the initiative to dance a traditional dance from his village to show the others how it was done—the proper way . . .! He hitched up his breeches and plucked up courage to stretch his tired bones like a twenty-year-old. With the long knife shining against the moonlight, he instructed the young musician to play a well-known folk dance. No sooner did the music drift into the air than he nimbly and bravely sprang to his feet . . .! The crowd formed a large circle around this dark-haired, haggard man with greying temples, and gave him space to dance. The children joined in by squatting around the circle, and spontaneously clapping their hands to encourage him, but Yiorkis did not need encouragement; *zivania* gave him ample strength and fuel to show these people how the dance-of-the-knife was done, even if he was dizzy from too much alcohol.

With the knife sparkling in his raised hand, he moved to the rhythm of the intoxicating music. He became one with the music, and could not see anyone . . . His vision turned blurry and his head was buzzing with the constant clapping and uproar of the spectators. Vasili handed him a glass of *zivania* for extra fuel. He gulped it down in one go and instantly threw the empty glass over his head and smashed it to pieces against a rock. He skilfully manipulated the sharp knife close to his chest and mouth . . . He jumped about in leaps and turns, like an elegant young gazelle, to the astonishment of everyone. With his open shirt hanging over his trousers, he raised his long arms in the air, kicked his legs and danced wildly with streams of sweat pouring down his rugged face. He could feel his heart pulsating like a wild drum wanting to burst out of his ribcage, and his lean body was soon bathed in sweat. After a while, he threw the sharp knife onto the ground and it instantly wedged itself into the earth. He briefly danced around the shuddering knife and then turned his back to it. With a swift jump, he did a somersault and picked up the knife with his teeth and, with another agile movement he sprang up to his feet again. That manoeuvre left everyone stunned. A deafening applause followed and everyone, young and old, praised him for such a feat, especially while being so drunk. His wife shook her head, as if to say, what a crazy husband she had married. But deep down, she felt quite proud of him. She gave him a gentle kiss on his sweat-covered cheek as if to say thank you, and then she went to join the other women who were beginning to get fidgety and tired.

It was well past midnight when everyone started to leave . . . Most of the men were completely drunk, but they had their wives to help them. They leaned on them for support, and clumsily walked away into the night. Others remained sprawled on the ground insisting to sleep it off until the next morning.

Food was scattered all over the place and the women decided to leave the clearing up for the next day when they would have their energy back and were clear-headed. Finally, one by one the guests departed and scrambled across the field to find sanctuary in their own homes, and nurse their headaches from over-indulgence in food, happiness and alcohol.

A blissful silence had fallen upon the neighbourhood once again, and a prevailing hush stretched its massive veil to engulf drunk and sober alike. It was soon replaced by the reverberating, all pervading sound of cicadas' and crickets' mating-calls that turned into a wild frenzy in their search for willing partners.

Daylight had finally decided to cast its first pallid light across the horizon, and a brilliant morning glow shone over the globe in full glory. A couple of hungry stray dogs appeared sniffing for scraps. They grabbed a bone each to gnaw upon and ran off.

CHAPTER TWO

THE WEEKS AND months monotonously rolled by and Yiorkis and his family settled down into their new environment. They were made to feel welcome and felt part of the community among people who shared the same fate. Everyone tried to cope with the pressures of unemployment and the struggle of earning a meal. Those who had a job to go to often laboured long hours for a pittance and others took any menial job they could lay their hands on.

Peasants from rural areas roamed the town in their thousands, searching for elusive jobs that rarely materialised. The majority, if they had no kin living in the main cities to help them temporarily, ended up in places like *Loukkos*. With no other choice, the destitute depended on willing landowners to permit them to put up a shack for a small fee. The lucky ones left the country, leaving their families behind, by emigrating to strange, distant places like Australia, America, England and other countries willing to take them in as cheap labour.

During the last war, as an inducement to join the British war effort, young lads and men were promised security and jobs after the war. In response, they volunteered by their thousands to join the British Cyprus Regiment. Nostalgia for freedom, being the inherited spirit of the Greek nation, motivated these men and women to join the Regiment and put their lives at risk for a mere promise. Some of the lucky ones returned to their families; others were left behind, in forgotten unmarked graves.

Upon their return, the only reward the surviving soldiers received was a complete disregard of all promises made by His Majesty's government, which conveniently threw these men to the turbulent winds of fate. Weak and vulnerable, they felt betrayed, but could not complain or demand their rights from the British Empire that chose not to honour its commitment.

As a result of this, they succumbed to their destiny feeling abandoned and whole families, heavily in debt, wandered on horse-drawn wagons throughout the island, trying to secure some kind of living.

Yiorkis decided to move and settle in the coastal town of Varoshia. Being blessed with deep port facilities and fertile vegetation, this town offered greater possibilities for employment and one day he loaded his wagon and moved there.

He knew it would be quite difficult at first, but he had determination and the willpower to make things happen. He always believed that good things happen because people make them happen, and bad things happen because people allow them to happen. Not shy of working hard, he had an industrious mind and he was never afraid of any obstacles that came his way. He was determined to make good things happen, and he would grab the bull by the horns and plunge into deep waters if it meant security for his family.

Back in his village, he learned the art of making ice cream, taught to him by an Italian friend. Making ice cream during the summer months became his regular profession. In the winter months, he prepared sesame snacks or candy and wandered on foot all over the town trying to sell them. It was not easy, but his vigour and stamina paid off; he could at least feed his family and would never starve.

In his many wanderings he frequently came across people in utter destitution, who could not feed their own families, and often felt touched by their misery. Generous and kind-hearted, he always tried to alleviate their pangs of hunger by offering them assistance if he could. 'Do a good deed and chuck it to the sea!' he always used to say to his wife whenever he came across someone who needed help. His wife would look deep into his brown eyes and nod her head with approval, knowing he would never allow himself to abandon his deep sense of generosity.

That was his character, and she felt proud of his considerate disposition towards others. He was a caring man, and he could not bear seeing others suffer if it was in his power to help those in a worse position. Often, he would come home and complain to his wife for not being able to help someone. All night he would feel guilty, and pace up and down, angry with himself for letting someone down. 'It's not within your power to help all those poor souls . . .!' his wife would say to him full of pity, trying to make him feel better.

Kyra-Soteria, his devoted wife, managed to secure a job washing linen in a local private clinic. Before sunrise she would get up, get the children ready and take off for work. She would toil all day, scrubbing by hand mountains of bloodstained sheets and nurses' uniforms and rarely return home before sunset. She frequently remained behind at the clinic till very late at night, with no additional pay, to ensure she did not give cause for the management to replace her. She was quite aware how vulnerable her position was, knowing that hundreds of other women were ready to take her place at a moment's notice. She worked very hard to the point of collapse at times, but she persevered and continued to get the job done well. Her hands, from constantly scrubbing dirty linen in hot water, always ached and in a matter of few months they had swollen and turned red. But she was not prepared to lose her job. She put up with the excruciating pain, and never complained; rather she was grateful that someone gave her the opportunity to work.

Like every other morning, Kyra-Soteria got out of bed and found her husband outside sitting alone in the yard, drinking a cup of coffee and enjoying the peaceful silence of early dawn. There were still a few faded, scattered stars visible in the morning sky, but these were disappearing rapidly against the rising glow of the morning sun. Not a single cloud was in sight—an indication that another hot day was about to emerge in its full glory to make their lives miserable.

Yiorkis was staring into nothing, in anticipation of getting his body off the chair and heading for the seafront to gather salt for the preparation of ice cream.

'You are up very early . . .!' she said to her husband, and stroked his hair lightly.

'I did not want to wake you up . . .! Today could be a busy day at the market.' he answered softly so as not to wake up the children. He was already dressed and ready to depart, but waited for his wife to get up so they could make small talk before leaving.

Somewhere in the shrubbery, a rooster started to puff out his lungs . . . craned his colourful neck . . . and raised his beak arrogantly in the air. Suddenly, he let out a piercing and prolonged crow across the neighbourhood demanding that everyone should wake up. His persistent, reverberating call continued for some time but, ultimately, he was confronted with stiff competition from another rooster at the opposite side of the enclave. Both took it upon themselves to ensure that no one stayed in bed, while the hens joined in and began to cackle about in search of food.

The couple sat next each other and shared a slice of bread and *hallumi* cheese. They talked for a little while, when both had noticed Ahmet in shorts cutting across the field and walking towards them. He looked sleepy and wore a red, sleeveless shirt that hung loose over his shorts.

'*Kalimera* Ahmet . . .!' Yiorkis said to him, as he joined them. 'What are you doing up so early?'

'It's Saturday . . .!' the boy exclaimed as a matter of fact, and stood in front of them with slightly puffy eyes and tousled hair.

'So it is . . .'

'Alexis and I want to help you collect salt . . .!' explained the boy and looked around to see if his friend was up. Realising he was still in bed he frowned and walked off to wake him up.

'He should have been up by now . . .!' young Ahmet muttered angrily to himself, and disappeared indoors.

Yiorkis looked at his wife and smiled at the attitude of the young lad, who was always at their house spending time with Alexis and the other children. They considered him part of the family, and they got so accustomed to him and missed him when he was not about.

'They are growing very fast . . .!' his wife said in a sceptical mood.

'Few more months and the boys will be out of school. Then, we shall see.'

'See what . . .?'

'What I mean is, we shall see what kind of job they will end up with, that's all . . .! he said.

'I am not worried about the two boys, you'll see . . .!' she said confidently.

There were a few voices heard momentarily from inside the house, and then the two lads, dressed in shorts, walked out and joined the grown-ups. No sooner had they sat down than Alexis' mother got off her chair so she could get organised and leave for work.

She picked up her straw carrying basket and put inside it a piece of bread, olives, cheese and a couple of tomatoes for her lunch. She covered the food-stuff with a towel and gently kissed both boys goodbye and took off for work.

They saw her disappear beyond the embankment, wearing her usual black scarf over her head for protection against the sun. She appeared to be dragging her feet, but she pressed on, undeterred by her slightly overweight condition that was beginning to slow her down. This had become her daily ritual, day in and day out, seven days a week. She longed for that one special day, when she would spend her remaining days caring for her children . . . but that was not to be. Only her heart was aware of such an unattainable dream, and she prayed to God to make a miracle and bring about that precious day before she died.

For the moment, she accepted her fate and could only hope for better days ahead. She grew older and lived with that one elusive dream, but, when she got distressed, she often cursed their predicament for living all these years in poverty. It seemed intractable, and was part of their lives.

Alexis hurriedly washed his face. He quickly picked up a piece of bread, stuffed it into his mouth and grabbed the clay water pitcher.

With a swift movement, he poured a long guzzle of cold water into his mouth, spilling most of it over his face. He had developed a lean physique and seemed tall for his age, with long legs and arms to match. With his brown hair cropped close to his head, his high cheekbones and facial features appeared chiselled and prominent while the hair at his temples had turned golden-blonde from the sun and match his well-defined sun-bleached eyebrows. His alert brown eyes appeared to be constantly on the lookout for something, and he rarely spoke without a smile. But above all else, he had a pleasant and likeable personality. Because of this, he quickly made many friends who kept visiting his home asking him to join in their activities. At the same time he was a sensitive, caring boy, 'taking after his father,' as his mum kept saying whenever his parents discussed the boys.

As soon as his wife departed for work, Yiorkis organised his rickety push cart and placed a couple of metal buckets inside the holding bay. Then he went back into the house to check on the young ones who were fast asleep and curled up close to one another. He decided not to disturb them and went outside where his two helpers waited patiently for his instructions.

'Are we ready?' he asked, and grabbed the handles of his cart

'Wait, I'll go pee first!' Alexis said and ran towards the bushes at the bottom of the hill.

'Me too!' said Ahmet and followed suit.

A few minutes later they both returned and the three of them took off on foot towards the seafront, pushing their cart along.

They passed the long row of the massive eucalyptus trees, that colonnaded both sides of the main road leading to the waterfront, and in no time at all they arrived at the King George Hotel—a favourite spot for British servicemen and their families. The hotel was sited directly on a golden, sandy beach and was constantly busy throughout the year because of its prominent beachfront location.

At this early hour, the crystal blue sea was always calm and tranquil. Not a single wave was visible. Only the soft swishing of the rippling sea breaking onto the sandy shore broke the silence of the morning. The sea breeze pleasantly filled everyone's nostrils with pure, unpolluted ozone, and the boys decided to splash their bare feet by walking along the shoreline.

They passed *Glossa*, another favourite spot with bathers, and then headed towards *Petres* where the Costantia Hotel stood proudly at the very edge of masses of shallow, sharp- edged reefs which acted as a safety barrier against the tidal waves of the open blue sea. Early risers had already picked their spot on the beach, and left their

24

towels unattended while taking a splash or a swim across the calm waters of the secluded crescent bay.

The boys paid no attention to them and continued forward to reach their destination. They left their cart behind, picked up their baskets and got onto the reefs, walking very carefully to avoid the sharp edges of the skin-tearing black volcanic rocks. There was hardly anyone about; they had the whole place to themselves except for a lone figure at the very end of the reef trying his luck at fishing.

'You start gathering salt, while I go and pick up a block of ice,' Yiorkis instructed the young lads, and turned to go back for his cart. 'Be on your look-out for coastguards . . .!' he warned the boys, while setting off for the ice factory.

With buckets in their hands, the boys began to scout the reefs for shallow still puddles, in search of white salt crusts that formed within these pools. It was not a difficult task mainly because these reefs were well known for their abundance of pure white salt granules and had become a regular spot for the locals to gather sea-salt. Now and then the boys would come across a small octopus or a crab, and would jubilantly pick it up and dump it in their bucket, securing their evening meal. They decided not to collect any sea urchins, but instead cracked their shells against the rocks and ate them on the spot as a morning treat.

By the time Alexis' father returned, the boys had two buckets full of sea-salt, a number of crabs and four small octopuses trying their hardest to suck their way out. Pleased with the catch, Yiorkis picked up one octopus at a time and started beating it against the reef until it moved no more.

'Your mothers will be pleased tonight . . .!' he said to the boys with a wide smile, and raised the tenderised catch high in the air so they could admire the limp octopuses.

The three of them began to make their way back to pick up their cart and head home before the sun was up. Yiorkis was pressed for time to prepare the ice cream, to catch the morning trade at the bus depot. There, a constant flow of buses congregated bringing workers from the outskirts to work in the town, and he did not want to miss the opportunity.

By the time they were halfway across the reefs, Alexis' father spotted two coastguards rushing towards them.

'We are done!' he said to the boys, who also saw the two officials approaching. 'Don't say a word . . .!' he warned the boys.

The two officials came and stood in front of them, dressed in their crisp uniforms and blue caps. They inspected the two buckets and realised exactly what these people were doing.

'You know it's illegal to gather salt!' the elder of the two men said to Yiorkis.

'We are newcomers in the area . . .'

'That's no excuse, it's illegal to gather salt throughout the island,' interrupted the same official who spoke in a firm voice to emphasise his authority.

'I make ice cream and I need salt to prepare it, how else can I get salt? Yiorkis said in a pleading tone realising that he could be sent to prison.

'You can buy it that's how you get salt, you don't just steal it!' interjected the other younger fellow.

'We are a poor family, who live at *Loukkos* . . . have mercy my good man. Have you ever met a destitute person with money? How are we stealing nature's gift to man? All I am after is to put bread on the table for my family is this a crime?', Yiorkis pleaded with the men, who stared, back into his eyes, contemplating what to do with him.

'Look friend, we don't make the law the English do, we are simply doing our job! The law says—no gathering of salt from the sea-shore—and if you do, this is a crime and is punishable under the law', explained the elder official, who had not yet made up his mind what to do with them.

He turned and stared lugubriously at the two boys, who stood aside with their mouths clamped shut not uttering a single word.

Alexis appeared to be worried, realising his father might be sent to prison, and a cold sweat had broken out over his fragile body. He could see that his father was also nervous, and he detected a slight tremor in his voice as he tried to get out of the situation. Their fate rested in the hands of these two men, who were simply doing their job.

'We will let you off this time but let it be a warning! The next time, you may not be so lucky.' said the man finally, while looking at the two boys who stared back at him imploringly. He felt sorry for the lads.

'Thank you my good man, thank you.' Yiorkis said with gratitude, relieved he was not charged with breaking the law.

'I know you'll be back but don't let me catch you . . .! Next time, I may have to report you, and I don't want to do this . . .! We too have families to feed, and we don't intend to lose our jobs over this, it's better for your wife to cry over you, than my wife over me . . .!' the official said and gave Yiorkis a stern warning.

As soon as the boys heard this, great relief overcame them as they realised everything was safe and they smiled at the two officials who maintained stern expressions on their sullen faces.

'On your way . . .!' ordered the official, and turned his back on them.

They both walked away and headed towards the port, talking with one another. Soon, the hum of their muffled chit-chat drifted with the wind, and was hardly audible through the thunderous crashing of waves against the reefs; the two diminutive silhouettes disappeared beyond a sharp bend in the shoreline.

Dawn with its crisp air began to fade away, making way for the morning sun to rule again. It gradually came into view from across the horizon, being most anxious to exert its perpetual dominance over the land and calm waters. Instantly, a blinding, brilliant reflection flooded over the azure calm sea. Sparkling like dazzling jewels skimming over the tranquil waters, the sun's reflection glided, undisturbed, until the first waves came to life demanding their rightful role of swelling and crashing against the shore and the reefs.

Yiorkis thanked the Almighty for lending a hand, and crossed himself three times for escaping the clutches of the law—for today at least . . .! The three of them quickly hurried home, fearful in case other officials showed up.

As soon as they arrived Yiorkis did not waste any time and began the time-consuming process of making ice cream. His speciality was the refreshing rose-flavoured type, the favourite for most of his customers. He quickly pulled out his wooden barrel and placed a tall, inner, metal cylinder inside it. With ice picks, the boys crushed the block of ice and filled the side gaps with chunks of it to the very top making sure the cylinder was freestanding and centred within the barrel. Carefully, they sprinkled plenty of salt over the ice, and Alexis' father began to churn the handle of the inner cylinder at a steady pace until the liquid ingredients of rose-water and sugar within the cylinder began to set. After a half-hour of steady churning, the rose-coloured sherbet was ready—refreshing, cool, icy and perfect for a hot day.

The noise woke up his other two children, and both came out to inspect the process with eyes gleaming, hoping for a taste. They mingled with the boys, and demanded a tasting session for their personal approval. Yiorkis played along with his children and scooped out large portions of sherbet, packed it into large cones as high as Mount Troothos, and handed them over to the outstretched hands.

'What are you two up to today?' Yiorkis asked Alexis, just before he was about to leave.

'We are visiting Ahmet's aunt over the Walls . . .!'

27

'When you finish you come and meet up with me.'

'Where?' asked Alexis.

'Where else, at the *Agora* . . .!' Yiorkis retorted, and looked most anxious to get going to catch the morning trade. He picked young Maro up in his arms and gave her a long cuddle, simultaneously warning Marcos to look after her during the day.

'Why do I always have to look after her . . .?' complained his son and stamped his foot. 'I want to go with Alexis . . .!' he insisted.

'You do what you are told and don't answer back . . .!' his father reprimanded him and slapped him lightly on the back of his head as a warning of more to come if he persisted.

Not interested in listening to his son's grumbling, Yiorkis pushed his rickety cart in front of him, and soon disappeared on foot behind the slope of the embankment, to earn his daily bread.

Early morning found Alexis and his friends walking barefoot across the stone bridge. A giant, arched tunnel across the long stone bridge dominated the rock-solid rampart. It was the main entrance to the Eastern Gate of the Walls of Ammohostos. Spyros, their other close friend from *Loukkos*, had also joined the inseparable pair. This long-legged lad was so light in complexion they nicknamed him '*Aspri*', and that name stuck to him like glue, to his chagrin.

Approaching the great Walls, they could hear the muezzin calling his morning prayers in a clear, mystic chant from the top of the minaret of Ayios Nicholaos church which had been transformed into a Turkish mosque centuries ago. His strong voice reverberated across the rooftops and caused a lingering echo against the stone fortifications.

These formidable Walls provided a secure enclave for the Turks of Varoshia. The enclosure was predominately inhabited by Turkish Cypriots who had chosen to make it their own quarter. Six centuries ago, in their attempt to repel the onslaught of Arab and Turkish attacks against their kingdom, the Venetians had constructed this fortress in huge blocks of carved sandstone. Masters of engineering, they had also dug out and built the deepest moat ever, around the massive Walls. When the wide, deep moat was filled with seawater, the fortress became impregnable and not even a fish could swim across it without been detected.

If only stones could speak they would tell a thousand stories each and every one of them, about these Walls that had withstood the onslaught of Time. They would say that great kings lived in splendour and grandeur and rich merchants roamed with a thousand servants in mile-long camel caravans. Rare spices, herbs, jewels and precious stones were exchanged as weddings gifts . . . and a multitude of foreign languages were spoken by visitors arriving from the four corners of the world. A human torrent would surge forward at the marketplace, in a wave of overpowering colours, crested with brilliant white turbans, some would be wrapped in shawls, others in tunics and long cloaks sweeping the ground. Others would proudly walk about with capes and togas adorned with ermine, in knee breeches and waistcoats encrusted with gold and belts bristling with razor-sharp scimitars. The women . . . those lustful creatures of men's own desires would glide forth with graceful movements, swathed in silken veils; the slender Negress wrapped in vivid coloured shawls and arms adored with jangling bracelets . . . a sequined veiled female slave . . . a Greek, with long flowing hair surmounted by a red cap . . . an Armenian, veiled in black . . . a Syrian, with gold-striped bands wrapped around her head . . . or a Bulgarian, in sombre-coloured tunic and tinkling jewellery . . . a Georgian, a Greek from Byzantium covered in lace, silver tassels and shiny buttons . . . an Albanian, or a jet black slave from Africa with sparkling white teeth and tattoos on her face. Petite Japanese maidens, dressed in vivid-coloured silk kimonos giggling as they stroll . . . and slender snow-white European ladies tossed about by the heaving masses in search of bargains. The deep port at the Northern Gate of these magnificent Walls would be teeming with vessels, loading and unloading their valuable cargo of wheat, barley, carobs, exquisite rare fine silks, and other merchandise. These vessels would anchor for days in the open sea waiting for their turn to moor in this deep harbour; as the main trading route to the East. This great city of splendour would be regarded as the kingdom of Jerusalem, where the standard of Saint Mark was hoisted for centuries; they would chatter of love, hatred and lust . . . and tell the story of Othello, the Black Moor who lost his mind for a beauty beyond compare and Desdemona's innocent blood that stained these stones; they would speak of brutality and anguish and they would also speak of barbarity and betrayal, in pursuit of wealth and dominance; they would call out against those who stole their magnificence, by dismantling these ramparts, and transporting their stones, one by one, to other lands for convenience. They would cry out with the pain . . . that of thousands of men who perished, building these massive fortifications; and, if the spirits of the dead could find a way to speak to the living, they would speak of death and misery, hardship and anguish that prevailed in this land of plenty. They will also say that thousands have died defending these Walls and that they saw the brutality of war, through greed and plunder; they will yell out of decapitations, and severed heads in their hundreds, sent to the Sultan as loyalty tokens. And, if that's not enough to make them cry . . . they would speak out of impalement and mutilation of noses and ears; the gouging of eyes, as well as of the cruelty of people flaying others while still alive. They would scream out about crucifixions, and of the blood of the innocent, as well as of that of the guilty, that blood flowed like rivers, and so drenched this earth of abundance. The enduring spirits of restless phantasms that long ago swarmed these Walls forever call out to be remembered but no one hears their cries, they are now but a distant memory, amidst the realms of times past. As for the weather-beaten stones . . . they proudly stand firm, as evidence to the living, recalling bygone eras . . . for they know too, that there is no future forgetting one's own past. And so . . . silently they stand erect, monuments of eons past, as a constant reminder to those who care to remember . . . and, warning to others who choose not to see, but would rather live in the house of the blind.

The Turks living within these Walls are the remnants of the past. Their roots are deeply entrenched with the soldiers of the Sultan, who fought and captured these Walls, for whom thousands died before they finally capitulated to the brute force of the invading army. One year of killing and counter-killing, at the loss of a hundred thousand lives, was the price of defending and capturing these Walls that have survived to this day . . . set to welcome the three barefooted lads, walking across its long stone bridge.

Eager for adventure, the boys entered the deep dark tunnel which traversed the thickness of the Walls. At the other side, they found themselves inside the Turkish community.

Crammed and congested with rundown houses, the neighbour-hood showed signs of plaster crumbling, paint flaking and utter neglect due to poverty and idleness. Narrow alleys entwined into a maze of cobbled pathways, stretching throughout the enclave with no beginning or end. Thin clothes-lines were strung across the alleys from one building to another on which women hung their daily laundry. Colourful windows were painted in bright red, yellow or green and decorated with ornate wrought-iron screens over them. Also painted in vivid colours, these screens identified each household from its neighbours.

The Turks had endured harsh conditions for generations and there appeared to be no future prospect of breaking down the barriers and shackles that dominated their meagre existence. Like their Greek compatriots, they toiled every day for a piece of bread, without expectations or better prospects. They survive with the dream and hope that, maybe one day, their fate will change and improve. But, until that day comes, they work hard, having lost faith in those who control their destiny. Dignity and poverty go hand-in- hand, and these poor people have learned to cherish dignity for they know that a man without dignity is a man without hope. For them, hope fuels their purpose in life and undeterred they continue their daily toil knowing that, everyone rich or poor lives on borrowed time.

At the bazaar, the boys encountered a kind of commotion they had never seen before. They could not contain their excitement and their eyes gleamed with joy, feasting upon the stalls loaded with curious merchandise and food stuffs.

Merchants pushed about carts laden with warm aromatic breads, while others peddled freshly-squeezed fruit juices and other traditional Turkish delicacies. They yelled and shouted in their attempt to outdo the competition by cutting prices and offering bargains for the day. Young *hanums*, wearing sequin-decorated veils and long colourful dresses, seemed to glide in their sandals from stall to stall, exposing their henna-painted toes, and trying their luck for bargains, hustling the merchants who often got angry with them. Men of all ages crowded coffee houses to sip coffee, or puff and smoke hookah through a long flexible hose attached to a bubbling water-filled glass bottle. The idle men or layabouts gazed at all this activity, eyeing lustfully the young *hanums* that mingled with shoppers. If their lust became unbearable, they would get up and visit their favourite local brothel and pay a prostitute to ease their pain.

Every Saturday, the brothels also did a brisk trade, knowing outsiders would visit the bazaar for shopping or peddling merchandise. In squalid alleyways, these women or young prostitutes would rise early and take up position in front of their doorways, revealing their own special brand of merchandise. Provocatively dressed, these ladies who have learned to have no shame would stare at men and try to lure them into their honey-trap.

'Who will be the first one . . .? The first one's always the lucky one . . .!' they would whisper at a man passing-by, and look at him imploringly to take a chance, promising not to disappoint him.

'Your wish is my command, *effendi* . . .!' they would insist with conviction, in order to earn their day's pay.

They would tell a thousand stories of how they ended up in such brothels, and they have learned to tell their stories convincingly. Young girls in their prime, who had chosen this profession, often came from rural areas and either because of lack of self-esteem or promiscuity had chosen selling their bodies for a price. For many, working in brothels was the only opportunity available to them to

31

overcome poverty or the scorn of their families. Others came into the profession by choice, enjoying the free lifestyle that offered them plenty of rampant sex with strangers. These brothels were brimming with women of all ages and nationalities, ready and available, as sex teachers to young lads who would not otherwise find release for their sexual drive. The women truly believed their profession was necessary, and they were doing a service to society by offering their bodies to men or women for a price. To become a prostitute was easy, but to overcome the stigma of being called a harlot was impossible in a culture where virginity until marriage was paramount. Losing one's virginity outside wedlock meant the girl had become a used commodity and she was not suitable for marriage. No young man would even contemplate or be permitted by his family to marry such a girl, and often girls were slaughtered like sheep to protect the family honour. To escape such a fate, many ended up in the only safe place available to them—the brothel—and as far away from their families as possible. Once they entered this milieu they were doomed to live a shameful life forever . . . but among their equals.

At the bazaar, the boys visited nearly every stall. People hurried about, buying live chickens or rabbits for a Sunday roast and large watermelons, fruit and vegetables and anything that would make their day more enjoyable.

By midday the square had reached its peak, and was jam-packed with men and women, foot-loose boys and girls, all in pursuit of a bargain. Horses, mules and donkeys loitered everywhere and constantly brayed and neighed as loud as they could, adding to the cacophony that was amplified above the rooftops of the busy square. The streets were littered with decomposing vegetables and horse dung that began to stink out the area, but no one cared. Shoppers and salesmen came from every alleyway, some riding their mules, others pushing carts or simply walking about, absorbed in the buzzing atmosphere. Old men, with carefully trimmed moustaches and beards, dressed in their traditional cassocks, tight black waist-jackets and red or white fezzes, mingled proudly among the throng, prompting the younger Turkish lads to make belittling comments and criticise them for living in the past.

Destitute souls stood on every corner, or mingled in the crowds with outstretched palms, pleading for generosity from unwilling shoppers. They were the beggars, the crippled and the disabled or the freaks of nature that depended on the kindness of others for their survival. They learned to endure the insults and verbal abuse of those who shunned them and pushed them away as the lowest class of their community. A number of those poor unfortunates, too proud to accept handouts, played musical instruments or sang dirges and languorous melodies as a way of making the people reach deep into their pockets and give them few coins. Dressed in rags, women begging for a living often learned the art of fortune- telling, and competed with the gypsies who roamed in groups, grabbing anything given to them for free.

Every Saturday, even Greek merchants travelled from Varoshia and neighbouring villages to trade alongside their Turkish compatriots in this hectic bazaar. The merchants made jokes with one another and exchanged stories and experiences as one unified community. They spoke each other's language albeit in broken dialect but there was a sincere camaraderie between the two communities. Over the years, living side by side, they had developed respect for each other's cultural differences, and were not bothered by such trivial matters. They intermarried, made friends with each other, worked together and cried for each other's misfortune. As far as they were concerned, they toiled equally to survive and this bazaar gave them the opportunity to meet old friends to gossip, and share a glass of *zyvania* and *meze* together, until the same was repeated again next week. Life for them meant living for the day, because they knew tomorrow might not come for some of those poor souls who had given up hope and the will to cope with the harsh conditions of the day.

Charon, the black ferryman of river *Styx*, had never been busier than recently. He wallowed in poor people's souls day in and day out without respite. Those who escaped his clutches tried harder than ever before not to come face-to-face with his huge appetite; and so they struggled with every bit of breath left in their lungs to keep him away from their doorstep. The lucky ones mingled happily in the crowded bazaar to live another day and tell their story, how they had cheated *Charon's* insatiable gluttony, to rip their soul apart. They were not ready yet for their final ferry-trip to his everlasting land of the black abyss, that recognises neither the rich nor the poor.

Ahmet met some of his Turkish classmates who were also killing time there, and the lads joined forces to scout the Walls and the surrounding area. Ahmet was most anxious to show his Greek friends the entire neighbourhood and, having had enough of the market place, the group decided to head off towards the Northern Gate adjacent to the harbour.

On their way there, they spotted an overweight man, pushing with great difficulty a push cart loaded with two glass cylinders full

33

of a milky-white yogurt refreshment. He appeared to be puffing and sweat poured down his chubby face as he pushed along the heavy load in his attempt to conquer the steep hill. Dressed in a pure white cassock and a bright red fez, he moved so slowly that even a tortoise could overtake him with ease. The youngsters felt sorry seeing such a pathetic sight and went to his rescue. They took charge of his cart and with a unified effort they quickly got it over the hill.

'May Allah, bless you all . . .!' he kept murmuring to himself, as he trailed behind, while attempting to wipe the sweat off his exhausted face and sopping armpits.

At the top of the hill, the man gratefully filled six glasses to the rim with the cold yoghurt drink and handed each boy a glass. The lads drank it down in one quick gulp and immediately departed, leaving him to go about his business. He pushed his heavy cart towards the direction of the bazaar and soon disappeared among the narrow alleyways.

In no time at all, the boys found themselves on top of the parapet of the ancient Walls, overlooking the harbour. A cool gust of wind blasted their bodies and nearly took their shirts off, but they loved every minute of it, and remained there watching the large ships in the harbour. There was a lot of activity below, and the people appeared like ants from such a great height, moving aimlessly about. Once in a while, the deafening blast of a ship's siren bellowed, and the boys would put their hands against their ears unable to bear the persistent roar.

Alexis let his eyes scan the unobstructed view over the scorching hot rooftops of the town of Varoshia. All this was a new experience for him, and he was captivated by the wonderful sight of the sea thrashing against the mighty Walls. He stared with awe and felt invigorated by the whole encounter.

Ahmet, who was standing next to him, decided that it was time for a swim and grabbed him by the arm, pulling him away from the very edge of the parapet.

'Let's go!' he said.

'Where to?'

'Swim!' he answered and pulled him towards the crumbling stone staircase. The boys agreed and flew down the stairs, jumping down each step in a hurry.

'Where shall we go?' asked one of his classmates.

'*Tripa* of course!'

'*Tripa*? It could be dangerous this time of the day.' the same Turkish lad added.

'Don't be silly, it's too early for that.' Ahmet replied and then turned to Alexis and Spyros. 'You will like the place, I always go swimming there, and there are plenty of urchins,' he said to them in a convincing manner.

'What are we waiting for?' Spyros queried. He was beginning to get hungry!

Once they reached the bottom of the long stone staircase, Ahmet and his classmates led the way forward. They entered the narrow alleys and headed towards *Tripa*.

'My uncle lives nearby, and we can pay him a visit after our swim . . .! Who knows, we might get some grub if my aunt is home!' Ahmet reassured his friends.

'She is always home!' interjected one of the Turkish lads.

'Six young ones, and your baby sister what do you expect?' another lad added, who knew his aunt well.

The sun was becoming unbearable, and the boys couldn't wait to dive into the cool water and splash about to alleviate the scorching heat of the day. They walked fast, not wasting time in case the tide came up and they could not swim. The sleepy neighbourhood seemed completely deserted with no one moving about, with the exception of a few stray dogs in search of scraps.

They were just passing a well-kept home with a trellised vine in the rear yard, laden with large clusters of grapes, when they heard a Turkish girl's mesmerising voice singing a dirge, and the sound of splashing water. A high wall surrounded the house, but that was no obstacle to the boys' curiosity. One of the Turkish lads approached the wall and listened with pricked ears.

'Be quiet!' he whispered to his friends, who had stopped in their tracks.

The singing continued in a pleasant Turkish voice, but the Greek boys could not understand a single word. All they knew was that it sounded very pleasant to their ears and they patiently waited to be informed what was going on behind that white-washed wall. The lad carefully raised himself up, assisted by his friends. He peeped across the inner yard, but kept his mouth shut and said nothing. Instead, he stared speechlessly across the back yard of the house.

'What do you see?' his friends, asked in urgent curiosity, mesmerised by the girl's singing.

'I see what my eyes are forbidden to see . . .!' the round-headed lad said without taking his eyes away from the yard.

'What you idiot?' they all whispered in one voice.

'. . . A Turkish siren!' he answered elusively once again, and looked at his anxious buddies with a gleam on his dark moon-face.

'Speak up, you idiot!' Ahmet said angrily, unable to hold back his curiosity.

'She's having a shower!' the boy finally said in a whisper.

'So?'

'So, she's stark naked like a newborn!' he added, with amazement in his voice.

'No way!' Ahmet said again, and looked at the others with dark eyes that sparked with curiosity.

'Allah has finally fulfilled my wishes' the boy said and stared imploringly into the sky in search of Allah.

Without wasting time, the boys hurriedly looked around the alleyway and found large rocks. They placed each one against the wall to give them extra height, and carefully balanced themselves on the wobbly pile. In total silence, they carefully raised their cropped heads and peeped inside the empty yard; their eyes nearly popping out of their sockets.

At the far corner, inside a makeshift shower enclosure, a voluptuous shapely girl, not more than sixteen years old, was having a shower. She shook her masses of long black hair that reached her slim waist, completely oblivious to her new admirers. She sang away, lathering herself with a bar of soap, producing a profusion of suds all over her slithery naked figure.

In total disbelief the boys stared, and stared, not quite sure if their eyes played tricks on them, or if the wonderful sight was real or not. None of them had seen a completely nude girl of that age before, and could not take their eyes away from her mesmerising movements and nakedness.

The corrugated-metal door of the shower stall was slightly ajar, and they could clearly inspect every part of this dark slim girl who moved and turned around like a nude goddess, not realising she was being watched. The boys ogled to their heart's desire and did not bat an eyelid, afraid they would miss something of significance. The girl let the water run over her firm body and, as she moved about, for a brief moment she faced the shower door. From the corner of her riveting black eyes, she spotted the six heads popped over the parapet, but said nothing . . . She smiled to herself, and continued singing, like a canary, pretending she did not see the boys.

She moved her wet black wavy mane about, and raised her slender arms which forced her breasts to cantilever even more, to the utter astonishment of the young lads. She was enjoying her new admirers and deliberately, but discreetly, pushed the shower door wide open with the tip of her toe so they could get a better view.

With the door flung wide open, she began to tease the boys seductively with her movements, pretending she did not acknowledge their presence. Stark naked, she stood in front of them, and moved about within the shower cubicle, exhibiting her nakedness and giving the boys the most revealing show of their young lives. Unblushingly, she began to touch her firm breasts that heaved up and down and she constantly kept putting her hands between her legs. She was pretending she was washing herself and like a slippery snake she began writhing and twisting her bare bottom. The water was splashing all over her smooth tanned skin, and she sang away to her heart's desire. Somehow, her singing became alive and she sang much louder and clearer, reaching new high-pitched notes she never knew existed before.

She happily twittered away in the lazy surreal afternoon, knowing she had a devoted audience to appreciate her exceptional qualities. Now and then, the young vamp would steal a glimpse at the boys, to ensure they were still feasting their eyes, and joyfully raise her arms in the air, leading them into temptation. This young seductress was playing games with them by using her bouncing breasts and body as a playing field; games they were yet too young to play . . .! She enticed them and refused to conceal her drenched, naked body, recognising that the boys were totally transfixed and gaped at her every move so as not to let her out of their sight.

The lads gazed speechlessly. They were stunned with delight at such a wonderful sight and new experience. For the first time, they realised what girls were all about . . .! The more they fixed their gaze at her, the greater the sensations flashed through their bodies. Unable to control their hormonal desires, they all became aroused and a pleasant new passion was bursting to come out. Not able to restrain themselves they all began to touch the front of their outstretched shorts while looking at the girl who was determined to give them an innocent, but sensual show.

Their small penises stiffened like darts and tented their shorts in a straight parade line like soldiers, in readiness to shoot.

Too absorbed with the girl's movements and melodious singing the boys failed to notice that her mother had spotted their heads over the parapet. Quietly, she picked up a broom, crouched and gently opened the front wrought-iron gate, gazing at them and not making the slightest sound. She carefully sneaked behind the boys, who were too distracted by their aroused penises and with her daughter's sensual exhibitionism.

With a giant leap, she pounced upon them, screaming as loud as she could, like a wild woman.

37

'You scoundrels! Get away from that wall!' she yelled at the top of her voice, and started beating anyone within reach of her broom.

Startled, the boys fell to the ground and saw a vicious, wild woman with fury in her eyes slamming the broom all over their skinny bodies. She was dressed in a black veil headdress that flew around with her every strike. She was determined to do as much harm to them as possible for their audacity in spying on her daughter. The racket caused other curious women to come out into the empty alley. Seeing what was taking place, they immediately came to their neighbour's support by bringing more brooms as ammunition and to join in and give the boys a good hiding—and a lesson they would not easily forget.

The boys scrambled up and took to their heels. They ran as fast as they could, and far away from these demon-witches who wanted to hurt them. They felt their heels touching their buttocks, and never stopped running for even a moment until they made sure the women had stopped chasing after them.

When it was safe, they stopped to catch their breath, but they could still hear the woman screaming her head off in the distance.

Suddenly their love-goddess burst out into deafening screams and piercing cries. She was getting a heavy thrashing by her furious mother. The sound of loud whacking against the girl's naked body was clearly audible from far away, and the slapping continued for the longest time. They felt sorry for their newly-found siren but there was nothing they could do about it, and moved on undeterred for their afternoon swim. Some of them had bruises on their arms and backs, and could still feel the pain of the broom thrashing down on them.

'Did you see the size of her tits?' asked Alexis, quite amazed with the whole experience.

'They were huge!' Spyros answered with exhilaration. 'Just like two melons!'

'How about down there . . .? It was like a forest . . .! I have never seen anything like it in my whole life. I got a bit scared looking at that forest!' exclaimed one of the Turkish lads.

'I have seen my sister's tits but they are like two small walnuts, compared to hers!' another interjected with amazement.

'How about her, behind, her rump?'

'Oh . . . that was heavenly curved . . . I didn't know girls look like that!' said Ahmet with amazement, and sighed loudly.

'Now we all know what is hidden underneath those long hideous dresses . . .!' said Spyros, who still could not believe he had seen a full-grown, naked girl for the very first time.

'Did any of you get your pants wet?' Ahmet asked his pals.

Everyone looked at each other, and nodded their heads negatively, feeling dejected that they had been interrupted by the girl's mother.

'I was so close but the broom shrivelled it up like a prune !' one of the Turkish lads said with disappointment.

In absolute exhilaration the lads approached *Tripa*.

Seeing this secluded place, Alexis recognised how it got its name. At the very base of the massive fortification, a breach was visible, big enough for a tall man to walk upright through. A sheer parched escarpment dotted with palm trees, ended at the bottom of the opening, making it difficult to go down the slope without falling to the ground. There, at the middle of *Tripa*, the earth formed a steep parched basin, and beyond the large gap, the open sea roared and crashed directly against the colossal Walls. Once the tide was up, there was no way anyone could get inside the fortification from this section of the Walls, unless one could fly or swim like a fish.

Gentle waves lapped and rippled against a secluded beach, while directly ahead a row of shallow reefs stretched and disappeared beyond the bend of the Walls.

'We have to be careful and keep our eyes on the tide' Ahmet, who knew this place well warned everyone.

'Is it that dangerous?' asked Alexis.

'One of my cousins drowned here, I warn you don't tell my uncle that we swam here, he'll go mad!'

'Why is it dangerous?' asked Spyros, who stripped naked and was ready to take a dive.

'When the tide comes up it is so high, *Tripa* is completely submerged and the water reaches as far as that high point inside the Walls,' Ahmet explained and pointed towards the peak line of the parched escarpment used as a playing field. 'No-one could swim that distance and people don't realise how deep the water gets and so, they drown! That's what happened to my cousin . . .!'

A couple of the lads headed straight for rocks to check out the shallow pools in their search for urchins wedged against the rocks, while others quickly threw their clothes aside and dived naked into the crystal blue waters. They remained there amusing themselves for a long time, until they got bored listening to Spyros' complaining. He was famished, and kept nagging everyone until they got fed-up with him and decided to take leave. Ahmet's Turkish classmates went their own way, leaving the three of them strolling through the narrow empty alleyways heading for the house of Ahmet's aunt.

As soon as his wrinkled aunt saw her nephew, her face lit up and she gave him a warm embrace. Realising there were guests about, his young cousins popped their heads out of every corner to see who paid them such an unexpected visit. Realising it was Ahmet they came out and jumped all over him amid joyful screams and yells and shouting at the top of their screechy voices. He could not restrain them and he fooled around with them until they had enough of his horse-play and went outside into the narrow alley.

Only his baby sister, a bubbly little girl with thick, long, black curly hair that reached down to her waist, refused to leave him alone. She stuck to him like glue, and stared imploringly at him, with her beautiful doe black eyes, pleading with him to take her with him. He held her tightly and tried to comfort her by explaining why she had to live with her aunt. Once she felt calmed and reassured, she gently slid out of her brother's arms and joined her cousins outside.

Pleased to see the boys, Ahmet's aunt quickly put together a modest variety of foods on a table outside under the shade of a huge fig tree and urged them to eat. They did not need much persuasion, especially Spyros who attacked the bread and green olives with passion. There was no stopping him!

They finished their afternoon nibble, and suddenly they all felt tired from doing too much in one day. The back yard was peaceful and quiet, exacerbating the need for a long afternoon nap. Well fed, they felt like a snake that, after a hearty meal, needs a long sleep but Alexis insisted they should go and meet his father as promised.

Reluctantly, they got up and left, leaving Ahmet's aunt and the army of his little cousins watching the three of them take off towards the Eastern Gate.

'Don't forget to tell your mother, that we are expecting her tomorrow . . .!' his old aunt yelled out as a reminder.

'I won't forget . . .!' Ahmet shouted back as they were turning around the corner of the narrow alley.

The boys arrived at the busy *Agora* of Varoshia late afternoon, and found that most of the shoppers were dispersing to go home. Barefooted lads on bicycles hurried back and forth delivering groceries as quickly as possible so they could return in time for their next job before this landmark building closed its massive doors. Men and women strolled about, carrying live dangling hens held tightly upside down by their legs, trying to sell the last few birds before going home for the weekend.

Wrinkled old beggars appeared everywhere, and swarmed the area in their last attempt to appeal for generosity. The destitute and sick or lame grouped together calling out for help, while the sick, covered in boils swollen with pus, the paralysed, handicapped and misfits, had no intention of moving until they earned their daily bread. Others stood around playing musical instruments, hoping someone would throw a few coins to them. Having no choice, many had accepted their lifestyles, and felt no shame in begging for a living.

The three lads found Alexis' father at the North Gate of the *Agora*, standing behind his rickety cart at the main bus depot. He looked tired and hot, with a scarf crammed with crushed ice cubes wrapped over his head to keep him cool. The melted ice kept dribbling over his face, and he loved every minute of it. Now and then, he would wipe the excess water off his forehead and continued his calls to attract customers.

As soon as he spotted the boys, a smile appeared on his rugged face, exposing his set of white teeth through his unruly, thick moustache.

'Here you are . . . did you boys have a good time?' he asked when they came up close. He noticed there was a jubilant spirit about them and were quite chatty.

'It was the best day ever . . .!' the boys answered and looked at each other, with a sly smile on their sun-tanned faces, remembering their Turkish goddess.

'I see you went swimming!' Yiorkis said to the boys, recognising the sea freshness about them.

'. . . We went swimming . . . visited Ahmet's aunt . . . investigated the bazaar inside the Walls and had an excellent time!' Alexis burst out jubilantly, and filled three cones with sherbet for him and his friends. 'How did we do today papa?' he asked while licking his sherbet.

'Nearly sold out!' his father answered, pleased with today's takings. 'You boys stay here I am dying to visit the toilet' his father added and took off. 'You continue selling while I am gone . . .!' he shouted back to them.

Not wasting any valuable time, the boys spontaneously began to yell at the top of their voices.

'Ice cream . . .! Ice Cream . . .! Fresh like a morning spring . . .! Ice cream . . .!'

They were eager to sell the remaining sherbet before Alexis' father returned, so they could all go home. They missed their afternoon nap, and the three of them felt tired and sleepy from the sweltering heat. Alexis took it upon himself to fill the cones, while his crew never stopped shouting at the top of their lungs, anxious to empty the two cylinders. The lively commotion attracted the attention of other children, who dragged their parents to buy the remaining rose-sherbet.

'Stop your racket!' passers-by kept shouting at the three lads.

It was getting quite late in the afternoon and they expected the siren to blast out at any moment, calling for everyone to vacate the building so the main doors could be shut for the weekend. The bus depot was crowded with shoppers, anxious to head home with baskets full of groceries, or carrying live hens, roosters or rabbits.

Without warning, the siren suddenly burst into a deafening roar; it was so loud it resonated for miles away. The boys placed their hands over their ears, and waited until it finally stopped. In a wild stampede, hurried shoppers crammed the exit doors. Like a herd of stampeding cattle, the steady surge of bodies bumped restlessly into one another, anxious to make their exodus and rush home.

Yiorkis was one of those who pushed through the crowds. From a fair distance away, he could hear his boys' voices, making such a spontaneous racket he could not help but smile at their determination. He walked up to them, opened the cylinders and could hardly believe his eyes; the containers were nearly empty.

'I should get you boys to sell ice cream instead of me . . .!' he said with amazement.

'We want to go home and take a nap,' Alexis said to his father.

'What are we waiting for, let's get going, enough for today . . .!' he agreed with them and began to organise his cart to take leave.

Soon the four of them were on their way home . . .

The siren roared for the final time, and in no time at all the whole area was deserted, with the exception of a few stragglers strolling about to get rid of their last merchandise. Some beggars walked aimlessly, in anticipation of earning a few extra coins, before they left and wandered into the empty streets with outstretched palms. The scorching heat persisted, and everyone was rushing to find comfort in their own homes under shade, and a large slice of watermelon to soothe their thirst.

In a matter of half an hour, the empty *Agora* transformed itself into a tranquil lethargic zone with hardly anyone moving about with the exception of a handful of belated people, lazily dragging their feet in anticipation of mastering the long walk home or the nearest coffee house.

At this late hour, only stray dogs and cats ambled in the empty streets in search of scraps. There was plenty of decomposing refuse lying about to satisfy their hunger. It was their turn to dominate the streets and they hurriedly moved in packs, always on a look-out for their dreaded archenemy; the dog-catcher. Each day without fail he showed up immediately after the massive dome-building shut its huge doors.

On foot, the dog-catcher would search out the enemy. He would skilfully balance the long pole over his shoulder and let the net swing back and forth at the rear, in readiness to pounce on the strays without pity. A dog caught in his net was as good as dead, no matter how much it howled or barked. The dogs were petrified and shuddered at the sight of this little bald-headed man dressed in rags, who had become such an expert at netting the strays. No dog would escape his clutches once he set his beady eyes on one. He would sneak behind the stray and freeze his stare at his target like a leopard, until he was positive the net would entrap his victim. With one agile manoeuvre the dog was doomed!

The pack of animals could smell his presence from miles away and always tried to avoid him at all costs. As for the dog-catcher, capturing these strays became an obsession and a daily ritual to catch as many as possible and throw them inside his large cart-cage for everyone to see and praise him. Once inside his cage, the dogs knew they were doomed and quickly lost the will to bark. Pitifully, they remained composed, with curled tails between their legs, realising their end had finally come.

Yiorkis together with the three lads pushed the cart along, and headed for *Loukkos*. On their way there, they strolled through an exclusive neighbourhood, crammed with luxurious homes, adorned with spacious verandas and gardens heaving with an array of coloured flowers. Beautifully painted, these homes became Yiorkis' dream, wishing that one day he too would have a house of his own . . . maybe not as grand, but at least a solid house built out of stones and not flimsy corrugated metal sheets; being too hot in the summer and freezing in the winter months.

'Which one do you like?' Alexis' father asked his son, and pointed towards the row of houses at either side of the road. He always asked the same question whenever they walked through this part of the town.

'You know the one I like' answered his son, playing along with his father's dream.

'When I grow up I will go to Lefkosia, and find myself a good job there' said Spyros, and stared at the beautiful buildings.

'Then . . .?' Yiorkis asked the young lad who turned red from the heat of the day.

'I will buy my parents a nice home away from *Loukkos* . . .!'

'I can't wait to grow up and move my mother into a nice neighbourhood . . . I hate *Loukkos*!' Ahmet interjected.

43

'Me too!' Spyros agreed with his friend.

'You have plenty of time ahead of you but remember, the most important thing in life is the family . . . as long as you love God, respect your family, honour the old, and have a good education . . . everything is possible. You don't want to end up like me who can hardly read or write!' Yiorkis advised the lads.

Slowly, they reached the familiar thoroughfare lined with its massive eucalyptus trees, casting their silhouettes across the scorching asphalt. *Loukkos* lay a short distance away and they headed for it, leaving behind the hot asphalt—which had turned quite unbearable to walk upon with bare feet.

They entered the well-known winding dusty trail, and the screeching wheels of their rickety cart soon disturbed the dust under their feet. A small cloud of dust began to drift into the sultry air behind them. Every time they took a step forward, their bare feet gently sank into the ground, and they could feel the soft powdery dust between their toes. Tired and worn out from the day's activities, the boys could not wait to collapse under a shady tree and take their long-anticipated nap.

Arriving at the embankment, with group effort they pushed their cart forward to overcome the small slope until they finally reached the very top. From there, they had a clear view of *Loukkos* below, crammed with its makeshift huts stretching into the distance as far as another sand dune that encircled the entire enclave.

Looking across the shacks, they noticed a commotion outside Ahmet's humble home. Crowds of people came into view, standing idly in groups, talking with one another. Their muffled voices were audible across the tranquil neighbourhood, but they could not understand what was being said, or why the crowd had gathered.

'What is going on?' perplexed, Yiorkis asked himself, wondering what the commotion was all about.

Sensing that something was not quite right, the lads instantly cannoned down the slope and into the open field below, not caring if the dry thorns pierced their bare soles.

Michalaki saw them running towards the house and rushed to meet his friends. They met half way across the field, and the boys saw that he was crying quite badly. His eyes were bloodshot and the trickling tears across his chubby cheeks left a mark down to his chin. He stood facing them, and stared ahead in a kind of trance, unable to utter a word.

'Speak up Michalaki! What's wrong?' Spyros asked impatiently, seeing that his friend was lost for words.

Instead, he burst out crying again, and his red eyes flooded with fat tears as he looked directly at Ahmet. He had a distraught expression on his young face and he tried hard, but in vain, to stop his tears.

'Out with it.' Alexis yelled at him, and gave him a heavy slap on the head.

'Don't hit me . . .!' he pleaded agitatedly.

Somehow the slap brought him back to his senses, and more composed he turned and looked at Ahmet.

'Your mother has died . . .!' he wailed and burst out in loud sobs again.

For a brief moment Ahmet appeared to be stunned and confused. 'My mother died?' he asked, not believing his ears.

'Yes! She's dead.' his friend shouted again at the top of his voice, trying not to believe it himself.

Suddenly, the four of them spontaneously shot across the open field towards the gathering crowd. Ahmet shoved the crowd aside, entered his home and discovered that the small room was jammed with women. As soon as they saw him, they squeezed aside to let him pass. He slowly walked towards his mother's bed and stood next to it. With a hollow stare he gazed at the white veil that covered his mother's motionless body from head to toe. Stunned, he was unable to utter a single word from shock. Instead, he stared at the white sheet and a thousand thoughts flashed through his young mind. He could not believe that under that piece of cloth his beloved mother laid dead . . . and he would never hear her voice again. He began to feel his knees weaken, and a sudden shiver flashed through him. His eyes were about to burst into a torrent of tears, enough to flood the entire enclave, when an elderly woman put her arm gently around his trembling body.

'She is at peace, my son . . .' she said to him kindly and lifted the sheet off her face so he could see his mother for one last time. 'She is with your father now, she always wanted this.' she added sympathetically, and wiped her tears off her wrinkled face while lifting the sheet up.

Ahmet stared at the lifeless, pale face of his mother and suddenly burst into loud, uncontrolled sobs. Panic-stricken, shocked, confused and traumatised, he could no longer look at his dead mother and pushed his way out, away from all these women.

He went straight to where his friends were waiting for him. As soon as they heard his uncontrollable sobbing, they too joined his grief and burst into tears. The four of them huddled together and sat on the ground, crying their eyes out, away from the grown-ups.

45

Yiorkis had finally arrived and was told the bad news. It left him speechless. A woman approached him, wanting to explain precisely how it happened.

'We were having a chat in my house when all of a sudden she felt dizzy and came back here! The next thing we knew . . . she passed away! God bless her soul, she was a good woman, kind and loving mother to her boy.' she explained and wiped her face with a handkerchief soaked in tears.

Yiorkis listened and a heavy sigh escaped his chest. The smell of death lingered in the sultry air and he could no longer stand it. He turned and looked at the four lads grouped together on the ground sobbing, and a heavy burden overcame his senses. He had to get away, and slowly he turned about and went back to his house.

He sat on a chair contemplating what to do, but above all he felt touched by Ahmet's miserable fate. He lit one cigarette and remained in contemplation until he smoked it in deep puffs. Shattered, he eventually got up again to join the others. He wished his wife was there to guide him and discuss the situation, but she was still at work and he decided to take the bull by the horns and do the right thing. He saw Vasili talking with one of the other men and walked up to him.

'We have to inform her family. I will personally go and do that,' he said to him volunteering for the job.

'What a catastrophe!' Vasili said and shook his balding head. 'That poor lad!' he added and looked at young Ahmet, who was still sobbing.

'You take care of things here!' Yiorkis instructed his friend.

Both men agreed and Yiorkis turned towards the boys, who remained seated on the same spot unmoved. He called Ahmet and the young lad got up and went to him.

'We have to let your uncle know about this.' he said to him and placed his arm around his shoulder to comfort the distraught lad.

Ahmet did not answer, but nodded his head in agreement.

'I will go too.' Alexis said and got up.

'No. You stay and look after Marcos, and your sister. They are around here somewhere!' his father said, in a firm voice.

'No. I am coming!' Alexis bellowed in defiance.

'Me too!' Spyros added adamantly and stood up.

'You are not leaving me behind!' Michalaki insisted.

'Let the boys go we will take care of the young ones!' Vasili interjected, knowing how good friends the lads were.

Without wasting time, the four of them were on foot again, heading towards the Walls. They walked fast, taking short-cuts, and the boys no longer felt tired. By late afternoon, they arrived at the small cramped house of Ahmet's aunt. His uncle was home and the couple were seated in the back yard enjoying their afternoon.

When Yiorkis broke the bad news to them, Ahmet's aunt took it very badly and started a prolonged lamentation that brought out her neighbours. They soon arrived in their dozens to console her. Losing her only sister meant that a piece of herself had died, and nobody could stop her expressing her bitter sorrow the only way she knew how. She sat on a chair and cried, while her six children gathered around her, clutching onto her long veil, perplexed at seeing her behave in such a manner.

Ahmet's young sister climbed into her brother's arms, and wouldn't let go of him. She was too young to know what was happening, but seeing the trauma around her she could detect that something was wrong and held onto her brother tighter.

His elderly uncle, Mehmet Nazim, as the head of the family and a devout Moslem, did not want to waste time and suggested that they both go to meet *hodja* and make the necessary funeral arrangements.

By the time they returned, it was getting quite late and Ahmet decided to remain behind with his uncle for the night while the rest took leave for *Loukkos*.

For Alexis, it was the worst night of his life. He could hardly sleep and his confused thoughts wanted to burst out of his tender young skull, longing to reverse his friend's predicament. Thousands of ideas flooded his head all night, until finally sleep overcame him.

The next day, he got up very early and joined the rest of the crowd who left on foot to arrive in time for the funeral and burial procession. At the cemetery, Greeks and Turks mingled together to grieve the loss of a kind woman, devout mother and neighbour.

After the interment, Yiorkis took Mehmet Nazim aside, wanting to have a private talk with him. They walked in the back yard of his house and away from the rest of the crowd.

'What is going to happen to Ahmet?' he asked the small man, dressed in his black cassocks and red fez.

'Allah, I don't know.' the man answered, being at a total loss. A melancholic expression had set on his sullen face. He was unsure what to do with the lad.

'He is a good boy . . . and it is a shame to be cast aside against the winds.' Yiorkis said to him.

'Twice he's an orphan. It is very unfair . . .! First, that dreaded widow-maker, Amiandos mines, snuffed the life out of his father— and a healthy young man at that—and now this . . .! What is going

47

to become of his boy now?' the small man said in perplexity and raised his arms into the air in despair. 'I have six mouths to feed, and Ahmet's sister, seven, how can I cope? How can any man cope, to feed so many mouths, nowadays?'

'Mehmet Nazim let me help. I have discussed the situation with my wife, and if you agree, we'd like to help!' Yiorkis said sincerely.

'How can you help, my good man?'

'We are not rich, but we get by. Ahmet and my son Alexis have become very good friends and seem inseparable. We like the boy very much. With your permission, we would like to adopt him if the boy agrees.' Yiorkis said in a firm voice.

'May Allah open his generous hands, and give you whatever you desire my good man . . .!' Ahmet's uncle said, and took both of Yiorkis' hands and held them tightly in gratitude. He could not believe his ears and felt a deep sense of humility at this man's suggestion.

'We just want to help and make sure the boy's life is not ruined. He deserves better!' Yiorkis said to him, pleased that Ahmet's uncle was receptive to his suggestion.

'It is a great thing that you and your kind wife are doing, I am sure one day the lad will repay your kindness many times over.'

They discussed the matter with Ahmet and he showed no objection. Pleased with the arrangement, Yiorkis and his family left the humble household of Mehmet Nazim, and headed back for *Loukkos* to give Ahmet the chance to spend time with his aunt and young sister until he was ready to move in with them.

As soon as they crossed over the Northern Gate of the Walls, the muezzin began to chant from the top of his fluted minaret calling his flock for prayer.

CHAPTER THREE

NATURE'S PERPETUAL CYCLE of life, like an infinite wheel in motion that never stops for a single brief moment, the long hot Summer had finally come to an end. With reluctance, it passed its supremacy over to Winter, which could not wait to reign supreme over the poor inhabitants. Year in and year out, these two battled it out as to which one of the two would cause the greater hardship during its reign.

Summer will ensure constant sweltering heat scorching everything in sight, while Winter will play havoc with people's lives on trying to warm themselves up. As extra ammunition Winter will bring out its reserves of fierce winds and rain to attack those who cannot protect themselves against its annual ritual. Irrespective of how much these two arch-rivals tried to break people's spirits, they in turn learned to cope with the onslaught and carried on with their lives. People had learned to persevere with the sizzling heat, and became accustomed to the downpour and bitter winter cold. They were not bothered with such trivial matters; their one and only serious enemy had always been prolonged poverty and famine. For years they struggled with no end in sight but lived in hope, that Fate would eventually see reason, and put its weight behind them.

Young Ahmet had moved in with Alexis' family, and he immediately became a welcome extension to the family unit and settled down well into his new environment.

Yiorkis made sure all the children attended school, and every morning without fail they would walk the half hour trek to the main cross-roads near the *Agora* and then split up; Ahmet would head towards the Walls for his Turkish school, while the rest continued on for their own school of *Ayia Katerini*. 'Education is the eyes of the blind and ignorance is the noose of the living!' he always kept reminding the children as a stern warning so they would never forget that education was a blessing.

An illiterate man himself, he paid heavily for not having been able to acquire an education. He had been forced to join the workforce at the tender age of eight in order to support his parents, earning a meagre living. The only schooling he ever received was from his village priest, but his real education came from life itself, and he quickly learned the craft of survival. As a caring father, he was determined that his own children would get a better chance in life, and he encouraged them to accept school as a means of escape from their present predicament. As parents, they often deprived themselves in their attempt to provide for the children's needs, especially school supplies.

It was not always easy. Many times they failed to provide all that was required of them but, seeing the young ones getting up each morning and departing for school, they felt a deep sense of pride recognising that their children were on the right path to a better future, irrespective of their economic shortcomings.

Every morning, the youngsters got up and prepared themselves for school, but the winter posed endless problems for them all. It was an ongoing battle to find heavy clothing, especially shoes, and today was no exception. Outside, the morning rain was coming down in a steady drizzle and there was no stopping it. Ahmet was barefooted, but Alexis managed to find a pair of his father's old shoes and put them on.

In readiness for school, they put a potato-sack over them like a poncho and headed out. They walked hurriedly to reach their school and get out of the drizzle, in case it decided to come down in buckets and they found themselves without protection in the middle of a heavy shower. There were dark clusters of clouds forming, and each one of them could suddenly burst out in a downpour.

'We might be lucky today.' Alexis said to Ahmet as they harried along.

'Why is that?' asked Ahmet while trying to hold the sack tightly over his head, to stop the pouring rain getting down the back of his shoulder.

'There is this rich lady who has promised to hand out shoes for the under-privileged,' Alexis explained, hoping he could chuck away the old shoes he was wearing.

'I am getting a pair too!' Young Maro shouted jubilantly in her squeaky voice in anticipation of getting a brand new pair of shiny shoes to wear the next day.

'Except me . . .' said Ahmet with slight jealousy in his voice for being left out.

'You can share mine . . . we are both the same size.' Alexis said to him.

'I am not wearing mine in the rain!' piped up young Maro. 'I want to save mine!'

'You wear shoes in the rain silly, not when it's sunny!' Marcos said to her.

'I don't care, I am not wearing them! I shall look after them forever!' she said with determination and paid no attention to her brother.

At their regular crossroads they split up, and Ahmet headed for the Walls, bundled up to protect himself against the rain that refused to subside. He held his books tucked tightly under his arms and soon disappeared behind the buildings.

By the time the three siblings had arrived at their own school, they were soaked to the bone and decided to stand temporarily under the long veranda to shake the rain off their clothes before entering their classrooms. But, as soon as they entered, their teacher called out the names of those who were to receive shoes and to go and wait under the school veranda.

Yiorki's children were among those chosen to receive a gift to mark the end of another school term. About thirty children from various classes gathered in one large group, excited that they were about to miss classes for the day. A great number of the youngsters were from *Loukkos*, and among them Michalaki, who was so thrilled he could not keep his mouth shut and kept picking on the girls. They remained under the veranda until the rain eventually decided to stop.

Happy at last with the weather, the teachers organised the pupils into one long column of two's, with the first-graders at the very front, and those of the sixth grade at the very back. The headmaster, a tall massive-looking man with thick bushy hair and spectacles, came out and issued a stern warning.

'Anyone not behaving gets nothing! Is this understood?' he bellowed.

'Yes Sir . . .!' everyone yelled in a deafening roar.

Intently the children listened in silence to their headmaster's lecture, and when he finished he blew his whistle hard in a long loud signal authorising the anxious procession to begin. An elderly female teacher led the way forward and they marched off towards the town centre, chaperoned by two other male teachers.

On their way there, the sun came out with a blinding brilliance causing the wet earth to produce a gentle grey steam across the wet fields. Soon the snails would come out and most of the youngsters after school would search the wet fields for the elusive snails and make a meal out of them. They will throw the captives into a large bucket, sprinkle flour over them, shut the lid tightly and put them on a strict diet and a self-cleaning process. After a day or two, the snails would be ready for cooking. . . .

Spyros was walking alongside Alexis and knowing they were about to receive a new pair of shoes, they chucked their old ones across an open field. Barefooted they walked across puddles and were not the least bit bothered with such trivial matters like having mud-stained feet.

After a long trek, the procession finally arrived at an exclusive footwear shop near the main *Agora*. The teachers lined everyone up outside the shop alongside the narrow shopping arcade until it was time to call them inside for fitting. Their chattering brought out the shop-owner, a podgy-looking man who appeared quite happy to see all the youngsters outside his shop. He recognised that they also brought him good luck.

Behind him emerged a small busty woman, who came out into the arcade to inspect the youngsters. She was wearing a pair of ornate spectacles that appeared to be too big for her face. They gave her heavily made-up eyes the impression of being smaller through the thick lenses. Immaculately dressed in a crisp white dress and a navy-blue jacket, she walked about in slow strides gazing at all the boys and girls. With a long cigarette holder stuck in her mouth, she puffed away tensely, allowing the cloud of smoke to gather over her red coloured hair.

'*Kalimera*, children . . .!' she squeezed out of her mouth, through her heavily painted thin lips, in a high-pitched voice.

'*Kalimera* . . .!' the children, yelled out simultaneously.

Their cries echoed across the shopping arcade, attracting the attention of other shop-owners who poked their heads out to see what was happening.

The woman gave them a smile and after a quick glance she walked inside again. She sat herself behind a desk and continued smoking and asked for the children to be brought in, two at the time. Happily, each child received the woman's gift, thanked her and walked back in line, carrying their valuable new possessions. Their faces lit up with excitement as they held their shoes tightly comparing them with one another. Marcos and his young sister received theirs, and rushed to the back of the line to show Alexis their brand spanking new shoes.

'Maro, they are beautiful red shoes!' Alexis said to his baby sister, and shared her sense of happiness and excitement.

'You have to look after them!' Spyros said to the young girl.

'I am not wearing them in the rain.' she warned in a whisper to him.

'You don't have to, Maro.' Alexis reassured her with a smile.

Finally, Alexis' and Spyros' turn had arrived and both walked inside the shop bare-footed. Their muddy feet stained the marble floor. They stood in the middle of the shop with a guilty expression on their faces, but quickly one of the lady assistants came to their rescue, and brought them a towel to wipe their feet.

The skinny lady had noticed the floor, frowned with her thin eyebrows, and nervously took a deep puff at her cigarette. Then she furiously raised her bony arms into the air in a gesture of disgust. Her wrists were covered in thick gold bracelets entwined with clusters of charms that jingled loudly like sheep bells whenever she moved them about.

'What is this?' she screamed out at the two lads. 'Couldn't you two get a wash?'

Alexis and Spyros instantly turned into stone and neither of them dared move an inch.

'Sorry *Kyria*! We got drenched this morning.' Alexis finally plucked up courage to explain. Humiliated, he bowed his head towards the floor, not wanting to make eye contact with this woman who appeared quite threatening.

Spyros, standing next to him, felt shattered at the lecture they were to receive. He glanced at his own feet and then Alexis' and realised the lady was quite correct; their feet were certainly muddy . . . but it was too late! She spotted them, and he reconciled himself to accept what was coming to them—as long as they walked away with a new pair of shoes.

'Look at your feet they are filthy!' she screamed again, but this time with uncalled-for fury, that not only startled the two motionless boys, but also the proprietor and his assistants.

'It is not a problem, Kyria-Pavlidou . . .' the proprietor said politely, and beckoned his assistants to hand the boys another towel each, to wipe their feet.

'Don't tell me what is, and what is not a problem!' she reprimanded the owner, who instantly shut his mouth, thinking that she might start attacking him for no reason. He could not understand her sudden unbecoming manner and decided to seal his mouth.

'We are sorry, *Kyria* . . .' both lads said, apologising to her in a low voice and feeling guilty and humiliated for being the cause of such a scene.

Their teachers remained silent and stood aside, watching the lads like hawks, which added to their traumatic experience. They appeared helpless to intervene and instead frowned and stared at the two pupils in embarrassment.

The woman's shrieking voice attracted the attention of the rest of the children outside, and they instantly assembled at the main entrance to see what was happening. They saw their schoolmates standing to attention and not moving a muscle. They eyed the lady lugubriously as she sat behind the desk.

Glaring through her spectacles, she fixed her sight upon the young lads. The look in those furious eyes sent cold fear down their spines. They knew they had not heard the end of it, and wished the earth would open up to swallow them down into its depths so they wouldn't have to listen to this lady's irritable voice. Trapped, they both swallowed their pride and waited in utter silence.

'Your parents should be ashamed allowing you to come here like this!' insisted the lady and re-examined them again from top to bottom, feigning disbelief.

'They are quite poor, Kyria-Pavlidou!' one of the teachers ventured. He decided to stand up for the two lads who appeared scared and lost.

'Where are they from?' she asked amidst a cloud of smoke.

'*Loukkos*.' the same teacher answered.

'Ah . . . That explains it!' she said and then gazed at the boys with a stern look. 'You are vagabonds . . .!'

'No *Kyria*, we are poor . . .!' Alexis said in a dry tone.

' . . . And because you are vagabonds, you expect handouts . . .!' she interrupted.

'No *Kyria*! We expect nothing!' Spyros answered in a calm, composed manner, while he looked her in the eye.

'Look at you, you are filthy and show no respect coming here like this . . .!' she added again and leaned back in her chair in an intimidating gesture to show her authority.

'We are not filthy *Kyria* . . . just wet!' Alexis exclaimed, trying to justify their appearance.

'You do not answer back!' she yelled. 'Where is your respect for your elders?'

By this time the atmosphere was tense and the children outside were speechless and shocked at what was taking place inside the shop. Marcos and his young sister, who was clutching her new red shoes tightly to her chest, pushed their way to the front and had a perfect view. They could hear everything that was said and felt offended, seeing their brother and Spyros being treated in such a humiliating manner.

Alexis could no longer take any more of this, and decided to put an end to it once and for all. He no longer cared if he received shoes or not. He realised this woman was a wolf dressed in sheep's clothing of the worst kind. She offered generosity at a price: subordination.

'*Kyria*, my father told me respect is gained,' he said in a calm tone, not knowing how those words came out of his mouth.

Totally shocked by the boy's comments, she blasted out furiously. 'Such insolence! Let your father buy you shoes then! Get out of my sight!'

The boys knew they were out of luck and turned to leave. They noticed for the very first time that the entrance was completely blocked by their schoolmates who had stayed put during the whole incident. Alexis saw his brother's tanned face at the front of the crowd, while his sister was standing next to him, looking inside with her dark, doe eyes, mystified and in a complete daze.

'Who is that boy's family?' she yelled at the teachers, who were standing aside amazed how this unhappy state of affairs had developed.

'Yiorkis' family.' answered one of the teachers.

'A rotten tree produces rotten fruit!' the lady mumbled to herself with indifference.

Over hearing those offensive words about his parents, Alexis' blood boiled and he could no longer take the woman's unwarranted insults. She had gone beyond permissible boundaries. She had entered into uncharted waters by insulting the proud family name.

Without thinking, he turned around, raised both his arms, and banged his fists hard on her desk, scattering everything off it. With a loud, echoing clatter, the glass ashtray full of cigarette butts shattered into tiny fragments across the marbled floor.

'You can insult me . . . but, never insult my family name . . .!' he burst out in a loud voice that took her by surprise. He was fuming with uncontrollable anger. His eyes flashed and his young face trembled.

He banged his fists one more time on the table. Instantly, the two teachers rushed to the lady's rescue and tried to put a stop to his unruly behaviour. They grabbed him by both arms and tried to pull him away from the desk.

'We may be poor but we have dignity, dignity *Kyria*!' he bellowed, at the top of his juvenile voice.

He wriggled about and struggled to break his teachers' hold, but they both held him tightly. He was no match against their strong arms.

Infuriated, the lady's face turned red with anger and shock. She was traumatised by the lad's audacity, and started to scream frantically at the top of her voice. Her skeleton-thin body shook like an earthquake with anger.

'Get them out of my sight! Now!' she yelled hysterically.

The children congregating by the entrance withdrew in fright, not sure what was coming next.

'Do you know who I am? I am Kyria-Pavlidou! Kyria-Pavlidou!'
She kept repeating in her horrid voice, trembling with fury.

Suddenly she lost her balance and tumbled flat on her back on the hard floor. She hit her head on a small stool, causing her spectacles to fly off and break into three pieces. A streak of blood began to flow over her heavily made-up face. That immediately sent fear into the boys' hearts as they realised the seriousness of the encounter.

At that precise moment, while she was flat on the floor, a middle-aged policeman attracted by the persistent screaming walked in. As soon as she saw him, she clumsily wobbled to her feet assisted by the two teachers, and instantly shrieked: 'I want them sent to a reform school!'

The policeman recognised her immediately. Observing the blood on her face, he carefully inspected her wound. It was only a slight scratch on her forehead, and he asked the assistants to clean it up. He then turned to the boys who did not move an inch so petrified were they at seeing him. He frowned with his thick eyebrows and gave them such a stern look that it seemed to pierce their fragile bodies.

'You boys have a lot to answer for!' he said to them in a tone of authority.

'Send them to a reform school, that's what they deserve!' the distraught, lady shouted with determination.

'Kyria-Pavlidou, that may be a little harsh don't you think?' the policeman replied in a calm voice.

'If you don't do your job my husband, the judge, can take matters into his own hands . . . I will make sure of that . . .!' she warned the policeman, arrogantly.

The boys felt their hearts pounding from fear of the possibility of being sent to a reform school, and panic had overcome them both.

'We did not mean any harm, it was an accident!' the boys pleaded with the policeman.

He on the other hand was quite perplexed what to do with the lads, considering the lady was the wife of a respected judge who exercised great influence over the authorities. In the end, he decided to let the boys go on the condition that their parents must come to the police station the next day and have a good chat with him and his superior. With nothing more to be said, the boys were allowed to leave the shop.

Standing at the entrance of the shop, Marcos and his sister had not missed a thing. Without hesitation, young Marcos picked up his new shoes and threw them inside the shop.

'I don't need shoes!' he said to the lady.

His behaviour stunned everybody, including the policeman, who shook his head not sure what to make of the boy's attitude.

As soon as his young sister saw her brother throwing his shoes, she took courage, hesitated momentarily, but then threw her own lovely red shoes on the floor next to her brother's.

'I don't need shoes . . .!' she repeated her brother's words softly at the lady, who by this time was fuming with anger. Frightened, Maro stood next to her brother for support.

'Ungrateful brats!' muttered Kyria-Pavlidou, and nervously lit a cigarette. She took a deep, lingering puff, and slowly released a thick cloud of stale smoke from her mouth, choking everyone in the room.

The incident came to an end, but the boys were in deep trouble and an uncertain future was looming over them. Scared, they did not even bother to return to school with the rest of their schoolmates, but decided to skip class much to their teachers' annoyance. They were devastated, confused and terrified at the possibility of being locked up in a reform school like prisoners. Only the worst delinquents were normally sent to reform institutions and they certainly did not deserve to be locked up with them. The outcome of their parents' reaction was obvious to both of them, and they expected some kind of punishment, but that did not worry them as much; only the reform school terrified them. To be confined in such a place meant to be stigmatised for the rest of their lives.

Alexis could visualize his father's face, fuming with anger for bringing such embarrassment upon the family's name. They already had plenty of problems to cope with, and for him to be the cause of additional trouble meant that he would never forgive himself for being such a fool. He realised that he had permitted emotion and pride to react excessively over reasoning, and felt shattered, but it was too late now; he had tripped with his tongue, rather than his feet. Distraught, he had to accept the blame and grim consequences of his irrational behaviour.

Early next morning, their parents went to the police station as instructed. The interview lasted for quite some time and their distraught parents had to practically go down on their knees and plead for leniency, this being their first misdemeanour.

The chief of police observed the lads' nervousness and noticed that they were speechless, fearful of uttering a single word. They appeared totally devastated by the whole episode, and the chief carefully considered their nervous dispositions, and felt sorry for them.

The judge's wife, on the other hand, insisted they should be sent to a reform school. But the head of police, a reasonable man, decided against such irrational and unwarranted punishment and refused to sign the necessary documents.

Kyria-Pavlidou did, however, successfully manage to influence the final decision and got the boys expelled from school.

Beaming with satisfaction, Kyria-Pavlidou in high heels wobbled out of the police station, knowing she had got the better of those brats. She had punished them for humiliating her in front of all those people . . . With her wounded pride restored, she strode arrogantly outside, without a streak of guilt, for bringing to tatters the boys' dreams and aspirations. After all, she was the judge's wife.

* * *

It took Alexis a very long time to accept that his school years were over for good. Devastated, he felt robbed of his youthful ambition. His pride had betrayed him, and disillusioned he entered the labour-force like many other boys and girls of a similar age.

He settled helping his father roam the streets selling ice cream and other home-made snacks. Time being the ultimate healer, the shoe-shop incident soon became a bad memory, but one that would follow him for the rest of his life.

Spyros on the other hand had decided to leave *Loukkos* for good and took off one day for Lefkosia, in search for work. He was told the capital had plenty of jobs for young boys, and without giving the matter much thought he left his family behind. He truly believed that his luck would change if he changed his surroundings, and two weeks after the expulsion he bid farewell to his friends and set off on foot to find his fortune. He was never seen again . . .

Ahmet did not last in school much longer either and he decided to forget classes, altogether. He could not bring himself to study while his friend was out working and putting food on the table. He developed a deep sense of personal guilt seeing Alexis and his father going to work each day, while he headed for school. One morning he decided his own school-days were over. 'I have learned enough, now I want to work' he said to his adopted parents.

Yiorkis on the other hand, a sensitive man, felt that his parental duty had not been fulfilled. He left no stone unturned in his pursuit of finding the boys a workplace so they could learn a profession or skill as the next best thing to an education. He certainly did not want them to end up like him, who had lost out on education. His wife urged him every day to do something about the lads' future and constantly kept nagging him to try harder.

'It's not from not trying, wife but there is nothing out there!' he would say to her, with bitterness and disappointment in his heart.

'There has to be . . .!' she would positively reply, knowing that her husband was capable of making good things happen.

After a morning's regular heated discussion concerning the boys, Yiorkis had enough of arguing and decided to take a day off. He instructed the lads to take care of matters and psyched himself up that today was the day; he was going to find his two lads a workplace.

'I am not coming home tonight!' he said firmly to his wife.

He combed his unruly moustache, put on his white short-sleeved shirt and hurriedly tucked it inside his black trousers, held up by braces. Immediately he took off on foot for the town, leaving his puzzled wife behind, watching him disappear beyond the embankment and wondering what he meant.

There was a spring feeling in the air, and as he walked along he could smell the first crocuses sprouting from deep inside the moist earth. The sudden aroma was overpowering, and each year he made a habit of clipping a bunch of perfumed stems for his wife knowing how much she loved flowers. For that thoughtful gesture, he would embarrassingly receive a gentle kiss on the cheek and a warm smile to see him through the day.

As soon as he noticed the cluster of colourful crocuses, he made a point of remembering to pick some up on his return, as a peace offering and to make amends. Soteria and his children meant everything to him, and he had no other reason for living except for his family. He would tear the world apart to protect them if necessary, and now he was determined to protect his boys by finding them a proper job so they could secure a future for themselves.

All day he scouted and visited workshops and other outlets, enquiring about job possibilities for his two lads. He didn't mind what kind of trade they learned, as long as it was a decent one. To be a master of a trade was good enough, knowing they would earn a fair wage and wouldn't be exploited. Tirelessly, he walked everywhere without success or prospect for finding a position for his lads.

Nightfall came, but he persisted and carried on, not prepared to give up so easily. The shops were beginning to open up their shutters for the evening trade, while many push-carts loaded to the hilt appeared everywhere among the cinemas and in the town square. A great number of oil lanterns were lit alongside the carts, illuminating the merchandise and attracting not only people, but also swarms of buzzing flies and moths anxious to do battle with the burning flames.

He was getting tired of walking and decided to pay a visit to Kosmas' garage as his last resort, before quitting for the night. The owner was known to him, but he also knew that he was not a prosperous man and had his doubts of success. But, undeterred, he headed towards his workshop. He approached the familiar grease-smelling arcade, renowned for its mixture of mechanical repair shops, and entered Kosmas' darkly-lit garage.

He saw the familiar small man with grey hair, bending over the boot of an old Hillman muttering to himself. As soon as he heard footsteps, the man turned his grease-smudged face and knotted his thick eyebrows into a prolonged frown to inspect the intruder.

'Who is that?' he asked, not recognising Yiorkis who was shrouded in the darkness of his dimly-lit workshop.

'It's me, Kosmas!' answered Yiorkis and got nearer to the light.

'Ah . . . *kalispera* Yiorkis . . .!' the man said, pleased, as soon as he recognised his late visitor and began wiping his hands with a rag. 'What are you doing here this time of the day?'

'I have a day off.'

'A day off? What's that?'

'I need to talk to you Kosmas, that's why I am here!' Yiorkis said and quickly added 'I have a problem.'

'If it's money, forget it!' interrupted the man who appeared older than he was, and pinned his eyes straight on his visitor.

'No. It's not money.'

'Thank God for that . . .!' exclaimed Kosmas with great relief, and walked towards the shop entrance, leaving Yiorkis standing on his own in the middle of the workshop. He poked his head outside, and yelled at the top of his lungs, 'Two Turkish coffees!'

'*Endaxi.*' a man responded from somewhere across the dark arcade.

Satisfied, he walked back and pulled up a chair for himself and another one for his unexpected visitor. They both sat down facing each other, among a pile of engines and grease-smelly scattered car parts.

'It's my boys, Kosmas, I need to get them into some kind of trade, so they can learn a skill.'

'You mean, your older boy . . . the one they threw out of school?' interrupted the man.

'Yes Alexis, and also Ahmet.' Yiorkis replied, slightly embarrassed by the man's comment.

' . . . the Turkish lad?'

'Yes, I want to ask if you can offer them a job.' Yiorkis said to the small man.

'The way things are . . . it's impossible!'

'They are both good boys, respectful, and will never steal a coin from you! I can vouch for them with my life!' stated Yiorkis, trying to persuade this sad looking man to give his boys a chance.

'I know the boys, they are good lads, but what can I do? Business is terrible, I can hardly make ends meet.' he answered apologetically, and raised his arms in the air.

At that moment, a young boy walked in bringing two coffees and two glasses of water. He left the metal tray on a grease-stained table and walked out again, without uttering a word. They picked their coffees up, took a long sip each and smacked their lips.

'You know I am not a wealthy man. . . .' Kosmas started to say in a serious tone.

'I am going to make you an offer you can't refuse.' Yiorkis interrupted.

'Meaning?' he asked suspiciously, knowing that nothing is for nothing in life.

'Both boys can work for nothing!' Yiorkis explained and looked at the man who appeared very shrewd. He waited for his reaction, but the man was taking his time to ponder on the situation.

'Yiorkis, I have seven children, and that's the result of marrying a woman fifteen years my junior! I often think of cutting my dick off, but she won't let me, so I work hard, not only in the garage but also in bed to prove that I still have some strength left in me to carry on. The result, I now have seven children—bless their hearts—and this garage is sucking the life out of me.' he said quite seriously.

'Kosmas, listen to me . . . My boys will bring new blood into your business, and in time you may slow down a little! We are not getting younger . . . New blood brings new life!'

'Like my wife did . . .!' butted in the worried-looking man.

'My boys are dependable, and will take care of your business . . . like their own two eyes! All I am asking from you is to give them a chance in life.' insisted Yiorkis

'You are putting a heavy burden on my shoulders, Yiorkis.' said the man somewhat sceptically, not being quite sure what to do.

'They will cost you nothing . . . The choice it's entirely yours, but give my lads a chance!' Yiorkis insisted, trying to be persuasive.

They both finished their coffee, but Kosmas was a reluctant player and appeared not so easily convinced about taking the plunge. But once he had given it serious consideration, he came to a decision and stood up. He looked Yiorkis straight in the eyes, and nodded his head, although still sceptically.

'I know your lads are both good boys, and I also know you as being an honourable man . . .! Poor, but honourable and your children can only be as honourable as you are! I will give them the chance you ask of me, but, if they are lazy and shy of working they are out . . .! I am not prepared to waste my time on lazy bones, crafty sods, or conniving and sly ones. I run an honest garage here and my reputation is unblemished, and as clean as a baby's bum . . . you tell them that . . .! You ask them to be here tomorrow at six in the morning sharp!' Kosmas declared authoritatively.

So pleased to hear those fine words, Yiorkis grabbed both of his greasy hands, and shook them wholeheartedly.

'Thank you Kosmas! Thank you! May God bless you, and your family! I shall always be indebted to you!' Yiorkis said, relieved that a heavy burden had just been unloaded off his weary shoulders.

Ecstatic, he walked out of Kosmas' garage and could not wait to get home and tell the good news to the boys. He reached *Loukkos* but, instead of going home, he decided to stop at their local coffee house to check if the boys were about. They were nowhere to be seen; only Vasili was there, sitting on his own out in the open air contemplating life.

He joined him under the vine-trellis, and Yiorkis announced the good news to him.

'I am going to face that problem next year, when Michalaki completes his school. Vasili said to him, openly pleased for his friend.

'It's not easy to be young in Cyprus.' Yiorkis said to him.

'It's not easy for anybody!'

'I am sure there are better days ahead!'

'You are an optimist Yiorkis; nothing will ever change as long as we are ruled by the British.' Vasili said and spat on the floor.

'We will never get rid of them, they are here for good! They suck the blood out of us day in and day out and that's a fact.'

'You are right at that.' agreed his podgy friend, and stared across the shabby enclave.

'In time Vasili, in time. One thing is for sure, there is always an end to a long cord,' Yiorkis said, to encourage his sceptical friend.

'It might be so, but we are getting old. I want to get out of this place before it's too late.' his friend added.

'There is a great future ahead of us. Our children are in good health, that's our future! Let's not lose sight of God's gift to us both.'

'God has nothing to do with it, my friend. It is man's own greed that plays havoc with our lives that bothers me,' Vasili said, with strong conviction.

62

'Mark my words, one day the British Empire would also come tumbling down, like all others. Then we shall be free to fight our own demons,' Yiorkis said, to reassure him that there is a slight hope ahead.

'Until then we are stuck here, in this miserable place called *Loukkos*,' Vasili interrupted. 'I hear they are opening up some parched land at Kato Varoshia, and they are selling plots very cheap maybe we should take a look at them.' Vasili added, attempting to influence his friend to get out of this miserable place.

'And how are we going to pay for them? Shirt buttons are no currency!'

'They are cheap and the owners are offering good terms.' Vasili persisted, being most anxious to get out of *Loukkos*.

After a lengthy discussion they both agreed to check it out . . .

With that in mind, Yiorkis left to go home and talk to the lads about their future. He found the boys lounging outside, enjoying the pleasant evening, topless and in shorts. He could hear his daughter nagging her mother about her school problems.

'I can't help you Maro you know I cannot read, go and bother your brothers!' she kept telling her daughter.

Yiorkis walked up to the boys, grabbed a chair and sat down next to them. He looked at the sprawled lads, who were beginning to wonder where he had got to by arriving at this late hour.

'I have good news for you two!' he said to them in a serious tone.

Hearing his voice, his wife came out, and Maro instantly jumped on his lap. She immediately began to bombard him with questions, but he had no time for her petty problems and told his daughter to speak to her mother, who had pulled up a chair and sat directly opposite him.

'These are for you.' he said to his wife, and handed her the few stems of scented crocus.

He kept one stem behind and handed it to young Maro. She gently held the yellow flower, smelled it, and in return gave her dad a tight squeeze for his tender consideration. His wife smiled and put the sweet smelling flowers close to her nose and contently began to sniff the bouquet.

'Come out with it *papa*!' Alexis demanded, curious to learn of his dad's good news.

'You and Ahmet are going to become car mechanics!' he said to them with an affirmative tone in his voice.

'Mechanics?' they shouted in one voice.

'Yes. Tomorrow at six o'clock sharp you are to go to Kosmas' garage and start your apprenticeship,' Yiorkis instructed and twirled his moustache.

Pleased with his achievement, he explained in detail how he had managed to secure the jobs for the boys. The two lads were absolutely over the moon to be given such an opportunity. They were so excited at the prospect of becoming mechanics that they began to jump up and down in leaps of joy and gave Yiorkis a loud smack on each cheek.

That night, everyone went to bed in full of excitement for being given such a positive, but rare, opportunity to turn a new chapter in their lives. These were cherished moments that were not always at hand around *Loukkos* . . .

CHAPTER FOUR

Athens, 1953

THE SCEPTICAL LITTLE man with a bowed head and hands behind his back walked slowly unaware of his surroundings. He often paused and murmured something to himself that only he could make sense out of his private jabber. Street-cars, pedestrians, cyclists and horse-drawn carts often confronted him, but he paid them no attention. He was too deeply absorbed in his own thoughts . . . At times, an incensed driver would shout at him, cursing the mother that bore such a louse, but he would pay no heed and move on, oblivious to the hustle-bustle of the morning rush-hour traffic.

The man, in his late fifties, was neatly dressed in a grey, wide-lapel jacket, a crisp blue shirt and a striped tie with a perfect knot. He wore perfectly pressed white trousers that made his shiny black squeaky shoes stand out and sparkle against the morning sun. His bushy but neat moustache was carefully twisted at either end, indicating that he was a man who took pride in his appearance. He walked upright like a proud man, with a touch of arrogance about him. Bald-headed, but with unruly thick eyebrows over his piercing brown eyes, he observed all that was going on around him. Undeterred he moved forward . . .

The car fumes and constant noisy commotion got on his nerves, but he proceeded, determined not to be angered by those who yelled at him. He had more urgent, burdening problems on his mind. His thoughts were on more serious issues that lives depended on, and lives could equally be lost and innocent blood staining the earth.

He had taken it upon himself to organise and mobilise a deadly force, and he battled with his conscience as to whether he had the right to undertake such a heavy task. His mission would certainly destroy families, create widows and cause many mothers to grieve for the loss of their sons. As an obscure career soldier, he truly believed lives were expendable as sacrifices in order to achieve one's own military objective. Throughout his inglorious military career he had seen hundreds of young men sprawled dead in forgotten lands and he was hardened by such emotional sights. He felt death was a price worth paying for freedom . . . and that one word motivated him to pursue his plan to influence others to see things in his way. He

65

wanted to recruit young men to train in the art of killing others, under the banner of freedom. It made no difference to him if those who died in battle were a child's father or a mother's son. He was used to such touching arguments and they did not bother him in the least; his objective was paramount.

His life as an active soldier had now vanished . . . As a retired military man and a failed politician, he had ample time to think of ways of rekindling that old vague magnificence. He was desperate to rejuvenate his cells and feel alive again, knowing that a man without a purpose or objective in life might as well be dead!

He wanted his name to be written in history books like Alexander the Great, Napoleon and other military heroes who had left their mark for others to study and admire. Swallowed up by delusions of grandeur, he had never managed to achieve that one special recognition during the last two wars, and time waited for no man; he was getting on in years. The glories of past battles never materialised for him, and time was running out. Death would soon come knocking at his door, and he was afraid to face it alone and in obscurity.

He wanted to leave his mark one way or another, and the small island of Cyprus could provide him with that immortality. This was his last opportunity; he had to grab it before it was too late. He truly believed that Cyprus could be freed from colonialism with him being at the vanguard of the struggle for the liberation. He would then die a happy man.

A stubborn disciplinarian, he had chosen the island of Cyprus as his gateway to immortality. He was on his way to keep an appointment to try and convince a dozen or so influential men to support his attempt to liberate Cyprus from British subjugation.

Today was a day of reckoning, and he hoped that crucial decisions would be taken which may ultimately transform the fate of the small island forever. He had been planning this crucial meeting for months, and had worked extremely hard to make the necessary arrangements. This was a serious gathering and a select number of men were summoned to express their views in anticipation that they might support his efforts to establish an underground Freedom Movement.

By mid-morning, he found himself climbing the marble staircase of a large block of apartments in the centre of Athens. The district appeared affluent, with impeccable houses surrounded by mature gardens colonnaded by large pine trees. He entered a long corridor on the third floor and lightly knocked at one of the white-painted doors.

Immediately, a middle-aged man with grey hair opened the door for him.

'*Kalimera*, Colonel . . .!' the man greeted him with a smile.

The two men walked along the lobby making small talk and entered a large room, crowded with other men seated on armchairs, sofas and wooden chairs . . . all waiting for his arrival.

At the end of the room, a long-bearded priest dressed in his clerical robe and black cap stood up and took a few steps forward to greet the newcomer. He wore his long greying hair in a neat knot at the nape of his neck, while his black cape was draped gently over his shoulders.

'Welcome Colonel.' the man of God said in a calm, soft voice through his massive unruly moustache that completely covered his upper lip.

'Thank you for coming, your Eminence.' he answered and reached for the Archbishop's hand. He kissed it lightly, and bowed in reverence as a sign of respect for the Archbishop.

'I could not miss this meeting, for anything.' said the Archbishop and took his position again at the head of the table. There was a serious expression on his face and he seemed bothered.

For a few moments, brief formalities and chitchat were exchanged between the men and it was quite obvious, that everyone in this room knew each other well. The men appeared sombre and seasoned professionals. Everyone knew precisely why they had congregated in this apartment, and the anxiety on their faces was quite obvious. The wrong decision could have dire consequences for the unsuspecting people of Cyprus, and great consideration had to be given to all relevant facts.

'Colonel, please share with us your plan of action so we may consider if the plan is possible, and deservedly offer our backing . . .! We need to be one hundred percent sure the plan is feasible because lives are at stake and it is not simply a war game.' the Archbishop said to the Colonel, and leaned back in his sofa in readiness to listen. He passed the floor to him so that he could speak uninterrupted.

'With all due respect your Eminence, I have never considered this undertaking to be 'just a war game'! On the contrary, I spend sleepless nights over this matter and I fully understand the seriousness of an armed struggle, given the fact that our resources are limited and difficult to come by. Yet, I truly believe we shall succeed!' answered the Colonel with strong conviction.

'I hope you are correct!' the Archbishop said to him with slight reservations, not convinced that an armed struggle was so necessary at this time.

The Colonel decided to take the bull by the horns and express his views with clarity in order to convince everyone in the room to support his plan. Without their wholehearted support or full backing his plan was as good as dead and could never materialise. This proposed uprising was his baby, and needed careful nurturing so it could mature.

To make his case convincing, he pulled some papers out of his briefcase and spread them across a small desk adjacent to the window. He stood upright alongside the table so he could see everyone's reaction. The men became all ears and waited in absolute silence for him to speak.

He glanced briefly at everyone, and in a calm tone began to present his case. He considered it wise to speak his mind on all matters relating to the Cyprus situation, before he entered into detail about his proposed uprising.

'As you all know,' he said, 'I am a man who believes in freedom and only for freedom shall I die. I have fought against the Germans, Turks, Italians, Bulgarians, Albanians and Greek Communists, for one reason alone and that is to preserve the inherited and most precious right to man; freedom! In the past, I have also joined forces with the British Army and received their support in hardware to liberate Greece from the Germans. But the time has come for that relationship to cease, permanently. We shall now face each other as enemies, rather than allies. I am ready to give up my life for the liberation of my mother country and I shall destroy—with your support—the shackles of the British yoke!'

'We are all familiar with how gallantly the Cypriots fought alongside the British troops in two world wars . . .! For their staunch support, Cyprus has been promised its freedom! After the war, the United Nations Charter proclaimed that all peoples should have the right to self-determination and yet, when the Cyprus delegation demanded that right to be honoured by Britain they were denied what had been promised to them! Am I correct on this point, your Eminence?'

'You are perfectly correct in your evaluation of the situation, and the answer to your question is, yes. London once again refuses to alter its present policy on the Cyprus issue. In my opinion, Britain plans to keep the island forever!' The Archbishop stated in agreement with him.

Pleased with the Archbishop's comments, the Colonel felt encouraged and continued to speak out his mind.

'The time has come to take back what rightfully belongs to us: Our Freedom! Such outright British intransigence shows that the only way Britain will relinquish her stranglehold over the island is through bloodshed! The British Empire will not succumb to gentle persuasion. I am prepared to make Britain come to terms and show that the Greek spirit is alive; it maybe half-asleep, but certainly not half-dead!'

When he finished what he had to say, he sat down on his chair and waited for a response. His listeners never uttered a single word while he was talking, but rather weighed his every word carefully. They appeared sceptical, and were unsure of the outcome of such a rebellious uprising that could easily backfire with devastating results for the whole island. The Archbishop seemed the most sceptical of them all, and was not so easily convinced by the Colonel's ambitions. If this turned out to be a mistake, the repercussions could prove disastrous for his people. As their spiritual leader he had a responsibility to protect them.

'I must admit, it seems a very dangerous undertaking to revolt against such a mighty power as Britain!' the Archbishop said to the Colonel. 'I am not a military man, but it seems to me that the odds are against any type of uprising, in such a small country. Mind you, I am not opposed to the idea but I do have my reservations and I need to be convinced.'

'How do you aim to achieve this liberation?' asked the former war minister, who was seated next to the open window so he could smoke without annoying the others.

'Guerrilla warfare.' answered the Colonel in two words.

'That would be suicide in such a small island . . . there are no places to hide!' interjected the Archbishop.

'Colonel, with all due respect, guerrilla warfare may be possible, but excuse me, you have not set foot on the island for thirty years. How can you tell us that Cyprus can be liberated and expect us to support such an undertaking, knowing that you don't even know the island yourself?' queried the war minister, not convinced about their speaker's initial proposal.

'I confess it has been many years since I visited Cyprus and I don't know each stone . . .'

'We don't care about the stones, but we do expect you to be familiar at least with the topography of the land if you are going to initiate guerrilla warfare!' interrupted one of the other men who didn't seem persuaded by the whole idea.

'For every obstacle there is always a solution! The liberation of Cyprus is within reach if there is strong willpower and a helping hand from the Almighty God!' the Colonel stated with determination and conviction.

'Leave God out, for the moment . . .' the Archbishop interrupted.

'We do not doubt your abilities. What concerns me personally is this: what if your enthusiasm turns out to be wrong and we enter into an irreversible sticky political situation that would drag Greece into a political upheaval with Britain . . . After all, we are allies, and Cyprus is a separate issue that needs to be treated with great caution,' argued the minister, and lit another cigarette to stimulate his thoughts.

'Don't expect Turkey to remain idle . . .! What would become of the Turkish Cypriots on the island?' one of the men butted in.

'Turkey has no jurisdiction over the island. My only worry is that Britain may use the Turks on the island to wedge a division between the two communities. That is how she operates . . .!' warned the former war minister again.

The tall dignified war minister had many dealings with the British establishment throughout his political career and knew by personal experience what he was talking about. He had fought in two major wars and had a long list of distinguished medals to his name that prompted others to pay attention to his every word.

'I am not bothered with the Turks on the island!' the Colonel interjected agitately, and then added quickly, 'Cyprus is a Hellenic issue and should put shame on all Greeks who accept the enslavement of their brethren, then, sit back and do nothing about it! Such attitudes incubate within the chambers of defeatists! If the Turks get in my way, I swear to you all that I shall fight them with all my might!'

'The question remains: can we do it alone?' the Archbishop asked everyone, and gazed at the faces of all the men in search of guidance, him not being a military man.

'That is the Colonel's department. But we certainly cannot involve the Greek Government in this matter. It would be political suicide to even think about it!' advised the seasoned politician and former war minister.

'Not openly.' the Colonel agreed, and then directed his attention towards the Archbishop. 'To your question: if we can do it alone, my answer is 'yes,' as long as the Greek government does not put any obstacles in our way.'

The Archbishop seemed worried and his vibrant, gleaming eyes were in constant motion watching everyone's reaction and body language. He was searching for some kind of sign to help him decide what would be the best way to handle this serious situation. He was not convinced.

After a long, heated discussion, the Archbishop sensed there was general consensus. They all agreed the matter required further consideration and that the liberation of Cyprus was possible with the right leadership and support. They came to the conclusion that the Colonel must visit the island, as a tourist, to make a proper study and report back before a final decision could be taken.

The Colonel was ecstatic about the favourable response and he agreed to visit the island immediately. It was crucial to make a proper evaluation of the situation and to work out how he could organise this new clandestine Organisation.

By late afternoon the secret meeting was over and crucial decisions were taken which satisfied most of the men. At the same time, many questions remained unanswered . . .

Before everyone departed, the Colonel rose up from his chair.

'Gentlemen,' he announced, 'today, we have made history! A revolution is born and we are its sentinels! With the help of God, we shall liberate Cyprus!'

*   *   *

The Colonel left for Cyprus immediately after the meeting. He arrived by plane at Lefkosia airport and felt a deep sense of patriotism seeing the land of his birth, after so many years of living abroad. His eyes filled with tears the moment his feet touched the soil of Cyprus. He was overwhelmed by mixed emotions that caused him to question why on earth he had never managed to visit his homeland sooner. He knelt down and kissed the earth. That gesture made other passengers think that he was either a fool or an over-emotional middle-aged man. Like a young child lost in a candy store, he couldn't get enough satisfaction from the sudden exuberance that had flashed through his body, by simply standing on the soil of his ancestors.

Aside from his brother and close family his main contacts on the island were members of the Cyprus Ethnarchy. He wasted no time in meeting a number of priests and other people who felt strongly about initiating any measures to unite Cyprus with motherland Greece.

He toured the island, taking notes and investigating every part of the small land. His task had also given him the opportunity to rediscover this beautiful country and the more he toured, the more in love he fell with this place. He noted that children toiled in the open countryside alongside the poor inhabitants to scrape a living, day in and day out, with little to show for their efforts. They worked hard but never lost hope or the spirit and determination to overcome their poverty, and so they ploughed the land even harder from sunrise to dusk. Seeing people's faces struggling so hard for a piece of bread on the table convinced him even more that what he was attempting to do was the right thing. Encouraged, he pursued his goal with greater determination and could not wait for the struggle to begin.

After two months of intensive reconnaissance, he returned to Athens and began to finalise a revolutionary committee by bringing more people in who would provide the movement with moral and material support.

He faced insurmountable obstacles wherever he turned for aid, especially arguments of political expediency or the Greek ethos of outright reluctance to fight against an old ally. The most familiar argument by government officials with influence, was always the same: 'We wish to assist but we cannot risk exposure as revolutionaries who are plotting against Britain, a friend and an ally.'

Under difficult circumstances, the first official meeting of a secret Liberation Committee was finally organised under the auspices of the Archbishop.

The new meeting was conducted in the same building as the previous gathering and the Colonel confidently presented his observations and discoveries during his stay on the island. To his surprise, none of the men expressed negative opinions. Even the Archbishop appeared to be swayed, and accepted the possibility that Cyprus could be liberated.

Encouraged by the men's attitude, the Colonel proceeded to explain his plan of action. His heavy task was made easier, by the unwavering enthusiasm of his audience to engage in a positive discussion.

'Our only chance of success,' he explained, 'is to initiate a two-pronged attack based on guerrillas in the mountain regions, and saboteurs in towns and villages. It's our only chance! All other attempts will end up in complete failure considering the British army is well equipped with unlimited resources and hardware. Our own limited resources can best be utilised by outsmarting the British army and attacking where they least expect it. Our hit and run tactics, together with cunning civilian involvement, will cause havoc to the army, which will be at a loss not knowing where the next attack will take place, and by who, or who in fact is the real enemy. When a well-organised army has to encounter elusive civilians as their enemy, they are extremely handicapped; they cannot kill the entire population in their attempt to get to the enemy. They are restricted, and will always be on the defensive while we shall have the upper hand, and always be on the offensive.'

He observed that the men listened to him with great interest and he had a gut feeling they were on his side. He presented his case convincingly. There was not much more to do except to sit down, and wait for their reaction. He gazed briefly at the men's sombre faces, took a sip of water and decided to give his closing statement.

'Gentlemen,' he said in conclusion 'give me your support and I shall give you a liberated Cyprus!'

The enigmatic Archbishop never missed a single word and could see that the Colonel was right. But, as a churchman, he was battling with his own conscience, knowing that innocent lives would be lost,and the uprising certainly would bring about harder times for his people. They already suffer enough, and to burden them with additional miseries because of an undertaking they had absolutely no say in bothered him deeply. If the revolution was successful it would be worth the struggle but, if it failed what then? Innocent people would clearly suffer. On the other hand, he longed to see his people liberated from foreign occupation so they could determine their own destiny free from oppression and exploitation.

He was on the horns of a dilemma, and it was not easy for him to reach a solution that would comply with his Christian upbringing. He looked at the men seated around the table, and could sense that the ultimate decision had been taken. Nervously, he began to twist his long beard and turned fidgeting and restless on his chair.

'It means the bloodshed of young lads' the Archbishop muttered, sceptically to himself, not happy with what was about to take place on the small island.

'It is our only chance!' answered the Colonel from across the table.

'Personally, I am always reluctant to attend the funerals of young boys and girls at the best of times . . . to be the cause of their deaths goes against my religious beliefs. Our boys are not fighters, nor killers; they are simple young lads. How can they be in a position to face an enemy such as the well-trained British army?' the Archbishop stated with strong conviction, desperately trying to seek out other ways than the one proposed.

'How long do you envisage for this struggle to last?' asked one of the men.

'If you are asking me for a timetable, I cannot provide such a schedule! All I know is the struggle has to continue until the enemy capitulates! That is my plan.'

'And if he doesn't?'

'Let me say one thing, all empires rise and fall, and now it is Britain's turn. They have lost Palestine, India, Egypt and they are going to lose Cyprus also. We shall liberate Cyprus!' answered the Colonel.

'How about if we sustain sabotage activities, and put aside the guerrilla part of your plan?' the Archbishop asked, wanting to minimise the bloodshed.

'Not a chance. I can assure all of you that I have considered all possibilities, and there is no point starting something unless one knows the end result. With a well-disciplined and brave fighting force, we shall defeat the enemy! I truly believe that Cypriots possess such qualities and in the end they would be victorious under my leadership.'

'His Eminence may have a point!' objected one of the other men. 'If we are to concentrate our efforts on sabotage activities—where there are plenty of targets as you clearly stated—we may ultimately win international consciousness. We may gain strong public opinion in our favour, to force Britain to seek out a political solution to our problem.'

'This is precisely how I personally envisage this uprising, and in doing so minimise the possibility of senseless bloodshed,' added the Archbishop, pleased that someone else saw things on his wave-length.

'Yes, a few bombs here and there and maybe the odd attack on military targets, surely they would bring attention to our plight.' another one agreed with the previous speaker.

'We shall fail!' interrupted the Colonel, sensing that the other men were beginning to agree with the Archbishop's point of view. 'Do you think Britain, a superpower at that, gives a damn about public opinion? If you believe that, then you all live in a dream world!'

'It may work . . . the United Nations . . .'

'. . . The United Nations . . .?' the Colonel abruptly interrupted the previous speaker with a slight anger in his voice. 'If you think those bureaucrats would put political pressure on the British Empire for the sake of our little island you are deluding yourselves. This is not a political game and empty talk, it is a struggle for liberation and no freedom has ever been won without sacrifices. Flowers need water to sprout but freedom demands blood. This is the reality of man's insanity.'

After a heated discussion, the newly formed Liberation Committee had unanimously decided that should the Colonel return to Cyprus and make the final preparations for the uprising. It was obvious that the Archbishop did not want a forceful solution, but he acquiesced by agreeing to a limited timescale of guerrilla tactics—initially a few months—and to reconsider the whole operation again once they had re-evaluated the British response.

Everyone was happy with this arrangement, and they poured a glass of wine to seal the birth of a revolution. There was only one thing left for them to do, and that was to take a solemn oath of secrecy and blind obedience.

The Archbishop got to his feet, put on his black cap and cape, and then picked up a small Bible. He raised it in the air and crossed himself three times.

One by one the men stood up and bowed their heads in reverence. The Archbishop softly muttered a short prayer, while the others humbly listened, in absolute silence. When he finally finished, he asked everyone to repeat the words of a solemn oath:

> *'I swear in the name of the Holy Trinity to keep secret all I know, or come to*
> *know about the cause of Enosis, even under torture or, at the cost of my life . . .*
> *I shall obey without question, the instructions given to me at all times.'*

Suddenly the Colonel's dream, from being a simple, abstract idealistic thought, had been transformed into reality, and into a tangible plan of action in which he was named the leader of this freedom movement.

*   *   *

The Colonel, the now sworn Leader of Liberation, found himself once again on an Olympic airplane heading for Lefkosia.

While flying, many perplexing thoughts were churning within his mind, knowing that a heavy task had fallen upon his shoulders. He was confident that he would prevail in the end, but he never believed for one moment that one could truly put a time limit on such an unpredictable undertaking. He very much doubted that the British would ever come to terms and negotiate a political solution. But at least, he was given the solemn support of the Liberation Committee to go ahead and make the necessary preparations.

With the Archbishop's backing, which carried powerful influence over the Cyprus Ethnarchy, he felt the sky had opened up for him. Without His Eminence's personal support, he could never initiate such a mammoth undertaking, not in a thousand years. At the same time, he did not blame him for his cautious attitude, and had much respect for him as a great man, and for his religious convictions. He was admired and loved by his people, and they were prepared to do anything for him. Such influence on the masses, through love and devotion, was very rare, and this pious man shared both those qualities. Having his personal backing meant that he would be able to move with ease throughout the island and have access to many safe places to hide himself and his fighters.

Engrossed in his thoughts, the plane landed on the runway at Lefkosia airport. He got off and hired a taxi straight to his brother's house which he was using as his temporary headquarters.

It was December, and already there was a strong chill in the air, an indication that a bad winter was looming. The capital was as busy as always and people went about their business as they had done for years, unaware that a very different type of storm was about to blow, capable of changing their lives forever.

For some this insignificant looking bald man, now walking in their midst, would prove to be their god-sent hero, offering them hope for the future. Others would consider him the dark merchant of death, who had arrived under cover of darkness to steal their children's lives and keep the grave-diggers busier than ever before. They would curse him for bringing such a catastrophe upon their mundane lives and question who on earth had given him the authority, without their consent, to encourage their children to take up arms and kill their fellow-men.

The storm had already started, and the first breezes began to blow gently in their direction without them even realising it. Like an elusive fox in the night, this small man had arrived shrouded in a mysterious silence. He came to scout his prey and pounce upon the naïve and innocent, eternally transforming their peaceful existence.

He tirelessly began to formulate the second phase, the foundation of his revolution by approaching leading citizens who shared the same objectives. He began to build his underground liberation movement from there. He was introduced to the two largest Christian youth movements, and their enthusiastic leaders selected a small number of reliable young men to receive and store guns throughout the island. These two movements were honey-traps, full of young boys and girls, ripe for picking and crucial for his organisation. He attached prime importance to establishing a strong youth movement, and he was convinced that these young boys and girls of school age would become the backbone of his organisation by putting them in the front line. His reasoning was simple: young people love danger and take risks to prove their worth. He picked the idea from the Nazi youth movement.

In a matter of few months the foundation of the Liberation Movement began to take shape. He appointed a head agent in each town whose main task was to choose a leader at every school, and in turn, each school leader chose a class leader. The cornerstone of his Liberation Movement was good intelligence and a rapid courier system, with messages delivered entirely by hand to minimise detection and ensure safe delivery. His network of youths provided the infrastructure necessary for his organisation. He was pleasantly surprised at seeing how quickly this web of young, industrious, and enthusiastic boys and girls spread their wings across the land like fireflies fearless of any danger.

The Colonel was anxious to mobilise the movement, knowing that a number of *Andartes* groups had also been set up and were in readiness for his final instructions to initiate the uprising. He could see that all was in place as he planned. But there was one last hurdle to overcome, and that was the safe shipment of arms into the island without detection. As a trial, a vessel loaded with pottery left from Greece towards Pafos, to allow the captain reconnoitre for adequate landing points. The *caique* arrived on the western coast of the island without difficulty and from a safe distance the captain scouted the shoreline. But the vessel's movements attracted the attention of the naval police who considered its presence suspicious and intercepted it.

After the incident, the first successful arms shipment for the organisation was transported by a small vessel, which landed safely on the west coast of the island. Under cover of darkness, the Hlorakas group unloaded the valuable cargo and hid it safely in the surrounding countryside. They received crates full of second-hand rifles, ammunition, hand grenades, uniforms and other small arms. But these were the bare necessities and more armaments were needed.

The Leader decided it was time for him to leave the island and return to Greece. He wanted to arrange for more arms and military hardware for his *Andartes*, his urban guerrillas and saboteurs in the cities. He was getting anxious to start the revolution . . .

*   *   *

Before his departure for Greece, and by sheer coincidence, he had learned that the Archbishop had returned from New York; the U.N. Security Council blatantly refused to even consider the Cyprus question for self-determination.

Hearing the UN decision, the Greek population spontaneously took to the streets in mass rallies against Britain and the United

Nations, demanding justice for Cyprus. Angry demonstrators burned American and British flags while shouting 'Betrayal' and 'Justice for Cyprus.'

Seeing the massive riots in Lefkosia, the Colonel wanted to discuss the situation in more detail with the Archbishop before leaving for Greece knowing that it may be the last time they would meet each other so openly. His next visit to the island would certainly not be as a tourist but, covertly as the Leader of the underground movement for the Liberation of Cyprus.

The meeting had been arranged to take place at Episkopi.

When he arrived there, he found the Archbishop in a sombre mood. He was seated in solitude under the arched veranda of the ancient Byzantine-style manor. He was gazing over the gardens, covered in tall palm trees and overflowing with vibrant, colourful flowers. The rear yard was divided by winding narrow footpaths that snaked between the many mature flowerbeds. Surrounded with such beauty, the Archbishop, a keen gardener himself, should have been thrilled. But instead, he appeared lonely and at a loss, smoking a cigarette and sipping mint tea.

Hearing the echoing sound of approaching footsteps against the veranda floor, he turned around to look at his visitor. He immediately stood up to welcome the Colonel.

'Come sit down my friend, we have plenty to talk about!' he said in his soft voice and showed the Leader a chair next to him.

He was not wearing his robes or his cap and his long, receding grey hair was tossed over his shoulder and gently drifting about, blown by the afternoon wind.

The Colonel had never seen him look like this before, and he was quite surprised by this new civilian image of His Eminence, who seemed so casual rather than his usual dignified self. He sat next to him, and detected that the Archbishop was quite distressed about the United Nations' affair.

'It's a bad day for Cyprus!' the Archbishop stated, and gazed at his visitor in search of some kind of guidance.

'Who was the devil who objected?'

'I give you two guesses' the Archbishop stated ironically, while pouring a cup of mint tea for his guest.

'America and Britain . . .?'

'You hit the nail on the head, but especially Britain, who tried to manipulate the political situation to protect its own interests. Do you know what they said?' the Archbishop asked with disappointment and disgust in his voice.

'No idea, but I can imagine.'

'The United Nations, whose job is supposedly to protect the weak and vulnerable, had *decided not to consider the Cyprus question further for the time being*. In short, they dumped us!' explained the Archbishop, and looked at the man seated next to him with his bloodshot eyes.

The Colonel thought for a brief moment while evaluating the Archbishop's statement, and then said in a calm voice, 'True, they dumped us for the 'time being', but at least we may get another chance at a later date.'

'Only those two specific words offer a glimmer of hope but most members seem to be on the British side,' replied the Archbishop disappointedly.

'Everyone knows the United Nations has become the lap-dog of the powerful. Its main purpose is to rubber-stamp the wishes of its Western paymasters' the Colonel said, convinced he knew how those paper-pushers operated. He had no time for them.

'It is about time we took our destiny into our own hands!' the Archbishop finally admitted, after he had weighed his companion's comments.

'We have no other choice. As a soldier, I have come to read those toothless paper-lions like a book. I have never trusted them and I never will. They speak with forked tongues,' he said, frowning.

'After our political humiliation in New York, the Greek Government—to my surprise—has now changed its mind, and decided to support us,' stated the Archbishop.

'That is very good news! At least now we can move forward with some kind of backing,' said the Colonel, pleased with the sudden change of heart.

'Unofficially, of course.'

'Your Eminence let this be a lesson to us.'

'What do you mean?' interrupted the Archbishop and looked at his companion in search of answers.

'The Greek nation has a contagious disease—*xenomania*.' the Colonel stated in a serious tone, and took a deep puff from his pipe.

'*Xenomania*?

'Yes . . . *xenomania*. Our proud nation has repeatedly failed to rely on its own strength, resources and capabilities. Because of weakness or lack of self-esteem or influence, the Greeks believe that anything foreign is greatly superior to ours. We allow those foreign powers to manipulate us. We trust them as loyal friends and we refuse to see the damage such one-sided friendship does to our nation. In a true sense, the Greek nation has no real friends and must learn to stand by its own strength if it's to survive as a free nation.'

'Explain yourself, Colonel.'

'It is quite simple. The Anglo-Saxon races have each other for support; the black races are united by their skin colour; the Asians have characteristics that bond them together, and the Arabs have their strong fundamentalist religion. What is it that binds the Greek nation with others? Nothing! Certainly not Christianity! As a nation we are certainly blinded by *xenomania*,' the Colonel explained with a certainty that showed he meant every word he said.

'You may be right!'

'Right? It is about time we tell all those foreign powers to mind their own business and stop meddling in our national affairs! As a proud nation, we are blessed with intelligence to differentiate between what is right and what is wrong! Only the weak, vulnerable and the defeatists plead to others to solve their national problems. As a nation, we have the right to defend ourselves and preserve our heritage handed down to us by our ancestors,' the Colonel patriotically spoke his mind.

'Yes, yes . . . we must learn to stand on our two feet.' agreed the Archbishop and continued in a serious tone, 'but, do you honestly believe that we can?'

'Of course, and we shall soon prove it! We are waiting for another delivery of arms to the island! With God's help, we may start the uprising soon after the shipment arrives. Then, we shall show the world that the Hellenes are a proud nation, ready to defend what is rightfully and morally ours.'

'May God help all of us.' muttered the Archbishop and quickly asked, 'Doesn't the organisation need a name?

'Yes. The name is *EOKA*.'

'*EOKA*? What does it mean?' the Archbishop asked curiously.

'*Ethniki Organosis Kyprion Agoniston* . . . '*EOKA*' for short.' he explained.

'It sounds good!' agreed the Archbishop, and smiled for the first time.

He appeared pleased and began to show more faith in the man seated next to him; this man who held the destiny of Cyprus in the palm of his hand. They talked for a long time, and covered all aspects of the organisation's structure from financing, to training. They also discussed the Liberation Committee's pledge that *Eoka* was to be included in any negotiated final agreement.

'I give you my word! No deal will be signed, unless you personally, as the Leader of *Eoka*, or your representatives take part in negotiating for a final solution to our plight. It is not up to me or you, or the politicians, to sign the fate of Cyprus. The final decision rests with the people, under the terms of a nation-wide plebiscite,' the Archbishop stated affirmatively.

'Your word is good enough for me, I would hate to find ourselves sidelined from any negotiations,' said the Colonel.

'Don't be concerned my friend. *Eoka* and the people of Cyprus shall decide, and not faceless politicians,' said the Archbishop to reassure him.

They finished their discussion and the Archbishop invited his guest to share a meal before departing for Lefkosia. He graciously accepted the invitation, and as they were walking along the veranda, the Archbishop stopped briefly and looked at his companion.

'Let's begin the uprising on the 25th of March, Greece's Independence Day!' he suggested.

'It is too late. We should try and make use of the long winter nights. As soon as the new arms shipment arrives, the struggle shall begin!'

'God help us all!' said the Archbishop and crossed himself. He then raised both of his arms in the air in search of the Almighty, making sure he was listening to his prayer.

Pleased with his meeting, the Colonel went back to Lefkosia with positive thoughts. Everything was falling into place like the pieces of a jigsaw puzzle and he could not wait to start the actual battle for liberation. His boys and girls were getting anxious and were raring to encounter the enemy. But he had to restrain their enthusiasm until he was sure all was in place. He needed one more shipment of arms, and then nothing was going to stop him from mobilising his young fighters into action.

He returned to Greece and plunged headlong into the cause to raise funds and purchase more arms for his revolution. Faced with the constant procrastination by reluctant officials, he finally succeeded in putting together another shipload of arms with the help of his ex-*Xhi* colleagues.

The urgency to move faster became obvious to him; he wanted to return to the island as soon as possible to start the revolution before the British realised what was about to hit them. So far, they detected nothing unusual, but as each day went by, the risk of discovery increased and he could no longer take chances. He knew of the dangers that lay ahead, but he also knew that great things are never achieved without great dangers and so, one sunny morning, he kissed his wife goodbye and set out for Cyprus. There was no turning back now . . .

'God guide me I leave with faith and courage. I shall succeed!' he said to her, and he set sail from the port of Piraeus.

He recognised that he was about to start the hardest task of his life, and with courage he entered a winding murky road, which may or may not ultimately lead to the freedom of his mother country.

Crossing the Aegean Sea, a storm began to blow fiercely and the small rickety fishing boat was blown like a small shell at the mercy of the huge waves that crashed upon it. The gale forced them to moor unexpectedly at Rhodes harbour until it subsided but the longer they remained there, the greater the danger of discovery or betrayal.

They waited ten days and nights while the rain and storm blew angrily. The sea whipped up huge waves that crashed with determination, like a bad omen to stop them casting off for the small island.

Eventually, the furious sea got tired and calmed down, calling its howling winds to ease up and offered the opportunity for their vessel to cast off at midnight from the small bay of Kallithea. It was not meant to be! Before dawn, a new gale arose more violent than the previous one. Huge waves were crashing over the fragile *Siren* as they were passing Kastelorizon Island, off the Turkish coast.

'We better stop!' the captain yelled at the Colonel, who was standing next to him on the bridge.

There was a grave worried expression on his weather-beaten face. He appeared to be constantly battling and steering the vessel to beat the oncoming waves. The fretful captain was a short hirsute man, with an unruly moustache that practically reached down to his solid chest. The fierce wind flapped his wild moustache over his shoulders and he felt great pride at feeling the hairs tingling against his rugged face.

'Did you hear me? We'd better find refuge!' The captain shouted again.

'Keep going!' insisted the Colonel determined to reach the Cyprus coast.

'We shall be crushed!' the nervous skipper called out again, concerned that they might all drown.

'I don't want to be in Turkish hands! Keep going otherwise we shall destroy everything we have achieved!' the Colonel insisted; not prepared to accept defeat so soon.

'Hold tight and enjoy the journey!' shouted the captain.

He grabbed the helm with both of his hairy strong arms, and pinned his eyes ahead like a hawk. He stared at the oncoming massive waves that shimmered against the night sky and stressfully shook his head. The waves showed no sign of abating. He took a few deep breaths, releasing a rush of adrenalin within his wide chest and stared at the huge waves. Undeterred, he expertly guided the vessel forward by turning the helm right and left and often letting it spin to overcome a persistent gigantic wave.

The entire party on the vessel were in a terrible state being sick and throwing-up over the side. Their stomachs constantly erupted like volcanoes as they vomited uncontrollably. The Colonel felt the wrath of the sea in the worse way and he lay on a bunk bed, with his eyes closed. He could hardly move a muscle, he was as white as a sheet, and remained motionless like a corpse on his rocking bed.

Slowly they fought their way southbound, and by dusk they arrived in the open blue waters of Cyprus. The welcome sight of the thin coastline had sent up a sigh of relief, knowing they had escaped the clutches of the angry sea. By nightfall, the waters eased . . . not a single wave was visible, only the majestic reflection of a glowing moon appeared to be floating on its swelling surface.

The Colonel and his companions, a mainland ex-military man, and one Greek Cypriot got into a small dinghy and rowed towards the remote rocky coast of Hlorakas. By then, it was pitch black, with not a single light detectable. When they approached the shoreline, a lone voice came out of the darkness.

'Who is there?'

'*Dighenis!*' shouted the Colonel in reply, using his adopted *nom-de-guerre*.

'*Akritas!*' instantly came back the correct password from the rugged coastline.

The three men stepped ashore, and were quickly guided on foot towards the village of Hlorakas. The evening breeze gently caressed their wobbly bodies as they walked on solid ground again and into the silent night.

Like a miracle, the storm had completely ceased to blow, replaced by a dreamlike calmness that engulfed the sleepy coastline. People snored peacefully in their beds, not realising a new storm was about to blow with greater vigour and far more destructive . . .

CHAPTER FIVE

IT WAS SATURDAY night, and Alexis was preparing himself to go out and meet his friends at *Salingari Taverna*. Every weekend without fail all the friends met at this tavern, their favourite rendezvous, to decide how to spend the rest of the evening. His mother had already pressed his white shirt and a navy blue pair of trousers and had carefully placed them over a chair in his bedroom. He was taking his time and was in no hurry, knowing the night was young. At the same time, he wanted to get going to avoid his brother's usual arguments with his sister. The sooner he got out of the house, the sooner he would hear less of their constant bickering.

From a skinny boy, Alexis had grown into a handsome youth, well proportioned with a solid physique. Muscles developed on his biceps and stomach . . . muscles that he never knew existed. Fit and agile, he always walked and rarely took a bus to go to Varoshia, preferring to stroll leisurely in case he met up with one of his friends. His thick dark brown hair was neatly trimmed and combed to one side, allowing it to fall slightly over his forehead. He was blessed with two thick black straight eyebrows like swords over his deep brown eyes and long eyelashes. Every time he smiled, his mouth caused small dimples at the sides of his cheeks, while his delicate straight nose was in perfect proportion with his face.

For a nineteen-year old he was quite mature, and the words coming out of his mouth were always polite and well spoken. Having to work from a young age, he had learned to take care of himself and never shied from responsibility. He had developed similar qualities to his father, a thoughtful, caring man who gained respect from those around him.

Alexis had developed into a tall, lean young man, but somehow he never managed to develop as masculine a physique as Ahmet, no matter how much he tried. But he was happy with the way he looked, especially now that local girls were beginning to pay attention to him.

One sunny day his family walked away from *Loukkos* which had been their home for four miserable years. His father, together with his loyal friend Vasili, bought a plot of land at Kato Varoshia, and had built a modest stone house each. Leaving *Loukkos* was like casting a heavy stone behind them for good. At long last, they were freed from such a wretched environment. But no sooner were they over the embankment than a new wagon appeared, carrying a family to take over their empty shack . . .

In their new neighbourhood, Yiorkis recognised the need for a grocery shop and managed to open up a small store. It was the wisest move he had ever made. It brought him financial security and his wife was able to give up her job and devote herself to the family. This had been her life-long dream. The day she quit her job, she prepared a huge feast for her family and friends, to celebrate her freedom from the daily drudgery of the steaming hot laundry rooms.

At the first pallid light of the day, she would rise, prepare breakfast, and put together a lunch-pack for her 'mechanics' and see them off to work. She loved her new freedom and proudly devoted her entire life to the well-being of her family.

As the years went by she grew heavier and tired quickly. She found it difficult to be as active as before, but her hands, those hard-working hands of hers, gave her the worst pain; they ached constantly. The years of scrubbing piles of laundry at the clinic had left its mark on them. Some days the pain was so excruciating she would place both hands inside a bucket of warm water with salt, to relieve the pain. It did not always work and she learned to live with the pain, day in and day out.

The only thing that gave her pleasure was her family, and she found happiness seeing that everyone was in good health and that they cared for one other. Her modest house was transformed into a lively centre for young boys and girls who congregated together nearly every day, bringing life to her household. She got great enjoyment out of mingling with the different age groups. She would gaze at their youthful, vibrant faces, and smile at their individual mannerism and child-like behaviour. She loved listening to their ceaseless chatter and vivacious laughter that reverberated throughout the whole house. Their vivacity always made her feel alive.

Today, there was nobody in the house except for her Alexis, who arrived early after picking up car parts from the wholesaler. Being Saturday, he knew the shower would be occupied forever once his sister and Marcos arrived home. Not risking his chances, he quickly jumped into the shower-room before they showed up. He had a slow shower and gave himself a clean shave, making sure that every bit of dark hair growth on his face was removed and his dark sideburns were absolutely straight.

Leisurely, he got dressed, posed and examined himself by staring in the mirror hanging behind the door of his room. He was very fastidious and wanted to make sure every bit of his clothing was perfectly in place. He put on a colourful necktie and it took him forever to master a perfect knot in proportion to his shirt collar. Being deprived of such luxuries in the past, he made sure now that he was working, to make up for all those lost years. He put on his black shiny shoes and walked into the kitchen.

He found his mother cooking while Maro, who had arrived without being noticed, was giving her mother a hand by peeling potatoes at the kitchen table and chatting. They both had their backs to him, and quietly he sneaked behind Maro, and wrapped his arms around her slim waist to give her a long hug.

'What's that for?' surprised, she asked, and continued peeling away without turning round to look at him. She knew it was her Alexis by smelling his cologne and the whiff of fresh soap.

'Oh . . . nothing special, I just wanted to tell you that I love you!' he said to her and gave her a gentle kiss on the cheek.

'Don't be silly!' she said, embarrassed and lowering her eyes while smiling.

At that moment Ahmet walked into the kitchen covered in grease, and instantly the room overflowed with the pungent smell of gasoline and grease combined. He went straight to Kyra-Soteria and gave her a little kiss, as he always did every Saturday after work. That had become his weekly trademark and a customary gesture. He then turned towards Alexis, surprised to see him already dressed up.

'Allah!' he said, surprised at seeing that he was immaculate and ready for action. 'What's the big rush?'

'I am sick of listening to those two arguing.' Alexis said and endearingly tousled his sister's hair.

'It's not my fault!' Maro complained, defending herself, and turned round to stick up for herself.

She looked at her brother with her vibrant black eyes and pushed her long tresses off her face. For a fifteen-year-old she was developing much faster than Alexis preferred, knowing that boys had already started hanging around the house just to take a glimpse of her. She was not ripe yet, but all the signs were there and it wouldn't be much longer before she was ready for the picking. He hated the idea, and he was always over-protective of his baby sister, who worshipped the ground he walked on and loved him dearly.

'Is Petros coming tonight?' Ahmet asked, while taking off his smelly overall.

'Of course! I'll get a table at *Salingari*, but don't forget to pick up Michalaki, he's not home yet.' Alexis said, in readiness to depart. 'How do I look?' he asked, wanting Ahmet's approval.

'Fine,' said Ahmet without paying attention and went to get into the shower.

At that precise moment Marcos walked into the room, wearing his favourite red striped shorts. He instantly sniffed his brother's cologne and pulled a long face.

'Why can't I come with you?' Marcos complained and joined them in the kitchen.

'Because I work . . . that's why!' Alexis retorted to his brother.

'But I want to enjoy life like you do . . .' complained his young brother.

'Seal it up Marcos!' irritated, his mother interjected. 'You are only sixteen and there is plenty of time for foolishness!'

'Yes . . .Yes,' he muttered to himself, and walked out of the room sulking. He banged the door behind him, and went looking for his own friends to console himself.

He had walked in like the wind, and walked out again the same way, but his departure brought peace and quiet back into the house. Just before leaving, Alexis put his hand into his pocket, pulled out a couple of notes, and handed them to his mother.

'Here take this *mama*,' he said, and passed over the notes to her.

She smiled at him and slowly stuffed the notes into her bosom. She turned around, raised her arms to reach his clean-shaven face and gave him a tender kiss on the cheek. She was very proud of her 'mechanics' who regularly gave her house money whenever they got paid, but in her own way she always gave it back to them, by buying socks or shirts for them.

'Don't be late!' she said to him, as he was about to leave.

'And you don't wait up for us . . . like you always do!' Alexis answered, but really knew better than to say that, and strode out of the kitchen.

Irrespective what time they arrived home, Kyra-Soteria was always waiting up for them, pretending she had endless chores to do or that she could not sleep. She would be seated in the living room, knitting or half falling asleep until they walked safely through the front door. Regardless of the late hour, she would be awake like a sentinel anxious to see her two young men walk through the door. 'Oh, You are home.' she would say softly once they appeared and then slowly raise her heavy body off the couch. Then she would drag her feet to her room and shut the door behind her, content that her boys were safe. In a matter of a few minutes, she would be in a deep sleep, with a sudden burst of snores escaping the room.

When he arrived at the tavern the place was quickly filling up with young people and off-duty British servicemen who had developed a taste for Greek food and culture. *Salingari Taverna* could accommodate more than one hundred covers, and offered excellent outdoor table facilities under two massive mulberry trees and an ancient fig tree. In the evening, a string of bare electric light bulbs, interwined throughout the gnarled branches illuminated the entire area. Apart from the customers these illuminations also attracted a myriad of fluttering moths and nocturnal insects that endlessly swarmed around the bright bulbs, often dropping to the ground like kamikazes.

Over the entire front courtyard, the tavern was blessed with a large vine over a vast trellised arbour, providing cool shade from the scorching sun. During the summer months, the vine was heavily laden with bunches of crunchy *verigo* grapes suspended in large clusters over the entire arbour. They attracted customers, anxious to get their teeth into those massive huge grapes. The classic old sandstone building with its red clay roof tiles, wooden window shutters, verandas and endless stone arches had gained a reputation for being one of the best authentic restaurants on the island.

Alexis saw an empty table in a corner alongside the fence, and went straight for it. He sat down and ordered a large bottle of Keo beer and waited for his friends to arrive. From where he was seated, he had a perfect view of the bustling street. The main avenue was crowded with people of all ages, leisurely taking a stroll in long lines at either side of the main promenade. They went back and forth to the seafront, until it was time for them to disperse by going into a restaurant, pastry shop or cinema in the main square of Varoshia. The busy square had become the hub of the city, especially during the evenings when it was chock-full of cart concessions and kiosks peddling anything one fancied. Flower-girls mingled among the crowds selling perfumed jasmine, strung together on fine thread, and people would wrap them around their wrists, or put them inside their shirt pockets to take a sniff periodically.

By eight o'clock none of his friends had shown up, and he was getting quite anxious. Restlessly, he ordered another beer and waited knowing they would soon show up to liven things up with their noisy compliments aimed at pretty *Gymnasium* school girls who walked by in groups dressed in their pristine school uniforms.

Alexis, with time to kill, watched the crowds going back and forth taking their stroll and enjoying the night breeze and hustle bustle of the evening. Suddenly, among the crowds he noticed a familiar face that towered over the others, and he quickly stood up. He could not believe his eyes. He quickly put his hands around his mouth and let out a deafening whistle.

'Spyros, over here' he yelled at the top of his voice. He received no response.

He called out again, but much louder this time, and gave out a prolonged whistle that made customers at nearby tables turn around and look at him as he kept shouting and waving both his hands like a madman.

Spyros had finally noticed him and smiled warmly on seeing his friend. He waved back and immediately walked towards him, pushing the crowd aside, and entered the courtyard. His tall, blonde friend, wearing a brightly coloured shirt, pulled up a chair and sat opposite him. He smiled, clasped both of his friend's hands and held them tightly, pleased that he'd finally met up with him after such a long time. They both gazed at each other, exhilarated, and their eyes glowed with warmth and sincerity at such an unexpected reunion.

'What on earth happened to you?' Alexis asked, being delighted to see Spyros again after years of separation. 'I saw you last . . .'

'. . . At the sea festival, remember? The fireworks?' Spyros answered and burst out laughing. He hadn't changed much in character. He was still the same jolly fellow that Alexis remembered from childhood. He had shot up like a weed and stood nearly six foot in height, with solid shoulders and piercing blue eyes.

'How could I forget! You caused havoc with those fireworks!' Alexis answered, and both burst out laughing remembering that day.

The waiter came and Spyros ordered a bottle of ouzo and *meze* to nibble on until the others arrived. The two friends conversed animatedly, reminiscing about the past and their youthful adventures. On a serious note, Alexis could not help but be curious and ask his friend what he had been up to in the past three years.

'You know me, I am still a printer but things have taken a different turn, and I have not been able to concentrate on printing lately,' he answered slightly nervously.

'Meaning?

'As a matter of fact you are the reason for my visit here!'

'How is that?' Alexis asked inquisitively and looked Spyros in the eyes.

'Alexis, there is a storm brewing, and I want to discuss this with you.' Spyros said to him and took a sip of his ouzo.

'What sort of storm? Speak up, I am all ears. We have no secrets from each other!' Alexis prompted him, realising that his pal had suddenly turned quite serious, which was out of character. He sensed there was something bothering him, and gave him his total attention.

'What I'm about to tell you is in strict confidence! Not a word to anybody and, I mean nobody! You give me your word . . .?'

'You have it damn you, out with it!' Alexis answered, bursting to learn what he had to say.

Spyros lowered his head and his blonde hair fell over his forehead. He was no longer joking, but in a serious mode. 'Are you happy?' he whispered.

'Of course I am happy! What kind of stupid question is that?'

'No, you don't understand, I mean the way people live in Cyprus?'

'I have never given it much thought, but, if you are asking me if I accept the living conditions here . . . no, I am not happy. But, you always knew that,' answered Alexis who had often shared his feelings with him and his close friends in the past.

The conversation had turned into a serious discussion and the crowded tavern seemed less important. People's voices became just a buzz, a cacophony, and the lads paid no attention to it. Instead, they got into an intense dialogue talking quietly so that only their ears could hear.

'Let's say this island rose up to struggle for freedom, what would you do?' Spyros finally asked his perplexed friend, who was totally puzzled by such double-talk.

'Spyros, you are talking nonsense!'

'What would you do?' Spyros insisted again, and his right eye twitched slightly.

'I would probably fight like others.'

'You mean that?'

'Of course I would!' Alexis reassured his persistent friend.

'Could you fight against the British army even if the odds were against such an uprising?' Spyros whispered and leaned over the table, his eyes staring directly into Alexis' without blinking.

Alexis looked at Spyros and realised he was quite serious. 'Of course I would!' he said to him, but could not fully comprehend what this conversation was leading to.

For the lads nothing of what was happening around them was visible or audible. The people transformed themselves into surreal silhouettes, that kept going back and forth with no purpose, and the melodic music drifting from inside the tavern appeared to be coming from somewhere beyond reality. They were in too deep a conversation to notice the crowds around them. Now and then, they lit a cigarette and took a sip of *ouzo* to fuel their discussion and carried on talking to each other.

'How would you like to join an underground organisation, to liberate Cyprus from the British?' Spyros finally popped the question, in barely a whisper.

Alexis looked at him, not sure if he meant what he said, but the expression on his face was so serious, it did not seem to belong to the same Spyros he once knew.

'I am interested.' replied Alexis, not realising the gravity of his answer. His wide brown eyes lit up in anticipation, and he nervously pushed back the hair off his face.

'I thought so . . . !' Spyros said, pleased with his friend's answer. He gave him a lingering smile.

'You are kidding me, of course?' Alexis interjected.

'I am dead serious . . . ! You have asked me what I have been up to . . . I have joined a secret organisation that will bring freedom to Cyprus! It is a new movement, and a number of select groups are now being formed across the island. The Colonel, our Leader, has been organising the movement, and soon it will go into action but we need more groups. I have spoken highly of you.'

'You can count on me! I'll do whatever it takes, to be part of this movement to rid our country of British colonialism. If you have joined, count me in!' Alexis said with assurance.

'I knew I could count on you!' said Spyros pleased with his friend's positive, patriotic attitude. 'Tomorrow you meet me here, at the same time and I will take you to join the movement'.

'I shall be here.' Alexis said, and nodded his head in agreement.

'This calls for a drink!' Spyros said happily, raised his glass of *ouzo* high and both clinked their glasses together, to seal the new relationship.

'I must remind you once again, not a word to anyone, not even Ahmet. If one word reaches the wrong ears we've had it! We are dead!' Spyros warned his friend, absolutely serious about what he said.

'I understand.' Alexis promised to put Spyros' fears aside.

They decided to end their discussion and waited for the others to arrive. By nine o'clock their three friends strode towards them. The moment they set eyes on Spyros, they all burst into spontaneous laughter. Their long lost friend had reappeared.

'*Aspris . . . Aspris . . . Aspris!*' they chanted aloud Spyros' nickname, unconcerned by the disapproving looks thrown at them by other customers.

Ahmet, who was walking in front of the others, immediately pounced upon Spyros, threw his chunky arms around his friend's waist and gave him a strong bear-hug. Michalaki and Petros instantly gave him a hard firm endearing pat on his shoulder.

In jubilant mood, they all sat down and ordered more *meze* and extra bottles of *ouzo*, knowing how much Spyros liked it. The unexpected, long overdue reunion had turned into a private feast not only of food and drink but also of camaraderie.

All night they drank, ate and made merry, but Michalaki got drunk silly, and demanded that everyone should go to the Walls and pay a visit to one of the brothels to seal the happy occasion between a woman's breasts.

'Why a Turkish girl?' asked Spyros who was also slightly drunk.

'Why not?' answered Michalaki, their chubby friend, and stood up anxious to get going.

'Greek girls, Turkish girls, English girls. Women are all the same under the darkness of passion!' Spyros ventured, lowering his voice and leaning over the table so he would not be overheard.

'I didn't know that.' Michalaki whispered and then started laughing aloud, being anxious to try and find out if Spyros was correct or not.

By one o'clock in the morning, half-tipsy and under the merry influence of *ouzo*, they all squeezed into Spyros' old wreck of a car and headed towards the Walls. Ecstatic at the unexpected reunion and aided by good food and plenty of drink, they managed to reach the Eastern Gate of the Walls.

They parked their car and, like a pack of lusting wolves on the prowl, rambled into the maze of darkly lit alleyways to seek out their prey. Like thieves in the night, they kept their silence so as not to wake up the locals who might chase them away. The nocturnal revellers stumbled about until they spotted a familiar red light, on one of the rundown mud-brick houses.

Without hesitation, they all went inside the modest house. They were delighted they had found a brothel operating at such a late hour. Inside, a number of skimpily dressed girls of all ages lolled on soft cushions arranged over wooden benches around a large lobby. As soon as the raven-haired harlots saw the pack of young studs, they quickly jumped up to welcome them by pressing their sweet-scented bodies against them. The girls knew what they were doing, and were most anxious to please them, but there was one girl short.

'No problem!' said a middle-aged madam, who woke up from her snoozing, as soon as she heard the clamour of the boys walking in. 'One of you can have me . . .at a bargain price . . .!'

The lads looked at the old broiler and would have nothing to do with her. They appeared to be scared of this woman who had a piercing pair of beady eyes and bright red hennaed hair. She picked up a comb and started combing her long fiery mane voluptuously to entice the lads, so that one of them would have her.

'We came here for spring lamb, not mutton!' Ahmet said to her.

'Don't be impertinent, young man! I am as good as any of them skinny bunnies, if not better! Here, you try me . . . then you can see what a Turkish hen can do for your hormones.'

'No way! You go and get us another young one or we shall all walk out,' Ahmet told her, in Turkish.

She locked her beady eyes with Ahmet's and realised he meant what he said. Not wanting to lose her punters, she shook her fist menacingly at him and walked out the front door, mumbling under her breath in Turkish.

A few minutes later she returned dragging a young Armenian girl with her. She appeared half-asleep, and was still in her white chiffon nightgown. She was a pretty girl with dark features and wild black hair, but she seemed quite upset at being woken up for duty. Madam held her by the arm with indifference, and shoved her to join the other girls who appeared anxious to get to work so they could please the boys and possibly go to sleep themselves. Madam grabbed the money from the boys, counted each coin and sent her girls off to work so they could earn their night's pay.

One by one the boys disappeared inside separate rooms, slamming the doors after them. Brief giggles escaped through the door cracks, then . . . silence!

*   *   *

The next evening Alexis went to meet Spyros as arranged . . . He got there early and had time to ponder what the future had in store for him, but he was quite excited knowing he was about to enter a movement that might make a difference to people's lives. He never in a million years could ever imagine that he would be part of such a revolutionary undertaking and the prospect filled him with confidence, as well as apprehension. How could he fight? He did not have the slightest idea about guns. Only once in a while would he borrow Petros' air rifle and go bird shooting with him. Could he kill another person? He was not able to answer that question, and did not want to ponder on it. He reasoned with himself that, with the right training, he might be able to pull the trigger. The idea of killing someone petrified him! Maybe it will never have to come to that.

With those thoughts in his mind, he observed the busy promenade crowded with people enjoying their Sunday evening stroll with families or friends. The night turned out to be quite warm and he took off his jacket and placed it over the back of his chair. He unbuttoned his white shirt halfway, to allow the breeze to caress his bare hairy chest and cool him down.

He noticed a couple of youngsters no more than ten years old, with cropped hair and dressed in rags mingling with the crowd selling peanuts in paper bags. With their heads raised, they tried to make eye contact and urged people to buy a bag for a few coins. Seeing the two skinny juveniles brought back memories of his own childhood, and he called out to the boys.

Hearing his voice, they both shot like a bullet towards his table, competing to get to him first. He picked up two bags of peanuts from each, and looked at them compassionately.

'Where do you live?' he asked the barefooted boys inquisitively. They already had their small palms stretched out, waiting for payment.

'*Loukkos.*' they answered with indifference, and quickly rushed off once they had been paid. He could hear their voices over the noisy crowd, but their cries soon faded into the distance.

He remembered the endless nights when he also had to roam these same streets selling snacks and ice cream dressed in a similar way, cocky and barefooted. Most of all, he remembered the blisters on the soles of his feet that never seemed to go away. Some nights, when he was not lucky in selling, he'd go home downhearted and curl up inside the chicken coop to sleep off his sadness. He could not fool his parents who got accustomed to his routine, and they would gently wake him up.

He hated those years! Maybe with the oncoming revolution, he would play a part and make a small contribution towards making life a little better for some other misfortunate youngsters. Things do not just happen without a purpose, and there is always a reason for all changes whether positive or negative. This new organisation might turn out to be the main catalyst to bring about positive changes so desperately needed on the island. The present living conditions were the direct result of years of Cypriot complacency, which permitted the foreign merchants of misery and suffering to wield their might across the land.

For every action there is always a reaction, and the British were about to feel the result of their own inadequacy and failure to help the poor inhabitants improve their living conditions. Instead, they pursued a policy of total exploitation, sucking the blood out of the poor peasant and leaving him in utter destitution.

Last night's conversation with Spyros prompted him to think of freedom and other issues he had never thought about before. He was grateful to his friend for sparking the flame inside his unblemished young heart. His words of patriotism made him realise that finally something was about to be done to remedy the British injustices of the past. He had come to recognise that it's within one's own power to make things happen, and one does not simply have to depend on others to alter one's destiny. He was now prepared to plunge in the deep end, and be part of this movement that was about to make things happen. For better or worse, he desired to be at the centre of this new uprising.

His thoughts were interrupted seeing Spyros walking between the tables and towards him. Spyro was anxious to get moving.

'Are we ready?' he asked his friend.

'More than ready! Let's go!' he answered and stood up. He picked his jacket up and both walked out of *Salingari* and into the crowded street.

Within half an hour they arrived at a sleepy neighbourhood and parked the car in an open field. They got out and followed a gravel trail until they stopped outside a house, surrounded by a high stone-wall. Leading the way forward, Spyros opened the sturdy iron-gate and both walked across the yard. He knocked at the door and in no time at all, they heard someone unbolting the entrance, and a young lady made her appearance standing at the threshold. She recognised Spyros.

'*Kalispera.*' she said in a deep resonating voice greeting the two lads.

She led them directly into the living room, where an older man was seated on a couch and two other lads sat at a table pushed against the wall. The moment they set eyes on the newcomers, they got to their feet and welcomed them both. They were expected. The older man seemed preoccupied, and had his nose sunk deep into some charts. He briefly glanced at the boys from above the rims of his eyeglasses, and smiled. He nodded his head at them in a welcoming gesture, and then continued examining the charts, without uttering a single word.

'I am *Aetos*!' the elder of the two lads said, introducing himself to Alexis.' You know why you are here?' he added, and beckoned the boys to join him at the table.

'Yes, Spyros has explained to me everything and I want to be part of this movement,' Alexis answered slightly nervously and sat down.

'We are glad to hear this. Spyros has spoken very highly of you.' and then went on to add, 'I shall be the only contact you will ever have with *Eoka*. You will receive and execute all orders given to you by me or the Leader and nobody else. Is this understood?'

'Of course!' answered Alexis with confidence, realising he was about to join this clandestine organisation. For the very first time in his life he felt that he was accomplishing something worth living for, and the idea of liberating Cyprus appealed to him with true conviction.

The man who was interviewing Alexis was no more than twenty-five years old. He had a pleasant smile and spoke softly without any aggression. He had a neatly trimmed, black moustache over a pouting upper lip, and a pair of piercing brown eyes that seemed to radiate kindness to those around him. He appeared to be a likeable person, and Alexis felt at ease talking with him and sensed that dealing with this man would not be difficult at all.

They talked for a long time of the need to liberate the island from British occupation and how this task could be achieved, while the older man on the couch had his ears pricked, listening. He got up, said nothing, and went into the kitchen. A few minutes later, he returned carrying a pot of coffee for everyone.

'Tell me young man, do you know what freedom requires?' he finally asked Alexis, while handing out coffee without even looking at him.

'Courage and love for one's country.' Alexis answered, quite surprised that this mysterious older man had finally allowed one word to escape his lips. His voice seemed domineering and Alexis recognised the Greek accent, rather than the Cypriot dialect. He instantly knew this man was not Cypriot, but was from mainland Greece.

'Do you have those qualities?' he asked again.

'Yes . . . and, determination to get the job done!'

'Freedom my son is like a weed, it does not need water to sprout, it demands blood! Are you willing to shed blood?' the man stated seriously and stared directly into Alexis' eyes, examining his reaction.

'To the last drop!'

The elderly stern looking man, who maintained his silence most of the evening, had now decided to take over the discussion. Seated at the couch, his shiny bald head captured the reflection coming from the light-bulb dangling from the ceiling, and every time he moved, the glow appeared to follow him.

He looked at the new lad seated at the edge of the table, and allowed his gaze to inspect the other three young men who also appeared to be determined and ready to give up their lives for their country. He recognised the burning passion in their eyes. He wished that he were as young as those boys, with equal vigour, zest and youthful enthusiasm, but, for him it was now too late. He was proud of all these boys who were fearless against all odds. With faith in God and without any demands, they were more than ready to take up arms against a mighty power such as Britain.

'You are about to enter into an organisation that will bring about the freedom of our beloved country and you will play your role, like all the other brave young lads who share the same aspirations as you do. It will be your duty to recruit and form other secret groups to fight for the liberation of Cyprus. Are you prepared to accept such a heavy responsibility?'

'With all my heart.'

'Very well then, we have just recruited another Area Commander to help us recruit other fighting groups.' the interviewer said to the others with a smile, impressed with Alexis' attitude.

Alexis felt relieved on hearing those words, and looked at Spyros to share his happiness. His friend remained silent throughout the entire discussion.

'One last thing, you trust nobody!' the man advised his new recruit.

The small room was choking with cigarette smoke and the other man—a lad with a thick neck on his broad shoulders—pushed the window ajar to let some fresh air into the room. With nothing more to discuss, *Aetos* asked Alexis to stand up and raise his right hand in order to take the oath of *Eoka*.

'*Eoka* is like a family and every family member must protect each other to the death. What unifies this family of ours is devotion to the freedom of Cyprus, supplication and love of our Orthodox Christian faith and unreserved allegiance to our Leader. To seal this everlasting bond you are required to take the solemn oath. These persons here are to witness your allegiance to *Eoka*,' *Aetos* said to Alexis, and asked him to repeat after him:

'*I swear in the name of the Holy Trinity that:*

I shall work with all my power for the liberation of Cyprus from the British yoke, sacrificing for this even my life;

I shall perform without question all the instructions of the Organisation which may be given to me and I shall not bring any objection, however difficult or dangerous it may be;

I shall not abandon the struggle unless I receive instructions from the Leader of the Organisation and after our aim has been accomplished;

I shall never reveal to anyone any secret of the Organisation, neither the names of my chiefs nor those of any other members, even if I am captured and tortured;

I shall not reveal any instructions which may be given me, even to my fellow Fighters;
If I disobey this oath I shall be worthy of every punishment as a traitor, and eternal contempt may cover me.'

Word by word, Alexis nervously repeated the oath with a slight tremor in his voice. Hearing those solemn words coming out of *Aeto's* mouth made him feel important and life appeared to mean something finally. He had a goal, and those around him, although strangers a couple of hours ago they had now become his brothers who were prepared to give up their lives for one another. A pleasant sense of bonding had overcome him, and after the swearing in, Alexis was congratulated with a sturdy handshake from everyone. Spyros gave him a warm hug, thrilled that his friend had joined the movement.

He was given his final instructions and the code name *Akamantis*, as well as points of contact in the event of an emergency and how he could approach *Aetos*, his District Leader. His training in explosives, guns and other urban guerrilla tactics was to begin immediately, so that he would be in a position to train others.

At about midnight everyone bid farewell and departed to go about their business across the island. On the way home, Alexis was curious about the older man who seemed the most unlikely person to be part of such an organisation as *Eoka*, considering his age.

'That bald man, who was he?' he asked Spyros.

Spyros turned his head and gazed at his friend while driving, and gave him a wide smile, exposing his white teeth that shone briefly in the strong lights of an oncoming car.

'I never saw a bald man.' he said quietly.

Alexis realised, that he had lots to learn and his training had just begun . . . He felt good, recognising that he finally had a real purpose in life—the liberation of his country.

He was driven home, but Spyros did not stop. He was anxious to get home the same evening and be with his family. They both said their goodbyes and he immediately sped off straight for Lefkosia, not knowing when they would ever meet again . . .

CHAPTER SIX

THROUGHOUT THE ISLAND a giant was born; a giant that sprouted through the earth's crust and prepared to destroy the shackles of oppression that had persisted for so many years. Discreetly, it stirred, impatiently fanning the flames of young people's patriotism to begin the struggle for freedom.

In secret, the teenagers had organised themselves, and learned how to prepare crude bombs with pipes and bottles and also how to handle guns, while others marked out possible targets, to be approved by the Leader or their district leaders. No more than a handful of lads made up the organisation, and these small select groups scattered across the island, anxiously waited for final instructions.

While *Eoka* was making preparations for an outright attack against the enemy, the British did not have the slightest idea what was churning in their midst. They were totally unprepared for the ominous uprising that was about to manifest itself violently. Badly organised, the authorities became complacent about the stranglehold they had on the island and never anticipated that a volcano was about to erupt.

The British had never once contemplated that the poor peasants would ever dare to rise up against the Empire. The Greeks may have been asleep for years, but they had finally woken up. It took one man's determined ambition to rekindle the smouldering flame that was burning within their souls and was now ready to blaze into a ferocious, unstoppable conflagration.

Alexis had a mission to accomplish and worked with astonishing vigour to recruit new members. He recruited Petros and Michalaki, but he needed more lads to join if he was to compose effective groups to combat the enemy. One of the main obstacles he encountered was that he was forbidden to recruit lads who were sympathetic to communist or leftist aspirations; that was prohibited by the Leader, who held a steadfast personal grudge against them and considered all such persons as his enemies.

Alexis did not understand much about politics. Many lads of his age group were prepared to fight the one common enemy to liberate their country, irrespective of their own personal political sympathies. To divide the nation into two separate political groupings he believed was wrong, but he had to obey orders.

Another restriction that touched him personally was the fact that the *Eoka* movement was not receptive to the recruitment of Turkish Cypriots, because the organisation was of a Christian origin, with *Enosis* aspirations to unite Cyprus with Greece.

Ahmet was his brother and he knew he would do anything to help the cause. But when he suggested the recruitment of Ahmet to his District Leader, he was flatly told not to entertain such an idea. Ahmet could be of help indirectly, as long as no secrets ever reached his ears.

Downhearted, he tried to find a way to break the news to Ahmet who begun to question him about his strange conduct sensing that something was not quite right. His behaviour not only astounded Ahmet, but also his family, who tried to find out why the sudden change in his character and mannerism. He wanted to explain to them what was going on, but he could never find the right words to tell them about the organisation, knowing how his mother would react to such troubling news.

Two months had gone by and he could no longer hide behind constant lies and excuses; he decided to have a good chat about it with Ahmet. He felt very uneasy discussing the subject openly, remembering the warning during his initiation that he should 'trust nobody'. But at the same time, he had an obligation to put his friend's mind at rest once and for all.

One Sunday, after church, they found themselves alone in their room and Alexis plucked up courage to talk with him about his new role. His mother was in the kitchen cooking Sunday lunch with Maro helping her, while Marcos was nowhere to be seen. His father had not returned from church, and like every Sunday, he'd probably met up with Vasili to pass the time at their local coffee house, gossiping to their heart's content, or playing cards.

He knew that Ahmet would be upset, and nervously psyched himself up to face his friend's reaction. They were completely alone in their own bedroom when he explained to him what was about to happen in Cyprus, and how deeply he was personally involved with the movement . . .

Ahmet was dumbfounded and could not believe his ears that Alexis, his brother had kept such a secret from him. A deep sense of betrayal overcame him, and he could not understand how he had not been trusted with the secret. Distraught and very hurt, he refused at first to understand Alexis' behaviour, and could not believe how this *Eoka* had suddenly appeared out of nowhere to come between them and transform their happy household into one full of suspicion and secrecy. Ahmet would be more than prepared to pick up the freedom banner himself and fight the British. But now, he felt wounded and betrayed, for not being given the opportunity to join the movement so they could both fight the enemy together. Alexis was in no position to alter the relentless course of fate that played havoc with people's lives.

Ahmet was seated on his bed in a state of deep despondency and a sad expression had come over his dark, handsome face. His curly black hair was tousled over his face and he stared with his wide black eyes directly at his friend, who was stretched across the opposite bed feeling very upset and disturbed. There was a strange sense of uneasiness in the air, and for the very first time they both felt uncomfortable together. If this was the result of growing up, neither of them had asked for it, but they had to accept the certainty that people grow up and choose different paths to follow. Nothing stays the same forever.

They both waited in anticipation for the other to break the icy silence. It was Ahmet who finally had decided to speak his mind.

'I may be a Turk, but I am a Cypriot. I feel the same way as you do about Cyprus!' Ahmet said softly with a deep sense of pain. 'Am I not a Cypriot?' he asked agonisingly.

'Of course you are but what am I to do? It is my duty to join *Eoka*.

'I understand that but it's not fair. Greeks and Turks should both fight British colonialism, not only Greeks! This land is your land and my land, it is our country!' he said, angrily raising his voice.

'You can help indirectly!' Alexis interrupted his troubled friend.

'How can I, if I am not even considered a Cypriot?' Ahmet queried, unconvinced.

'I don't make the rules. It's all political shit why Turks are not to be involved, but you can still help me even if you are not an *Eoka* member.'

'As you said, it's all political shit, once you touch it you get your hands dirty! I am hurt but I shall always stand by you.'

'Let's not dwell on it and allow this to come between us.' Alexis suggested to his unhappy friend, eager to make amends.

'Nothing can come between us!' Ahmet interrupted defensively.

'All I ask of you is to be there for our family, in case something happens to me!'

'Don't talk nonsense!'

'It is not nonsense! Anything is possible, this is war!' Alexis insisted

'Don't worry, you just take care of yourself and I will take care of the rest.' Ahmet said, to reassure his friend.

Ahmet got off the bed, lured by the whiff of Sunday roast drifting through the kitchen. Alexis also got up and stood in front of Ahmet and stared straight into his jet black eyes. He detected that his friend had reluctantly accepted the new situation, but he also recognised that he was not pleased either.

'You promise to take care of our family?' Alexis insisted, without taking his eyes off him.

'I promise! You do what you have to do but I just pray to Allah this is over soon!' Ahmet said, and put one arm affectionately around Alexis' shoulder to reassure his friend of his devotion.

'Let's go and eat!' Alexis suggested, relieved that at last he had this discussion with Ahmet.

A great burden had lifted from his chest, but he was still bothered about how to break the news to his parents. He was certain they would not react in a similar understanding manner, especially his mother who'd probably burst into a river of tears. Her wrinkled face would instantly bloat and turn beetroot red.

They both headed for the kitchen to join the two ladies who were preparing the Sunday lunch. The whole house was overflowing with the appetising aroma of the mouth-watering roast baked in cinnamon and clove-scented potatoes. The boys could not wait to get their teeth into this troublesome rooster that pecked every hen in the neighbourhood! Marcos had chased it across the fields until he caught it by its legs and handed the doomed bird over to his mother, who quickly slit its throat.

Maro carefully placed the bird on a big platter surrounded by potatoes, bay leaves and rosemary that gently dispersed aromatic steam into the air The victim was now glowing crispy golden brown on a plater in the middle of the table.

The lads took their seats until Marcos and his father had arrived, both famished. The sharing of a Sunday meal bonded the family even more tightly, and today was no exception. They chatted between bites until the rooster was devoured, and settled down to a stimulating conversation about 'respect', which turned into an argument between Marcos and his sister.

They could not agree whether respect for the elders is inherent because of one's age or earned through one's righteous character. Tired of listening to the young ones arguing, particularly after such a hefty meal, drowsiness overcame them, and one by one they went for an afternoon nap.

*   *   *

As the weeks had come and gone, Kyra-Soteria had noticed the obvious change in her son's character. She kept her observations to herself, thinking it might simply be a temporary phase he was going through. But she was bursting to discuss the issue with her husband, an issue that was troubling her deeply. Alexis was going out practically every evening, and kept giving her a barrelful of excuses, while Ahmet was frequently excluded from his mysterious activities.

One evening, when everybody was out of the house, she embarked on disclosing her observations to her husband while sipping coffee on the veranda.

'They are young, and young people are always puzzling.' he said and tried to comfort her by shrugging off his son's strange behaviour as part of growing up.

'I don't like it. Call it a motherly instinct or, call it what you like but I don't like it! Mark my words, something is going on. They talk in whispers. When was the last time Alexis had spoken in such a manner?' She insisted pleadingly, in search of moral support, or at least comforting words to put her mind at rest that she was not imagining things.

'If there is something going on, Alexis will tell us. He is a sensible lad and he knows what he is doing.'

'I hope you are right, but I sense a big catastrophe is heading our way. All of a sudden, there is too much secrecy in my household, with doors shut and whispering, I tell you, I don't like it!' his worried wife insisted.

'You have a suspicious mind wife, the lads are young and need room to grow and breathe , free from their mum's apron-strings, let it go!'

'I can even see this catastrophe in my coffee cup!' she stubbornly insisted, and stared intensely with knitted brows into her empty cup. Then she raised it closer to her face, to inspect every detail. 'Here, look for yourself!' she added, and showed him the blurry images of coffee grounds stuck to the side of the cup.

Yiorkis stared into the coffee cup, and shook his head in disbelief at how his wife could believe in such absurd fortune telling.

'All I see are coffee-grounds!' he said to her.

'Don't you see them dark clouds?' she insisted, 'and look at those mangled trees, there is definitely a hurricane on the way!'

'Soteria . . . it is only coffee-grounds, don't worry! Alexis will outgrow what is bothering him, you just wait and see.' he said to her, and smiled affectionately, for having such a caring woman for a wife whose main purpose in life was the welfare of her children and her family.

'I hope that I am wrong.' he muttered unconvinced.

As a mother, she had a gut feeling that all was not well, but she accepted her husband's explanation. Meanwhile, she resolved to watch in silence and see the outcome of her son's irrational behaviour. She also observed that even Marcos was acting strangely but kept her mouth shut in case her husband thought that she was losing her mind for imagining such things about her sons. She knew that a mother's intuition was rarely wrong . . .

*   *   *

Alexis worked night and day, and he had successfully put together four fighting groups across the town of Varoshia with each group leader answerable directly to him. It was a demanding undertaking considering all those new members had to be trained under strict secrecy and dangerous conditions.

He formed his own special underground cell, made up of Dimitri,—a butcher's son—a stocky but loud lad of eighteen, Petros and Michalaki. Another member chosen was Andreas, a tall cheerful boy, who was always game for a good joke, and their muscle-man Adamos, a short but fierce looking lad who could lift practically anything with his bare hands. He appeared not to have a neck with his head practically part of his massive, shapeless shoulders, spreading fear whenever he frowned. He was paired off with Dimitri, to form the group's execution squad, while the rest, together with Alexis, handled the task of sabotage.

So as not to raise suspicion, Alexis showed up for work each morning. Together with Ahmet, he would open up the garage and carry on working as usual, but once he received instructions from his District Leader, he'd make all sorts of excuses to leave work. The charade was maintained for weeks on end, and he felt confident seeing that all was proceeding as planned.

On a drizzling grey morning his courier, a boy with cropped hair, no more than twelve years old, was seen standing outside the garage, waiting for his arrival.

As soon as Alexis saw him, he quickly parked the old car he had recently bought from Kosmas in a nearby open field. Ahmet opened the metal shutters of the garage, while Alexis went to the boy who handed him an envelope. Immediately he took off on his bicycle like lightning into the pouring rain. Alexis entered the garage, read the message and then tore the paper into tiny fragments.

'Ahmet, I have to go!' Alexis yelled out, and his voiced echoed across the high concrete ceiling.

Ahmet came out of the small toilet that served as a changing room dressed in his blue overalls.

'Are you off?' he asked, and walked to where Alexis was standing.

'Yes. Urgent meeting.' he answered, and went out into the rain. He got into the car and drove off, leaving his friend watching him disappear round the bend.

He sped through the streets of Varoshia and headed out of the town towards the ancient ruins of Salamina. The first buses and trucks of the morning rush-hour appeared heading towards the town centre. He paid no attention to them and drove against the oncoming traffic until he reached the main road-junction of Salamina.

He immediately turned left, entering a gravelled, narrow, bumpy road full of potholes and puddles. He drove through them, forcing the pools of water to take to the air either side of the car, in splashes of muddy water. The rain had no intention of subsiding and the wind-screen wipers furiously moved from side to side, attempting to clear the screen without much success.

Alexis had just passed the holy landmark of the sanctuary of *Apostolos Varnavas'* tomb, where he was once taken during a school outing to pray at this holy shrine of the most celebrated saint of the island.

It was here that Apostolos Pavlos and Apostolos Varnavas, together with his nephew Mark, first introduced Christianity to Cyprus, not long after Christ's crucifixion. The discovery of Apostolos Varnavas' body, tightly holding the original Gospel of St Matthew, was of paramount importance to the island. It confirmed that the Church of Cyprus was very much an Apostolic Foundation. The island was also blessed with many saints such as Ayia Katerini, Ayios Epiphanios, Ayios Minas and many others who chose to preach the Word of God across this special land, making Cyprus the first nation to be converted to Christianity.

The Church of Cyprus was declared *autocephalous*, and was granted imperial privileges so that: Only the Archbishops of Cyprus had the exclusive honour and privilege of signing their names in red ink could wear purple robes during religious festivals, and carry a sceptre instead of a pastoral staff.

The sarcophagus of Apostolos Varnavas was laid at rest where his body was discovered, inside a small cavern sited alongside the muddy road that led to the monastery.

Encased in a glass cask, the shrine attracts hundreds of pilgrims each year; they arrive by foot or buses in great numbers to pay their respects and pray to this holy person who had introduced Christ's teachings to the island.

For Alexis, his tomb represented man's determination to change things for the better, and every time he passed by this holy site, he crossed himself as a sign of respect and humility. Approaching the cavern, he briefly stopped the car, turned to his right and gazed at the isolated escarpment; he crossed himself three times, as always, and then drove off again.

Momentarily, the centuries-old Byzantine monastery of Apostolos Varnavas came into view at the very end of the road, which terminated at its churchyard. Arriving there, he hastily parked the car outside the main forecourt and quickly ran across the inner cobbled courtyard. Under cover from the pouring rain, he strode along the arched colonnaded portico, passing the massive fountain at the centre of the inner yard, and headed towards a low wooden door at the far end. He raised the large iron doorknocker, banged it once, and waited for a response. There was not a sound to be heard inside the yard, except for the constant rain making rhythmic splashes on the ground.

Suddenly, behind the solid door, faint echoing footsteps were heard. Instantly the snapping noise of someone unbolting the door supplemented the noise of the torrential rain. A cloaked graceful looking elderly monk, with a massive pure white beard and unruly moustache, appeared.

He was totally surprised to see the lad out in such a terrible weather.

'My name is *Akamantis*.' Alexis said, and entered the dark corridor.

'Ah, yes! I will be right back.' the timid monk softly said and walked off.

A few moments later, he returned carrying a sealed envelope and handed it to Alexis.

'Come inside, and have a coffee until the rain stops.' added kindly the old monk, inviting Alexis to keep him company for a while.

'I have no time.' Alexis answered and kissed the monk's hand in supplication, before taking off.

Inside his car, Alexis read the coded message requesting his immediate presence in Lefkosia, for a most urgent matter. It was from his district leader and it was signed, *Aetos*.

He started the car up and headed for Lefkosia without wasting a single valuable moment. He drove in the rain for about an hour and a half, until the familiar outline of the capital came into view.

The rain had finally stopped and he parked the car outside a small house in the old district of Enkomi, renowned for its narrow, winding streets and alleyways, crammed with mud-brick houses. He knocked at a blue door, and a boy about ten years old appeared and asked him to follow him. A few minutes later, they arrived in an affluent part of the capital and the boy showed him a house surrounded by a large hedge and a mature garden. Immediately, the boy took off again, leaving Alexis standing there alone.

He approached the house, and a middle-aged woman led him into a big living room, where about a dozen young men congregated. His own District Leader was present, his friend Spyros, and the elderly man he had met during his initiation but most of the others were not familiar to him. Greetings were exchanged, and Alexis sat next to his friend.

From the expressions on the young men's faces, he immediately sensed that something was not quite right. There was an obvious chill and tension in the air. He examined the other lads hoping he could detect some give-away signs, but saw none. The only thing that became apparent was that, everyone appeared to be curious about the urgency of calling this sudden meeting of leading *Eoka* members under one roof, and risking the chance of detection.

The elderly man stood up, took the floor and let his deep-set eyes gaze at the young men's faces, so that they gave him their absolute attention.

'I will get straight down to business.' he said and gently stroked his bushy moustache. 'Obviously you must have heard the news this morning, the shipment of explosives and ammunition we have been waiting for the past five weeks has vanished for good!'

The lads stirred agitatedly, not sure what to make of his comments. They all recognised the importance of this one crucial shipment before the uprising began. They had depended on that consignment, and suddenly they felt at a loss and spoke loudly to each other trying to find some kind of a solution.

The speaker's face was troubled, and he stared at his audience as if to plead with them for help. Distressed, the man asked them to stay calm and, once they became silent, he went on to explain the situation.

'Someone had betrayed us! *Agios Georgios* has been intercepted by a British destroyer off the West Coast and both the crew and the landing party have been arrested. This is a grave set-back! If the British smell an uprising, we shall lose the element of surprise, crucial to our struggle! We must therefore find other means to arm ourselves, and begin the battle for freedom as soon as possible?' he explained, and let his eyes take in everyone's reaction. He then knitted his brows into a deep frown.

Silence fell upon the room. Everybody was flabbergasted by the bad news, but none of them could offer immediate answers to such an unforeseen and devastating hindrance to their plans.

'We must find a way to lay our hands on explosives and get them soon! We can no longer wait for the next shipment. Do any of you have any ideas?' he asked again trying not to disillusion his young audience.

Everybody looked at each other in bewilderment but, after a short pause, a curly haired lad, not more than twenty years old, stood up and took the floor.

'Colonel, we can steal dynamite from Amiandos mines. We have members who work inside the complex and we could steal as much as we need.' he said with confidence.

'That's good, very good!' said the man, pleased, and smiled, nodding his head in agreement.

Alexis, for the very first time, suddenly realised that this elderly man standing in front of them was their Leader. He could not believe his eyes that he had the privilege of meeting him in person. He recollected his discussion with Spyros, and remembered his friend's reluctance to disclose anything about this man after his own initiation into the movement. He now recognised the importance of the need to work in complete secrecy, and how easy it is for someone to betray the cause for a handful of coins. Confidently, Alexis stood up immediately after the previous lad had finished explaining his plan.

'I am aware of fishermen diving off the Paralimni coast, salvaging explosive material for fishing.' Alexis suggested.

'Well . . . well . . . Things are not as bad as I thought' the Leader said, and rubbed his palms together in excitement. 'Is there a lot of material there?'

'Apparently. There is an endless source of discarded shells and mines at the bottom of the seabed dumped by the British after the war,' Alexis told him, pleased that his Leader had responded favourably to his suggestion.

'Can you swim young man?'

'Like a fish, sir!' answered Alexis with confidence.

'Then you take care of it! Provide a progress report to your district leader at all times. It is a matter of urgency that we must start to make our own crude bombs immediately! We desperately need material to be shared between us either stolen, or salvaged. Soon, we shall begin the uprising, and show the British that the Greek spirit is alive and well and nothing can deter us from gaining our freedom!' instructed the Leader and lit his pipe, pleased with the outcome.

He considered the risk worth taking, given the alternative, because without explosives the initial impact against the enemy would be undermined, if not laughed at by those who would be against the struggle. He was not prepared to give up so quickly and calling for this gathering had proved to be the right decision.

He knew that he could count on his young warriors, who exhibited resilience and appeared more than determined to initiate the first blow against the enemy. He had to hold them back and restrain their eagerness until the right moment. He reassured them that *Eoka* would become the nemesis of the British army in time, but one must not rush! Those who rush often trip prematurely and he did not want his boys to trip, for it may be their last trip in life and he wanted to protect them. He also emphasised the need for secrecy, and could not stress the point strongly enough about this other enemy who may dwell in their midst; this most unlikely enemy might pose a greater threat than the British soldier. It could show itself in many guises—as a loyal friend, a relative or even a brother or sister. For money, or other personal reasons, people were prepared to carry out desperate actions and pass on information to the enemy. They would not be the least bit concerned by the consequences of their treachery. That is what happened to *Ayios Georgios* . . . it had been betrayed for a price.

The secret meeting ended, and one by one the boys departed discreetly to fulfil their mission. Before leaving, Alexis was approached by his District Leader, who appeared impressed by his positive attitude and the heavy responsibility that fell upon his young shoulders.

'How long do you think it will take to recover these mines?' he asked.

'Probably a couple of weeks at the most.'

'That's good, but be careful, it is a dangerous job!' he warned, concerned for his safety. Then he tapped Alexis lightly on the back as a sign of friendship and approval.

Alexis took leave accompanied by his friend Spyros who insisted they must go and have a bite to eat before he drove back to Varoshia. They casually strolled to Metaxas Square, adjacent to the busy shopping area of Palea Yitonia, and grabbed an empty table alongside the sidewalk overlooking the main bus depot.

This corner restaurant known to everyone as 'bohemian,' was always busy and the owners, to gain additional seating space, had conveniently used the sidewalk to accommodate their loyal customers. The dense smoke from grilling pork and lamb drifting in the wind constantly attracted customers from all corners of the neighbourhood, while others drove up for a take-away.

They ordered a plate of barbecued ribs of lamb each, side salad to share and sat in the open for about an hour. At four in the afternoon

Alexis got into his car and headed for home, leaving Spyros behind; there was no time for socialising.

*   *   *

For days, Alexis and his dedicated fellow members plunged into the shallow waters in search of explosives lying on the seabed. The task was not difficult, because of the crystal clear azure waters and white sands which enabled the divers to easily spot the discarded materials. Their diving board was a ramshackle, paint-peeling fishing boat that belonged to one of the members. It served them perfectly well for the job at hand.

Eight sun-tanned lads kept diving during daylight, bringing up rusty mines and shells, covered in barnacles and tangled in masses of seaweed, and transported them to various hide-outs across the town. From this source, they built new, crude bombs to be shared with other members throughout the island. For two weeks the lads worked like busy bees night and day to accomplish their mission, knowing how crucial their task was to the success of the organisation.

One early morning, Alexis' courier appeared unexpectedly while he was diving, bringing a message to him from his District Leader instructing the group to abort the mission and be prepared to receive final orders to start the uprising. He passed on the message to his group leaders, who could not contain their excitement that, finally, the time had arrived to take an active role in the liberation of their country. Everything was going according to plan, and the interception of *Ayios Georgios* had become a bad memory now they had secured enough explosives to start the uprising.

The enslaved giant had suddenly stirred out of hibernation and broken out of his cage, invigorated and full of life, and no longer asleep. He now demanded justice for all those years he was held in shackles . . .

The month was coming to an end, and while Cypriots soundlessly slept in their beds, a devoted select group of young boys and girls stayed up, preparing for that crucial moment to put into practice what they had learned over the past few months. They were getting impatient, but they knew the time was getting nearer, and nothing could hold them back. They anxiously waited for the final order from their Leader.

They didn't have to wait for long . . . By the third week of the month, their long anticipated orders were issued by *Dighenis:*

Freedom or Death: 24.00 hours, 31ˢᵗ of March 1955.

110

Each *Eoka* group knew their assignments well and went about like professionals, gathering the right explosives and guns that were to be used against the chosen targets. The propaganda section of the organisation began to prepare printing presses to produce thousands of leaflets to be scattered throughout the city, while school boys and girls of tender years got their paint and brushes together to daub slogans on walls. In every village and town throughout the island, similar activities were initiated in total secrecy in readiness for the oncoming zero-hour.

*   *   *

Alexis, like all other *Eoka* members, called for a final meeting to be held at his house, before they took off for the initial attack against the enemy: to blow up the Four-Mile Military Base.

Finding a strange commotion going on in her house, Kyra-Soteria could not understand what was happening, but detected apprehension on the faces of the lads who congregated in her son's room, talking in whispers. They behaved seriously and none of them joked with her, especially Andreas who always picked on her. She was not an educated woman, but nor was she stupid and she knew something was not quite normal.

Agitatedly, she paced about the house eager to learn what the lads were up to. Rather guilty, she would lightly knock at her son's room and ask the boys if they were hungry, or wanted something to drink as an excuse to nose. It was ten o'clock and the lads were still up engrossed in their own world while her other two children were fast asleep. Her husband was in the kitchen smoking and trying to read a newspaper although he was barely literate.

A light drizzle began to fall, but did not last for long. The boys went over and over each detail of their mission until they were exhausted. Ahmet was to be their driver and lookout to allow the others to execute their assignment more effectively. He often helped out by doing odd jobs on behalf of Alexis, but he was always kept in the dark about the organisation's structure. He was only permitted to have this small role because he was a childhood friend and the group had total trust in him. Ahmet's involvement was their private secret.

'I see that *mama* is nervous, maybe this is the right time to talk to her.' Ahmet had suggested to Alexis, recognising that the matter had to be discussed sooner or later and tonight was a good time to put his mother's mind at rest, in case something went terribly wrong.

'You come with me!' Alexis said to him, needing moral support and not sure how his parents would react.

111

They both walked into the kitchen and found Alexis' parents sitting opposite each other at the table, making small conversation. The boys pulled up a chair each, unsure how to begin a discussion that would probably transform their lives. Alexis looked at his elderly parents and a sense of guilt overcame him, seeing how peaceful they both appeared. His mother wore her usual scarf over her greying hair, and was dressed in her long nightgown, while his father still had his working clothes on.

Alexis finally plucked up courage, stared at both of his parents and said somewhat hesitantly, 'I have some news to tell you both, you may not like it but you have the right to know . . .'

They pinned their curious gaze on him and then looked at Ahmet. They waited for their son's words to sprout out of his mouth, but instead, he stared at them both intensely. He gave a big sigh and took his mother's hand in his own.

'Speak up son. What is it?' his father demanded, sensing something was bothering the two lads.

'I have joined a secret organisation and we are about to start the liberation of Cyprus from British rule.' he finally spat out, drawling his words.

A sense of relief triumphed over his entire body. He gently squeezed his mother's rough palms as a gesture of comfort, anticipating that she might start sobbing.

'What are you talking about?' his father asked, not sure what he meant, and put his paper aside.

'I am a member of *Eoka* . . . '

'*Eoka*? What is this *Eoka*?' his father interrupted, with a frown, in total disbelief. He then gave his son a stern look.

'It is an underground movement dedicated for the freedom of Cyprus.'

'Ahmet, did you know about this?' Yiorkis asked, and gave him a piercing stare which sent a shiver down his spine through guilt at keeping such a secret from them both.

'Yes.' he answered, and a lump rose in his throat.

'When is this to happen?' his father asked harshly, and his bottom lip quivered in anxiety.

'Tonight!' Alexis answered dryly, but firmly.

'I knew there was something brewing in the pot, remember the coffee cup?' his mother burst out in a trembling voice engulfed in apprehension.

'By tomorrow you will hear all about it. I had to do what I believe is right and liberating Cyprus is the right thing to do. There are many others who have joined this organisation, not just me.'

112

'Michalaki, Petros and them other lads, are they also involved?' his father interrupted and pointed towards his bedroom where the other boys remained inside.

'Yes.' Alexis said, nervously twisting a lock of his tousled hair.

'Ahmet . . . are you part of this?' he inquired, and stared at him sternly demanding to know if he was personally involved with this organisation.

'Not exactly, it is only for Greeks.' he answered and shook his head negatively.

'Curse the scoundrel who fired up this catastrophe, and brainwashed our children to become killers!' his mother erupted, raising her voice.

Instantly, a torrent of tears flooded her tired eyes and trickled down her wrinkled face that turned red.

Yiorkis examined the boys' faces sombrely and detected the determined spirit and unwavering conviction in their alert eyes. He nodded his head thoughtfully and lit a cigarette, trying to analyse this grave situation.

Marcos and his sister were awoken by their mother's voice and walked into the kitchen half asleep, curious to find the cause of this brouhaha.

'You two get back to bed!' their mother screamed at the top of her voice.

Seeing the fury in her eyes, they retreated from the kitchen without uttering a word, stunned at their mother's strange behaviour. They did not want to add to her torment, realising how upset she was about something. Marcos went into his sister's room and both began to talk in whispers, curious as to what had suddenly happened for their mother to behave in such a way.

'Do you think it is the right thing to do?' Yiorkis asked his son, once things calmed down again.

'Yes, *papa*!' Alexis answered with conviction.

'Then you do what you have to do. You are old enough to know what is right and what is not. Your mother and I can only pray to God that you are kept out of harm's way,' his father said to him, realising how deeply involved his son was with this underground Organisation.

He paused briefly, got to his feet, approached his son and gave him a kiss on the cheek.

'I cannot stop you, may God protect you and all the others, son.' he said softly and gave him his blessing.

Alexis was deeply touched by his father's unexpected gesture, and his throat went dry. He wanted to shed a tear, but controlled his childish emotions. His father then went over to where Ahmet was seated, and repeated the same gesture and blessed him the same way. When he finished, he turned to his wife who was still crying, and placed his heavy hand over her head lightly, to comfort her.

'It will be all right, Soteria . . . Don't cry . . . The boys have to do this, it not within our power to stop them . . . Let's offer them our support and blessing. That's the only thing left for us to do.' he said to her, and stroked her head gently.

Downhearted, she nodded her head, accepting her husband's decision. She realised that she was not in a position to change destiny. She heaved her heavy body off the chair and stood in front of her son. Gently she raised her arms and gave him a long embrace and a kiss on both cheeks. Alexis felt her warm tears on his face and the slight tremor in her arms brought about by fear and by anxiety.

'Don't worry *mama* . . .' he said to her comfortingly. 'Everything will be all right . . .'

'I hope so son, I hope so . . .' she muttered, sounding devastated, and slumped her body down on her chair conceding defeat. 'May God protect you!' she added, and sighed deeply.

Petros walked into the kitchen and instantly sensed the tense atmosphere. He looked at Kyra-Soteria and Alexis' father and could not help but feel sorry for their anguish. Their sadness touched him deeply because he considered these two kind people as part of his own family. Seeing them in such a distressed state, he wished the clock could be turned back, but it was too late.

'It's time to go . . .' he said softly to Alexis and pointed at his wrist-watch.

Alexis nodded his head and stood up.

'We have to go.' he said to his parents, who continued to stare at him.

At that moment, they knew their son's destiny had suddenly been transformed from one of stability and security, to uncertainty. They were powerless to change his mind, and both succumbed to this new reality that was about to nibble away bit by bit at their mundane existence. Their son's commitment did not surprise them, knowing his sensitive character, and no matter what they attempted to say to him would not make any difference. He had decided he had a mission to accomplish, and independently he had made up his mind to pursue his heart's desire towards an ambiguous future. Only time would be the judge of his action, and they had no alternative but to remain silent, whole-heartedly support his dream, and pray to God that no harm would come to him.

Alexis put his jacket on, and called out to the others. One by one, they came out of his room and congregated in the living room in readiness to depart. Because of the commotion, young Marcos and his sister had joined the lads, absolutely puzzled as to what was happening, but nobody had paid any attention to them. Alexis' distraught parents were also among the lads, wishing to bid them farewell and sensing they were about to do something dangerous.

Kyra-Soteria looked at the faces of these lads in their prime, and deep sadness had overcome her. She recognised their innocence would be destroyed for good, after tonight's activities. She did not want to know details, but she could anticipate what was about to happen and reluctantly restrained her emotions.

'You tell your mother to come and visit me tomorrow,' she said in a troubled voice to Petros, who was standing nearest to her.

He felt terrible seeing the old lady crying.

'I will make sure she comes this Sunday.' the young lad reassured her, and gave her a gentle, endearing pat on the shoulder to ease her anxiety.

Without wasting valuable time, the boys walked out of the living room and went outside where their car was parked. The time was past ten thirty. Ahmet immediately started the engine up, while the others squeezed inside the car, seated on top of each other like sardines in a can. The rain had decided to stop, but the night sky was pitch-black with hardly any stars visible through the dense clouds. They hurriedly bid farewell to Alexis' parents and drove off, leaving the elderly couple and the young ones standing silently on the front veranda, watching the car disappear into the distance.

'God protect them . . .' Kyra-Soteria muttered to her husband, and both walked inside to ponder soulfully. These new developments came to them like a violent thunderbolt as they both realised that, from this moment on, their lives were to be turned upside down.

Within half an hour the group had arrived at the isolated military compound and got out of the car, leaving Ahmet behind to act as a watch. They had thirty minutes to spare before zero hour, and from a distance they discreetly scouted the barbed-wire perimeter fence. They knew precisely what to do and where to place the bombs, having reconnoitred the area many times over, with the help of Andreas, who worked inside the compound as a labourer.

Their first task was to black out the entire compound by cutting the main electricity supply. That was Petros' job, and by eleven thirty he approached the tall pylon located about twenty yards away from the barbed-wire surrounding the camp. He began to prepare himself for the climb. He wrapped one end of a long thick rope around his waist, and by twining the rope through his leather belt he made a thick solid knot. Then he placed the rest of the bundle of rope over his shoulder and waited for the appropriate time for his climb.

The others entered the compound by snipping through the perimeter fence, and they began to plant bombs in strategic locations deep inside the camp. Like shadowy ghosts, they hurried around in pitch darkness determined to plant each and every one of their explosives. Swiftly they moved about in absolute silence, placing time bombs and pressure mines, in anticipation of keeping their deadline.

Petros checked his wristwatch, decided it was time for him to execute his task and carefully began to climb the slippery tall pylon. He reached the top and waited for Alexis' signal to proceed with the cutting of the thick transmission wires. A pair of strong clippers was carefully secured around his wrist to safeguard them dropping from his hand during the cutting process. At that great height, the evening air was bitterly cold and Petros could feel the crisp chill on his face, making his nose run.

The sound of a long dog-whistle echoed into the night. Petros heard Alexis' signal, and hastily wiped the snot off his nose with the back of his sleeve. He planned to secure his body against the metal pylon to allow both of his hands the freedom to sever the electrified transmission wires. Without hesitation, he picked up the loose end of the long rope from his shoulder and with a quick thrust he swung the rope over the wires, not realising that the rope was slightly damp. As soon as the moist rope made contact with the live wires, they exploded in blinding sparks, forcing the compound lights to flash and flicker on and off.

The electrical current instantly engulfed Petros' body in a ball of fire, and he tumbled down off the pylon in convulsions and screams. With a loud thump Petros' motionless burning body landed over a small bush.

On the ground, his electrocuted body remained tightly attached to the electrified flaming rope that refused to disconnect from the high voltage wires above. The current continued to travel across the rope consuming his dead body. The high voltage instantaneously transformed it into a black carcass.

Petros' burning body and the blazing rope had caused nearby shrubs to catch fire, and the stench of Petros' burning flesh quickly reached the boys' nostrils. They knew that something had gone terribly wrong and their friend was in trouble.

In a panic, they hastily discarded the remainder of their explosives and frantically ran to escape, and see to their friend. As they made their escape, suddenly loud explosions echoed into the silent night from various parts of the army barracks.

The intermittent but deafening explosions, together with the ongoing flickering lights, caused the British to jump out of their beds. They came out into the open, yelling and shouting in total disbelief at what was happening. The army barracks' siren instantly roared and searchlights were switched on, flooding the entire compound with their powerful beams. The dark night had suddenly turned into daylight and there was absolute confusion and mayhem within the barracks, with soldiers and other personnel running in disarray to investigate.

Alexis and his friends rushed to the pylon and were faced with the charred body of Petros sprawled on the ground completely black, engulfed by burning shrubbery. The stench of his smouldering body was too much to bear and they ran in horror to where Ahmet had already started the car engine, in preparation for their escape.

They jumped into the car and made their escape as fast as they could. Things certainly did not go well! Most of the explosives failed to explode and they could not understand how Petros had got electrocuted.

Crammed in the back of the car, Michalaki was squeezed between his friends. Without warning, he burst into loud sobs, crying his heart out, traumatised by the sight of his childhood friend's charred body. None of them expected such a bad incident on the very first day of their mission, and they were in total shock. They had no idea how to cope with such an experience and they all turned hysterical. In total panic, they yelled and shouted at each other in search of answers.

Ahmet drove like a maniac to get away from this terrible place that was to remain embedded deep in their psyches forever. It finally dawned on their naïve minds that struggling for one's freedom meant the sacrifice of lives, and Alexis remembered their Leader's words to him that: *'freedom needs blood to sprout.'*

Devastated by the traumatic incident, the boys made their escape. They also realised that this was just the beginning . . . They had to accept a new pragmatism, of encountering more deaths of other friends in the future. They felt shattered and recognised the hardest part of tonight's mission was not over yet; someone had to break the terrible news to Petros' parents!

After a heated shouting match and argument, they decided to allow the authorities to be the messengers of doom, in case their own identities were revealed to the British authorities.

Alexis was completely overwhelmed, and felt weak and broken by the mishap. He personally felt responsible for Petros' death for introducing him to *Eoka*, and he could not get his friend out of his tormented mind. Stunned and horrified, he remained silent most the journey and gazed at Michalaki, who continued his uncontrollable lamentation for the loss of his close friend. Their chubby pal could not get over this dreadful experience and, haunted by the sight of Petros' charred body, he kept bursting into heart-rending sobs. The others did their best to console him but their efforts, had no effect on their sensitive friend.

Ahmet drove each lad home and by two o'clock in the morning he found himself with Alexis in their room shattered to bits. They stayed up all night, talking quietly, until they heard his mother moving about in the kitchen preparing coffee for her and her husband. They remained motionless over the bed covers unable to face anyone. But by six in the morning their eyelids shut, although sleep did not come easy.

They tossed and turned restlessly, until the first rooster started to crow, commanding everyone to rise and face the dawn of a bright new day.

CHAPTER SEVEN

THE PEOPLE ON the island woke up and turned a new chapter in their lives, one full of confusion and apprehension, not sure what had transpired during the night. They were mystified by the multitsude of slogans painted in blue on walls throughout towns and villages across the land. The words *EOKA* and *ENOSIS* appeared on every street corner in large lettering, while other slogans demanded that the British get out of Cyprus.

The events confused not only the Cypriots, but also the British authorities, who had no idea who the culprits were, or how much of a serious threat the manifestations of the night were. The morning newspapers in large headlines reported what had happened and wondered who was behind the sabotage activities that had destroyed many installations, including the government radio station in Lefkosia, and the looting of a great number of police stations.

When the markets and shopping squares opened up, schoolchildren mingled in the crowds, hurling bundles of leaflets over people's heads, and quickly disappearing into the throng. Unsuspecting citizens picked the scattered leaflets and read the message:

PROCLAMATION 1st of April, 1955

With the help of God, with faith in our honourable struggle, with the backing of all Hellenism and the help of the Cypriots, we have taken up the struggle to throw off the English yoke, our banners high, bearing the slogan which our ancestors have handed down to us, as a holy trust—Death or Victory!

Brother Cypriots, from the depths of the past centuries, all those who glorified Greek history while pursuing their freedom are looking at us; the warriors of Marathon, the warriors of Salamis, the 300 Spartans of Leonidas and those who, in more recent times fought in the epic Albanian war. The fighters of 1821 are looking at us—those fighters who showed us that liberation from the yoke of rulers is always won by bloodshed. All Hellenism is looking to us, and following as anxiously but with national pride.

Let us reply with deeds. Let us be worthy of them. It is we who showed the world that international diplomacy is unjust and in many

119

ways cowardly, and that the Cypriot soul is brave. If our rulers refuse to give us back our freedom, we shall claim it with our hands and with our blood. Let us show the world once more that the neck of the contemporary Greek refuses to accept the yoke. Our struggle will be hard. The ruler has the means and he is strong in numbers. We have the heart, and we have right on our own side and that is why we will win.

Diplomats of the world:
Look to your duty. It is shameful that in the twentieth century people should have to shed blood for freedom, that divine gift for which we fought at your side and for which you at least claim that you fought against Nazism.

Greeks:
Wherever you may be, hear our call: Forward all together for the freedom of our Cyprus.

EOKA
The Leader — Dighenis

Everyone read the leaflets with astonishment, asking each other if Cypriots truly dared to rise up against the colonialists. People gathered in groups, discussing the events of the night, and expressing their opinions. There were many dissenting voices and a great number of people disagreed, while others welcomed the prospect of fighting for their freedom. They bought the morning papers and read every line, while others had their ears glued to the government-controlled radio, broadcasting and condemning the activities of those 'hooligans' who aimed to destabilise society and bring greater hardship on the poor inhabitants. The fact that a dead body was recovered, and installations across the island blown to smithereens, indicated that these *Eoka* resistance fighters meant business.

The uprising took the world by surprise, but none were more shocked than the British officials who ran Cyprus in absolute complacency, on the assumption that Cypriots would never dare to confront their authority. The attacks reverberated like a massive storm-wave throughout the island, and these were not simply isolated incidents but well-planned assaults, causing the British authorities and Whitehall a new problem; one they had never anticipated.

British military advisers appeared stunned and panic-stricken, realising they had an uprising on their hands. They were not properly prepared or equipped and hot cables were transmitted back and forth from Whitehall and the Colonial Office. These transmissions showed what a state of turmoil the British authorities were in as they attempted to find ways to put down this revolution before it got out of control.

Efforts were immediately taken to recruit and arm Cypriot civil servants into a special constabulary to guard government buildings. Simultaneously, the authorities began a massive propaganda campaign, condemning and branding the attacks as the work of vandalism.

The first *Eoka* assault inflamed young people's spirits for freedom, and many rushed to join the movement by taking up arms. They came from all walks of life and various ages, eager to be part of this movement. The organisation quickly mushroomed into a strong but determined force to be reckoned with. School-children were keen to join and, the bolder ones were instantly promoted to join the fighting groups. Others joined the propaganda and courier network of *Eoka* which was equally essential and an important mission. Without the secret courier network, the Organisation could not function effectively, and those boys and girls accomplished their missions with enthusiasm, at the risk of being incarcerated.

Nightly the attacks continued, shattering and blowing up power plants and government buildings, while the execution squads of the resistance in towns began to show their strength in combating British military personnel.

In mountainous regions, a handful of small bands of *Andartes* set up cunning ambushes against military convoys, and they frequently entered into sporadic armed battles with the unprepared army. *Eoka* action plans were strategically executed with precision, and these unlikely bands of rural warriors often blew up army transit vehicles indiscriminately. They were an easy target. In a state of alert and disarray, soldiers no longer walked unarmed, and they took precautions to safeguard their lives whenever travelling in their jeeps and cars by encasing their vehicles in chicken wire to repel the bombs unrepentantly thrown at them.

Exacerbating the authorities' problem, mass demonstrations were organised practically each week, straining their military resources to their limit, while the police could no longer control the school-children from demonstrating in their hundreds, demanding freedom and blatantly calling out in public their wholehearted support for *Eoka* and its fighters. Many times the British Army were baffled to find that the enemy throwing bombs at them were sixteen-year-old schoolboys, and those distributing leaflets were ten-year-olds from primary school.

121

The civilian Governor was at a loss, and was sent thousands of additional highly trained soldiers from Egypt to boost his forces, in his attempt to put down this insurgence that was becoming more brutal and decisively effective as time progressed.

The summer of 1955 came to an end and the struggle for liberation grew into a colossus, full of vigour ready to tear anyone apart who stood in its way. The prisons on the island were crammed with boys and girls under suspicion of being either *Eoka* members or sympathisers to the cause of liberation. Without trial, they were thrown into prisons to keep them off the streets in the hope that the tide of revolt might subside. Their incarceration was strategically planned to serve as a deterrent in the hope of dissuading others from joining the movement.

The name *'Dighenis'* had become an enigma and was on everyone's lips. Nobody had the faintest idea who this elusive man was and everyone wondered where on earth he came from to transform the island into one powerful force, strong enough to stand up against British Might. He mobilised the entire nation, supported by the undiminished Cypriot spirit for freedom . . . This indefinable enemy was beginning to cause havoc for the rulers with the loss of British lives and the destruction of government properties.

The Colonial Office and Foreign Office was at a loss. The matter was debated in the British Parliament, and it was decided that a more determined and dynamic Governor was needed, one who had the military expertise and a cunning enough mind, to become a worthy adversary of this elusive *Eoka* Leader. It was essential to put someone else in charge and solve the problem once and for all. The present civilian Governor was losing the battle. They certainly did not want another international political humiliation like their most recent one when they were booted out of Egypt and Palestine.

A new political strategy was required, one that would serve the interests of the British Empire and not waste valuable time and money, dealing with irregular bands of hooligans who might bring about another unexpected humiliation of the Empire. The urgency to tackle the problem decisively had become paramount, and the Colonial Office had no time for reconciliation. They needed someone to lead the battle with ruthless fortitude, clip the wings of those insurgents who dared oppose their authority, and deal with them without a grain of pity, smashing their aspirations for good.

The ideal candidate for the task was a highly decorated Field-Marshal and career military man who had commanded British troops in North Africa, Italy, India, Germany and the Far East colonies. He was also privileged to be a member of the Imperial

General Staff, and his experience of warfare tactics was well recognised throughout the Empire. If anyone could accomplish the job in hand, he would be the right person.

He was summoned to the opulent offices of the War Office in Whitehall, and was installed as the new Military Governor of Cyprus. He was under strict instructions that *Eoka* must be dismembered permanently at all costs. Foremost, he was ordered to ensure the Empire reinstated its full control and authority over this crucially strategic colony, irrespective of what it took. In order for his mission to bring about positive results, he was also empowered with unlimited authority to stamp out the *Eoka* uprising, and destroy all adversaries of the Crown.

'Use your military skill and crush the enemy,' he was ordered by the Colonial Secretary. 'We cannot afford another Egypt or Palestine on our hands!'

'To achieve results, not only must we use military tactics, but we must also capitalise upon those who are opposed to the uprising!' the new Governor opined.

'You have dealt with such matters before. Utilise every means at your disposal, even if you have to deploy one sector of the community against the other, as long as we are not humiliated again. The Turkish Cypriot community is perfect! Use them to our advantage.'

'With my government's permission, using the Turkish community would make my job much easier. For a start, Cypriots are impoverished and we can recruit hundreds of collaborators from either community by offering financial rewards for their loyalty. Simultaneously, we can manipulate and encourage the Turkish community to aspire nationalist ambitions mainly because *Eoka* calls for union with Greece. These are good military tactics to use against the enemy. For certain they would bring about positive results,' suggested the Field-Marshal.

'Are we correct to assume that you are proposing to introduce our 'Divide and Rule' policy?' The Colonial Secretary asked.

'Precisely! A wedge between the two communities will serve us well. We have always used similar tactics in other colonies and they have never failed us yet, why not in Cyprus!' said the new Governor with determination.

'Yes. Why not.' agreed the Colonial Secretary in support of their new Military Governor. 'You are the Governor, and you are in charge! Crush the enemy!'

As soon as the new Govenor and Field-Marshal set foot on the island in late September, he wasted no time in crushing his enemy, and immediately set up a military dictatorship. Overnight, he became the judge and the jury, who instantly attempted to maintain total control over people's lives. His unyielding ruthlessness had quickly become evident and touched without pity everybody across the island. With an iron fist he set out to destroy the spirit of freedom, and he introduced punitive fines on poverty-stricken villages, reminiscent of Nazi collective punishment. He built up an intelligence network composed of Greek and Turkish Cypriots, to spy and act as informants, lured by financial rewards. Hundreds had volunteered for this most inexcusable job as a means of overcoming their appalling living conditions or simply because of outright greed.

To maintain his authority, he indiscriminately sent suspected sympathisers to jail without trial, and condemned imprisoned young lads to be hanged on suspicion of being *Eoka* members. No male was safe, whatever his age. Determined to crush *Eoka*, he also introduced the torture and beating of children. But his most effective tactic to control the masses was the introduction of week-long curfews, which he imposed with an iron fist upon the civilian population.

He was empowered to rule the island by decree, and he censored the press in order to prevent the printing of unfavourable articles. Political parties, unions and cultural organisations were abolished, and the flying of the Greek flag was prohibited as well as all public aspirations of union with Greece. Disobedience meant instant imprisonment. Priests, civilians and bishops were deported each week, while political speeches in public were outlawed and the ringing of church bells forbidden. The police were also granted unlimited authority of arrest.

The people of Cyprus had come to realise that this man meant to destroy the insurgence for good, and in order to achieve his goal he denied them their basic fundamental human rights. He treated the general masses like a herd of sheep that he could dispose of at will, by releasing his wild dogs to pounce upon the guilty and the innocent, in his attempt to stop their bleating hearts.

Eoka retaliated with vigour and did not succumb. Instead, it unleashed its own warriors to attack his authority with more determination than ever before. In the absence of justice, violence became a necessity, and explosions together with arson had become a daily occurrence, while the execution squads of *Eoka* set about to execute known collaborators, who had become an unlikely additional enemy of the organisation.

Those informants who had escaped the firepower of *Eoka's* guns were swiftly transported secretly abroad, under cover of darkness.

Once the British authorities had squeezed out all the information from them, they were discarded like so much baggage. Certainly they were not to be trusted, for if they volunteered to betray their own people for a price through greed and by dubious actions, these characters were clearly untrustworthy and most unreliable. A vast number of them including their families were relocated to Britain, Australia, and South Africa to find sanctuary and anonymity.

The death of young Greek lads or lengthy imprisonment and torture did not perturb their conscience. Abroad they felt safe and secure being among friends . . . and far away from harm's way . . .

* * *

Alexi's household was in complete turmoil . . . Marcos and his sister got out of bed at the first pallid light and groomed themselves to participate in their school's parade, in celebration of the Greek nation's defiant 'No' to Hitler's ultimatum for surrender.

Kyra-Soteria got out of bed before her children woke up and quietly put their blue uniforms and blazers neatly folded over the back of two chairs in the living room. She tenderly pressed Marco's white shirt and grey trousers, and then did the same to her daughter's blouse and pleated skirt. As a caring mother, she wanted to ensure they looked perfect for the annual celebration.

She could hear Marcos in the bathroom having a shower, while Maro kept pressuring him to get out so she could use the bathroom. Puffing and huffing, she moved about the house stamping her feet with fury.

'We are going to be late!' she kept shouting at the top of her voice.

'You have plenty of time . . . it's not even seven o'clock.' her mother reassured her each time she screamed at her brother.

When he finally came out, she cannoned into the bathroom fuming with anger at him for his lack of consideration. Unable to remain in bed because of the constant noise, Alexis and Ahmet got up, and walked into the kitchen.

They made themselves a cup of coffee anxious for Maro to finish, so they could use the bathroom. Yiorkis rose out of bed and joined the lads, also waiting in line to use the bathroom.

Alexis had noticed that his young brother combed his black hair into a perfect sleek style, and he observed for the first time how handsome his young brother was becoming. A sense of pride overwhelmed him seeing him smartly dressed in his pristine uniform. He helped him tie his school tie and then handed him pocket money for spending.

'You two be very careful! There might be some trouble today.' he advised his brother.

'There are rumours the British might assault those in the parade.' Ahmet added, concerned for their safety.

Maro decided to take her time, and the rapid splashing sound of the water coming from the shower sounded like torrential rain. She was in heaven whenever she was in the shower, especially when taking care of her thick, wavy mane that reached her slim waist.

'If you detect trouble, just walk away!' his mother advised him.

'Don't worry *mama*, I am old enough to take care of myself.' Marcos said to her.

'The Devil has many claws and strikes when you least expect him!' she insisted with apprehension.

Alexis did not speak much that morning. He was anxious to use the bathroom and patiently waited for the splashing of the water to stop. The sound of running water made it even harder for him to restrain his bloated bladder from bursting, and he sat in silence.

Alexis' father reached over the window ledge and tuned his small radio on, eager to listen to the news. He carefully manipulated the tuner knob across the wave bands and locked onto Cyprus Broadcasting Corporation.

The news was in progress, and a male announcer was broadcasting the Governor's orders for the public to refrain from participating in this year's October festivities and that '*Eoka* ambushed a convoy at Morphou with two British fatalities, one guerrilla fighter was apprehended. Early this morning the first execution of two *Eoka* members, twenty-two year-old Michalis Karaolis and Andreas Demetriou, had taken place in Lefkosia . . . they were executed by hanging on the prison gallows, and their bodies were refused to their families, the terrorists' remains were buried within the prison compounds . . . '

Yiorkis had heard enough and switched his radio off. Fury had overcome his wrinkly face and banged his fist on the table.

'Barbarians!' he muttered softly with disgust, 'they went ahead and hanged the poor lads without pity like carcasses that hang on a butcher's hook!'

He was so upset his lower lip quivered and both of his hands trembled. He lit a cigarette and gazed with emotion at the young lads seated around the table. He sighed loudly, but kept his thoughts to himself, realising this was just the beginning. His wife shook her head in astonishment at such callous action by the authorities and could not believe her ears that hangings had already began.

By eight o'clock, Marcos and his sister said farewell and departed to catch the bus for the *Gymnasium*. At the bus stop, they met up with other friends, all excited by the pending activities of the day. They talked jubilantly in anticipation of participating in the parade, knowing hundreds of people would be watching and admiring their performance undaunted by the Governor's order.

* * *

To assert his authority the Governor had authorised, on that very special day, to execute by hanging the two young lads held in captivity. He adamantly refused to listen to reason, or respond to the desperate, humble pleas of the boys' distraught parents. Even the Archbishop had intervened, asking him to grant the lads leniency and spare them from the gallows. All efforts to save the boys had failed . . .

In absolute stubbornness, he had gone ahead and executed his first victims to serve as an example to others. By placing a noose around the young lads' fragile necks he had hanged them like rags.

The news quickly spread like a wildfire, inflaming people's hatred of the British rulers. World leaders and the public expressed their abhorrence and shock at the two hangings, while in Athens thousands of demonstrators took to the streets expressing furious anti-British feelings. The Mayor of Athens, livid with anger, hammered and chipped to splinters a marble plaque of Queen Elizabeth and Prince Philip. Hundreds of demonstrators were imprisoned for civil disobedience, while seven lost their lives during the angry riots that swelled throughout Greece. The British press condemned the hangings, with bold headlines, and the Sunday Times lambasted the government on its front pages: '*History shows over and over again that when the imperial power shirks its responsibility, nothing but evil follows and the worst sufferers are the people governed.*'

When the news had spread to every corner of the island, the people could not believe the Governor's insensitivity and brutal decision. They were appalled by his total disrespect for the boys' lives. But he was not bothered. He was determined to stamp out the movement, and he did not care about people's feelings or what they thought of him as a man. His priority was to ensure the explicit instructions issued to him by his government were implemented, and in doing so preserve his own military integrity without a black stain marking his character. To accomplish his objective, he relied entirely on his own instincts and self-righteousness and he was not concerned or bothered with other people's opinions; he knew how

127

to deal with insurgents and nobody could tell him how to do his job.

In total defiance of his authority, the islanders prepared themselves to hold their annual parades, irrespective of his threats. Defying the Governor's orders, *Eoka* encouraged the public to make this year's parades a symbol of their determination for freedom; the Governor could not possibly imprison or massacre the entire population for a simple parade . . .

Ever since the uprising had begun, people had woken-up and had come to realise that no power was strong enough to subdue their aspirations for freedom. One may successfully kill thousands in the process of controlling the masses, but one can never destroy an idea—being God's precious gift to mankind! Cypriots had already spilt their own blood across the fragile soil of their land, and were more than prepared to shed a river if necessary in their attempt to tear away the shackles of British colonialism.

Motivated by the undiminished spirit of all those fearless *Eoka* fighters, who confronted the enemy with fortitude, the masses raised their fists in absolute rebelliousness and they no longer cared about saving their skin. There was no stopping them now because the idea of freedom had embedded itself deep within their souls, and a great number of them had sworn to give up their lives for this noble idea of liberation inherited down to them by their ancestors.

*   *   *

The students gathered within the grounds of the *Gymnasium* of Varoshia in preparation for their parade. Dressed in their pristine school uniforms, neatly groomed boys and girls lined up by age group, while the bands tuned their instruments in readiness to start marching beyond the school grounds.

A boy of sixteen proudly held the flag-pole tightly, secured by a leather strap around his waist and at the very top the blue and white massive Greek flag fluttered gently in the wind.

It was a perfect, bright morning for a parade, with not a single cloud in the vicinity. There was only a mild breeze that blew from the coast. By nine-thirty, the never-ending preparations were completed and the headmaster, standing at the top of the stairs, blew hard on his whistle. He let out a long piercing blast for the parade to move forward.

Instantly, the drummers played a long drum-roll accompanied rhythmically by hand-held cymbals. The parade began to move ahead like a winding snake towards the main school gates. The sound of trumpets and the band playing drifted on the wind, dispersing its message across the town and calling others to come out and celebrate.

The parade moved steadily towards *Ayia Katerini's* church, and crowds jubilantly stood alongside the main thoroughfare cramming the sidewalks, clapping their hands and bursting out in welcoming cheers. They proudly admired the well-groomed flowers of Cypriot youth who marched in unison not missing a step. The spectators shouted and whistled in utter exuberance, encouraging the marchers on by raising their hand-held flags high into the air, while young children standing at the forefront gazed in wonder.

The marching footsteps of the students and the band playing echoed across the town, insistently demanding that no citizen missed out on the festivities. The parade had reached the familiar cross-roads of the main thoroughfare, when suddenly the whole area was cordoned off by hundreds of British soldiers with guns and truncheons pointing at the oncoming marchers in readiness for a combat. Every avenue was completely blocked off by the army, and the soldiers in their combat gear waited in total silence and apprehension for their next orders.

The marchers stopped and stared with anxiety at the soldiers, expecting the worst to flare up at any moment.

The band was briefly silenced, and the young flag carrier turned his head for a sign of guidance, but he heard and saw nothing except for total silence and fear in people's eyes. He gazed at the army cordon blocking his way, and remained motionless, unable to decide what to do next. Confronted by the enemy, he felt a deep sense of patriotism and held the flag tighter with both hands. The honour of carrying the flag suddenly dawned on him and he had to make a split second decision on how to act. He took a few steps forward . . . and the drummers hit their sticks on their drums once forcefully, to give him encouragement to continue and lead the parade forward.

The blue and white flag fluttered with the wind and people began to chant, 'EOKA!' 'ENOSIS!' Their chants reverberated across the rooftops forcing the British soldiers to line up in readiness for confrontation.

'Go home! This is a curfew . . . curfew . . .!' a Greek policeman shouted loudly and persistently into a megaphone.

The crowds would hear nothing of it and continued their endless chanting of anti-British slogans, thus causing the soldiers great anger and anxiety; they moved agitatedly holding their fingers tightly on the triggers of their weapons.

Encouraged by the constant, thunderous slogan chanting, the flag-carrier advanced a few steps, and was followed immediately by those behind him. In total defiance, and complete disregard for the soldiers' presence, the school band began to play a modified version of the Greek national anthem, infuriating the soldiers even more.

Four armed soldiers moved forward and tried to remove the flag from the young lad's tight grip, but he angrily retaliated and tried to break free from their clutches. Other students rushed to his rescue and tried to help him out, entering into a brief scuffle with the soldiers. The teenager managed to outmanoeuvre the soldiers' grasp and took to his heels, with the soldiers chasing after him. Immediately, a pack of students raced after the soldiers in support of their flag-carrier.

The megaphone incessantly blasted the policeman's angry yelling, ordering the crowds to disperse and go home before they ended up in prison. The crowds ignored it completely and maintained their constant clamour.

Suddenly, hundreds of leaflets were hurled discreetly above people's heads. Everyone in close proximity of the cloud of floating leaflets raised their arms to grab and read them knowing they were *Eoka* fliers.

At the sight of these leaflets, the soldiers plunged into the crowd to apprehend the culprits by furiously hitting anyone with their truncheons who got in their way. They collided with the assembled swarm and thrashed at them indiscriminately. As a warning a volley of rapid gunshots were fired into the air, forcing the demonstrators to stampede and run for safety. They scattered throughout the area, stepping over others and jumping over fences in fear of their lives.

In the confusion, the young flag-carrier outsmarted the soldiers, managed to break through the army cordon, and dashed towards the church. He found himself running on his own, holding the flag-pole tightly and proudly waving the flag about, making it flutter even more. In hot pursuit, the soldiers kept barking in English for him to stop, but the lad was too excited to listen to their warning and quickly gained ground between them.

The soldiers stopped, raised their rifles and aimed directly at the lad who was leaping ahead with agility, zigzagging his way in front of them. Four shots rang out and a single bullet penetrated the boy's back. The force of the bullet caused him to stumble for a moment. But, unaware of what happened to him, he moved a few yards forward. Four more shots were fired and the flag-carrier felt his legs give way as another bullet blew a large gash in his stomach that tore his skin apart. Suddenly his young legs gave in, and he stumbled to the ground, causing one end of the pole to penetrate the open wound in his stomach. Like an impaled carcass he lay motionless on the tarmac. The bloodstained pole pierced through his back like a large spear. He remained still on the ground, covered in warm blood that quickly formed a puddle around his dead body. The school cap that lay next to his corpse was gradually submerged by the flow of blood that gushed out of the fist-size wound in his belly.

The soldiers converged on the splayed body and confirmed the lad was no longer alive. One of the soldiers quickly ran back to his superior and a military ambulance was rushed to the scene blasting its siren. Two young soldiers hastily carried the limp body into the ambulance, and quickly drove off at a high speed anticipating that a riot might flare up.

They were not wrong. The moment news flashed across the crowds that their young flag-carrier was shot dead, pandemonium broke out and scuffles erupted between soldiers and civilians. Stones were thrown and chairs flew in the air, but bare hands were no match against steel and the heavily armed British army who fired their guns into the air to control the angry masses. The jubilant parade had turned into complete mayhem, with screams and raised fists.

By early afternoon the riot had subsided, and the town-centre transformed itself into a deserted battlefield with hundreds of protesters—men, women and children—thrown into waiting trucks, to be locked up in detention camps and prisons.

Under a State of Emergency, a strict curfew was immediately imposed throughout the city. Bustling Varoshia had turned into a ghost town, with not a soul moving about, except for the armed patrol brigades that stormed the empty streets.

*　　*　　*

Not knowing how long the curfew would last, Alexis and his family settled indoors waiting for the town's confinement to be lifted. All they could do was listen to the radio for news and kill time by playing cards, or chatting with one another.

Marcos was shattered by the incident of the parade, and he could not get over the fact that the British killed one of his schoolmates. The whole family congregated in the living room but Marcos was constantly fidgeting, pacing back and forth not knowing what to do with himself. He sat between his brother and Ahmet on a couch, while Maro remained in the kitchen keeping her mother company and listening to their small radio.

131

'He was only sixteen, how could they kill him?' Marcos kept muttering to himself, in search of answers to the recent tragedy.

'There is no law against them, they are the law!' Ahmet replied, while reading and not bothering to raise his eyes from his magazine.

Marcos kept silent for a moment, weighing Ahmet's words. 'They should have captured him not kill him like a dog.' he mumbled again.

'What's the use of talking about it. More lads will end up in a similar fate—may God save our youth!' his father said to him with a fretful expression on his wrinkled face.

'Did you hear that?' Maro yelled from the kitchen and came out to join them. 'We are to get identification papers once the curfew is lifted!'

'Like dog-collars, to keep track of us!' Alexis said.

'It was expected.' his father stated as a matter of fact, and not surprised at all.

'How about the curfew?' Ahmet enquired, anxious to get to work, instead of being confined within four walls.

'They said nothing about that.' Maro answered, and sat on a rattan chair facing her brothers.

Maro had grown into a beautiful young lady, adorned with masses of black hair that she constantly kept squeaky-clean. She would spend hours looking in the mirror, messing about with her mane, attempting to create new hairstyles and presenting Marcos with an excuse to tease her and start up an argument.

'How about telling us some war stories *papa*?' Marcos burst out and looked at his grey-haired father who was staring out the window, where not a soul was moving about. The entire neighbourhood was deserted with everybody shut indoors, desisting to come out in case the convoys patrolling the area spotted them and sent them to prison.

'There is nothing to tell.' Yiorkis said to his son, and gazed at his youngest.

'Oh, yes there is!' his mother shouted from the kitchen and came into the living room, 'none of you were born when your father carried a gun. You were not even a sperm then.' she added, and sat next to her husband and looked at his tanned face with devotion.

'Like all women, you over-exaggerate.' he said to his wife, trying to avoid discussing the past.

'Please, *papa*.' Marcos, who always enjoyed his father's stories, insisted. Unable to brush away his son's persistence, Yiorkis had decided to talk to them about his war years as a fifteen-year old soldier, and a muleteer who fought alongside the British army, against the German oppression that nearly swallowed up most of Europe.

'Oppression is a terrible thing *papa*. Marcos stated when his father finished telling them about his war experiences.

'It certainly is son.' his father answered. 'No man should have to resort to such barbarism, in order to remain free. Common sense, decency and justice must be aimed for at all times if people are to live in peace. Unfortunately, one of the results of excess power is the ability to take what belongs to the weaker but, I always believed that people, irrespective of ethnicity are all equal.'

'You are becoming an idealist, *papa*!' Alexis butted in.

'I tell you, there are no winners in wars, only losers. When this *Eoka* struggle comes to an end . . . you will understand what I mean. The people on this island shall never be the same again. Do not be misled, there is a darker side to every struggle, one that the politicians never disclose because if they did, no one would take up arms. At the end of the day people naively die for a noble idea and that grand idea, is exploited by those dark shadows that remain hidden like wolves, during liberation struggles! Young boys and girls shall spill their blood and others shall wallow in luxury and glory.'

'Well said, my husband, you tell them what war is all about.' Kyra-Soteria stated, agreeing with her husband.

'It is different now *papa*!' said Alexis, who realised that the conversation brought back troubled memories to his ageing father.

'Aggression, does not solve problems, and *Eoka* has chosen aggression as a means to an end!'

'We have no choice . . . '

'Everyone has a choice.' his father interrupted. 'This uprising will bring about misery for many innocent souls! Wounds will flare up and shall never heal, followed by new and more treacherous wounds in the future.'

'What misery, *papa*? Cyprus would be liberated!' Curley-haired Marcos interjected. 'We live in misery now surely it cannot be worse.'

'We may live poorly, lads, but certainly not in hatred for one another. This type of warfare will divide families, it will put brother against brother, cousin against cousin and the whole community will never be the same again! Once innocence is replaced by the art of killing shrouded in secrecy and manipulation, our simple society will never be the same again.'

133

Yiorkis, not wanting to elaborate further, slowly raised his body off the chair and stood up. With head bowed, and in a sceptical mood, he walked straight to his bedroom, eager to close his eyes and forget the present. He was quite familiar with the morbid outcome of all wars and this uprising was deeply bothering him, knowing his son was involved.

The curfew this time was a lengthy one and there was no intention of it being lifted. People became prisoners inside their own homes, forced to make do with the provisions they had before the curfew was enforced. The empty streets became no-go areas and posed serious consequences for those who dared to defy the British order. Desperate people would risk captivity and sneak outside to visit their neighbours in search of food, to get them through this seemingly endless confinement.

The threat of detection was everywhere because of the constant appearance of military trucks packed with armed soldiers patrolling every locality. The familiar military jeeps and trucks became an eyesore to most people, who watched them with utter disgust through their window blinds as they slowly drove by on the look-out for possible culprits. Only dogs and cats seemed to have escaped the curfew.

If coping with the curfew was not bad enough, the winter rains came down with a vengeance causing greater hardship for those trapped. Like helpless sheep they were penned within their homes.

It was getting very late at night and the heavy rain was coming down in bucketfuls, turning the earth into endless muddy puddles. Rapid roadside streams rippled and flowed, dragging anything that could float along with the torrent. It was a miserable winter night, and being indoors, it was the best place to be under the warmth of a burning fire.

Everyone had decided to call it a night and departed for their own rooms when a faint knock at the back door was heard.

'Who can that be this late at night it's past eleven o'clock?' Soteria asked her husband who had his pyjamas on and preparing himself for bed.

Quietly, he went to the door and saw a young girl standing outside, soaked to the skin. He recognised the petite creature; it was Xanthia, Alexis' friend and sweetheart.

'What on earth are you doing here, child?' he asked, totally surprised seeing her at this late hour and risking captivity by the army. He hurriedly ushered her inside.

'I must see Alexis!' she answered in a quivering voice.

She didn't have to wait for long. Alexis came out to see who had arrived so late at night. As soon as he saw Xanthia, he went and gave her a light kiss on the cheek.

'Have you gone mad?' he said in a reprimanding tone.

'I have a message,' she said to him between the chattering of her teeth.

She pulled out a piece of paper from inside her blouse and handed it over to him. She was shaking and Kyra-Soteria quickly took her into the kitchen and turned on the gas burners of the stove. She took her coat off and hung it aside to dry, while Alexis handed her a towel to dry herself.

'What happened to the courier?' he asked, concerned about her safety for risking coming all the way from Varoshia on foot.

'He was apprehended at the parade.' she answered, while towelling her masses of black hair.

Xanthia's unblemished olive skin was marked with a tiny beauty spot above her right cheek, and she was blessed with the longest eyelashes anyone had ever seen. She was a delightful, chirpy girl full of smiles and hardly shy but when she smiled, her eyes squinted slightly, causing a gentle tempting aura about her. She was a shapely girl, with a small waist, slim neck and delicate high cheekbones, but her eyes—black as ravens—were alert and full of life.

A childhood friend of Alexis from *Loukkos*, she had joined the movement about the same time as Alexis did. She was deeply involved with the propaganda section of the organisation by secretly mobilising rallies and setting up the printing of leaflets. It was her last term at the *Gymnasium*, and she planned to enter the teaching profession once she completed her studies, but ever since the uprising had begun, she had little time for studying, much to the disappointment of her parents.

Strong minded and determined, she put all her efforts into the organisation, knowing Alexis was also involved. She cherished the ground he walked on. The relationship between the two had steadily blossomed, but their sweet love had been platonic and remained so by choice. They were restraining themselves until the proper time arrived so they could have a traditional church wedding. They wanted their first night together to be a memorable and a blessed one.

Alexis read the message from his District Leader and his face lit up. On a piece of paper three words were written—*Forward to Victory*—and signed by the familiar scribble *'The Leader-Dighenis'*. He knew exactly what those words meant and could not wait for the curfew to be lifted.

The rain had no intention of stopping and continued to pour down. At the far end of the house, wedged among the dense shrubbery, the hens were safely locked up inside their coop, unable to shut an eye because of the noisy rain. They constantly stirred, disturbed by the ongoing downpour. The ancient rooster in their midst tried to crow prematurely, disturbed by the stormy conditions, but soon gave up. Instead, he decided to peck with his sharp beak against the coop-wire.

Like its owners, he could not wait to be let out of the pen and roam freely in search of fresh worms, or copulate with a willing hen. He craned his neck and tried to crow one more time, but he quickly changed his mind and, ruffling his feathers restlessly, shut his eyelids . . .

CHAPTER EIGHT

T HE DAY AFTER the curfew was over, citizens young and the old congregated at the court houses and police stations to be issued with their identification papers. They were given one week's grace to acquire these, and anyone caught without them after the deadline would receive an immediate prison sentence. Within a week, every living person over the age of ten years old was issued with an ID card.

In retaliation to the two brutal hangings, the Leader had authorised the execution of two British soldiers who were held as hostages for a possible exchange for Greek prisoners. The Governor refused to negotiate for the lives of his young soldiers, and they were immediately executed.

The Governor laid his traps to destroy his enemy but as clever as he was, he forgot the first rule of human behaviour: that violence begets violence and one does not need a stick to bring out a snake—coaxing and honey will do. In desperation, he unleashed his armies—under the code name 'Operation Kingfisher'—to comb the mountain regions in search of *Andartes* and their hideouts by using thousands of troops and tracker dogs. For this task, he relied upon crucial information provided by highly paid informants to guide his every move.

To terrorize peasants, the army frequently cordoned off entire villages, and gave a free rein to hundreds of threatening troops, to make house-to-house searches of entire villages, arresting the young on suspicion of being *Eoka* sympathisers. The Governor's main objective was to capture, dead or alive, this illusory but credible military adversary who called himself '*Dighenis*', and who had become his archenemy and a legend to his people. He put up a forty thousand pound reward for his head, hoping some traitor would be lured and betray his whereabouts. But all his efforts had failed to yield fruit and had gone in vain.

If he was going to be successful, he needed more help from those Greek and Turkish Cypriots who were opposed to the uprising, or from those who did not have any scruples about pointing a finger at others for a price.

He introduced a cunning system to attract and recruit collaborators and simultaneously protect the identities of those who aspired to become informants. While villages were cordoned off, soldiers and police handed out blank pieces of paper and envelopes, demanding that every household write down any information or knowledge they may have about *Eoka* and its members. If they refused to provide information, they were incarcerated and punished for refusing to cooperate with the authorities. In a matter of a few weeks, his network of spies and traitors grew into a fine web that touched every sector of society.

In reprisal for the loss of a British life, military convoys would systematically storm into a village, and viciously attack its inhabitants and beat up the young and old with sheer brutality. At gunpoint they would force the entire population, like a herd of animals, into the village-square or churchyard, and have them stand there for hours. They would enter houses and ransack them, while others would empty whole sacks of grain on the ground and pour paraffin, oil or wine over the grain, rendering it useless, as punishment. Lorries full of produce or crates packed with grapes and melons would be tipped over the side of the road, in search of illegal arms.

But all these tactics, intended to frighten people off, had failed miserably to bring about positive results for the authorities. The greater the mistreatment of the innocent, the greater their hatred for the British army grew. Winning the souls and minds of the people was anathema to the Governor's policy, and he totally failed to grasp or understand that the more he mistreated people, the worse they were likely to retaliate.

The Governor was a desperate man, and desperate men often make fatal mistakes. But he could not see that. In his desperation, he authorised a great number of new detention camps to be constructed throughout the island, to house thousands of innocent inmates. No sooner one was built, it was quickly crammed with prisoners, and new ones had to be constructed. Special torture chambers had been built by the intelligence service and these detestable chambers were equipped with the latest torture apparatus imported from Britain. The Governor believed that the only way to destroy the enemy was by brute force and absolute fear of his mighty authority. He never understood that the idea of freedom never dies and is indestructible.

The British press maintained its barrage of damaging reports, calling for a political solution and self-determination for the people of Cyprus, as it had been promised to them for their loyalty and staunch efforts as allies during the last two world wars. Heated debates flared up and mixed views were expressed in the House of Commons. A great number of MPs called for an immediate solution to the problem because of the daily news reports of British soldiers dying at the hand of a band of hooligans and terrorists.

Cyprus had suddenly become a painful thorn to the government, and it sought ways to pull out this stubborn irritant to ease its pain. For this task it relied entirely on the expertise of its Military Governor of Cyprus to restore the tainted glory of the Empire and crush this petty insurrection.

*   *   *

The Field Marshal did not waste any time and called for an urgent private meeting with a number of prominent Turkish community leaders. The secret meeting took place at Government House in Lefkosia and, as planned, he prepared the ground to sow the seeds of division between the two ethnic communities.

At the meeting was a man named Osman, leader of the entire Turkish Cypriot community, and a young stumpy looking fellow and law graduate, who came along to act in the capacity of legal observer. A senior Turkish policeman was also invited, as well as two labour union officials and a tall *iman* accompanied by an overweight *hodja*. The group represented the backbone of their small impoverished community on the island.

None of them had any idea why they were suddenly summoned to see the Governor, especially under such mysterious conditions. Puzzled, they congregated in a spacious conference room and waited for the Governor to ease their curiosity.

They did not have to wait for long. The Governor arrived dressed in pristine military uniform and shiny, high leather boots and sat himself at the head of the conference table so he could have direct eye contact with everyone. He had an aura of arrogance and pompousness about him that was quickly picked up by his poorly dressed guests. Three other British officials joined the conference, and once the formalities came to an end, the Governor went straight to the point.

'As you are aware, we have a serious situation on our hands,' he began to explain, 'if not tackled decisively, it could pose serious consequences, not only for us but also for your community. The reason why you are summoned here is to discuss the present situation and, with your community's assistance, we may stamp out this insurrection by these Greek terrorists, who are calling themselves *Eoka*.'

The men stirred. The Governor realised they were taken by surprise, and gave them plenty of time to dwell upon what he said. He leaned back in his chair and waited for their response.

'Forgive me sir, but we are a small community and a poor one at that. What can we offer the Empire that it cannot handle on its own?' Osman asked, in absolute puzzlement.

'This Greek insurrection should also concern your community,' stated the Governor convincingly.

'We cannot see what this has to do with us!' the Turkish leader said, not sure what this man was up to, and continued to speak his mind. 'This is a matter between your government and the Greeks, who demand self-determination, for the island. Our small community is no different than all the other minorities who reside here.' After all, Cyprus has always been a Greek nation, why is our community special? And why are the Armenians, Maronites or the other ethnic minority community leaders not summoned to partake at this gathering? They too are inhabitants of Cyprus!'

The Governor did not expect such an answer and was taken by surprise.

'You are the largest single ethnic community on the island, and the most vulnerable! The Greeks are calling for self-determination; *Enosis*, union with Greece. In anticipation of the Greek aspirations, my government is gravely concerned about the long-term effect such aspirations may have on your community' the Governor continued to explain in a persistent manner.

One of the men, the union man, coughed once to clear his throat and looked at the Governor straight in the eyes.

'With all our respect, sir . . . ' he said in a heavy accent, somewhat suspiciously 'we as a Turkish community do not have problems with the Greeks in Cyprus! We live as brothers, Greek boys marry Turkish girls, and Turkish girls marry Greek boys.' We subsist in the same villages, we share the same food, and when our unions - which you have abolished and declared illegal - demand better wages and improved working conditions these demands are for the benefit of all workers, Greeks, Turks, Armenians and all Cypriots alike! Why the sudden interest for our welfare?'

'Simply because in the event my government decides to make reconciliatory concessions for a political solution directly with the Greeks you will be left out on the fringes without any say in the matter. Surely you can see the consequences of such a scenario!' answered the Governor, knowing full well that he had not yet convinced his audience.

'We do appreciate your government's concern for our well-being! But, what we don't understand is quite simple; what do you expect from us?' Osman asked, not quite sure what this man had in his mind.

'Our objective is to put down this insurgence either through peaceful means, or by brute force if necessary. The Greeks cannot win this uprising. They delude themselves if they believe that they can succeed, your community however, can safeguard its future by supporting our efforts to bring peace on the island!' stated the Governor.

'If we understand this correctly, your government wishes that we should join forces and rise up against our Greek compatriots.' stated the union man, furrowing his thick eyebrows, not happy with what was asked of them.

'To be quite blunt about it, yes; against *Eoka!*' answered the Governor firmly.

The Turks began to talk among themselves in Turkish, not sure what this man was setting them up for, and they were certainly not convinced. They were not happy with what they had heard so far and became agitated. They recognised that this official with his mighty authority was ploughing the ground to split their peaceful communities apart. They were perplexed by his comments, but they also realised there might be some truth in them. They were in a dilemma, but they were not stupid either; they knew that the Governor was planting the seed of division between their communities, and that bothered their sense of dignity and justice.

'I emphatically disagree with such a venomous plan!' retorted the union man after considering the proposal. 'I have a brother married to a Greek woman and my neighbours are all Greeks. How can I justify this ridiculous and sudden change of our friendly relationship? I say this is a matter between the British and *Eoka*, and it has nothing to do with the Turkish Cypriots!'

'My government has been in discussions with Ankara and Athens, and I can assure you they both support our efforts to put down this uprising, that threatens to destabilise the region. Ankara is behind us and has no objection to implicate your community in a peaceful capacity, to bring about order in Cyprus.'

'Ankara has no say in our community's affairs or how we choose to live! They never cared before, why the sudden change now?' Osman bellowed, interrupting the Governor.

'If the Greeks persist with this uprising my government might have to come to a political solution in order to stop the bloodshed but what's worrying us, the Greeks may start to make moves against your community, since their main objective is union with Greece,' the Governor said, in an attempt to raise fear and suspicion.

'Does the British government really care about our poor community? Osman asked again, with slight anger in his voice. He

141

felt hot and his face was suddenly covered in sweat. He nervously started to wipe his forehead with a white handkerchief.

'Of course my government cares!' insisted the Governor assertively.

'We have seen nothing so far to justify your fears!' butted in the union man again, quite upset, and in a trembling voice. '*Eoka* has never tried its hand on Turkish citizens on the contrary, they publicly proclaimed that this uprising is specifically aimed against British colonialism, and not against anybody else!'

'I can assure you, they will turn their guns against you, when the time is right . . .!' insisted the Governor putting terror into the men around the table.

'But as you rightly stated there is no chance of this happening!' butted in the long legged *iman* who had remained silent so far.

'*Eoka* will never succeed but in politics, anything is possible. That is why we must not leave things to chance. We must integrate our efforts and stop this insurrection and, as far as I am concerned, the sooner the better for both our sakes!'

'What do you expect from us?' Osman finally asked bluntly.

'We plan to establish a new armed Auxiliary Police Force alongside our existing Mobile Police Force. This new force would be made up of approximately ten thousand men. Its purpose is to maintain peace and order. Since we cannot count on Greek participation we have no other choice but to recruit Turks to do the job. We are bringing five hundred experienced police personnel from England to oversee the training of all new recruits,' explained the Governor, convinced he was beginning to win his audience over by mentioning the creation of these new jobs.

'Are you saying that this force will be composed entirely of Turkish–Cypriot recruits?' the Turkish leader asked, quite impressed by the new job opportunities being handed to them on a platter by the Governor.

'Yes!'

'I don't like the idea!' the union man said, displaying great misgivings about the whole proposal.

'What is it that bothers you so strongly?' the Governor asked this man, who always appeared to be so negative.

'Governor sir, I will tell you what bothers me.' answered the union man firmly in his harsh accent. 'The instant we put on a uniform and arm ourselves we shall become enemies of our compatriots and friends. We lived together for nearly eighty years without any problems between us, why change now and impel us to fight your battle?'

The union man was quite blunt, but he appeared quite distraught and lit a cigarette to calm his nerves. He worked in the Amiandos mines owned by the Anglo–American Mining Corporation, and knew first hand how miserably the British authorities treated the Greek and Turkish miners. He did not trust this man's words. He spoke with a silver tongue in his mouth and was completely ignorant of reality, of how people lived on the island. He did not trust him at all . . .

'We do not expect you to fight our battle.' answered the Governor, intimidated by the man's tone which questioned his military authority. 'With or without you, we shall establish this Auxiliary Force. I am giving you the opportunity to get involved and secure a decent livelihood for your families. Either way, we shall recruit Turks . . . but with your personal support, as leaders of your community, it will expedite our objective. But above all else you shall have my government's gratitude and unwavering support in future developments. On the other hand, I do not have a crystal ball to tell the future, but should you offer my government your loyal support, you shall be well rewarded, politically and economically.' added the Governor, using a carrot and a stick to influence his audience.

The men switched into Turkish, and there seemed to be a brief argument developing between them. The Governor remained silent to allow the Turks enough time to debate the situation, realising they had to discuss the matter between themselves. After a heated discussion, Osman, their spokesman, turned and looked the Governor straight in the eyes and in a sombre mood . . .

'Do we have your government's guarantee that you will not forsake us in the event the Greeks take reprisals against our community?' he asked in a serious tone.

'It is with my government's full support that you have been summoned here! That in itself should indicate to you our loyalty and commitment!' the Governor replied, recognising he had them in the palm of his hand, like a lump of clay to manipulate in a shape of his own choosing.

'As you have correctly stated, no-one can foretell the future, but for us it could turn disastrous if we are left to hang dry, without your support . . . after all, we have to live with the Greeks every day.' Osman reiterated, demanding more assurances.

'There are forty five thousand British troops stationed on the island, that is your guarantee!' the Governor reassured him assertively.

'I will have nothing to do with this Anglo–Turkish conspiracy.' the union man objected.

143

'You may call it what you like but, this is survival of the fittest.' the Governor said to him with indifference.

After another lengthy discussion and argument between themselves, the spokesman of the group stood up, and went over to the Governor's chair. He stretched his arm out.

'You have our support.' he stated, and reached out, to exchange a handshake with the Field Marshal.

Pleased with the outcome of the meeting, the Governor stood up and stretched his own arm out and reciprocated with a lengthy handshake with everyone present.

The conference ended, adding a new dimension to the Cyprus situation—one full of uncertainties for the future. The only person who seemed opposed to the whole betrayal was the union man, who did not trust the Governor's word. He smelled that a hidden agenda was in the making, and showed great misgivings, and did not hesitate to speak his mind. He felt that they had just betrayed their Greek compatriots, in exchange for jobs.

He was too upset to even shake hands with the Governor, and he was the first one to walk out the door, wanting to breathe some fresh air, feeling that the air inside that room was stale and reeked with betrayal.

*   *   *

In a matter of a few weeks, hundreds of Turkish Cypriots rushed to join this new Auxiliary Police Force. The response was beyond the Governor's wildest expectations and, after a brief training period, he armed and sent the poorly trained units across the island, to patrol the streets and guard government buildings and installations.

Greeks had suddenly found themselves in a confused and unwarranted dilemma. Overnight, a new enemy had suddenly appeared out of nowhere, one that *Eoka* had never anticipated, and this adversary was well armed and prepared to execute its duties with efficiency and without scruples.

Among the ranks, the Turks organised their own clandestine organisation to counter the *Eoka* aspirations. They named their organisation *Volkan*, and systematically set out with vigour and by intimidation to command their own people to segregate from Greeks and relocate within the Turkish–Cypriot controlled villages and enclaves.

The Governor was pleased with his manipulative master plan, and he could not have been more thrilled, having created an additional force to combat his enemy. With the Turks on his side, he was positive that the enemy would soon buckle at the knees and give up all hope of any success. He turned a blind eye to this new Turkish clandestine organisation, and gave them total freedom to move against the enemy, as long as they met his own objective: to crush *Eoka* for good . . .

Volcan had grown very quickly into a strong force. It was capable of mobilising the Turkish masses to take part in demonstrations and rallies in direct opposition to Greek aspirations.

Almost immediately, many Greek and Turkish households, fearing for their lives, chose to relocate among their own people. Simultaneously, *Volcan* set the wheels in motion to incite the Turkish community to aspire for the partitioning of the island. In a matter of a few months the two friendly communities began to segregate, to the delight of the Governor. He had both ethnic sectors in the palm of his hand to manipulate on his own terms.

The Archbishop, on the other hand, was stunned by these unexpected developments, and realised the struggle for independence had taken on a new dimension, one he had not anticipated. He suspected these new realities had received the Governor's blessing, and he was distressed how easily the Turkish community fell into this man's trap. The Turks had chosen to accept a gift from dirty hands, not realising their own hands would be soiled.

He was also puzzled by the Turks' behaviour, and wondered what had been promised to them for making such a drastic decision. As a devout churchman, he was a neophyte in political manipulation and he was at a complete loss what initiatives to undertake. He desperately wanted to bring the Turks back to the Greek side. Disillusioned, he recognised that the Governor had proved to be a formidable manipulator who gambled with people's lives without conscience.

In search of an amicable peace settlement, the Archbishop had decided to enter into negotiations with the Governor to discuss the issue of self-determination and try to find ways to reach a favourable solution to the Cyprus problem.

He wanted these killings and destruction halted and to come to an end.

At the Archbishop's request, *Dighenis* had ordered all military activities to stop, as a gesture of goodwill in order to assist His Eminence's negotiating position. But, while these negotiations were in progress, the Governor candidly refused to honour his end of the agreement and maintained the imprisonment of civilians and daily arrests, to the bitter disappointment of the *Eoka* Leader.

Dighenis was furious at the outcome of these shallow talks, and he soon realised they were nothing less than delaying tactics by the

British. This Field-Marshal had dishonourable intentions; he was never interested in peace, but rather maintained a policy of deceit and trickery in his attempt to crush his adversary.

Anxious to talk about these matters with the *Eoka* Leader, the Archbishop called for a secret meeting to take place at the isolated Stavrovouni monastery. In addition to this, he invited the Bishop of Kerynia, and two other church officials involved with the struggle so that they could formulate a unified front, to combat the unexpected developments brought about by the Governor's cunning policy of division.

Perched on the peak of Mount Troothos amongst the dense Pafos forest, Stavrovouni remained for centuries in complete isolation, surrounded by the wildest countryside on the island. Gracefully, it overlooked across the sloping hills and ridges, sheltered by timeless scented pine, fir and cedar trees. From its summit, the wild forest below rolled in the distance as far as the eyes could see, pierced only by endless mountain peaks, inhabited by wild life and circling eagles. There is always a majestic sense of silence about the place that causes one's ears to hum with tranquillity. The rhythmic throbbing of a person's heartbeat is the only sound audible in this magnificent still forest, carpeted thickly by dried pine needles.

Ayia Eleni, the Byzantine Empress and mother of Constantine the Great, founder of *Ayia Sofia* in *Constantinoupolis,* was responsible for commissioning the building of this shrine more than a thousand years ago, as proof of her devotion to the Christian faith. On her return from the Holy Land, she fell in love with this mountain peak and dedicated the shrine to *Panayia* - Mother of all mothers and Mother of Jesus.

The Archbishop frequently visited this place to find solitude and peace, in order to gather his thoughts whenever he was troubled. Recently, his troubles had become insurmountable and surpassed all others. They demanded his urgent consideration, to find a viable escape from the present predicament that occupied most of his time. He was constantly distressed, and became worried about the welfare of his people, realising that he was crossing murky waters infested with writhing underlying dangers in every step forward.

Dighenis was the first to arrive at this monastery, driven by a loyal female member of the organisation. He was disguised as a woman and as soon as he arrived, he quickly changed his clothes, embarrassed by the way he looked. As his face appeared on posters everywhere, he could not risk recognition or captivity. Therefore, he often resorted to strange disguises as the only way he could move about freely when necessary.

He changed into an abbot's cloak and no sooner had he a chance to settle down, the sound of another car was heard coming up the long driveway. An elderly Bishop got out of a black car, followed by two other companions who appeared much younger than the dignified looking Bishop.

The men congregated in a large dining hall scented by the overpowering smell of incense burning. They were served lentil soup and roast chicken for lunch, prepared by a tall hunched-back skinny abbot, who kept coming in and out of the hall to ensure all was fine and the food was to their satisfaction.

Between mouthfuls, the five of them had plenty of time to discuss the imminent situation that was troubling their minds. They sipped *Commandaria*, brewed by the monks at the monastery, and entered into a heavy debate which offered no easy answers to their plight. Only the Leader fully understood the eventual result of this new Turkish Auxiliary Force that came out of nowhere to haunt them. He could smell the stench of the Governor's plan a mile away.

'No more games . . . this is survival!' *Dighenis* finally spelled out his thoughts. 'I have never trusted politicians and I am not about to start now! The British have decided—and succeeded, I might say—in splitting our two communities apart so they can manipulate us both by setting one against the other in order to control us. The fact that they are threatening to bring in mainland Turkish and Greek Commissioners to assist the Governor—supposedly—to rule our country clearly indicates that they have decided to partition the island! They pretend to ignore our existence . . . and by doing so they insult our intelligence! Because of these British moves and their persistent attacks on our civilians—while under a cease-fire—I have called off the cease-fire, as of today! *Eoka* is back in action again! I am not prepared to allow my fighters to become sitting ducks and be killed at the whim of this pompous autocrat!'

'What do you think is behind this new British plan?' asked the Archbishop in a perplexed manner.

'It's quite obvious . . .! The British have decided to internationalise the Cyprus issue, and transform the problem into one between Turks and Greeks, exonerating themselves from their responsibilities! They plan to tell the world that our struggle for liberation has no legitimacy and their military actions are to maintain law and order. It is a clever move, because they have now decided to implicate Turkey and Greece in our affair and I can assure you they have already negotiated a secret deal to carve up the island between the three of them. I am not ready to accept defeat yet! So far not a single Turk died from a Greek bullet but sadly, this will not last forever, not unless the Turkish community changes its stance and position.' explained *Dighenis*, and rubbed his thick moustache in agitation. He frowned and gazed at the men of God.

'Can *Eoka* cope?' asked the elderly Bishop of Kerynia and stroked his massive unruly white beard that moved about when he spoke.

There was an aura of omnipotence about him and he did not speak much but when he did speak, his spoken words were well targeted and meaningful.

'*Eoka* is growing as we speak!' answered *Dighenis*. 'We have twenty *Andartes* groups in the mountains made up of approximately three hundred fighters. We can resist until the last drop of our blood is drained from our bodies.'

'Against forty-five thousand troops?' the elderly Bishop asked, somewhat perplexed.

'Yes!' asserted *Dighenis* with conviction. 'We can resist because we are fighting for our liberation. The only thing that bothers me is not to fall into British political traps and they are going to produce many such plans as time goes by! The grey men of Whitehall for sure would come up with grand ideas, how to maintain control over the island and in doing so try to persuade us that they are doing us a favour.'

'What can we do about the Turks?' asked the Archbishop.

'If they start to attack our people we shall fight them also! The choice rests entirely with them and not us! We did not start this state of affairs and they bear full responsibility for their actions!' *Dighenis* stated flatly, and did not seem to be bothered by the new developments.

'Colonel we are to fight the British army, the Turks, a network of traitors and those Anglophile Greeks who prefer to live under British rule?' queried the Archbishop, in a mystified manner.

'We shall fight them all and we shall succeed!' interrupted the Colonel.

The men around the table appeared bothered, but none offered a better suggestion or a way out of their predicament, except for the Bishop of Kerynia who decided to speak his mind openly.

'Tomorrow we are to meet with the Colonial Secretary, obviously he will bring with him a British proposal!' he began to say.

'Don't trust him!' *Dighenis* interrupted him firmly.

'Even so, in order to give peace a chance under what terms is *Eoka* prepared to suspend all hostilities and put down its arms?' the Bishop asked.

'You know my position! I will not rest until Cyprus gains the right of self-determination! But, if I am to make reconciliatory concessions

148

before I will even consider the idea of telling our fighters to give up the struggle, I have four requests.'

'They are?' the Archbishop asked softly, anxious to see the end of the bloodshed that had persisted for so long.

'I will lay down my arms only if the British provide a cast iron guarantee that they will honour any agreement reached, the additional British troops brought to the island to be removed from Cyprus, a complete amnesty for all our captured fighters, and the release of all our prisoners. And finally, internal security of the island not to be left in the hands of the British! If those terms are met, there might be a chance for *Eoka* to cease its hostilities. But I can assure you, the British will not accept our terms! They have other plans and the Turkish situation clearly exposes their trump card!' *Dighenis* said with complete conviction.

'Let's see what the Colonial Secretary has up his sleeve.' the Archbishop stated, and went on to add, 'I too believe they will not accept the conditions you have just stated.'

'So be it. But my advice to you is: don't agree on anything, unless they meet our conditions. Just be sure you do not fall into a British trap.' *Dighenis* said to him in a warning tone, recognising this man of God was most anxious to find a solution to the ongoing struggle.

'Rest assured Colonel, we shall outfox the fox but what troubles me most of all is the Turkish situation,' the Archbishop said, not quite accepting what had emerged through deviousness on the island.

'I can handle the Turks.' he said to him.

'May God have mercy on us all, we began with a dream, and that dream has now turned into a nightmare!' the Archbishop stated distressfully, realising the ominous consequences.

The men of God and the Warrior spent all afternoon analysing their predicament, and by six o'clock they had come to a unanimous decision; to tread with caution and see what transpires out of tomorrow's private meeting with the Colonial Secretary.

By late afternoon, the *Eoka* Leader was driven by his female companion directly to his hideout in Lemesos. He planned to remain there in hiding until he received news from the Archbishop before disappearing into the hills to join his *Andartes*. He was anxious to use his military skills against the enemy, and he felt inadequate from idleness brought about by the unproductive ceasefire.

*   *   *

Early next morning the priests were greeted by a glorious day, one full of vigour and life. A flock of birds stormed upon the nearby orchards, weighing the tree branches down, twittering gaily and chirping away in search for food. They flapped their wings and hopped from branch to branch, exposing their tireless wings with an array of colours that contrasted against the lush green background of almond and olive trees.

From the hills beyond, a thick cloud of brilliantly-coloured butterflies appeared from nowhere and settled temporarily in the orchard. They flapped their delicate wings momentarily, stormed about in their thousands briefly, but soon flew off again as quickly as they had arrived.

The morning sun began to emerge gracefully over the mountain peaks, emitting piercing spears of sharply-edged shafts of light between the branches, forcing the morning dew to ascend gently over the trees as a shade of mist. The smell of fresh pine was invigorating, and the abbots soon came out for their daily morning ritual of taking deep breaths to welcome the dawn of a new day before serving breakfast. The monks stood in a long line watching the beautiful flock of birds, and admiring in wonder, God's creation of life.

At ten o'clock, a highly polished black car arrived, and the Archbishop sat in the front passenger seat, as he always did, while the Bishop of Kerynia and the two other officials sat at the rear.

Immediately the car drove off and headed towards Lefkosia to keep their appointment with the Colonial Secretary and the Governor, in anticipation of coming up with some kind of a solution to their political differences.

They passed the mountainous region of Pethoullas and headed through the dense Cedar valley for the isolated village of Kakopetria, perched among high peaks of green forests. Peasants stopped and waved at the passing car once they recognised the Archbishop and the other passengers. He responded by smiling and waving back at them.

The car rolled gently down the endless hills and dangerous sharp bends, when the driver noticed a military roadblock ahead blocking the main cross-roads of Kakopetria. He slowed down and brought the car to a halt a few yards away from the armed blockade.

A young British soldier wearing shorts quickly approached the car and the Archbishop craned his head out to see what was happening.

'Is there anything wrong?' he asked in his heavily accented English.

'No trouble at all, your Eminence.' the soldiers answered politely, recognising the Archbishop. 'We have instructions to escort you to Nicosia and have been looking out for your car.' he continued, pleased that he was able to intercept the entourage.

'There is no need my son. It's a wonderful morning and we have been enjoying the slow morning drive,' the Archbishop said to him, not pleased that his trip was interrupted.

'I have my orders your Eminence,' answered the soldier 'Please follow us.' he added and walked back to where the other military vehicles were parked crammed with armed soldiers.

Without much choice, the Archbishop obliged and their car followed the two vehicles leading the way forward. Sandwiched between the convoys their car moved forward at a snail's pace.

One hour later the entourage reached the outskirts of Lefkosia. The men had noticed that instead of driving directly to Government House, the long convoy headed for the airport.

'Maybe the Colonial Secretary is there,' said the Bishop, trying to justify the sudden change of route.

At the busy airport the convoy headed straight for the runway, and stopped alongside a plane that had its engines roaring and propellers rotating fast in readiness to take off. The four churchmen, dressed in their black robes and caps, were guided towards the noisy plane. Their driver was left behind scratching his head in puzzlement at the sudden change of plans.

Under armed escort the men were guided into the plane.

Inside, the cabin crew asked them to pick any seat of their own choosing, as they were the only passengers on the flight.

No sooner had they taken their seats than a British official arrived in a hurry, carrying a sheet of paper. He called out their names and ticked each one off his list, without saying a single word.

'What is going on?' the Archbishop asked him, realising something was not quite right.

'You and your companions are being exiled from Cyprus. The plane will take you to the Seychelle Islands in the Indian Ocean, until further notice.' the official said, without further clarification.

'Are we being kidnapped?' bellowed the Archbishop in total disbelief.

'These are our orders,' answered the official and turned to depart.

'I demand to speak with the Governor!' shouted the Archbishop, fuming with anger.

'It was his orders,' stated the official, and walked along the aisle towards the exit.

'I am the Archbishop! We are not criminals!' His Eminence objected, yelling at the top of his voice and realising the seriousness of their predicament.

His black cap fell off his head, exposing his long, dishevelled, greying hair and receding hairline. One of the stewards picked it up and handed it back to him. He fell into his seat, in absolute disbelief at what was happening to them.

It was no use. The official disappeared as quickly as he had arrived, and completely ignored the Archbishop's objections.

'Some rise by sin, some fall by virtue,' the Bishop of Kerynia said calmly, accepting their fate. He crossed himself three times.

'May God help us all,' the Archbishop murmured softly. He leaned his head back against the cushion, and stared ahead in bewilderment.

'God help us,' repeated the others in unison.

The instant the official left, the military crew shut the plane door tightly and it was immediately given clearance to take off. The plane rolled across the runway with its engines reverberating and steadily moved forward. It briefly came to a stop on the main runway. With a roar, it accelerated forward and picked up the necessary speed for take off.

Once airborne, the plane steadily climbed to a great height, leaving the four kidnapped men staring in absolute bewilderment. They peered through the small cabin windows, and gazed at the diminishing outline of their beloved island below. It was disappearing fast. In a matter of a few minutes the land had completely vanished from sight. They could no longer see anything except the vastness of blue sky.

Suddenly a flock of pink flamingos appeared across the skies flapping their long wings in synchronicity heading towards the salt lake of Larnaka . . .

CHAPTER NINE

AT THE NEWS of their Archbishop's exile the people of Cyprus went wild with anger. But they were not as livid as the Leader of *Eoka* who immediately gave orders for all clandestine activities to escalate to teach the British and their sympathisers a lesson they would never forget. As far as *Dighenis* was concerned, there was nothing more to discuss and all barriers were down: this was war! His *Eoka* fighters together with the *Andartes* groups in the mountain regions embarked on an unrelenting offensive against all enemy targets. Explosions, ambushes, executions and angry mass riots became a daily occurrence, stretching the Governor's resources to their limit.

Simultaneously, *Eoka* had called for passive resistance by ordering all civilians to boycott British products and to remove all English signs from shops and buildings throughout the land. With the signs removed and replaced by Greek ones, the island began to look Greek again, as it always had been. The repercussions for disobeying *Eoka* directives were extremely harsh, often resulting in death for persistent offenders. Chaos had touched every part of the island, with little chance of the merciless attacks and counter-attacks coming to an end.

As an area commander Alexis ordered his urban groups to carry out their missions in any way they saw fit, as long as they produced devastating results. He on the other hand, was constantly on the move. Most evenings, he would be out all night arriving home late, often distraught and other times happy. As always, his mother would be awake waiting for him, simply to say, 'Oh, you are home.' and raise her heavy body off the couch, and disappear into her own bedroom content that her son was safely home.

Tonight, he was to meet up with his own group and decided to go ahead before the others had arrived at the small barn that had become their hideout for storing ammunition and explosives. As customary, before setting out for an assignment, the group met to discuss details and pick up the necessary arsenal.

The isolated citrus barn constantly reeked with the stench of decomposed citrus fruit, and was located deep in the centre of a massive orange grove. It was very easy for anyone to become lost in this dark and densely planted grove. Alexis' group had dug out a large pit under the floor alongside a huge fireplace that had become

153

their bomb-making factory. The old, dilapidated citrus barn had become their second, private home, and they spent endless hours inside this place.

The interior of the pit contained a simple wooden counter covered with tools and a few low wooden crates strewn across the floor to sit upon. The lads proudly hung Petros' school photo on the wall directly above the counter so they could always have sight of him. On either side of their dead friend's photograph, they folded a Greek flag as a shrine to him. Every time they climbed inside the pit, the boys greeted their friend as a matter of respect and to remind them how easy it is to lose one's life, through a simple error of judgement. Below his photo, Michalaki, their sensitive childhood friend, had written in bold lettering—*We shall never forget.*

Alexis' new target was a slightly frightening but an important one, the destruction of which would cause a serious blow to the enemy. It was his friend Spyros who first mentioned the target to him, and they often discussed its feasibility. He was positive the sabotage mission would be successful and expressed his feelings to Alexis, who instantly agreed to take part and join his group in a common effort.

Arriving at the hideout he sat outside on the ground, resting his back against the thick-walled barn, and started at the dark sky covered with brilliant stars. As he waited for the others, he was becoming impatient and anxious to disclose the night's operation.

With nothing to do but wait, he cogitated upon the organisation and the dangerous assignment he was about to undertake, recognising it was probably the most dangerous mission he had ever been involved with and was prone to high risks. His mind drifted to his family and how understanding they had been since the uprising had began, by not interfering with his activities, but rather remaining supportive and keeping their reservations to themselves. He could tell his mother was deeply worried, and tried hard not to give her unnecessary grief, often lying to her. But, with his father it was a different matter, he could not fool him. Even so, he never tried to stop him, knowing that nearly every youth on the island was involved with *Eoka*.

In the verdant orange and lemon groves, Xanthia flashed through the dark corners of his mind, and he felt quite upset they were not able to spend more time together. Before, they would frequently sit next to each other at home, making plans for the future and dream of an eternally blissful life together. Between their chitchat, they would steal a small kiss from one another, and resume their conversation oblivious to their surroundings. That gentle closeness had recently become a rarity and he missed those cherished moments terribly, but he could not turn the clock back.

His pleasant thoughts were interrupted by the sound of the movement of branches, and he realised that someone was approaching through the thick orchard. It was his punctual friend Michalaki, and he came and sat on a crate next to him, swearing at the same time, angry that his shoes were covered in mud. He began to wipe the mud off his soles using a stick and moaning about the terrible catastrophe that had befallen upon him.

'I hate mud!' he muttered to himself, forcing Alexis to smile with compassion for his sensitive childhood friend.

Adamos and Dimitri, the group's execution team, came soon after Michalaki, and both joined the two lads. Gathered together amidst the dark shadowy groves, the boys waited for Andreas to show up. He was never punctual and had a thousand excuses, for turning up late. They were accustomed to his unorthodox disposition, and never questioned his punctuality, but rather played along with him, often teasing him about it. Irrespective of his punctuality handicap, he was totally loyal to his friends and would never let anybody down; his word was his bond and for that quality his friends loved him.

As soon as he arrived, the boys removed the secret hatch from the floor, and climbed down inside their hideout using a small wooden step-ladder already in position at the bottom of the pit. Once inside, Andreas hastily lit the glass oil lantern adjacent to Petros' portrait. The warm flickering flame instantly illuminated their friend's photograph, and cast a soft yellowish-red glow on their faces.

'Greetings, Petros.' said Andreas, and gently touched the photo with his hand, with deep respect for his dead friend.

One by one they followed suit by greeting their deceased friend and then settling down on wooden crates to discuss the assignment of the night. Michalaki was seated next to Andreas, and kept moaning about his shoes and began to clean them now that he could see better under the light.

'You are thick, Michalaki!' burst out Andreas, annoyed that he kept moaning about his stupid shoes 'Why clean them, they are going to get smothered again once we get outside.'

'Yes, but not as much.' he replied not paying attention, and turned to Alexis 'Where is Ahmet?' he asked.

'His sister is in hospital.' answered Alexis, who sat at the far corner of the damp cavern.

'What's wrong with her?' Michalaki asked curiously, concerned about the girl's condition. He regarded her as his baby sister.

'They say its her appendix but they are not sure.'

'What's up, Alexis?' fearsome Adamos interrupted with his reverberating voice, anxious to find out about the mission.

'We are going to blow up some planes tonight and destroy a runway.' Alexis answered and waited to see their reaction.

'Where? There are no runways here!' Dimitri said in total disbelief.

'Akrotiri . . .!'

'Akrotiri . . .? That's on the other side of Cyprus!'

'We are going to join forces with Spyros and blow up these planes inside their own military compound. Everything has been arranged and we should be in Lemesos, by two in the morning,' Alexis explained.

'Inside the air base and how do we get out?' Michalaki asked in astonishment, at such a daring undertaking.

'Never mind that. How do we get in?' added Andreas, and looked at his friend seated next to him.

'Don't worry everything is under control!' Alexis said to ease their minds, and set out to explain in detail the overall plan.

The lads listened with total devotion and became quite excited about the prospect of destroying such a valuable target. They had absolute faith in Alexis' capabilities, trusted him with their own lives, and were convinced without a doubt that the mission was well planned.

'Just think Michalaki we might get a commendation from the Leader, if we blow up them planes.' Andreas said to his chubby friend, and slapped him on the shoulder.

'Not likely!' he answered with indifference.

'I also have some bad news . . . '

'Don't spoil it Alexis, we don't want to know!' Dimitri interrupted, and sprang up ready to go.

'*Aetos*, our District Leader has been betrayed by someone in his village. But the British failed to capture him. He has now joined the *Andartes*.' Alexis continued, not paying attention to Dimitri.

'Them traitors need to be skinned alive!' bellowed Michalaki, and banged his clenched fist against his other palm, fuming with anger. His face turned red, like an over-ripe tomato.

'I will skin them inch by inch!' Dimitri added between clenched teeth, and meant every word of it. As a butcher's son, he had become a master and an expert of handling knives by skinning animals on a daily basis for his father's butcher shop.

Once Alexis finished with his instructions, the lads went about the business of opening up crates and hastily gathering the necessary arsenal; grenades, a couple of ancient pistols, bullets and a number of time bombs together with detonators. They carefully packed everything inside two leather grips, and one by one climbed up the small ladder and set off towards Alexis' house where his car was packed.

Following one another, they cannoned into the dark thick grove. The endless low branches seemed to find their target with their every move, and constantly hit them in the face. Michalaki kept moaning as always, and became relieved once they finally entered the open fields behind Alexis' house and he could see where he was stepping.

The full moon turned the night into day, and the boys could see their way clearly by following their own moon shadows and cutting across the vast turnip plantation. Blind bats whizzed by them swiftly in search of food, and appeared to have taken control over the night sky. They constantly flew in flocks of hundreds, and fluttered about emitting a blizzard of high-pitched shrieks into the silent night.

Treading over the green vegetation, the five lads reached Alexis' house sited at the edge of the huge plantation. The kitchen light was turned on and they all headed for the back door, while Alexis together with Adamos went directly to the car, to stow away the two carrier bags packed with explosives. They carefully concealed the bags under a false compartment inside the boot of the car, and then joined the others inside the house.

Kyra-Soteria was up waiting for her husband to return from his local coffee-house, and as soon as she saw the group of boys, she sensed they would be going out again for some kind of mission. She kept her thoughts to herself, and tried to offer the boys food, but they all politely refused her hospitality, except for Michalaki who picked up a slice of *hallumi* cheese on a piece of bread. She had known all of these raucous boys since they were children, and had watched them growing up into the young men that were now crowding her living room. Whenever they paid a visit, she treated them as part of her own family and never refused their wants, be it food or refreshment. She took pleasure in feeding these boys, and the happiest moments of her mundane life were to see them stuffing their mouths. They often brought her a small present or a bunch of flowers in gratitude of her kindness, and in return she would smile and quietly disappear into her kitchen, totally embarrassed, and dish up a feast for them. That was her character, and remained so all her life, finding great pleasure and self-satisfaction in giving rather than receiving.

Marcos and his sister were up and joined the lads, making small talk with them. They knew they were about to go for an assignment, but they never questioned the fact, being quite accustomed to their brother's commitment to the uprising. All they could do was to wait, until he returned safely home, and their anxiety for him would then be over. Both of them had developed great respect for their elder brother and cherished the ground he walked upon. For them, he was their hero.

After a brief stay, Alexis decided it was time to take off and went to his mother and gave her a small kiss on the top of her head, as she was so short. '*Mama*, you are always shrinking' he would frequently tease her.

'Don't wait up for me I will be probably late.' he said to her and felt kind of sorry for her, knowing she would stay up all night waiting for him to return.

'Go with my blessing.' she said to everyone, while they exited from the front door. She tried hard not to show any misgivings.

When they got outside, she went and stood out on the veranda to see them off. Next to her stood Marcos and his sister, who had their eyes fixed on the boys who scrambled inside the black old Consul. Alexis took the wheel and Andreas sat next to him having the longest legs of them all. He turned the engine on and was about to take off, when he heard his brother's voice calling to him.

'Do you have your papers?' anxiously he asked, while standing on the veranda.

Alexis and his friends quickly stirred about and checked their pockets. All was in order and he immediately drove off, leaving his family standing behind on the veranda watching the car going round the bend.

Once the car disappeared, Kyra-Soteria went straight into the kitchen, and took the small glass jar out of *Panayia's* shrine that was hanging in a corner of her kitchen wall. She carefully washed the jar, and then filled it half way up with water and topped it with olive oil. Gently she placed a floating wick in the centre of the jar, and by striking a match she lighted the wick inside the shrine.

Without uttering a word, she knelt down on her heavy legs and began to whisper a prayer to *Panayia*, Mother of all mothers, who understood the suffering of mothers for their sons' well being. She remained there for a long time, until she completed her prayers and then went into the living room, plunging herself into a chair. She would remain there all night if necessary, until her son returned home safely . . .

The car sped steadily towards Lemesos. Within half an hour they left Varoshia behind and entered the open countryside engulfed in complete darkness. The headlights of their car flooded the narrow road ahead guiding the boys forward. The odd tree quickly flashed by the speeding car like a sentinel, guarding the long isolated road that snaked through the roaming hills and remote landscape.

By the time they reached the sleepy town of Larnaka, hometown of *Zenon*, the ancient stoic Cypriot philosopher, heavy rain started to pour and a howling wind rose and blew from across the open sea. It seemed that the dawns of heaven had been ripped apart letting the heavy downpour come down in buckets. Driving alongside the seashore, they saw that angry waves had swollen to great heights, crashing with might against the rocky shore in a thunderous force, rarely seen at this small town.

Andreas opened the car window slightly, and a rush of salty wind blew in. He was anxious to fill his nostrils with fresh ozone, and rapidly took a few deep breaths. But he quickly shut the window again to accommodate his friends' objections.

They passed Larnaka, and by one-thirty the first scattered lights of Lemesos appeared in the distance. A great number of ships moored in the harbour became faintly detectable through the pouring rain. The lads knew they were finally approaching their destination. They were making good time and Alexis headed directly for the waterfront where Spyros was to meet them.

It was with great relief that they saw his tall figure standing alone, attempting to hold his coat together tightly, against the violent wind and pouring rain. Alexis stopped the car, got out and handed Spyros the steering wheel. He squeezed between his friends in the back seat allowing Spyros to take over the driving, as he was familiar with the town and the target location.

Spyros drove the car through the narrow back streets of Lemesos and headed straight for Akrotiri RAF base. Twenty minutes later he approached a small van parked on an isolated side road. He brought his car to a stop and turned off the headlights. Behind the steaming windows, two boys were vaguely visible crouched in the front seat, smoking and waiting for their arrival. As soon as they saw the car, they came out into the rain, exchanged a few words and then quickly got into their car again.

'Two of you go with them.' Spyros said to the lads who were crammed into the back seat of Alexis' car.

Without hesitation, Adamos and Dimitri got out and got inside the van. Immediately it took off, followed by Alexis' car at high speed. Fifteen minutes later, the dim lights of Akrotiri Air Force Base came into view. In complete isolation, the huge military base sprawled forever, complete with buildings, tarmac runways and massive hangers.

The two cars drove forward until they came upon a small hill and then parked at a short distance away from the massive razor-wire fence and rolling barbed wire, which surrounded the Air Base. The compound appeared deserted, with nobody moving around at this hour, except for the tower search light that moved slowly, emitting its powerful flood light across the camp illuminating everything in its path. The lone tower sentinel did not pose a threat for what they hand in mind, and the boys quickly gathered their explosives and walked ahead, guided by one of Spyros' lads.

The other lad together with Michalaki remained behind on guard duty, in case it was necessary to make a speedy getaway. They sat inside one of the cars, and carried their pistols in readiness . . .

Drenched to the skin, the boys walked a fair distance away from the stationary cars, and their guide finally came to a stop at an isolated part of the compound. Spyros approached the open end of a two-foot diameter protruding storm drain-pipe and turned his torchlight on. A torrent of rainwater was gushing out of the pipe and disgorging into a ravine below which was overgrown with thick bamboo canes, cactuses and dense impregnable undergrowth.

'That's how we get in and get out.' Spyros said to the others and pointed his hand-held torchlight at the concrete pipe.

The boys stared at the pitch black pipe wondering if they could fit inside its small diameter, carrying explosives at the same time. Andreas went close to it and shone his own flashlight inside the endless long pipe, to give it his personal inspection. He shook his head not sure if that was such a good idea.

'I have tried it!' Spyros said to reassure him.

'Did you come across any rats?' Andreas asked.

'No rats.' Spyros added, and went to explain the operation. 'There is another pipe further along, beyond those trees, and both of these pipes cut across the main runway. About three hundred yards of crawling we shall reach a metal manhole grating. Pavlos works as an electrician inside the camp and he has already unbolted the screws of both gratings this morning. When we reach these covers, just push them up and we are inside the compound. It is safe to come out, especially with tonight's weather conditions. I will lead one group to the main plane hangar, and Pavlos will lead the other. We have thirty minutes to complete our mission and then, we must get the hell out of here! Set the time bombs for precisely one hour from now and don't forget the last person on the way out has to leave explosives inside the drain to blast the runway!'

Like professionals, the boys listened without uttering a single word, set their watches and formed two separate groups; Alexis, Spyros and Andreas formed one group, while Pavlos together with Adamos and Dimitri formed the other. They split up.

Once the light signal was flashed twice from Pavlos' group confirming their position, the lads attached a leather bag of explosives each to one foot, to help them drag it along inside the concrete pipe.

'Remember not a sound.' Spyros advised.

He immediately climbed inside the pipe, flat on his belly. He started to crawl inside the dark void, submerged to his chin by the gushing cold water. Alexis and Andreas crawled right behind him, and the three of them moved along, by using their elbows to push themselves forward. It turned out to be a much slower process than anticipated, with hardly any space for manoeuvrability, especially with the torrent of water blocking their mouths. They constantly had to raise their chins up to take deep breaths of air, and then proceed with their faces partly submerged. Like writhing worms they slid forward, inch-by-inch, soaked to the bone. But the prospect of blowing up the planes encouraged them to move on with determination. Their adrenaline was surging, and they became fearless of the enemy who possibly lay ahead. That did not scare them, as long as they fulfilled their objective. They were prepared to sacrifice their own lives if necessary and with those thoughts in mind, they wiggled in the darkness, encased within this solid concrete pipe—their only safe way to reach their target.

Fifteen minutes later, Spyros reached the metal grating that was letting in a torrent of rainwater. He twisted his body inside the pipe, and turned on his back, facing upwards towards the grate opening. He raised his back and stretched both his arms and grabbed the cold metal, allowing the oncoming water to surge over his face. Carefully, he pushed the cover and felt it move slightly. With great relief, he pushed harder. The lid moved and came out of its concrete tray. In a swift movement he pushed it aside and a dark open hole appeared in front of him.

'We are in!' he whispered to his companions.

He popped his head out like a rat, and inspected the area. He saw nothing suspicious but an empty camp with some isolated, scattered lights shining from the nearby buildings. He raised his body, crawled out of the down-pipe, and found himself inside the pitch black camp.

'All clear!' he whispered to his friends. He then stretched his arms to them and helped them out of the pipe.

The three of them quickly untied the bags of explosives from their legs, and ran across a muddy field towards the isolated, massive hangar that stood about fifty yards away from the manhole. As soon as they reached the structure, they squatted alongside its high, corrugated wall waiting for the others to catch up with them.

They did not have to wait for long, as three figures like dark silhouettes in the night were seen running towards them from the furthest drain, located alongside the long runway about one hundred yards away. The closest tower sentry with his powerful searchlight did not pose a threat from this angle. They were well protected and overshadowed by the sixty-foot high hangar.

Re-grouped, the boys were ready for the next part of their assignment, but they became concerned, noticing that some lights were visible from the side windows.

'Don't worry they are nightlights.' Pavlos said to them quietly. 'They always leave those on at night, just follow me.' he then added and moved alongside the wall.

Cautiously, everyone walked behind him until they came across a small door, midway along the long hangar. Pavlos pulled out a forged key from his pocket and carefully unlocked the metal door with ease. He slowly pushed the door ajar, and the boys found themselves inside the huge silent hangar and clear of the downpour.

Astounded, they remained there for a moment, confounded by the sight of the large planes that filled the hangar. There were four planes inside, including a fighter plane that stood in isolation for repairs, with half of its nose exposed. They remained motionless momentarily to ensure that nobody was around. Pavlos was correct . . .

Without wasting valuable time, the lads set the bomb-timers, quickly ran across the hangar and in complete silence they began planting the magnetic explosives directly under the bellies of the fuel tanks and inside the cabins. The fighter plane received four bombs directly inside its exposed engine, and they also planted incendiary explosives in the main fuel control valve, hoping it would blow up the main fuel deposit tank outside. Pavlos knew every inch of this hangar and guided his friends where to plant the bombs for maximum impact.

In minutes the bombs were in position and they quickly made their exit towards their escape route. Outside, the rain seemed to have abated somewhat but continued to drizzle. One by one, the lads rushed across the muddy field and climbed down inside the drain-pipes again.

Alexis' task was to plant the bombs inside the drain, and he waited until the others disappeared inside the void. When it was clear, he ran across the dark open space and placed both his feet over the manhole and slid down. His right back pocket was caught on one of the protruding bolts, and he forced himself to one side. In doing so he ripped his pocket in order to free himself.

Once he was free, he proceeded to enter the dark tunnel carrying the remainder of the explosives. Being the last to enter, he carefully replaced the metal grating concealing their route of entry, and began to crawl out as quickly as possible. As planned, he carefully planted the remainder of his bombs inside the long dark void.

Twenty minutes later, the lads found themselves standing safely outside the open end of the large concrete drain. They hardly spoke, and quickly hurried across the muddy terrain. A great relief overcame them all knowing they had accomplished their mission.

As soon as they saw their friends running towards them, Michalaki and the other· driver turned their car engines on, in readiness to take off.

'Good luck!' Spyros called out with excitement. There was no time for talk, but rather speed away as quickly as possible from this place.

'Until next time!' Alexis replied, equally excited and sat next to Michalaki, who instantly drove off like a maniac.

'We have done it!' Alexis yelled out with enthusiasm and gave Michalaki a loud smack on his chubby cheek.

Soaked, they all began to sing a merry song and sped for home to get some sleep . . .

* * *

Marcos could not believe his eyes and burst into Alexis' room, anxious to wake his brother up. He jumped on his bed determined to have a chat. Alexis stirred and turned the other way. Marcos would have none of it and kept pestering him until he could no longer ignore the persistent voice that pierced his ears.

'Get up! Get up!' Marcos kept insisting and pulled off his bed covers. He then pushed a newspaper in his brother's sleepy face.

'Why aren't you in school?' angrily asked Ahmet who was sleeping in the next bed. 'Curfew.' Marcos answered, and showed no intention of leaving the room.

Without any choice, Alexis got out of bed and put on his trousers still feeling quite tired and unable to get his senses together. His whole body felt heavy and his knees ached from crawling inside the drain-pipe. But realising he was not about to get extra sleep, he put on a shirt and went into the living room. Clumsily he dropped himself on the couch. He could smell the frying of eggs coming from the kitchen and became ravenous. He wanted to have a good breakfast to give him plenty of stamina to deal with his brother.

Marcos immediately went and sat next to his brother and persistently shoved the newspaper on his face. Alexis finally picked it up, and a smile flashed over his face. In large bold lettering, the main article described the devastation of the Royal Air Force military base at Akrotiri. The article went on to describe in detail the destruction of four Canberra bombers, a Vernon jet fighter, and the total obliteration of the hangar and main runway.

Alexis could hardly contain his excitement. He was over the moon their assignment had been a success.

Suddenly he was no longer sleepy. He put the paper aside, and looked at his young brother, who stared at him imploringly with his dark eyes, anxious for him to say something.

'Well?' Marcos demanded.

'Well, what?'

'Did you do it?'

'Don't be stupid, that is Akrotiri, not Varoshia!' Alexis said to his brother to put his mind at ease.

'I think that you blew those planes up, that's what I think!' Marcos said, not believing his brother.

No one could fool Marcos. He knew that his brother had something to do with the Akrotiri job, but he finally dropped the subject and went into the kitchen to pester his parents. It was a glorious morning and as soon as Marcos walked into the kitchen, his father got up and went outside into the garden, to weed their small patch of vegetables and till the ground.

Yiorkis enjoyed spending time in the garden. It gave him a sense of achievement, watching the seedlings sprouting into full-grown plants and flowers. Before leaving for work, he would spend at least half an hour each morning looking after his patch of garden, and admiring his handiwork. His greatest satisfaction was to share his produce with neighbours and friends, feeling proud of his green fingers, especially if they happened to praise his gardening skills. This morning, the weather conditions were perfect, the soil was moist from the night's rain and the warm sun dominated the blue sky with not a single cloud in sight . . .

The boys went into the kitchen and sat around the square table. The fried eggs and sausages smelled wonderful and the lads began their breakfast, when Maro appeared half asleep carrying a book under her arm. Her pretty face was barely visible under her messed-up mane, and she appeared not in a talkative mood. She grabbed a chair and sat next to Alexis, without uttering a single word.

'*Kalimera*, Maro.' Ahmet greeted the young lady, and pushed her hair off her face, so he could take a better look.

'*Kalimera*.' she said in a dry tone and picked up a slice of toast.

'You always carry them damn books.' Marcos said to his sister who refused to talk.

'Can't someone have breakfast in peace?' Maro objected furiously to her brothers' taunts.

'For a seventeen-year-old you have a big mouth.' Ahmet said to him, and slapped him lightly on the head as a warning.

Maro got fed up listening and got up and went into her room to find peace and quite. She took a slice of bread and locked herself in her own world, absorbed amongst her books.

Like a young cub, Marcos had too much energy to burn, and demanded that he and Ahmet had a wrestling match after breakfast. Ahmet accepted the challenge anxious to teach him a lesson, and before finishing his breakfast he got up and went outside into the back yard. Marcos immediately followed him and in no time at all, they were both entwined in a battle of wits. The noise brought out their next door neighbours who gathered along their fence watching the two lads wrestle until one was ready to give up.

Yiorkis stopped his weeding and took it upon himself to become the referee, by supervising the two combatants who grabbed each other in combat with jovial cries. Marcos constantly complained whenever Ahmet had the upper hand, and being younger, pleaded for fairness. But Ahmet would have none of it. He wanted to teach him a lesson worth remembering. Kyra-Soteria came out and sat on a chair next to her husband excited by the morning's unexpected activities. He on the other hand was too absorbed with the battle of wits, and kept shouting endless instructions at them. Maro stopped her reading and joined the rest outside who appeared over joyed by the bout. She took Ahmet's side.

'Marcos' being brave again.' Maro said to her mother, who was ecstatic watching her young boy standing up for himself.

'Ahmet give him one, he deserves it!' Maro kept yelling, to get her own back at him for his impertinence.

'He deserves it!' agreed her mother, and clapped her hands with excitement.

Marcos was in difficulty and sought support from his brother who remained impartial and was rather enjoying the wrestling match.

'Give up Marcos!' Ahmet kept urging him.

'Never!' Marcos repeated stubbornly.

Both lads rolled on the ground, clutched at each other's hands or legs and squeezed one another, until their faces and hair were covered in mud. Their clothes turned muddy-brown and fused onto their skin that had instantly turned slippery and difficult to grip. The next-door neighbours appeared to take Marcos' side, but they could not help him no matter how much he yelled for assistance. They stood aside appreciating the morning mud-wrestling by encouraging the two lads to fight on.

Kyra-Soteria smiled contently seeing her family in such a happy atmosphere, one full of life and vitality. She was thoroughly enjoying this lively bonding activity, while her husband kept urging for the fight to continue. She sat on her chair clapping her wrinkled hands, and periodically giving out a loud whistle, like a young girl.

Suddenly, persistent knocks on the front door were heard. Someone was banging so loudly it nearly brought the door off its hinges.

'See who that is, Maro!' Yiorkis instructed his daughter, surprised that someone dared to defy the curfew. He was not prepared to miss the final result of the wrestling.

Maro went inside the house and opened the front door. A young boy in shorts was standing at the threshold, panting and gasping from running. She recognised him. It was Lambraki, the baker's son.

'What are you doing here Lambraki, don't you know its curfew?' Maro asked, in total shock, that this boy run all the way from his house.

'The English are asking for Alexis, I have come to warn him.' he spat out between gasps.

'Are you sure?' Maro asked, and fear swept over her whole body.

'They are doing a house-to-house search and keep asking where he lives! Tell him to go, now! They will be here soon!' the boy continued, and ran off as fast as he could to avoid captivity.

In the distance loudspeakers were warning people to remain indoors. Maro looked across the empty neighbourhood and not a soul was visible. She noticed an oncoming long line of military cars, driving fast towards their own locality. She turned petrified and ran to the back of the house.

'Alexis . . . Alexis!' she called out frantically.

Instantly the boys stopped their wrestling, realising there was something wrong. They remained motionless covered in mud and looked at Maro who was practically in tears. She rushed to her brother, grabbed both of his arms and started shaking them over and

166

over again in fear for his safety. Petrified, she could not utter a single sound.

'What is it girl, speak up!' bellowed her father in an angry voice, seeing that his daughter was lost for words.

'Soldiers are asking for Alexis!' Maro burst out, and tears flooded her eyes.

'*Panayia* . . .!' his mother screamed out loud, sensing the terrible outcome and quickly got up and off her chair.

Suddenly, the happy occasion had turned into a nightmare. Their next-door neighbours instantly departed and shut themselves indoors, realising what was about to happen.

There was no time for procrastination and Alexis had to act quickly if he was to save his life. They all hurried inside and Alexis' mother felt her legs give way and sat on a chair. Distraught, she stared at her son, with anguished eyes.

'Quick, my son, go . . .! Go now . . . before it's too late . . .!' she yelled at the top of her voice, and broke into loud sobs. Thick tears flooded her eyes and came down in bucketfuls over her wrinkled face. She lost the strength to rise up, and remained slouched on the chair shattered by the idea of losing her son.

Alexis went to her, held her tightly and kissed her wet cheeks. He then quickly put his arms around his father and kissed his stubby unshaven gloomy face.

'Farewell . . . *mama* . . . *papa* . . .' Alexis said in a broken voice and then grabbed his young sister who was in tears and gave her a long embrace.

She would not stop crying and wouldn't let go of his arm. She wanted to feel his arm as means of reassurance. Gently he pushed her away and looked into her tear-drowned eyes. He pinched her cheek lightly and then grabbed his young brother and gave him a tight hug. His brother was stunned and didn't know what to say or do, but remained motionless covered in mud and too shocked to utter a word. Then he turned quickly to Ahmet and saw him standing next to Marcos in complete bewilderment, realising the moment had come for the two to part. His black curly hair and clothing were covered in mud, but Alexis no longer cared, and put both his arms around his friend's wide shoulders in a warm clutch. Ahmet returned the gesture and both stood for a brief moment in a tight brotherly embrace.

'Look after our family! No harm should come to them, do you promise?' Alexis said to him as he gazed into his wide black eyes that were ready to burst into tears.

'That's a promise!' he answered and urged Alexis to take off.

Alexis turned and headed towards the back exit and everyone followed after him. At the outer edge of their back yard, he stopped briefly and looked at his speechless family, who remained in absolute shock, eager to take a last glimpse of him. He raised his arm and waved it in the air and without a word, he ran off as quickly as possible. With agility, he jumped over the small wall and cannoned towards the adjacent dense orange grove. His svelte silhouette, dressed in his white short-sleeved shirt, soon disappeared into the thick grove . . .

* * *

No sooner had Ahmet and Marcos time to wash and change their clothes, screeching cars suddenly came to a stop outside their house. Instantly, English and loud Turkish voices filled the air, together with the clatter of soldiers moving about and yelling at the tops of their voices, spreading fear at the mere sight of them. The vicious barking of tracker dogs added to everyone's terror, and neighbours peeped through their windows to see what was happening. In anguish, onlookers realised their neighbour was in trouble. Instead, they stared in puzzlement expecting the worst for the poor family . . .

Petrified, Alexis' family remained still, grouped together in their living room, when the front door was abruptly kicked open by two soldiers with guns at the ready. Other soldiers including Turks burst in, pointing guns, and kicking every door of the house wide open in search of their quarry. In a matter of a few seconds the house was overrun by the military, while others surrounded the house outside and the nearby streets in readiness to shoot at anyone who posed the slightest threat.

'Where is he?' an English soldier barked at everyone in a threatening manner.

The entire family stared at the soldier without uttering a single word.

'Search the entire area stone by stone!' he ordered his men realising no-one was prepared to speak.

They immediately started ripping the house apart for any kind of evidence or concealment of weapons. Outside, a crowd of soldiers, in a combined effort with the Turkish auxiliary police, checked out the grounds and began to smash anything they came across, including the chicken coop, forcing the hens to jump out in fright and scatter aimlessly around the yard in search of safety. For ten minutes the mayhem continued without results and a young soldier came into the house to report to his commander.

'Nothing here, serge!' he said in a disappointed tone of voice
'Release the dogs, they will track him down if he's nearby!' the tall,
skinny sergeant screamed, ordering the soldier to get moving. He
then turned his attention to Ahmet.

'So you don't know!' he asked sarcastically.

'No, he hasn't been home for two days.' Ahmet answered.

'And how about you?' he barked, staring fiercely at Marcos
sending shivers down his young spine.

Marcos looked at the threatening soldier and shook his head
negatively. Without a word or any pity the sergeant clenched his fist
and punched Marcos hard in the stomach. He immediately bent
down holding his belly with both of his hands in agony, but his pride
did not allow him to utter a single word.

As soon as his mother saw her son in pain, she screamed loudly
and tried to go to her son's assistance, but the soldier pushed her
away. She tripped and fell flat on her face on the hard marble floor,
prompting her husband to rush to her rescue. She appeared helpless
lying on the floor and her headscarf flew off her head, letting loose
her long, grey hair.

'Barbarians!' he burst out aloud, and rushed to help his pitiful wife
off the floor.

'Shut up old man!' yelled the same soldier and pointed his gun at
him, in readiness to fire if the man gave him an opportunity to test
his patience.

Yiorkis gave the soldier a stern fiery stare full of hatred, but kept
his mouth shut, recognising the possible outcome. He was trapped
and in no position to win this battle, faced with such a trigger-happy
enemy. He admitted defeat and proceeded to help his wife, assisted
by a tearful daughter. They both helped her up and sat her on a chair.

Distraught, Kyra-Soteria looked around her house, and felt that
her privacy had been raped by the presence of all these foreign
soldiers who invaded her peaceful surroundings. Her eyes stared
ahead, bewildered by the sudden catastrophe that had befallen her
household. She felt that a sharp knife had pierced through her heart
to shatter her family apart. She could not alter the course of fate, and
sat on the chair traumatised, unable to say a word or raise an
objection. She began to shake her head slightly in a nervous reaction.
Her lips started to quiver and a slight dribble began to streak down
her chin. Without realising it, both of her arms that were resting on
her knees started to shake uncontrollably and she could not stop
them.

'Where is your son, old woman?' the sergeant yelled at her in a
threatening tone, and took a few steps closer to her, compounding

the terror that had consumed her meagre existence.

Kyra-Soteria raised her tearful eyes, gazed at the soldier and shook her head harder.

'She doesn't speak English can't you see that?' Ahmet said angrily and came to her rescue.

'Well you better give us some bloody answers!' barked the English commander and grabbed Ahmet by the neck and squeezed his hands around his throat.

'He's not here!' he answered choking.

'I can see that, but we'll catch the bastard. He's an *Eoka* is he not?' bellowed the commander angrily.

'He's not in *Eoka*!' Ahmet insisted with a serious expression on his troubled face.

'How do you explain this?' the commander said and showed him Alexi's mud-covered ID card.

Ahmet looked at the card and realised his friend was in deep trouble with the authorities, but said nothing.

'Take them both!' he ordered in a threatening tone.

The soldiers grabbed Ahmet and Marcos and pushed both of them outdoors where a crowd of soldiers stood on guard with guns in readiness. With hands above their heads the two captives were directed under escort towards one of the nearby jeeps and forced to climb in the back and lie down flat on their faces. Neighbours gazed through their shut windows and cursed the soldiers between their teeth for apprehending the two local lads.

Kyra-Soteria burst into loud sobs realising her young son was to become a prisoner and feared for his life. Losing two sons in one day was too much for her, and she began to yell hysterically at the top of her voice in total anguish and despair. Her husband, together with his daughter, went and put their arms around her shoulders to comfort her, but it was pointless, only a mother understands the pains of losing her off-spring. Traumatised, her shaking had suddenly escalated into continued tremors, and there was little chance of calming her pain down.

Yiorkis was at a total loss and felt powerless to help her. All he could do was to say a few comforting words and allow her to cry. The soldiers paid no attention to her screams, and continued their search throughout the house, oblivious to her condition; she was not their problem . . .

Ahmet and Marcos, they lay motionless in the back of the open jeep, while soldiers and Turkish policemen sat around guarding them with guns pointing at them. The scorching metal deck of the jeep was unbearable and whenever they attempted to lift their heads , a heavy boot came down on them hard, forcing their face to absorb the full impact of the sizzling hot metal against their tender skin.

'What are you doing here with the Greeks?' one of the policemen asked Ahmet in Turkish.

'None of your business!' Ahmet answered him, unwilling to discuss his life with him.

'Get ready for some pain.' The same Turk said to him and kicked him on the face.

An hour later the convoy departed and sped across the empty streets, leaving behind a shattered family in total anguish. The two boys were taken to one of the interrogation compounds at the main police station near the courthouse, in close proximity to the general hospital of Varoshia. They locked the prisoners in a small, windowless cell, and left them there in isolation seated on a narrow wooden bench staring at the bare stonewalls.

The place reeked of urine, while the air felt stale from lack of ventilation. Marcos seemed scared, not knowing what was going to happen to them once the interrogators walked into the room. He sat quietly and anxiety shrouded the curly haired lad. His unblemished, handsome face was traumatised by the experience, and he pinned his stare on Ahmet in search of answers and support.

'What are they going to do to us?' he asked Ahmet, who appeared quite composed.

He looked into Marcos' eyes and he sensed that fear had overcome the lad. He gently put his arm around his shoulders to comfort him.

'Don't fret little brother . . . Be strong!' he said to him.

'Do you think they caught Alexis?'

Ahmet shook his head, unable to answer his question and stared ahead deep in thought. 'He will join the *Andartes*.' he added softly, as if he was talking to himself.

They did not have to wait for very long to find out what would become of them. A tall Englishman dressed in civilian clothes walked in, followed by two Turkish policemen with pistols in their holsters. He was massive with wide shoulders, and a square face covered in freckles. His deep-set eyes instantly spread fear on Marcos. He briefly looked at the two boys and stood in front of them, his legs slightly apart and systematically began to tap his long, black truncheon.

'We don't want to hurt you . . . just tell us what you know about this Alexis and *Eoka*,' he said to both of them, and hit the truncheon against his leg.

The boys shook their heads negatively and looked at this tall man who held their lives in the palm of his hand.

'I hear that you are a Turk surely you must know something living with the Greeks.' he then asked Ahmet.

'I live with them but I know nothing about *Eoka*.' Ahmet answered, and looked at this man who had so far remained composed and had not raised his voice at them.

'My wife has just had a baby and I have promised her that I will not inflict pain on anybody for this one special day, but you must talk! One way or another you will talk so make it easy on yourselves, and tell us what we want to know!' the English interrogator explained.

'We speak the truth' Ahmet answered in his soft voice.

'Do I look like a fool? Stop lying to me it will do you no good' the interrogator barked, interrupting Ahmet, and he stared at them angrily for insulting his intelligence. He nodded his head and walked towards the exit.

'Have it your way!' he said with indifference and left the room, leaving the two Turkish policemen behind standing on guard, with hands on their pistols.

No sooner had the Englishman left than a burly looking Turk appeared. He walked straight to where the two prisoners were seated, and stared directly at them without uttering a single word. He appeared to be studying them.

He looked fierce and wore a thick black moustache that curved at either side of his mouth over his wide upper lip. His thick eyebrows practically joined one another above his nose, like a mono-brow, and concealed the greater part of his eyes. He was a tall hunky fellow with an upright, solid posture and had muscles that seemed ready to burst out of his tight shirt. His wide shoulders seemed like a powerhouse and the mere sight of him spread fear over those around him. Nobody in his right mind would dare consider giving this giant reason to upset him. He seemed capable of killing a mule with a single blow, with his long, thick hairy arms.

As soon as the two boys took a glimpse of him, terror set upon their faces in anticipation of what he was about to do to them.

'What am I to do with you two studs?' he asked himself in a deep voice, and stared at the boys who were in absolute fear of him. He turned his attention towards Ahmet.

'Why are you mixed up with the Greeks?' he asked Ahmet not mincing his words.

'I was adopted by Marcos' parents.' Ahmet explained and pointed at Marcos.

'You were adopted by Greeks?' the interrogator said and frowned, not believing his ears.

'Do you not have any people in the Walls?'

'Only a poor, old aunt, Mehmet Nazim's wife who lives near *Tripa*.'

'I know Nazim, he's a good man. Are you a Moslem?' the interrogator asked.

'Yes, I am a Moslem.' Ahmet answered.

The Turk shook his head surprised by Ahmet's words and could not decide if he should proceed with his job or not. He felt uncomfortable torturing someone of his own blood, but at the same time he was responsible for dragging out from the boys' clamped mouths everything they knew about *Eoka*. It was his job . . .

'And this Alexis, is he an *Eoka* man?'

'I don't know.'

'You don't know? You don't know?' the interrogator suddenly yelled, bringing fear into the boy's soul. 'I tell you what, you know plenty but refuse to talk, that's what I say!'

'You are a Turk . . . you understand how a Turk feels! You can break our bones, but we know nothing.' Ahmet stated stubbornly, and expected the first blows to begin raining down on them. He psyched himself to receive the first blow from the club-hand of this giant.

'You are very lucky that you are a Turk. I can make you spill everything out but I am not such an animal to torture one of my own.' the interrogator said to him, and then turned to Marcos. 'As for you, I would also make an exception because of your family's kindness to an orphaned Turk.' he said to him.

The boys were relieved by his attitude and didn't know how to interpret his sudden change of heart. They expected at least a hard beating.

'Why are you doing this?' Ahmet asked in shock at the man's unexpected behaviour.

'Because us Turks, we must stick together and you will be useless to us if I break your bones.' the man answered.

'I don't understand?' Ahmet said surprised.

'You will find out when the time is right. But I have to do something first.' The Turk said.

Without warning, he raised his hand and gave Ahmet a hard punch in the face. His return second blow found Marcos' face, forcing both of them to fall off the wooden bench. They did not expect this and the interrogator continued kicking them while they were on the floor. He began to throw punches at both of them, while the other two policemen stood aside watching. He yelled something to them in Turkish, and both walked out of the interrogation room.

'Scream you bastards, scream!' he kept yelling at the top of his voice, 'especially you Turkish traitor!' he barked, and concentrated his punches on Ahmet's body.

The lads were in excruciating pain and could no longer cope with the constant thrashing. They began to scream, sending echoing sounds of agony along the corridors. They felt his every punch. Suddenly he grabbed Ahmet by the scruff of the neck, and pulled his head tight against his body. Ahmet expected a volley of punches, but instead the Turk held him tight.

'Keep screaming . . .' he said to him in a low voice and then gave Marcos a wink, and a short quick smile exposing a gold upper tooth.

In total puzzlement at the man's extraordinary behaviour, the boys complied and immediately began to scream. But Marcos' screams of pain were for real. The charade continued for a while and their deafening screams attracted the attention of the English interrogator who walked into the cell. He saw the boys sprawled on the floor, holding their stomachs and pleading aloud for mercy.

'Did you get anything out of them?' he asked without emotion or any pity showing on his expressionless face.

'Nothing, sir . . . but I think they are telling the truth.' answered the Turk and gave one last kick on Ahmet's backside. 'Shall I send them off to the detention camp?' he asked his superior.

'No, let them go . . . after all, I am in a good mood today.' he instructed the Turk, and walked out of the room with indifference.

'This must be your lucky day!' the interrogator said to the boys, and asked them to stand up. He called in the two policemen who were standing on guard outside, and ordered them to drive them home to avoid being recaptured by the curfew patrols.

The boys were about to leave when the interrogator turned and looked at Ahmet.

'We shall meet again, remember *Volkan!*' he said to him and walked out of the room.

'What did he mean?' Marcos asked while they were being escorted to a jeep parked outside.

'Who knows.' Ahmet answered indifferently and kicked a loose stone.

The stone landed on a dog's back, and with a quick jerk the animal limped across the street barking with pain . . .

CHAPTER TEN

ALEXIS ENTERED THE grove and ran for his life . . . He cannoned into the orchard not caring about the thrashing his face received by the endless branches. Apprehension fuelled his legs when he considered the ominous alternative if captured. The final result was obvious to him; death by hanging . . .! 'I am too young to die,' he thought to himself and sprinted even faster.

He plunged into the trees like they were not there. Half-an-hour later, he noticed the familiar farmhouse owned by a well-known merchant perched amongst the orchards. He by-passed it but somewhere between the trees, a fierce dog sniffed his scent and embarked on a ferocious barking exercise. The lone dog was quickly joined by two others in an equally ferocious mood. Alexis could not see the dogs, but thinking it might be the police unleashing tracker dogs on his trail, he panicked and ran even faster to gain distance between himself and the barking dogs.

Roaming about in bright daylight during curfew was suicidal, and he had to find a place to hide until nightfall so he could reach Apostolos Varnavas monastery and make contact with *Eoka*.

He thought of many places to hide, but none of them gave him the assurance he was after. He must hide until precious night comes . . . but where? 'In a church? Yes . . . it will be the safest place.' he reasoned.

The ancient, deserted cavern of Chrisospiliotissa flashed through his mind, and he headed in its direction avoiding open spaces. He convinced himself that he could reach the church in safety if he continued from grove to grove. It was a longer route, but it would ultimately take him outside the tiny, unused cavern, minimising his chances of being detected by search parties and military convoys.

Hundreds of thoughts flashed through his mind. He imagined the mayhem at his house, stormed by troops and policemen turning the place upside down, while his mother would be in tears, devastated by the sudden catastrophe that he had brought upon the household. His father would be standing next to her, trying to comfort her, but none of his comforting words would assuage her anguish, not unless her son was there with her. Next time he met up with Ahmet, he would thank him for insisting he did not leave any incriminating evidence in the house of his involvement with *Eoka*. If the army were

175

to find anything, for certain his home would be razed to the ground before the evening was over and his family would be made homeless. By late afternoon, black and white posters with his picture printed on them would be plastered throughout the city, offering a handsome reward for his captivity.

Ever since he joined *Eoka*, he never anticipated for once, or even imagined, that one day he would take leave so abruptly from his family, without saying a proper goodbye. When would he see them again? Next week? Next month? A year from now? Who knows! He could never imagine the prospect of not seeing his family again, or the loyal friends he grew up with. They were part of his life . . . Andreas, Adamos, Dimitri, Michalaki, Spyros, they all came into his mind, and he speculated how they would respond once they learned of his escape and of becoming a fugitive with a price on his head. He was certain they would take revenge, especially Michalaki and Spyros who thought the world of him and loved him dearly. He could visualise the angry reaction of both of them, and Andreas would insist on finding targets immediately and go out on a rampage, planting bombs and blowing up installations. Dimitri on the other hand, together with their muscleman Adamos, in retaliation would certainly seek out the enemy and take revenge.

Confused and scared, he crossed a vast number of orchards, petrified of captivity. Like an agile gazelle running for its life pursued by an angry pack of hungry jaws, he did not stop running for a minute, knowing everyone would be out searching for him. At the same time, he had to watch out for prying eyes who could betray him by reporting his whereabouts to the authorities who would close in on him, making it impossible to escape their net.

His legs began to ache, but the thought of captivity gave him stamina to move ahead anxious to reach the small cavern. His face was scratched and dried streaks of blood marked his cheeks and exposed arms. But that did not deter him or make him slow down in his attempt to reach safety under the shroud of darkness. Dried leaves and small sticks found refuge in his tousled black hair and he noticed that his white shirt was ripped into shreds. The watering puddles of each orange tree made his shoes gather a mass of mud, the extra weight making it harder to run. He frequently slowed down to wipe the mud off the soles of his shoes, and remembered Michalaki, who always complained about it.

By the time he entered the last grove he was panting like a dog with his tongue hanging out. Sweat covered his entire body, soaking both his shirt and trousers which fused with his drenched skin.

Dragging his feet from exhaustion, he cut across the steep grove and stopped at the very edge of the massive orchard surrounded by a high wire fence. He could see clearly the main tarmac junction ahead. It was completely deserted and there was nobody to be seen not even a dog. A great relief had come over him realising that he may have escaped the clutches of the army.

He gazed across the street and saw the familiar sheer rock formation, ascending steeply directly from the edge of the road. He recognised the narrow steps leading to the cavern. All he had to do was to rush across the road, and sanctuary was there, waiting for him!

Without hesitation, he climbed over the wire fence and quickly ran to the other side of the road. He leapt up the steep stone steps and entered another narrow staircase at the top of the mound of rock. The steps led deep inside a narrow passageway that terminated directly outside the cavern entrance. He quickly climbed down the steps, opened the tiny wooden door and entered the pitch black secluded cavern. A sudden sense of relief had overcome him . . . safety at last!

Unable to see inside this dark cave, he temporarily left the door slightly ajar and piercing shafts of bright daylight flooded its interior. He crossed himself three times, and walked inside the tiny incense-scented shrine, carved out of the solid rock eons ago. His head was touching the arched ceiling and had to crouch to move about this tranquil, holy cavern.

Every inch of the perimeter walls were covered with ancient hand-painted icons that had faded with the lapse of time. The rough, chiselled floor sloped away towards the end of the short cavern and, at the very end, a large icon of *Panayia* holding baby Jesus dominated the entire facing wall. At the foot of the icon, two small wooden crates were positioned on the floor covered with wax candles, and shallow glass wick holders. He approached the icon and lit an oil lamp and a long candle, by using a matchbox he found on top of the crates. He crossed himself again and humbly kissed the icon.

Immediately the eyes of the icon seemed almost to have come to life from the flickering flame. Seeing the icon, he felt at ease, and a pleasant, warm feeling overcame his tired body. *Panayia's* vivid compassionate eyes appeared to follow his every move, and solemnly he went and shut the entrance door behind him. He felt content that he had finally found sanctuary and safety under Her protection.

The strong smell of candle wax and incense burning from centuries past permeated against the hard rocks. Fused together, they emitted an everlasting lingering scent within this solemn shrine.

He felt completely isolated from the real world outside, and a sense of false security overcame him, being surrounded by these solid walls. For a moment he forgot why he was there, but the sounding of a siren outside brought him back to reality and fear set in again. He had to remain in hiding until nightfall and then try to make his way on foot to Apostolos Varnavas monastery, where his fate and destiny would be decided.

With time to kill, he sat on the floor and studied every detail of the small cave, illuminated by the flickering candles. He remembered this place very well, and being here again brought back memories from when he was a young boy visiting this cavern with his mother. They were still living at *Loukkos* when his mother brought him along to pray to *Panayia*. She dragged him away from playing, insisting that he must come to light a candle and say his prayers, so he would grow into a healthy young man. He was warned that, if he was a good boy, and placed a coin on the holy icon, the coin would never fall . . . The Holy Mother then would always protect him; but if the coin did not stick, it meant that he had not been honest, and *Panayia* would never accepts gifts from dishonest hands. That day he had knelt and prayed for a long time, and when he finished, he had reached out and placed his coin on the surface of the icon. Disappointed, he saw his coin drop off but he tried and tried many times over without success. He even tried to dig it into the oil paint of the icon, but that too failed. Downhearted, he left with a deep sense of guilt and he had never returned to this place again. Whenever he had to pass by the cavern, he always chose a different route, to avoid being seen by *Panayia*, in case the Holy Mother of Jesus recognised him, as she had been blessed with everlasting memory.

He was now seated on the floor of this tiny sanctuary, that had traumatised him when he was a young boy and, observing it closely, the lifeless icon had remained unaltered and exactly the way he had always remembered it. With his back resting against the wall, he stared at the timeless icon and could detect the precise spot where he had tried to stick his coin years ago. *Panayia's* soft eyes gazed back at him in a mesmerising stare, and for a brief moment he felt like a child again, wanting to try the coin one more time. But instead he stared back at the icon with its golden gleaming halo and vivid oil colours that dominated the entire wall. Spellbound, he let his thoughts drift to his present predicament.

He thought of Xanthia. Once the curfew was lifted, he imagined her shapely silhouette walking towards Kosmas' garage to look for him and he could also perceive the river of tears in her beautiful eyes the moment Ahmet tells her about Akrotiri and his sudden disappearance. Devastated, she would scamper home and stubbornly refuse to speak to anyone for days, she would lose her appetite and refrain from eating through anxiety for his safety but, as an *Eoka* member herself, she would try to understand, and pray that Harm does not stretch its claws to hurt her beloved one. Thinking of her, he wished that she were seated next to him, so they could hold hands. He would miss her soft scent, and the smell of her lustrous hair, but above all he would miss her lively character and happy disposition. When would their lips meet again? When would they embrace tightly or, simply be near each other, without uttering a word?

He was in no position to know the answers, but while staring at the icon, he made a vow that he would make it up to her with a wedding ring on her slim finger, when all this was finally over. *Panayia*, seemed to approve of his inner thoughts and fixed Her hypnotic gaze at him. He looked deep into those compassionate brown eyes and a sense of surreal calmness engulfed his exhausted body . . .

'No! No!' he yelled out of fear, and a cold chill flowed rapidly across his whole body.

He ran outside into the empty streets! It was a run for his life, and he dashed all over the abandoned town with troops chasing after him, anxious to capture him at all costs. The angry troops persistently fired at him with deafening gun blasts, while bullets whizzed about his body in hundreds, all missing their target. Petrified by the prospect of being captured, he ran even faster feeling the heels of his shoes touching his buttocks. The persistent firing coming from behind kept up with the pace of the wild chase, and sent shivers down his spine knowing the army was closing in on him. His only companion was the thumping sound and constant pounding of his heart against his own ribcage, reverberating like a drumbeat and never missing its cue. Terrified, he criss-crossed the empty streets at lightning speed to avoid captivity, until he finally came across a narrow alleyway that showed a likely prospect for escape. Without hesitation, he entered the elongated, cobbled alleyway and sprinted across its stone surface, amplifying the solitary sound of his shoes with every sprint forward. Strong sunlight flooded in, and created a blinding reflection against the whitewashed, single-storey row of houses that faded away into the diminishing distance of this strange place. Alexis found himself running halfway across the long but narrow street, flooded with a blinding, strong light. He noticed that not a soul was moving about, except for the clattering of his own footsteps. His long, jet-black shadow stretched forward in parallel to the mysterious houses of the empty street. The gunshots from behind had no intention of coming to a halt. With sweat pouring down his handsome face, he went deeper into the narrow, puzzling maze, when suddenly Petros' face appeared in the distance. The strange image of his dead friend's head seemed to be elevated, and swallowed up by a churning white cloud that floated in mid-air across the alleyway, trying to block his way forward. Stunned, and in total shock, he slowed down and inspected Petros' face which appeared powdery white, with part of his head cracked and smashed at the right temple. His young friend stared at him, and a smile developed on his pale white face, exposing his teeth that grew bigger the longer he maintained his grim smile. He stretched his white arms out to take his childhood friend with him, but Alexis resisted, recognising that *Charon*, dressed in his black cloak, was standing behind Petros urging him on to grab Alexis before he escaped. Alexis shook his head, and started moving backwards to avoid his friend's outstretched arms, but Petros persisted and kept coming closer and closer . . . Seeing that Alexis was reluctant to join his friend, *Charon* stood up tall, and gave out a deafening, roar of laughter that echoed across the vast sky. '*You too shall come!*' he bellowed, causing the ground to tremble. Alexis decided to run back the way he had entered the alleyway and turned around . . . He saw a great number of soldiers in formation, and in a slow motion they were closing in on him, blocking his only possible escape route. He was trapped between the two, who both seemed determined to destroy him; the first to snuff his life away, and the other to grab his soul. In total silence, the soldiers blocked the entire street and slowly moved, in formation and loud footsteps, towards him with guns aimed . . . Petros kept calling him to join him, but Alexis repeatedly shook his head, refusing to go . . . *Charon* in his long, black cloak and black head-dress, continued his endless laughter vibrating every roof-top and shattering windows. Knowing there was no escape from the two, Alexis, in total panic and desperation, began to bang with his fists at any doorway that was nearest to him, pleading for someone to let him in. People's scared faces appeared behind the windowpanes, staring at him with hostility, while children inside began to cry out loud, flooding their innocent faces with tears. With no-one willing to help him, the trap was closing in on him and desperation had set in. He recognised that his escape was no longer possible. Trapped, he looked around in search of one last chance for escape, but there was nothing in sight, except for a drainpipe. He ran across the cobbled street, put both hands around the pipe and began to climb, while people stared through the windows in astonishment at his determination and daring attempt to escape captivity. Halfway up, the clay pipe gave way, and Alexis came tumbling down, falling flat on his back, skewed across the alleyway. He found himself staring helplessly into the sky, unable to move. He was ensnared for good, with no chance of escape! He gazed up, and saw Petros' frightening chalk-white face, and right behind him stood *Charon* with absolute supremacy over everybody's lives. He was laughing in a bellowing roar that shook the windowpanes and he knew that he always wins in the end. People forever try to escape his clutches, and get up to all sorts of conniving plans to miss his net, but they all fail . . . rich and poor, kings and paupers, thieves and priests, they all end up delicacies for his pet worms. Lying flat on his back, Alexis looked up and saw an army of guns pointing at his face, while *Charon* writhed with joy, that a new customer was on his way and a young one at that. Realising the lad had not escaped, the people looked down from inside the safety of their homes and burst into a spontaneous chuckle that grew louder and louder, transforming itself into euphoric hysteria and ecstasy. They jumped up and down with joy and yelled out loud, while *Charon* roared the loudest of them all. The racket grew so loud, that it pierced Alexis' ears, forcing him to place both his hands over them to block out the clamour. But it was no use, the sound penetrated well into his eardrums. Helpless, he noticed that Petros bowed down towards him with outstretched arms; his eyes turned bright red in contrast to his pale white skin, while a trickle of blood poured out of the wound at his temple, forming streaks of red across his cheeks. The soldiers on his other side stretched their own arms to pick him up. In absolute panic he shook his head, not prepared to die yet. He was too young, but he was in no position to do anything about it; the end was near! The rowdy crowd, hiding behind closed windows, suddenly stopped their laughter and after a moment of absolute silence, they spontaneously began to chant teasingly in a cacophony of sounds, and loudly clapped their hands together in a strange wild frenzy . . .

'What a foolish boy you have been . . . what a silly boy with a dream!' They chanted in a unified uproar.

'No! No!' Alexis screamed at the top of his voice and woke up.

He was covered in sweat and felt a slight chill all over his body. He looked across the tiny holy cavern and saw that *Panayia* was staring at him motionless as before, and realised he had had a terrible nightmare. The light of the candle was out, but the dim flickering flame of the oil lamp was trying to stay alight. He got off

181

the stone floor, walked across the cavern and stood in front of the small wooden crates and lit another candle. With the candle burning, the cave seemed to have come back to life again and he humbly kissed the divine icon of *Panayia* for the last time . . .

He crossed himself and then headed towards the entrance. He opened the solid wooden door and climbed up the narrow stone staircase. Outside, he stood briefly at the top of the stairs and inspected the area. He was delighted that finally the night had arrived to give him the cherished cover he was after.

Famished, and always on the lookout for military patrols, after a four-hour walk Alexis managed to reach the ancient ruins of Salamina. In the distance, across the escarpment he could make out the dim lights of the monastery of Apostolos Varnavas, surrounded by an arid thorn-covered landscape. His legs ached, but the sight of the monastery gave him hope to push harder, knowing salvation was at hand the moment he entered that divine place.

He walked in complete isolation across the barren landscape, accompanied only by his sharply-edged moon shadow that followed him everywhere. The cool evening air caressed his tired body and he often took deep breaths to give him strength. He went over rocks and shrubbery, entered ditches and got out of them again knowing that every step forward would bring him one step closer to safety.

Half-an-hour later, he reached the monastery and a sense of security had overcome him the moment he picked up the heavy doorknocker and banged it hard. The empty courtyard ricocheted with the sound of his hard knock, and he stood anxiously waiting for the door to open. Momentarily, he noticed a dim light escaping from under the threshold accompanied by the dragging echoing sound of footsteps coming from within. They stopped behind the door.

'Who is it?' a tired voice was heard from the inside, and someone started to unbolt the heavy wooden door.

'*Akamantis!*' Alexis answered, using his pseudonym, and feeling relieved that he had finally reached his designated safe house.

An old monk dressed in his white nightgown opened the door, and remained standing at the threshold carrying a flickering candle in one hand. Immediately, a sudden gust of wind tried to blow the flame out, but the smouldering flame refused to die. Instead, it cast a yellowish glow on the serene face of the elderly monk. A sudden draught blew his unruly white beard aside, but he remained steadfast and stared curiously at the young intruder.

Alexis recognised the elderly monk. He was the same monk who handed him an *Eoka* message in the past.

182

'Yes?' he said, and frowned, trying to make out who had arrived so late at night.

'I am on the run.' Alexis said to him, realising the old monk did not recognise him.

'Well . . . don't just stand there, come in, come in.' the monk said softly and stood aside, to let the young stranger enter.

With his arm stretched forward and carrying his candle, he led the way into the long corridor. They walked side by side along the empty, marble passageway that amplified the sound of their footsteps. There was blissful silence within the interior, and not a single sound was audible except of their echoing footsteps. Alexis' nose detected the familiar scent of candles and incense burning, but it did not seem to be as pungent as the overpowering scent of his last sanctuary, at the cavern.

The monk entered a warm room where a fire was burning. At either side of the fireplace, two other monks with spectacles were comfortably seated on low chairs. Under candlelight, they were absorbed in their own private reading, and they too were dressed in long white nightgowns that touched the floor. Their massive white beards mingled with their unruly grey hair, and only their smooth shiny cheeks were visible to the naked eye. It seemed that their parents had decided to form a mould and produced these pious-looking monks as identical triplets. Seeing the three of them Alexis instantly recognised that these fragile ancient men were brothers.

As soon as they saw the newcomer they stood up, pleased that an unexpected guest had arrived. They welcomed their stranger who had appeared from nowhere to break the monotony of their evening.

'This young man is a fugitive,' the monk carrying the candle explained to the others, and put his candle on the mantelpiece.

'Welcome son, I am Father Socratis, the youngest.' said one of the elderly monks and stretched his hand out to Alexis for a warm handshake. He stared with astonishment at his dishevelled state.

Once he was over his initial shock on inspecting the scruffy lad, Father Socratis went on to introduce his brothers; Father Grigoris, a slightly heavy looking man who loved cooking, and Father Apostolis the eldest, who had opened the door for him. The latter was a timid looking gentle man with hardly any flesh on his fragile body.

Alexis felt comfortable among these three ancient sentinels, who instantly showed heart-warming hospitality towards him. But, above all else, he felt secure under the roof of God. He looked at the three elderly monks and noticed they had their deep-set eyes pinned on him, assessing him. A pleasant feeling overcame him, knowing he had escaped the clutches of the enemy. He felt like kissing the three pious monks, they were his saviours.

'Look at the state of you! We can't have you going about, dressed in those shreds,' Father Socratis said to him, shocked by Alexis' appearance that reminded them of a destitute beggar. 'There is a shower-room at the end of the corridor, you go and get cleaned, and I shall see what we can do for clothing,' he then added and showed him the way to the shower room.

Under proper light, Alexis noticed that he was caked in dirt, with legs covered in mud and his clothes shredded to pieces from top to bottom. His face and exposed arms were inundated with deep, crusty, blood-stained scratches and cuts. It was no wonder the monks kept staring at him.

After he had a good wash, Alexis was given a monk's robe to wear. He felt very strange wearing such a garment, but he soon got used to it and joined the three elderly monks in the warm room. He sat next to them, and being famished, gulped down two bowls of chicken soup topped with crusty bread, which delighted Father Grigoris who made the soup.

The pious looking monks hardly spoke with one another and seemed very content with their lives. They had no demands or expectations out of life, just the choice to devote their entire lives to serve God. They lived a divine, solitary life, and needed nothing else, as long as they had the Almighty in their hearts to guide their every action in life. They were most revered by everyone, and they had achieved an indisputable reputation throughout the island for being the finest icon painters in the land.

Having had the warm soup, Alexis felt good and rested. He let his eyes take a glimpse of an unfinished canvas resting on an easel, depicting faintly the icon of *Panayia*. The painting vividly portrayed the exact same warm eyes as those of the faded icon in the cavern that had gazed back at him, and kept him company for the entire day.

'You will have to remain here until I make contact with *Eoka*.' Father Socratis said to him and then asked him curiously, 'Why are the British after you?'

'We blew up the planes at Akrotiri,' Alexis answered with pride.

'So it was you!' exclaimed Father Apostolis, impressed that they had a real hero in their midst who had caused such great damage to the enemy.

'There is a thousand pound reward on your head! How did you do it? Father Grigoris asked who appeared to have taken a liking to Alexis for wiping the soup bowl clean.

Alexis entertained the monks by describing how he and his pals had executed their mission. The three of them sat speechless, and listened to him with absolute concentration. They were amazed how a small group of young lads could have caused so much damage, but most of all, the elderly monks were astounded by their determination and courage in undertaking such an assignment against insurmountable odds. When he finished, the monks stared at him in complete amazement.

'With young lads like you we shall free this land!' Father Socratis said with a deep sense of conviction.

It was getting quite late, and Alexis realised the three of them were showing signs of drowsiness. Their old eyes kept closing and he wanted to tell them to go to bed, but, as a guest, he could not make such an impolite suggestion. He too was tired and could not wait to put his head on a pillow to have a good night's sleep. He was relieved when Father Apostolis, the timid, finally decided to stand up.

'*Kalinikta* my son.' he said softly and walked out of the room.

'*Kalinikta* Father.' Alexis replied and stood up.

As soon as he left for bed, the others followed and Alexis spend the night in a small room furnished with a single wooden bed and small side table. He lay on the hard planks and immediately sleep overtook him from sheer exhaustion.

*   *   *

Before the sun had the chance to rise in its morning glory, Alexis was awoken by a nasty cockerel crowing persistently at the top of his lungs, with no intention of stopping his restless racket. Half asleep, he walked out into the inner yard, and saw Father Grigoris cleaning a row of hen cages at the far side of the building, while Father Apostolis was busy scattering corn across the yard for the hens.

Hungrily, the birds nibbled at the corn off the floor, often pecking one another as a warning to keep off their patch. The timid monk looked like a mother-hen himself, surrounded by birds of every size that followed his every move. A hen waddled about pecking seeds off the floor and was trailed by an army of bright yellow chicks, eager to learn the correct way to peck.

It was a beautiful still morning that made one feel lucky to be alive. Kissed by the sun's morning rays, the moist earth across the yard began to dry out, causing wisps of vapour to gently ascend in a cloud of mist.

Dressed in his monk's robe, Alexis went to join his newly-found friends who were engrossed in their morning chores. Father Grigoris saw him first, and stopped his work. He straightened his back and called out to him.

'*Kalimera*, come and give me a hand!' he said quite loudly, pleased there was someone else to share his workload.

From a distance his brother spotted their young guest and waved his arm to Alexis, muttering a greeting that only his ears could hear. Hunched, he continued his feeding of the ravenous chicks and hens that strutted around his timid body, forever tangling themselves between his legs. His daily routine was to feed the hens and he enjoyed every minute of it, especially being surrounded by the lively hens that cackled and followed him everywhere. He had maintained this daily ritual for years, and had got to know each and every one of his hens by name. But his greatest joy was collecting the warm, freshly laid eggs immediately after the hen had cackled, announcing that she had just finished her own part of the job.

Alexis did not waste time and he picked a besom. He went in the cages and began to sweep the hard earth floor that was chock-full of chicken droppings. When he had finished, he filled two buckets of water by manually pumping water from a bore-well, alongside a circular fountain full of red carp. He sprinkled the entire floor with water to keep the dust under control.

'Where is Father Socratis?' he asked his work companion, realising he was not about.

'He left for Enkomi, the village over the escarpment,' Father Grigoris said to him.

'How about the curfew?'

'It doesn't effect us . . . that's the privilege of being a monk. He has gone to make contact with *Eoka*,' he answered, and stopped briefly to take a rest.

He was slightly heavier than his brothers but had a noble expression on his face, accentuated by a white beard and unruly moustache that covered most of his shiny wrinkled face.

They spent over two hours cleaning and taking care of their daily chores and by mid-morning Father Apostolis spotted a truck heading towards the monastery. He recognised the truck and walked up to Alexis who was standing by the fountain admiring the carp that swam aimlessly within the shallow waters of the circular pool.

'That's Hambi,' he said to Alexis, 'he's your contact, and he will take you to your *Limery*.'

As soon as the dust-covered vehicle arrived, Father Socratis got out, followed by the driver, a man dressed in traditional peasant's clothing, and wearing long black cassocks that nearly touched the ground. He had a black waistcoat over a collarless white shirt that appeared too tight for him, stretching the row of small shiny buttons to their limit. A massive, thick embroidered sash was carefully folded and wrapped around his waist to secure his baggy cassocks in place. Both sash ends draped loosely over his garment to expose the intricate interwoven beads that dangled every time he moved about. The man appeared to be very proud of this costume which gave him a sense of self-esteem and identity.

'The curfew is over, and Hambi will take you with him tonight.' Father Socratis said and introduced the man to Alexis.

Hambi extended his hand and gave Alexis a sturdy handshake, while inspecting the lad's eyes. He was a small man of medium height, in his late forties with a mass of spiky brush-like hair on his head. His delicate thin face was dominated by a thick black moustache that was neatly twisted at both ends.

'So you are one of the lads that blew up Akrotiri!' Hambi exclaimed, most impressed by the sight of this lad dressed in monk's clothing.

'We did our best.'

'Your best? My . . . my! If everyone did what you lads did in one night, we shall liberate Cyprus in no time at all!' Hambi said in a jovial manner, and smiled at Alexis.

'Hambi will take you to meet up with the *Andartes*.' Father Socratis advised.

By mid-day, they all shared a bite to eat in the open air under the shade of an ancient eucalyptus tree that grew massive in height at the far end of the inner yard. The tree had not been planted, but had grown naturally and had become a central gathering place for the monks and others during the hot summer months. Pilgrims had spent endless hours under the blessed shade bestowed by its long thick leaves that rustled in the slightest breeze, fanning the entire area.

Hambi took off immediately after lunch, but returned the same evening around midnight to take Alexis on a long trip; a trip into the unknown . . .

The car sped forward along the long dirt road dotted with never-ending potholes and puddles, shaking their insides out. With great relief they finally reached the main highway alongside the coastline, and Hambi put his foot down hard on the pedal. Highlights at full beam, the car picked up speed and headed straight into the long, empty road. At this late hour they had the entire road to themselves and Hambi drove steadily into the night.

'The Leader has arranged for you to join the Pitsilia group,' he disclosed for the first time.

187

'I have never been to that part of Cyprus before.' Alexis said.

'It's not a bad life if you like mountains. As for me, it's the only life that suits me best, I am a shepherd you know.' Hambi said, and lit a cigarette.

Between chit-chat, they travelled for about one hour into the night, often going through isolated darkly-lit villages and climbing over gentle hills that seemed to go on forever. His companion was absorbed in his driving, especially when he entered steep narrow and winding roads that posed danger. With a cigarette hanging from his lips, he would steer the car forward, and fix his stare ahead like a hawk until the car got into a straight stretch of road. Then, he would relax again and start conversing with ease.

Alexis noticed that Hambi suddenly accelerated, contorted his face and gazed ahead without uttering a word.

'Missed it!' he suddenly yelled disappointingly.

'What?' Alexis asked.

'I missed it! Did you not see the hare?' shouted his companion again, for losing a delicacy and banged his hands against the steering wheel.

'I was day dreaming.' Alexis said, disappointed at missing the chance to share Hambi's excitement.

'Nothing wrong with that.' Hambi said, while trying to master a sharp bend. 'A man without a dream might as well be dead. There is no hope for someone, without dreams, you remember that!'

'I was thinking of *Eoka*, family and friends.' Alexis admitted.

'And so you should!' Hambi interrupted and went on to add, 'Cast any doubts that you have aside and have courage! Believe in yourself! There are plenty of boys and girls like you, who are prepared to give up their lives for a dream and liberate our country. That takes courage, greater courage than you think! Personally, I admire and respect those brave lads, who do not flinch in the face of death. After all, what lives must die, so we might as well die for an honourable cause and, what is more honourable than dying for the liberation of one's own country. Can you name one?'

'You are right, there is no greater honour.' Alexis agreed.

'And do you know why? Because we fight for justice!' Hambi interrupted. 'I am a simple shepherd, illiterate and hardly one who can be called sophisticated. There was no need for me to join the OKT force. But I have joined because I believe in justice, and I detest oppression! Oppression under any guise is a cancerous disease. There is no cure for it, unless one destroys the cause of the disease. When a crafty wolf attacks my sheep, I pick up my shotgun in readiness to destroy him, if not, he would return for more.'

'And so you should!' Alexis said in agreement with this undemanding but dedicated man, who simply understood right or wrong, justice or injustice, and nothing between.

'The British colonialists are no better than them wolves. They suck the blood out of us and try to justify the indefensible through injustice. They deserve what they've got coming to them but I can tell you; they are craftier and more cunning than any wolves or foxes that I have come across. Look what they have done to us with the Turks, for instance.'

'Do you believe the Turkish problem will escalate?' Alexis asked

'Escalate? We may have to pick up arms and face each other in battle.' Hambi said with certainty.

'You are not serious . . .!'

'Not serious? You wait and see! Mark my words! Very soon, we shall face the Turks as enemies and start killing each other!' Hambi stated with great emphasis. He turned his head and gazed briefly at his passenger, nodding his head to stress the seriousness of the matter. 'I blame them deceitful British for splitting our peaceful communities but, I also blame the Turks for siding with them!'

'Not everybody!' Alexis disagreed.

'It may be true . . . I have many Turkish friends, and they tell me . . . there is a deadly storm heading our way and all because of them deceitful foxes. They stirred people's passions with dirty hands and they are about to bring everlasting misery and hatred to our country, for generations to come!'

'You truly believe that?'

'Yes! From rivalry and blind passion comes hostility my friend and the process has been set in motion.' Hambi stated. 'You are young and have youthful, idealistic thoughts about such things— nothing wrong about that—but, in the real world, ideals are thrown out the window. Lad, don't ever forget, we live in a jungle and only the law of the jungle applies, where the fittest survive.'

'You may be right Hambi but . . . '

'Right? Of course I am right!' he interrupted by raising his voice and gesticulating frantically. 'How do you think the British created an Empire? It was their ability to take what belongs to the weaker. They systematically create poverty purposely by exploiting the weak and vulnerable through insatiable greed, in order to rule over the destitute. And, by doing so they are able to sustain and replenish their overflowing coffers with the sweat and blood of others less fortunate. Look at the Crusades for example . . . for queen, king, country and faith, they went on a rampage to loot and rule others in foreign lands. Them plunderers, ruined our small country and they plan to continue to do so today.'

'There is something in what you are saying, but that's in the past.' Alexis said to him realising this peasant was not as stupid as he pretended to be.

'In the past? Never forget the past son. That's your passport to the future. Ignore it, and you are doomed. I just pray to God that you lads do not give up your lives, for others to dance gloriously on your graves when this is all over, because that's what normally happens.' Hambi stated, and, then went silently into deep thoughts.

Alexis listened to this man who spilt his heart out. He could not fully agree with him but, at the same time, he could not simply disregard his ideas as nonsense. There was some truth in what he was expressing, especially with the recent events in the way the Turkish Auxiliary Police Force behaved towards the Greeks. He could see his reasoning.

The car roared forward, and travelled deep inside the pitch black forest. The invigorating smell of fresh pine filled his lungs and nostrils, and he could detect the air was thinner at this great height. Tired from travelling, they were desperate to get out and stretch their legs but Hambi persisted with his driving.

They were approaching the final stretch of their journey amid the peaks of pine forests, vast valleys and sheer cliffs. The winding, narrow road seemed endless, and the car pushed forward slowly, reaching a yet higher elevation. Hambi locked the first gear in place to give him additional power, to overcome the steep stretch of road ahead. The car crawled forward at a snail's pace with its engine roaring and discharging a grey smoke from its exhaust pipe.

'We are nearly there.' Hambi finally said in a tired voice. His neck and shoulders ached and he kept rubbing them to relax the muscles, but he never complained once. Without a fugitive sitting beside him, the return trip would not be as stressful.

Alexis saw nothing but trees engulfed in total darkness. He felt relieved they were about to arrive at their destination without encountering any military patrols or blockades on the way. At the same time, he was quite excited that shortly he would meet new faces—lads like himself, who were devoted to the cause of liberating their country. He had no idea what to expect, but one thing he was sure of, those lads known only as *Andartes* had become the scourge of the British army. They managed to spread fear amongst disciplined troops, and they seemed to have gained the upper hand over them. Being so close to his new lifestyle, he cast aside his personal predicament, and felt privileged that he was about to join those dedicated heroes. If he was going to make an impact on the enemy, this was the place to be and devote his life for the ultimate goal of Freedom.

Hambi finally stopped the car in a lay-by on top of a steep hill, and turned the engine off. A heavenly silence fell upon them both, but they could still hear the roar of the engine throbbing deep inside their ears. They couldn't wait to get out of the car and stretch their legs, but remained seated until contact was made. Hambi signalled their presence with his headlights and waited . . . No response! He tried again, but no answer.

'I hope they are not asleep.' he muttered in a tired voice, and flashed the lights again, this time with agitation.

There was still no response. Instead, their tired eyes feasted on the darkness of the abyss that had totally engulfed them. The stars appeared to be brighter at such a high elevation, but the moon was nowhere to be seen; it was well hidden behind dark clouds. Hambi was becoming impatient, and pressed hard on the horn by blasting a deafening sound over the steep valley.

A response came back immediately; a light flashed intermittently in the darkness.

'They must have been asleep.' Hambi said, pleased that his part of the job was finally over.

They immediately got out of the car and stretched like lazy cats while watching the single dim light approaching them. The dark silhouette stopped at a safe distance and whistled once. He waited for a response. Hambi whistled back and immediately a man approached them, and shone his light on his face.

He couldn't have been more than twenty years old and was dressed in a military uniform and boots. There was a beret on his head, and he had a rifle strapped over his shoulder.

'Have you been asleep?' Hambi asked him.

'Yes, I dozed off.! I wasn't sure what time you would be arriving,' he said, and turned and gave Alexis a stern look. 'What, a priest?' he asked surprised at seeing Alexis' monk's robe.

'This is *Akamantis*, and he is not a priest but a fighter like you.' Hambi said and introduced his companion.

'*Ola-kala*.' the young man said.

Immediately, Hambi got into his car and started up the engine. He reversed and stopped momentarily to gaze at the two boys who were standing in the middle of the road, watching him manoeuvre the car, ready to drive off. The headlights flooded the area briefly as he swerved around, and he paused for another moment to look at the lads for one last time.

'Good luck to both of you!' he shouted, and drove off into the night.

In no time at all, the car disappeared beyond the steep hill. Its distant roar soon faded away, substituted by the dead silence of the night. Once again, a veil of pitch blackness had engulfed the rugged terrain.

A night owl swooped across their path, and disappeared into the dark . . . a bad omen . . .

CHAPTER ELEVEN

WITH THE TORCHLIGHT guiding their way, the two lads started to walk side by side along the isolated road. With long strides, and rifle over his shoulder, Andonis advanced with absolute confidence, being familiar with every nook and cranny of the entire area. Dressed in his combat uniform, he personified a professional soldier, and Alexis felt slightly embarrassed, if not intimidated, wearing the monk's robe. He could not wait to put on his own *Andarti's* uniform and be part of this cell of rural fighters who had mastered the vast mountain regions and surrounding countryside.

After a long trek, they left the main road behind them and entered the wild forest. 'Just follow close behind!' he advised Alexis once they got into dense terrain with low branches thrashing their faces.

'I can't walk in these damn robes . . .!' Alexis complained, restrained by the long garment over his legs.

'Cut it off!'

'Have you got a knife?' Alexis asked.

'Have I got a knife?' Andonis answered, and handed him a sharp military blade, with a serrated edge. He then shone his torch on Alexis' legs.

Alexis quickly ripped off the bottom of the robe just above his knees.

'Now you've made a skirt.' Andonis teased his new recruit.

He led the way forward and proceeded to tackle the seemingly endless forest. They felt as if they were walking on thick soft cushions, whenever they treaded over the strewn pine needles that had accumulated on the ground. The scent of fresh pine was overwhelming and Alexis felt alive and invigorated trekking in such an unspoiled environment. He was no longer tired and moved with fortitude to keep up with his companion. Now and again they talked anxious to get to know one another.

'Now that you are an *Andartis*, tell me, what brought you here?' Andonis asked, curious about their new recruit.

'We blew up some planes'

'The Akrotiri job?' Andonis interrupted.

'Yes!'

'Well done!' he exclaimed, totally surprised and directed the light on Alexis' face to take a better look at him. He stared at him briefly and muttered 'Ola-kala.' and moved forward.

'How many are in the group?' Alexis asked him once they got to a clearing.

'Five. There is Yiannis, our musician who plays the harmonica, Andros my twin brother, Aris the Englishman . . . '

'Englishman?

'We call him that, because he is blonde, like an Englishman and of course Alexantiou, our *Mastro*. He is twenty-six and older than the rest of us, but he has plenty of experience. He trained with the Greek army and he's also very close to the Leader,' Andonis explained.

They entered a ravine and walked carefully down the steep slope. A gentle rippling sound suddenly became audible, and they headed directly for it. At the bottom of the ravine, engulfed by a thicket, a wide stream flowed rapidly and snaked down the gorge. They went into the ice-cold stream, and cautiously crossed over to the other side.

'Our *Limery* is just over that slope,' Andonis explained.

About thirty minutes later, they approached a well-hidden hideout, dug out of the side of a slanting ridge that overlooked the vast valley below. By the time they reached their tranquil *Limery*, the first pallid light of dawn had begun to appear over the horizon, and a few early birds started to twitter gaily. The morning dew gathered upon the leaves and pine needles, glistened in the early light of day. Across the valley, a mass of cliffs rose stiffly and a spectacular scenery loomed out of the haze, that lingered between the peaks of an inaccessible gorge.

They approached the entrance of the hideout, and Andonis removed a loose wooden door made up of planks and camouflaged by a mass of pine branches. In a crouched position, they entered the dark, musty cave. Three bodies could be made out sprawled on the floor fast asleep, oblivious of the new arrivals. Careful not to wake them, Andonis gestured to Alexis to stretch out in a corner, and handed him a blanket. He did not need much persuasion. He immediately crashed on the floor beside one of the other lads, and deep sleep overcame him the moment he shut his eyes . . .

Alexis was awaken by the smell of broiled smoked wine-sausages. He got off the floor and went outside and saw the four lads seated on rocks, gathered together around a small wood fire, chatting and waiting for the sausages to cook. Dressed in their combat uniforms, as soon as they took a glimpse at what their new recruit was wearing they burst out laughing. Alexis responded by laughing with them, recognising how ridiculous he looked with his half torn monk's robe.

'Please give me a uniform.' he pleaded. 'I want to become an *Andartis*.'

He sat among his new companions, anxious to get his teeth into the sausages. The smell of burned meat instantly titillated his taste buds and exacerbated his hunger. Andonis gave him a combat uniform, and he immediately put it on eager to get rid of his silly garment. He proudly posed in front of everyone, in anticipation of all sorts of comments, but instead his new friends clapped their hands, in a welcoming gesture.

'*Ola-kala*, you are an *Andartis* now.' Andonis said to him approvingly, and tossed a black beret over to him.

His new companions were a lively bunch and they all seemed about the same age, with the exception of Aris, who had just turned twenty-one. Seeing Aris, he understood why they called him the 'Englishman'. He was a lean lad, with long legs and blonde hair with bleached streaks highlighted by the sun. He wore his hair long and it touched the nape of his neck reminding him of Spyros. His unblemished, tanned skin was fair, but his eyes were the deepest blue colour Alexis had ever seen. Over his upper lip, a blonde moustache was also sun-bleached matching his tousled hair. His posture and handsome looks personified the idealistic image of an ancient Greek god. He spoke softly with a deep voice, and constantly smiled. That smile of his had become his trademark.

Yiannis appeared the smallest of them all, but he made up for his lack of size, by being both wild and brave. He was a determined, dashing lad who had no fear of anything. Dark skinned and with masses of black curly hair and black moustache, he was often taken for an African, and his friends often teased him about it. He loved music and constantly played his harmonica. Positive in his way of thinking, he was the life and soul of the group, and everyone loved him for his kind nature and his absolute dedication to *Eoka*.

Andros was the spitting image of Andonis, being his identical twin. Medium in height with broad shoulders and solid arms, they both looked like two bulldozers, but Andros was less talkative. He hardly spoke and kept to himself. He was the only married one of the group and had a baby boy he had not seen for five months. That troubled him constantly. Every now and then, he would pull out from his pocket a creased photo of his young wife and baby boy, and stare at them for ages without uttering a single word. Then he would put the photo away and proceed with his task with a sad expression on his face. Andonis, on the other hand, was a more open character and he made friends easily with others. He often spoke in riddles, his best one being, 'Ola-Kala'.

The boys welcomed their new member with open arms, and told him about the life of the *Andartes*. The group was responsible for inflicting as much damage as they could to the enemy within their region, by setting up ambushes against army convoys, dynamiting transformers, cutting power lines, attacking police stations and stealing arms and explosives to build up their own arsenal. They were constantly on the move, hiding in other hideouts across the region. Their biggest problem was the risk of being betrayed and they were always on the look out for collaborators.

Food was provided for them, by civilian members, and dropped at designated locations. The monks over at Maheras Monastery, four miles away, also provided them with food, provisions and other assistance. But nobody knew the precise whereabouts of their hideouts that were scattered across the region. They as a group had never met the *Eoka* Leader. He was an elusive man, and kept strict control over their activities through their *Mastro*, who authorised their missions. As for their *Mastro*, he often disappeared for weeks sometimes, to train other *Andartes* across the mountains or meet up with the Leader.

Alexis spent three weeks with his new companions and had never met their *Mastro* during the entire period. He was somewhere in the mountain region of Pendathaktilos, training a new group of *Andartes* and while he was away there was very little that they could do, except to wait for his return for new orders. They spent their days and nights as lookouts, keeping notes of troop movement across the region. Other times they would break into a police station stealing guns and ammunition but taking little chances. All they could do was to wait until their *Mastro* showed up.

On a bright morning, their *Mastro* appeared dressed in his combat uniform and carrying his machine gun. As soon as Alexis saw him, his eyes lit up; *Mastro* was none other than *Actos* his District Leader, who swore him into *Eoka*.

Alexantiou went up to him and embraced his new recruit in a heart-felt gesture.

'Welcome to our group *Akamantis*, or should I say Alexis!' he said and greeted the new member.

'This is a pleasant surprise!' Alexis said and gave him a great smile.

Alexis couldn't believe his eyes that fate brought him close to this kind man again. Since the day of his initiation, they had worked together for more than ten months, fighting the enemy on a daily basis. And yet, they never actually had the chance to meet each other in person, not since their last gathering in Lefkosia. They exchanged messages on a weekly basis through their couriers, and had developed a genuine respect for each other's dedication to the cause of liberation.

That unexpected meeting with Alexantiou was months ago . . . Now, he had become a seasoned fighter and had learned all there was to know about the life of *Andartes*. He received plenty of survival instructions from his new friends and learned to love his new lifestyle. The isolation did not bother him, but on the contrary he enjoyed the freedom of living without rules and pressures of the daily struggle. Each day posed a new experience without conditions or plans for the day and that suited him fine.

On a wet miserable day, Alexantiou, their dedicated *Mastro*, arrived back from one of his missions with a distressed look on his handsome face. He appeared worried about something. The group immediately sensed that something was not right.

As soon as he arrived he glanced at his young warriors who turned all ears to hear what he had to say to them. He had an aura of authority about him, and spoke with confidence, and yet, he was not much older than the rest of them. For a twenty-six-year old, he had become the right-hand of their Leader, from whom he had gained the Leader's absolute respect and trust for having a strategic mind. Like Alexis, he had a price on his head. Posters with his name, photograph and a reward were plastered everywhere, and he could never travel in the open in fear of betrayal by someone who wanted to pick up the bounty on his head.

'We have to split up the group.' he finally instructed them. 'Our Leader's hideout over at Spilia, it may have been betrayed, and we need to get him into safety and away from the area. He is stuck on the summit.'

'Yesterday and last night we noticed a great number of troop movements throughout the region,' Andonis reported, having realised that the extra troop movements may possibly have been intended to do just that.

'Yes, I have also noticed that on my way here.' Alexantiou said apprehensively.

'Our hideout is a long way off from Spilia.' stated Aris, who knew the region well. 'It's too risky to bring him here . . .!'

'You are right but first things first.' Alexantiou said to his fighters, being anxious to get moving.

'I will take Andonis with me and meet up with the Leader. Alexis, Aris and Yiannis you three go to Scara and join up with our contact,

Ilias. Help him to organise and establish a new hideout. He's expecting you at the usual place. Andros, you remain here to keep an eye on things.'

'Let my brother stay here.' Andros objected, wanting to go with him instead.

'No! You are married and have a child, you stay put!' Alexantiou ordered, not wanting to argue.

They did not waste time, and immediately set themselves to work in preparation for their new mission. Like professionals they gathered their weapons, bullets and few hand-grenades with hardly any discussion between them. They checked and double-checked their weapons and stocked up with as many bullets as they could. In half-an-hour they were ready to leave.

Before departing, Alexantiou turned and looked at his young fighters, dressed in combat gear in preparation to enter into battle if necessary, and felt very proud of them. The odds did not dismay them, and they were all psyched up and ready to face the enemy head on.

'Remember . . .' he said to them. 'We are each other's keeper, ready to give up our lives to protect our brother *Andarti*!'

The lads raised their fists in the air, and repeated in one voice. 'Each other's keeper!'

One by one they climbed up the steep rampart and split up, leaving Andros behind in a brooding mood, to take care of the *Limery*. Alexis with his two companions headed for Scara village, and Alexantiou together with Andonis entered the forest to reach Spilia as quickly as possible. They had a long journey on foot ahead of them, and they anticipated that by nightfall both groups would reach their destination.

*   *   *

Alexantiou with his hunky friend Andonis, moved forward with great anxiety for their Leader's safety. They wanted to reach him as soon as possible before it was too late, but crossing the precipitous ground ahead was not an easy task. This mountainous region posed great dangers with every step, making their journey a slow undertaking. The greatest fear that plagued their minds was the prospect of being confronted with a military patrol each time they crossed an isolated rural road. But worse still was the fear of someone detecting their movements and reporting them to the authorities. Always on the look-out for dangers ahead, they crossed over ridges and valleys, eager to meet up with the Leader.

By mid-afternoon, a drizzle started, accompanied by a thick, swirling mist that made it even much harder to move easily. At such a high altitude, the thick mist covered the trees and the entire area. It appeared like a dense smoke that lingered and hovered over the wet, sludgy ground. Visibility was impossible, but that did not deter them. With unflinching determination they proceeded northwest to reach *Dighenis'* hideout at Spilia.

From a safe high distance, they detected a steady movement below of convoys jam-packed with armed troops, snaking down the narrow winding roads and causing them great apprehension in case they had arrived too late.

Seeing the threatening convoys, they increased pace and plunged into the forest like it was not there. They strode on with agility, and did not care if they fell over loose branches or hidden ditches. They would get up and carry on with only one thing in mind: to reach their Leader.

He depended on them to guide him to safety, and Alexantiou felt responsible for his personal security. His Leader was not familiar with these wild regions and he could easily fall into a British trap, trying to make his escape. He imagined that *Dighenis* would be sitting tight in great anxiety, waiting for his arrival to guide him out of his predicament. It had become apparent that someone betrayed his whereabouts. A forty thousand pound bounty, dead or alive, was a good enough reason for a traitor to spill his guts.

By three in the afternoon, wet, tired and exhausted, the two *Andartes* came across a familiar narrow trail at the very edge of a dangerous cliff with a long sheer drop to the right. The mist was as thick as ever and they could hardly see in front of them. But Alexantiou knew this place well and confidently led the way forward. They followed a winding, sludgy, trail along the edge of the summit and climbed even higher. On their right side, the sheer vertical drop presented danger at every move, while the left side of the trail was no safer, being a wet slippery slope with hardly any vegetation to grab for balance or support. Halfway up to the summit, their trail was blocked by an enormous boulder. It cantilevered over the hazardous, precipitous rock-face exposing a sheer bottomless drop. One wrong footing and they were doomed.

Alexantiou stopped at the base of the boulder and looked up towards the summit and over the tip of the huge rock. He placed two fingers in his mouth and gave out a piercing whistle as a signal of their arrival. He waited for a response, but did not have to wait long. Immediately, a similar whistle sound was heard beyond the boulder.

'Thank God for that!' Alexantiou said to Andonis, relieved that, after all, they were not too late.

'*Ola-Kala!*' Andonis replied, pleased their mission had been accomplished.

They by-passed the boulder by negotiating the steep slope surrounding it, by using both hands to grab onto exposed roots. When they reached the top, they took sight of their Leader standing upright in the distance, slightly in front of his companion.

They were both dressed in combat gear, ready to fight the enemy if necessary, but their faces showed anxiety and a sense of helplessness. They remained at the top of the hill with weapons in their hands and, as soon they saw the lads trying to master the slope, they gave a big smile at the two young fighters who were soaked to the bone. *Dighenis* put his pistol back in its holster and raised both hands into the air.

'Salvation has arrived at last!' he yelled with joy, and his face lit up, pleased to see his right hand warrior.

'Welcome lads.' *Dighenis*' companion of similar age shouted in a harsh voice, and took a drag on his cigarette.

'We have no time to waste. The army is encircling the summit.' Alexantiou called out to them.

When they finally mastered the slippery slope, they came face to face in a clearing surrounded by tall pines, shrouded in grey mist. Their meeting was a great relief, and the fear of danger seemed to have vanished now there were four in the group.

'They are casting a net around the summit.' Alexantiou said to his Leader.

'What do you think their plan is?' *Dighenis* asked.

'There must be two thousand troops and my gut feeling tells me they are combing the entire summit, checking every rock,' his young lieutenant stated, confident that's what the army was doing.

'It is obvious, we have been betrayed.' *Dighenis* said, in a worried tone of voice. 'The question is, how do we get out of their net?'

'We have no choice but to go west.'

'Explain.' he interrupted.

'This summit—I know for a fact—is encircled by a narrow road at its base, except to the west which is inaccessible by road. The west side of the summit continues and joins up with another ridge equally treacherous. I cannot see the British risking their men on the ascent from there.' Alexantiou explained with confidence.

'The army will attempt to comb the mountain from the bottom up, hoping they will trap us at the top.' said Andonis, who knew the region like the back of his hand.

'Andonis is correct, I believe the army will set up two operations!'
'You are familiar with this region, is this your best evaluation of our predicament?' their Leader asked, anxious to get moving before it was too late.

'Yes. I am sure one group will move from the north, combing the whole mountainside until they reach the top and the other will proceed from the south and then, both shall meet at the peak. As they move upwards, the army will spread out its net to cover the inaccessible west side. We certainly cannot risk heading eastwards, they'd be waiting for us! Our only hope, I believe is to act quickly before they close their net across the west side and trap us on our way down.' Alexantiou explained, anticipating the British plan of action.

'It sounds a feasible plan. It seems that our friend the Field Marshal is determined to capture me this time but we are going to disappoint him.' *Dighenis* said, with the utmost scorn for his arch-enemy.

He knew that the Governor has been trying in vain for months to capture him dead or alive, but all his efforts had failed, and he was becoming a bitter man.

'God is on our side and has sent us this thick mist.' *Dighenis'* mainland Greek companion said, and looked around examining the entire area. He was thrilled that the mist had no intention of clearing.

'*Ola-kala.*' Andonis muttered.

'*Ola-kala,* Andonis, let's go!' Alexantiou repeated teasingly, and took the lead forward.

In single file, they began to descend cautiously, trekking along the winding trail to get away from this place as quickly as possible. Visibility was poor and every step along the edge of the steep cliff threatened danger, but no more danger than the one that awaited them if they were captured by the army. They hardly spoke, and maintained complete silence in case some sharp ears overheard their suspicious movements. Despite their age difference, *Dighenis* and his companion maintained the pace and kept up with the lads. They never once fell behind the younger legs.

The drizzle came down steadily, making the precipitous ground slippery and muddy. With every step their boots sunk into the sludge, making the perilous descent even more difficult. The persistent, heavy mist aggravated their problem by restricting visibility.

They walked for about an hour without incident and felt confident that they outsmarted their adversaries. Half way down the mountain, they entered less hazardous terrain, but the mist continued to linger above the ground. This Godsend mist helped to conceal their movements, and they were able to move even faster now the treacherous cliffs were behind them.

Alexantiou was not wrong in his evaluation of troop movements. They executed their operation precisely as he anticipated, and the British spread their net across the entire summit to cover the inaccessible, but possible, escape route through the west side.

By five o'clock, the mist started to thin out and the four men became completely exposed, making it harder for them to hide. Soon they began to hear soldiers' distant voices coming from the right as well from the left. As predicted, the army was closing its net using hundreds of soldiers who were climbing steadily upwards, while they, tried to break through it, on their descent.

Soldiers' voices became clearer, and the men could now hear clearly the movement of branches and shrubbery. Apprehension began to set in, realising they might have been too late, and captivity was imminent unless a miracle was sent by God.

'Avoid firing, unless we have to.' *Dighenis* whispered to his companions.

They all agreed, but the enemy was closing in on them very fast. In the distance, they began to detect soldiers moving around, disturbing bushes in search of hideouts. It was becoming unsafe to walk in the open, and *Dighenis* decided their best option was to hide temporarily among thick bushes. With crouching movements, they approached a thicket and fell flat on the wet ground. They quickly scattered loose branches and pine needles over their bodies to camouflage themselves and maintained absolute silence.

In the distance, the voices of the soldiers grew louder, but they were still far enough away to pose an imminent threat. With the mist gradually being lifted, they could now see clearly around them and lack of visibility was no longer a hindrance.

Motionless, they remained flat on the ground, hoping the threat of danger would pass them by so they could slip away and reach the other side of the valley in safety.

Suddenly, a woman's faint call was heard in the far distance. The men raised their heads slightly and then looked at each other in puzzlement, not sure what to make of this unexpected development.

'Kook. Kook. Kookoo.' the woman's call persisted.

A rustle of bushes was heard ahead of the nervous men, and out of nowhere came two goats moving about, with bells round their necks tinkling. The goats nonchalantly craned their necks and grazed on leaves.

'Kook. Kook. Kookoo.' the woman's voice was heard again, but louder this time.

The men could now see the woman clearly through the undergrowth. In the distance, a middle-aged peasant, dressed in black garments from head to toe, was climbing the hill and moving in their direction. She carried a long stick and flailed it about agitatedly.

Oblivious of their mistress's call, the goats moved up the slope and slowly ambled towards the men's hiding thicket. Lazily, the brown and white goats came and stood directly in front of them. They came so close that the men could smell them. The animals moved their heads about and spotted the men on the ground. They timidly stared at them with glazed eyes and refused to budge. At a loss, the men tried quietly to shoo them away, but the goats fixed their stare directly at them not willing to move a hoof.

The woman had seen her goats and started walking towards them. 'Here you are!' she said to her goats, and began to climb closer.

She was still at a fair distance, but the likelihood of her spotting the men was high. She might scream from sudden fright and expose their location. Certainly her screams would bring the entire army upon them.

In a split-second decision, *Dighenis* pulled out his long serrated army knife in readiness to pounce upon the woman before she got a chance to yell.

'What are you doing?' *Dighenis'* companion asked, realising what he had in mind.

'If she yells we are finished! *Eoka* is finished!' *Dighenis* whispered, and pinned his eyes straight on the woman, like a lion that locks its gaze on its prey ready to pounce on its helpless victim.

The woman steadily came towards them but her goats remained still, staring at the men and stubbornly refusing to move an inch. She approached closer . . .

Dighenis was about to flex his muscles, while the other men remained in total silence expecting the worst to happen at any moment. An innocent life was about to snuffed, for simply being in the wrong place and at the wrong time.

'Here you are, come here you run-a-bouts!' the woman screeched, and threw her stick at the two goats. That did the trick.

Abruptly, the goats turned their heads and retreated in the direction of the woman, trekking clumsily downhill and away from the men. They gave a sigh of relief that the death of an innocent woman had not materialised. They waited until she had withdrawn beyond the slope, and decided they had no other choice but to risk it, and get moving. It was no longer safe. The troop movements posed a greater danger, and they were moving rapidly to close the net. The men had to move fast before it was too late.

They got off the ground, and began their descent by entering a dense thicket. They had managed to cross it and were about to leave it behind for good, when at the other end they suddenly came face to face with a young startled British soldier.

Both combatants froze temporarily, but not as much as the young soldier who turned yellow with shock, the instant he saw the *Andartes*. Panic-stricken, he hesitated and stared at the men who had their guns pointing directly at him. Another soldier's voice was heard calling him, but he remained planted on the ground, speechless and unsure of his next move. He sensed that he was in a no win situation. His life was threatened and he realised his end was near. At the same time, his adversaries were also in a precarious situation. If they emptied their guns at the young lad, the shots would bring the whole army on top of them.

In absolute silence, they both stared at each other trying to anticipate each other's next move. Eventually, without uttering a single word, the young soldier lowered his gun and turned away from them and headed towards the direction where his colleagues were calling him.

'Your mother loves you.' Alexantiou said to him in English.

The young soldier looked back at them for a moment, and disappeared into the forest, blessing his lucky day for not having his life snuffed out.

The men did not waste time, and hastily picked up pace to get as far away as possible from this place. They knew they had escaped the troops' net, but did not want to hang about in case their luck might not hold out for much longer. Eventually, they entered a stretch of roaming hills, covered with carob and olive trees that offered them adequate protection. Recognising they had escaped from the danger-prone summit, they were ecstatic in their success at out-manoeuvring the Governor and his troops.

In a composed and less stressed-out manner, the men walked until they reached a gentle ridge and climbed to the very top. Standing at its peak, they surveyed the horizon and turned their attention to the distant summit that nearly brought about their downfall. Half way up the mountain, the mist prevailed like a thick cloud making visibility practically impossible.

Tired, they rested momentarily on large rocks and gazed across the peaceful, lush surroundings. No sooner had they time to catch their breath, than the blissful silence was interrupted by a sudden burst of rapid gunshots over the distant summit. Loud shots echoed across the valley, bursting from different directions and coming from the north and south side of the mist-covered mountain.

The deafening explosions of hand-grenades blasting, together with prolonged rifle and machine-gun fire, had turned the whole mountain into mayhem. It appeared that the soldiers were firing wildly in different directions, without any coherent plan. Within minutes, the clear mountain air had turned into a stench of gunpowder drifting across the valley. Desperate yelling and soldiers' screams filled the air, amid the deafening sound of gun-fire. Pandemonium and panic was in progress, exacerbated by the lack of visibility and steady drizzle.

'My God! They are killing each other!' *Dighenis* said astounded, while watching through his binoculars. He had realised what was taking place across the valley.

'Idiots!' Alexantiou said, quite shocked by the loss of innocent lives, even though they were the enemy.

'*Ola-Kala.*' Andonis said and shook his head, amazed by the whole scene.

The mayhem continued for more than half-an-hour, until it eventually came to an abrupt stop.

Immediately, the four men took leave and headed for a safe house in the remote tranquil village of Kakopetria, perched between the high peaks of mount Troothos.

On their way there, the Leader had changed his plans and wanted to reach his hideout in Lemesos in order to re-evaluate the present situation in a coherent manner. He had a feeling that unforeseen developments might come about, due to this British military blunder, and he considered it necessary that he should be in a position to mobilise his forces across the island at a moment's notice. Being at Lemesos would offer him a better and faster means of direct communication with his District Leaders, and he could assess crucial intelligence much more quickly.

'Once we reach Kakopetria you two go back to your *Limery*. Don't move until you receive my new instructions. I will make my own way back to Lemesos.' *Dighenis* said to Alexantiou.

By midnight, they had arrived exhausted at a safe house. After a hot cup of coffee and a bite to eat, Alexantiou together with Andonis immediately left on foot for their *Limery*; their Leader was safe and well.

* * *

By late afternoon, Alexis and his two companions, Yiannis and Aris, left the forest behind them and reached the outskirts of the hillside village of Scara in the district of Solea.

The long trek on foot was a strenuous one, and by the time they arrived at the dilapidated storehouse, they felt worn-out. Soaked, they entered the musty, empty building perched on a gentle hillside. They sat on the floor to take a breather, away from the drizzle that persisted ever since they left their *Limery*. After a short break, Aris departed to make contact with Ilias by cutting across plantations and fields to avoid detection.

At the bottom of the hill, they could see the winding gravel road that snaked across the open countryside, and which eventually disappeared between the first visible houses of the tranquil village. From the storehouse, they had a clear, unobstructed view of all traffic movements going in and out of the village, and they felt quite safe inside the walls of this rundown building. It offered them ample protection against the elements as well as the enemy, but it also provided a perfect surveillance position over the main road and the entire village below.

Peasants working in the countryside were returning home from the fields. On foot, they guided their donkeys and mules forward by constantly prodding them with a stick. Some of the animals were laden with firewood, while others had sacks full of carobs piled on their backs like massive towers, to be used as animal feed or sold. At a snail's pace, the animals trekked ahead, anxious to reach the comfort of their barn and have the load removed from their back. Other locals travelled along the road in two-wheeled, mule-drawn wagons, often with a number of kids perched at the front, constantly calling out to the animals to go faster so they could reach home before nightfall.

Alexis peeped out the window, examining the unfamiliar rural community that appeared to be blessed with plenty of water and breathtaking, fertile scenery that stretched for miles across. The rain came to a stop, but outside he could still hear the rushing of water flowing rapidly over loose rocks, creating channels like tiny ravines and gullies that rippled swiftly down the slope.

Yiannis did not move from his position, but pulled out his harmonica and began to blow into it softly. A melodic sound drifted into the air and echoed against the bare walls of the storehouse. Alexis listened to him playing, and looked at his young friend, who was completely engrossed in his music. His curly black hair from under his beret was soaked and fell over his face, but he paid no attention to it. Instead, he carried on playing his harmonica oblivious of his surroundings. He always seemed to repeat over and over again the same old haunting melody that stuck in everyone's ears which he named 'Yiannis' melody.'

206

While listening to the pleasant melody, Alexis kept his eyes pinned in the direction in which Aris went, in case he appeared in the distance. He stared ahead, with his deep brown eyes but instead of seeing Aris, he noticed a large military convoy heading towards the village.

'Yiannis, we have visitors.' he said to his friend, and began to count the vehicles.

Yiannis immediately stopped his music, sprang off the ground, and stood next to Alexis alongside the window.

'How many are there?' Yiannis asked, observing the long convoy that was moving towards Scara.

'I have counted twenty so far,' Alexis said, and continued counting. 'Twenty eight!' he added, once the last car of the convoy came into view.

'Something is brewing.' Yiannis said, apprehensively.

Before Yiannis had time to say anything, Aris and Ilias walked in. They had used a different route to approach the storehouse. Ilias, a skinny man in his late twenties, walked with a limp, and that immediately made Alexis feel sympathetic towards the new arrival. He had trouble with his right leg and dragged it along slightly, as he walked. Dressed in a heavy turtleneck pullover, his head appeared to be half covered as if he was afraid he might catch a cold.

'It is not safe here.' Ilias said, and went to check the other side of the storehouse facing the distant forest. 'If they cordon off the area, we are in deep trouble' he added, while inspecting the surrounding valley.

'Our only hope is to sit it out and hide, until they move out.' Aris advised.

'Certainly not here but Aris is right. I suggest we wait until nightfall and then sneak back to my house. I have a concealed hideout under the floor and we can all squeeze inside it, until the army moves out.' Ilias suggested.

Having no other alternative, the boys agreed to sit it out and wait for nightfall before they made a move. Like hawks, they were on constant lookout for troops approaching the storehouse. But their fears did not materialise and by nine o'clock they left for Ilias' house.

Under the cover of darkness, they arrived at Ilias' farmhouse, surrounded by a stonewalled enclosure dotted with cypress trees. His house was in a prominent location, perched at the top of a hill not far off the main road and overlooked the entire village below. Across the valley, dim scattered lights were visible, flickering through the night, escaping from the houses beyond.

With his limping gait, Ilias led the way forward, and entered the adjacent barn. In complete darkness, three mules stirred the moment they sensed their arrival, but remained in a far corner surrounded by fodder. The place reeked with pungent dung which, through the years, had permeated the earth floor. The obtrusive stench was exacerbated by the overpowering presence of scattered hay and urine-covered carobs, making the barn unbearable.

Ilias approached an inner door in the back wall and opened it up. It led directly into another smaller room used as a laundry, and he led his friends inside this dark, narrow place. A small, shuttered window overlooked the orchard beyond. With the help of his friends, Ilias removed a marble slab from the floor, and then picked up a stubby torch resting on the window-ledge. He turned it on, and directed its beam inside a narrow hole in the ground.

The boys peeped into the hole to inspect Ilias' hideout.

'Can we all fit inside?' Alexis asked, as the hole seemed quite tiny.

'For sure.' he answered. 'The pit gets bigger once we get to the bottom, it's like a crater under the fireplace of my house,' he reassured them.

'Ilias, it's not a grave, is it?' Yiannis said to him, not impressed with his friend's masterpiece.

'Don't be silly! Come . . . let's go and tell my old lady that we are here.' he said to them and led the way forward.

Everybody left their weapons behind, piled in a corner of the small room, and followed Ilias. Outside, they crossed the yard and went inside the adjacent arched building. As soon as his mother saw the lads, she stopped her needlework and got off the chair to greet them. The elderly lady knew precisely what they were up to seeing them dressed in combat gear.

'*Mama*, my friends are going to hide in the barn until the soldiers leave,' he said to her.

'Welcome, boys' she said, and looked at the three new lads. 'Your father is not back yet and I am worried about him with all them English about,' she continued in a soft voice.

'Don't worry, *mama*, he's too old to cause trouble for the English.' Ilias said to her, trying to alleviate the obvious anxiety that was written all over her wrinkled face.

'You don't know the English' she muttered under her breath. 'I am going to the square to see what is going on' she insisted, and walked into her kitchen.

The boys heard the clattering of plates. A few minutes later, she returned carrying small dishes filled with cracked green olives, cheese and smoked dry-cured pork. She gently placed the food on the table, and then wrapped herself in a thick woollen shawl and put a black scarf over her face. She meticulously covered her mouth with the long end of the scarf and immediately left for the long trek to the village square, worried about her husband's safety.

The boys hardly had time to finish their snack, when they heard the familiar sound of a loudhailer, announcing in broken Greek that a curfew was in progress. The announcer was a Turk, and he kept repeating warnings in a harsh voice for everyone to stay indoors or else they would be arrested.

'Bastards.' Alexis swore, realising they might have to remain there indefinitely, until the curfew was lifted.

'So much for our Leader's hideout.'

'We have to sit it out.' Yiannis said, and reluctantly submitted to their predicament.

Half an-hour-later, they heard the footsteps of Ilias' mother stamping across the veranda. Her son immediately opened the door for her. His father was not with her, and she seemed distressed. She sat on a chair and started to sob, unable to contain her emotion.

'Where is *papa*?' Ilias asked.

'They've gone crazy son, they are herding all the men in the dark, into the school . . .'

'Father too?' Ilias interrupted his mother.

'Yes son, they took the old men too may God curse the lot of them.' they have killed Vasillou, poor woman!'

'Moutta's wife?' Ilias cried out in shock, at the loss of such a loveable woman who would not harm a fly.

'*Katares! Katares!*' the old lady wailed loudly and there was no stopping her.

When she composed herself, she was anxious to tell the lads everything to relieve her anguish. She leaned back in her chair and looked at the boys who stared at her in great sympathy.

'My old eyes have seen terrible things son. I need to go to church and pray! May God have mercy on us all' she said imploringly, and raised both of her calloused hands into the air.

'Tell us, *mama*!' insisted her son, anxious to find out what really happened in the square.

'*Endaxi, Endaxi!*' she bellowed out.

'The English,' she began to explain, 'asked her young son Savvaki to take down a Greek flag from the church, but he refused. Two soldiers picked him up and began to give him a good hiding, but the boy would not budge—you know how stubborn he is—Vasillou, like a mother hen . . . and ready to give birth . . . attacked the soldiers with her bare hands, screaming to make them stop, but they punched her and she fell to the ground. Mouttas, seeing his pregnant wife on the floor, ran to her rescue, but the soldiers grabbed him . . .

I don't know how he managed it but in desperation, he stabbed one of the soldiers with a knife and he ran off to escape. They shot him in the back like a dog! Vassilou lost her mind and went crazy to reach her husband but the army restrained her, poor woman. All the neighbours came out of their houses and the women grouped together and started throwing rocks. Chairs and broomsticks flew at the army. The soldiers—God curse them all—panicked and herded all our men like cattle inside the churchyard and held them there with guns pointing at them. Like a desperate beast, Vassilou, seeing her husband motionless on the ground, started to scream and pounced on them again and then the English cowards together with the Turks, climbed into their cars and started firing at the women. A bullet went through Vassilou's eye and she fell down and died. Many women got injured, but poor Vassilou and her unborn baby, they are both gone. May God bless them eternally!'

Traumatised, the old lady kept shaking her head, in disbelief at her terrible experience.

'They are animals! Animals!' she muttered between her few teeth. 'You boys are not safe, you'd better hide, and don't come out until I call you' she then burst out at them and started to shoo them off.

The lads did not argue with her and left to hide under ground, leaving the old lady to ponder in grief.

Ilias' mother maintained her vigil and between loud sobs she kept muttering to herself: '*Kateres*, five orphans . . . *Katares!*'

The boys climbed down inside the musty hole in the ground, and to everyone's surprise, the hideout was quite large. They could easily fit inside, but there was not enough headroom to stand upright. The low roof was covered with planks of wood supported on posts to hold the weight of the soil above, while the perimeter walls were left bare. Ilias had a stash of candles in a leather pouch hanging from one of the posts. He lit a thick candle which instantly illuminated the interior of his masterwork.

'I told you we could all fit!' Ilias said to them, feeling proud of his work.

'Let's hope we won't have to remain here for long.' Alexis said to everyone, anxious to proceed with their mission and establish their Leader's secret hideout.

The ongoing clinking of footsteps on the marble floor above, were distinctly audible within the confined space of the small hideaway. The lads could detect that Ilias' mother was pacing back and forth, frequently heaving a loud sigh of distress. Her son felt sorry for her, but he was in no position to help her or relieve her anxiety. Only the return of his father would pacify the traumatic experience she had encountered that evening.

They spent the evening inside their burrow like rabbits, crouched and curled on the floor with blankets over them to keep away the damp. To their disappointment, the air quickly turned stale through lack of adequate ventilation. The small clay pipe that ended outside by means of the chimney breast above was insufficient to service four big lads.

They constantly moaned about it, but Ilias shrugged it off, and soon fell asleep. He started to snore, and that triggered the others into closing their eyes and nodding off, leaning against each other in complete darkness . . .

CHAPTER TWELVE

THE FOUR OF them were suddenly awoken by a loud commotion coming from upstairs. They could hear Ilias' elderly mother shouting at the top of her voice in a distressed manner, while a Greek was trying hard to calm her down. Loud footsteps and English voices amidst a Turkish dialogue were also audible from within the boys' burrow.

They realised the army had taken over the house. They were trapped in their musty hole unable to make a sound, let alone make a break for it. As long as the army did not search the house inch-by-inch, they were safe for the time being, but their lives were in danger.

Panic-stricken, they were at a loss for what to do about their unexpected predicament. They knew the slightest sound would betray them to the army. Uncomfortably crammed together, they pricked up their ears and listened, trying to anticipate what was happening above their heads. All they could hear was endless muffled voices and footsteps echoing back and forth against the marble floor. They could no longer hear Ilias' mother, and they assumed that she had been thrown out of the house until the army had finished its temporary occupation.

The army was in fact using the premises for questioning, and the boys often overheard the grilling of locals by Turkish or British interrogators, who were trying to extract information about *Eoka* activities in the area. Greek interpreters did most of the questioning, aimed at convincing the villagers to speak against their neighbours.

Squeezed tightly against each other, Alexis and his friends listened to the continuing shouting, yelling and agonising screams. Someone had lit the fireplace above and, in no time at all, their pit became a torture chamber itself through heat. Sweat started to pour down on their faces and they were all gasping for fresh air. Trapped like rats, they crouched next to each other wishing that nightfall would come soon so they could try and make their escape out of the hole which might prove to be their mass grave.

As time went by, they could no longer cope with their parched throats, rumbling stomachs and the stiffness that had beset their entire bodies. They moved as much as space permitted, but there was no way they could stretch their legs to alleviate the rigidity in their joints. They did not even dare to close their eyes fearful they might snore and bring the troops on top of them. If any one dozed off, he would soon get a nudge from the others to keep him awake.

The noise from above subsided as the night progressed. There was not much activity except footsteps and small-talk in Turkish and English.

They assumed that the enemy was getting tired and sleep was getting the better of them. In the next couple of hours the occupiers would certainly fall asleep. When that happened that would be the right time for them to make their break. In the event that they had to battle their way out, they were well stocked with ammunition and were confident that, with the help of God, they would escape the clutches of the enemy. They certainly could not last another day inside their roasting, stifling hole without water, food or sleep.

A sudden outburst of commotion disturbed the silence of the night. A volley of shouting and yelling shook the walls and Turkish voices roared with anger, while a Greek captive pleaded for mercy. There appeared to be a scuffle and the lads listened, trying to make out what was taking place. The captive's agonising screams made the hairs on their arms stand on end. The sound of punching, slapping and hard beating became evident and the boys were fuming with anger but felt powerless. They remained packed like sardines in a can, confined in Ilias' musty hideout.

The beating carried on for a long time, but the captive refused to give any information about *Eoka*. More hurried footsteps were heard, and a Greek spoke to the captive.

'Tell us what you know about *Eoka*. I know that you are a member!' he yelled in a harsh threatening voice.

'Traitor! Take that mask off, and show your face. I want to curse the wench that bore such a scumbag of a man!' the captive shouted at the top of his voice.

The apprehended man kept his mouth shut and his mistreatment continued. He insisted that he knew nothing about *Eoka* but the traitor knew better, and kept insisting that the torture should be continued until the man broke down.

The lads were no longer tired or sleepy. The mistreatment inflicted upon the man got them so angry, they completely forgot their own precarious situation, and wanted to kill the Greek collaborator.

There was a brief scuffle across the floor and suddenly the captive yelled.

'You! My own butcher, why Christophore, why?'

The tortured man somehow must have exposed the identity of the village traitor.

'Shut up!' the traitor yelled back, upset that his identity had been revealed. 'You shall pay for this, bastard!'

'You are a dead man Christophore, you can no longer hide behind that mask of yours, you are dead!' shouted the captive.

'Do you know him?' Alexis asked Ilias in a low voice.

'Of course I know him!' Ilias answered, shocked by what he had just heard.

'I know him too.' Aris said in a whisper. 'He's as good as dead the bastard! I am going to kill him!' he added, and gnashed his teeth in anger.

After a little while, the clatter and noise came to an abrupt end, and the boys assumed that the captive had probably been taken away and sent to a detention camp for more interrogation.

Peace and quite finally reigned once again. It was well past midnight and silence fell upon the entire house with hardly any movement. This was the chance they had been waiting for . . . and, by one in the morning, they were ready to make their escape. The only safe place for them was their *Limery* and the surrounding dense forests that would offer them ample protection.

They carefully climbed out of the hideout gasping for fresh air. They gathered at the small window facing the apple orchard and took deep breaths. Once revived, Ilias carefully opened the wooden shutters and looked outside into the pitch black orchard engulfed by the dark night sky. There was not a single sound except of a lone frog that raucously croaked away to his heart's content.

They picked their guns and arsenal in readiness to make their escape.

'You know I cannot run.' Ilias said reminding them of his handicap.

'Ilias, you must try this is not the time to think about your leg,' Aris said to him and put his semi-automatic over his shoulder.

'I will go first.' Alexis said, and started to climb out of the tiny window. With one agile movement he found himself standing out in the open, facing the vast orchard.

Aris climbed out next and both started to walk carefully towards the orchard. Yiannis, with his rifle over his shoulder, followed suit and the three of them walked quietly like three dark mysterious shadows into the night.

They approached the first row of apple trees, when out of nowhere they suddenly came across a Turk who was urinating and had spotted the three shadows.

'Allah, who goes there?' he shouted, startled by the sight of the three faint silhouettes.

214

Aris immediately pounced on him, assisted by Alexis. He began to shout in Turkish and the three of them fell on the ground. The Turkish policeman, fearful of losing his life, managed to pull out his revolver, and pulled the trigger once. A harmless but loud shot rang out from his pistol and echoed into the silence of the night.

Instantly, voices were heard coming from the house, both in Turkish and English. The Turk never got the chance to fire his pistol again. Aris hit him hard on the head with the butt of his sub-machine gun, and he fell unconscious on the moist ground.

The lads waited momentarily for Ilias to climb through the window, but he was having a difficult time and was struggling. He looked at his friends and realised they were all exposed to imminent danger.

'Make a run for it, I cannot run!' he shouted.

'Try Ilias, try!' the three of them shouted back, urging him to try harder.

They were in a life and death situation and every second counted. They heard hurried footsteps coming from inside the house.

'No I cannot make it!' their trapped friend shouted, and disappeared behind the dark window.

The lads took to their heels, and cannoned into the orchard. Suddenly a series of deafening gunshots were heard coming out of the barn. The boys realised that Ilias had made a diversion to give them time to escape. He decided to battle it out with the army.

Immediately, a fierce gun battle began between Ilias and the army, but Ilias knew he was in a no-win situation. He continued to fight for ten minutes, while his friends managed to cross the orchard.

Then out of nowhere, a large explosion shook the ground. The lads looked back and saw directly over the barn huge flames that lit up the dark sky. Amidst the conflagration, the panic-stricken animals neighed and whinnied in desperation. In shock nearby residents, came out of their homes to see what had suddenly disturbed their sleep. Loud voices, shouting and endless instructions in Turkish and English were shouted frantically into the night. But shots persisted from inside the inflaming barn. Five minutes later, the shots stopped . . .

Pandemonium had set in. Soldiers rushed everywhere to capture the other *Eoka* fighters, while cars drove off in a hurry to block their escape route, by trying to encircle the lads. The constant sound of machine-gun fire ricocheted through the area in the hope that the hail of flying bullets would hit their target in the dark.

The lads ran as fast as they could, and realised that the army was right behind them. Aris often let out a spurt of bullets from his sub-machine gun, and the other lads followed suit by firing towards the dark threatening shadows that were gaining ground on them. A brief exchange of gunfire ensued, but the boys knew they were no match for the well-trained army, which was stocked with an endless supply of ammunition.

Running was their only means of escape. They jumped over fences into neighbouring yards, causing the animals and hens to scatter in panic. Frightened locals poked out their heads to investigate what was happening this late at night. They all realised that a battle between the army and *Eoka* was in progress. They knew that blood was about to stain the fertile earth and crossed themselves fearful for the lives of their patriots.

The lads came across a stone wall and like gazelles, Alexis together with Aris, quickly got to the top of the wall, and jumped over to the other side. Yiannis made the climb and as soon as he reached the top, he leaped into the air but a stray flying bullet hit him directly on the head. Without a sound he fell flat onto the ground.

Alexis noticed him motionless on the ground, back tracked, and rushed to him not knowing he had been shot.

'Yiannis get up!' he roared.

His friend didn't move . . . He tried to drag him by his arm, but Yiannis remained still with his face flat on the ground.

Aris went to help out but immediately realised what had happened.

'He's dead!' he called out in anguish. 'Let him be!' he yelled at Alexis.

Aris desperately pulled him by the sleeve so they could take off before they ended up the same way. They took to their heels again by crossing back yards and jumping fences.

They could hear the sound of running boots and soldiers shouting in English right behind them, while deadly bullets were flying all around them. Suddenly Alexis felt a thump across the right of his stomach. He put his hand over it and felt something wet and warm.

'Aris, I've been shot!' Alexis yelled to his friend.

Aris stopped to take a look. He put his own hand over the wound and felt Alexis' blood on his palm. But there was no way of establishing how serious the damage was in the dark.

'Can you move?' he asked

'I think so.' Alexis answered.

'Keep your hand over the wound and let's go before we end up like Yiannis!' Aris insisted frantically.

216

They swerved about in the night but Alexis was having difficulty running. Aris often slowed down to help him. Then a miracle happened—the soldiers seemed to have lost them amongst the maze of narrow cobbled alleyways and stone walls. They could no longer hear the threatening footsteps and considered themselves lucky, for the moment at least.

Aris led the way forward and Alexis tried to keep up with him. He was in great pain and anxious about his injury, especially as he didn't know how much damage the bullet had caused. He could still move and that gave him encouragement but the warm blood, relentlessly dribbled down his thigh.

Fifteen minutes later Aris entered a well-kept yard of a large house located at the very edge of the village, surrounded by tall pine trees. He headed straight for the front door and banged on it impatiently. Then he tried the doorknob. The door was not locked, and they burst into the house and found themselves in the kitchen.

An overweight woman in her late fifties was standing boiling a pot over a small stove in the corner. Startled at the sight of the two intruders, she began to scream loud enough to wake the dead. She was petrified as she recognised that the lads were *Andartes* by their uniforms.

'Shut up!' Aris yelled at her, filling her with fear.

A thin-looking man with a sullen face, and half asleep, walked into the kitchen to investigate what was happening in his house at this late hour. As soon as he saw the lads in combat gear, fear overcame him, realising that *Eoka* had just paid him a visit.

'Christophore?' Aris yelled at him, as soon as he set eyes on the small man with a hooked nose.

'Yes.'

While Alexis was crouched holding his wound, Aris did not wait for another word from the man's mouth and sprayed his sub-machine gun into him. Riddled with bullet holes, the man fell flat on the floor with blood pouring out of his wounds. His body jerked momentarily, he coughed few times, and then remained motionless.

Like a wild beast his wife hissed like a snake, grabbed a large butcher's knife and shrieking frantically she pounced on Aris from behind and dug the blade deep into his back. He gave out a loud scream and before he had a chance to stop her, she pulled the blade out of his back and continued ferociously stabbing him across the chest and hissing at the same time.

His lean body collapsed onto the floor jerking spasmodically. Instantly it was covered in a pool of blood. His head and body shook

217

for a moment, then, there was no more movement, except for a minute twitch of his fingers.

In the traumatic confusion, Alexis managed to pull out his pistol with one hand, and while holding his wound with the other, he fired directly into the woman's face. Her knees buckled and she fell like a sack next to her husband with blood spreading across the marble floor. The woman's face was shattered. Bits of her flesh and bones were scattered over the kitchen walls and pine cabinets.

Alexis was at a loss and knelt next to his motionless friend and saw his blue eyes stare past him. He took his head in his arms and, for the first time ever, examined his face closely. The stubby beard on his handsome face had grown thick and his blond hair was covered in mud and soaking with the red blood that spurted out. He gazed at him briefly and then gently closed his eyes unable to look at his lifeless blue eyes. Carefully, he laid his head on the floor and replaced his black beret over his face.

'Good-bye my friend.' Alexis muttered to him.

He had never seen death so close and he was having trouble coping with his emotions. Shattered, he got to his feet anxious to take off.

Under the kitchen light, he looked at the wound in his stomach and for the first time, he was able to examine the open gash closely. He had a deep, five-inch gash across his right side where the bullet had penetrated from his back and ripped his skin on its way out.

Confused and distraught by the senseless loss of two of his close buddies, he pulled himself together and by stepping over the three dead bodies he clumsily rummaged inside the kitchen drawers. He moved as fast as he could in case the army surprised him, attracted by the gunshots. After scattering the contents of a few drawers, he found some wooden clothes pegs. Scared, he carefully clipped the open wound together with the pegs and then wrapped a kitchen towel tightly around his waist to slow down the bleeding.

Panicked, he looked at his dead friend for one last time and walked out of the back door. The only safe place for him was his *Limery*. The monks at the nearby monastery would know what to do, and would fetch a doctor to see to his injury. The only obstacle— aside from the army—was the long journey ahead. He wasn't sure if he could make it in time, before losing too much blood and his condition becoming beyond salvation.

Like a wounded animal, he staggered into the night across endless fields until he finally entered the edge of the forest. He wanted to leave death behind him and staggered with fortitude to reach the safety of his hideout knowing that his friends would be there for him. Being so close to death, he no longer feared it, but Aris' and Yiannis' faces haunted him constantly. He could not understand why he had been spared and why he had not met the same fate as them. He should also have died he thought to himself, and felt guilty for being alive. Why was he spared? He did not have the answers . . .

With those thoughts, he climbed dark, treacherous hills and ravines anxious to reach safety. He lost all sense of time and had no idea how long he had been travelling, or if he was heading in the right direction. As time progressed, his eyesight turned blurry and his senses were gradually leaving him. Numbness started to set in over his entire body. The thunderous sound of gunshots never left his ears and they seemed to have lodged themselves deep into his eardrums.

Unable to see Yiannis' dead face in the dark, nor even Petros' for that matter—his electrocuted old buddy—their deaths had not had as much of a devastating emotional or psychological impact on him as Aris' death had. With Aris, it was a different story . . . he had seen his riveting blue eyes under a bright kitchen light without a speck of life in them. He had never before encountered the traumatic experience of death at such close range. He had truly seen death in Ari's, blue eyes and that scared him . . .

He ran into the forest to put tragedy behind him for good, but nothing was so easy; everything was closing in on him.

The pitch black sky suddenly appeared to be so low, he was under the illusion that he could reach out and touch it. As he wobbled forward he felt dizzy and his weak body constantly shuddered. While trying to climb a steep slope, he stumbled and fell backwards. He let out a helpless cry into the cold, silent night and, like a rolling boulder, he span down and crashed into the bottom of a ravine. There was no one to hear his faint cries.

All of a sudden, he was engulfed in pitch blackness . . .

* * *

Newspaper headlines described in detail what took place at the village of Scara, but reported that only two bodies were recovered. The army was searching the entire area for the third body, which they were sure would be found somewhere in the nearby ravines. With third-degree burns, the fourth terrorist, named Ilias, was apprehended and sent to the infirmary while his entire house was razed to the ground as punishment for his active involvement with *Eoka.*

News had also reported that more than fifty British soldiers had lost their lives in vain from friendly crossfire, due to their own officers' blunders over at Spilia summit.

The Governor was in no mood to accept such a black mark on his impeccable reputation. He was desperate to redeem his tainted reputation, and the success over at Scara motivated him to act with brutal decisiveness. He gave orders to use any force necessary to impel people to inform on any *Eoka* activities, or to turn in known members. The prisons and detention centres were filled to the rafters, but he was sure his methods would ultimately bring about positive results.

His brutal tactics provided him with some positive results and many *Eoka* members were apprehended, while a number of hideouts occupied by the *Andartes* fighters were discovered and blown to bits across the Troothos and Pendathaktilos mountain range. His methods under Operation Kingfisher were beginning to pay off and he did not want to lose the impetus of his sudden victories; he demanded that entire mountainsides be combed inch-by-inch to flush out the enemy. Thousands of troops were designated for this purpose, and all collaborators' reports of *Andartes* sightings were taken seriously and acted upon immediately.

The names on the Governor's most wanted list that demanded the highest rewards were the *Eoka* Leader himself, otherwise known as *Dighenis*, and his right hand-man and commander, Alexantiou. Recently, his soldiers had killed Drakos—another notorious guerrilla fighter—in an ambush and he wiped him off his list. But he was desperate to remove those other two notorious names. Futile searches for those two had been going on for months, and the Governor was quite frustrated by their cunning and elusiveness. He knew that if he caught those two, *Eoka* would probably fizzle out and become no more than a distant memory.

On a cold February morning, a peasant informant handed the Governor Alexantiou's name on a platter. He had informed him of a number of guerrilla movements in the Pitsilia region. He believed Alexantiou was one of the fighters. All he knew was that a hideout was located around the Maheras area, but he was not sure of the precise location.

The Governor's eyes gleamed with joy at the prospect of eliminating one of his most wanted adversaries. He immediately sent his army to capture or kill this lad and his group which had caused so much havoc to his troops.

A convoy of well-armed soldiers, supported by a long line of back-up trucks, snaked up the winding dirt roads to reach Alexantiou's possible hiding place. They steadily reached higher ground and entered a dense forest of large, ancient pine and cypress trees. By ten in the morning, five thousand troops had been dispersed into the countryside surrounding Maheras, and systematically combed every inch of the terrain in their attempt to find his hideout and flush him out. On foot, and in mile-long search parties, the army thrashed through wet shrubbery and thickets throughout the entire valley in pursuit of their elusive prey.

Alexantiou and his two companions had no idea what was about to descend upon them and made the most of their time, while waiting for instructions from the Leader.

They were devastated by the incident over at Scara and were at a total loss over the death of three of their group members. Despondency and depression set in, and they lost the will to eat or even talk with one another. Andonis with his brother could not come to terms that they would never see their friends ever again or, listen to Yiannis playing his harmonica to them.

Downhearted, the group continued to live the life of *Andartes*, and anxiously waited for the Leader to send them new recruits so they could become a strong fighting force again. Every day, they waited and tried to maintain a sense of normality with their activities, but they knew getting new recruits would take time.

As always, Andonis took the first watch. He got up early and headed for their lookout post at the bottom of the winding gravel road that led to the monastery. There was no activity or movement at this isolated part of the countryside except for monks cycling or trekking peacefully towards the monastery.

He sat on a boulder watching the entire valley, with its spectacular scenery, and listening to the twittering of birds in the bushes. The brimming landscape and breathtaking panoramic views intensified his deep sense of patriotism and his love for this troubled land. He was captivated by the hovering and gliding of a lone eagle in the far distance, like a dark speck in the grey February sky.

His thoughts were suddenly interrupted when he noticed a monk riding his bicycle. He was having a difficult time with the steep hill and eventually dismounted and proceeded on foot. The panting monk came closer, and Andonis climbed off the boulder to have a chat with him.

As soon as the monk set eyes on him, he stopped in the middle of the road. He recognised Andonis as one of the *Andartes* group he often provided supplies for.

'There is a lot of military activity in the area. Take care.' the young monk warned him fretfully.

'How far away?' Andonis asked, and put his rifle over his shoulder. 'They are over the hill and there are thousands of them!' the novice answered, concerned for their safety.

Before the monk had time to say any more, they heard the roar of a helicopter hovering low to scout the mountainside and its deep, inaccessible valleys and gorges. Like a flying ant, the helicopter appeared over the ridge across the hazardous valley.

The pilot noticed the cloaked monk and his companion and headed straight for them.

Andonis quickly plunged at the side of the road and tried to hide among the bushes. He pointed his gun to the sky and waited. The helicopter approached, hovered briefly above the monk, and then turned its nose and quickly disappeared beyond the hills.

Andonis came out of hiding not sure if he had been spotted or not. He quickly took to his heels to warn the others, leaving the monk to head on foot for the monastery.

He took to the road and ran as fast as he could. But no sooner was he half-way there than he saw the long convoy in the distance, snaking closer. He knew they were in trouble; there was no way the three of them could fight off hundreds of troops. Their only salvation was to go into the forest to outsmart the army. He ran even faster, but every time he turned his head to watch the convoy, the less optimistic he became of being able to out-manoeuvre the rapidly approaching army.

The army spotted the lone figure on the run, and picked up speed.

He could enter the countryside, but that would slow him down and give him little chance of warning the others. At the risk of getting a bullet at his back, he decided to continue on running along the dirt road. A few more hundred yards and he would reach the safety of their hide-out, and then Alexantiou would decide their next move.

The engines of the advancing trucks grew louder, but they were forced to slow down to overcome the steep hill. They continued at a snail's pace and steadily snaked their way towards him. The convoy must have been a mile long because he could see a never-ending stream of military vehicles appearing one by one from behind the distant bend in the road.

As soon as he saw the familiar surroundings of the hideout, he dived into the bushes and fell down the slope. He tumbled over but managed to grab onto exposed roots to stop him from rolling to the bottom of the treacherous ravine.

Andros and Alexantiou saw Andonis tumbling down the slope and rushed to help him. Immediately, they sensed that something was wrong.

'We are trapped!' cried out Andonis as soon as he got to his feet.

Alexantiou looked across the gorge and spotted the long convoy that was snaking towards their direction but was not sure if they or their hideout had been spotted.

'We have been betrayed!' said Alexantiou apprehensively, 'there is no way of out-running so many troops, we would be pinned down like dogs trying to escape.'

The convoy stopped a few hundred yards away and a stream of soldiers hurriedly jumped off the trucks and took up combat positions throughout the immediate area. They could not see the three *Andartes*, but they knew they would be somewhere around these parts. All they had to do was to search the entire area and flush them out. In a matter of minutes, hundreds of soldiers had begun a thorough search of the valley and nearby hills. Loud voices echoed across the valley as the soldiers systematically moved about in search of their prey and their lair. They knew it would not be far away . . .

Alexantiou and his two friends went into their hideout to consult and come to a decision on their next move. As long as the hideout was not discovered, they were safe, but they knew that their luck would not last for long. Split-second decisions had to be made if they were to save their lives, and not end up like their friends who had perished overnight. The two brothers gazed at their troubled *Mastro* who was trying to evaluate the situation.

After a brief moment, he made up his mind.

'I am doomed either way. If they catch me, they will hang me. I will not give them that pleasure. I shall fight to the end, and I shall die!' he said to his two friends, who were rendered speechless by his decision.

Andonis looked at his brother and realised that he was devastated by the sudden predicament they found themselves in. None of them had ever contemplated that they'd be trapped in such a way. They did not fear death, but now that *Charon* had come knocking at their door thousands of thoughts went through their minds.

'Don't worry brother, our deaths shall fan the flames of freedom.' Andonis said to his worried twin brother.

'No-one shall die, except me . . . ' Alexantiou yelled at them.

'We are staying, like it or not!' Andonis interrupted, determined to stand by his *Mastro*.

'You are not throwing us out, get that into your head!' his brother agreed.

'It is you, who always said to us that, 'there is no greater honour for a man to lay down his life for his country or his friend' . . . We are going nowhere . . .!" Andonis insisted and shouted at his *Mastro* with anger.

'You two must give yourselves up. We are in a no-win situation! You have a family Andros, think of your child as for me, my fiancée would eventually get over it,' Alexantiou said, trying to make his friends give themselves up.

'I have no wife, no fiancée and, not even a dog! I am staying till the end,' Andonis insisted determinedly. 'As for my brother, I agree that he should give himself up.'

'Don't speak for me,' his brother objected, distressed. 'I shall fight with you two!'

'If I have to shoot your legs I shall do so. You are not going to die today!' their *Mastro* stressed, not prepared to see his two young fighters lose their lives.

Alexantiou was very upset, but there was a determined spark in his eyes knowing that he was not going to be hanged by the neck today. He made up his mind to fight on, at all costs. His warm smile had suddenly disappeared from his handsome face, replaced by a serious troubled expression. He looked at his two buddies and he desperately wanted to protect them.

Paying no attention to him, Andonis went to the entrance and saw a group of soldiers coming towards them.

'I can see them coming this way.' he said apprehensively.

The soldiers were moving slowly, thrashing through the bushes in their attempt to find their hide. Their voices were quite loud, and the boys knew the time was approaching for the imminent battle. Alexantiou grabbed his machine-gun and stared at a group of soldiers below the slope. He had also noticed that others were approaching from the left. Both groups were closing in on them.

'You two get out!' he yelled, and ordered his two young fighters to give themselves up.

They would not budge, but positioned themselves at the entrance and aimed their guns towards the approaching enemy. Suddenly, Andonis fired a round of bullets purposely at the approaching soldiers. The shots sent the army into a panic and the troops scattered to find cover.

Their hideout had been discovered, and the soldiers immediately returned the gunfire aimed at their direction.

The *Andartes* had a good field of view, and were able to see all movements below the steep slope. But they were dangerously restricted from seeing army activities above and beyond their hideout, obstructed by the steep slope. They responded to the volley of army bullets, but were pinned down inside their hideout, unable to ascertain their situation properly.

They exchanged fire for more than an hour, without much success. The army was determined to flush them out, maintained steady gunfire and threw many hand-grenades at them. Their hideout began to fall apart. The bushes of the surrounding area were ripped to shreds by the spray of bullets that never seemed to stop. Bullets kept raining down on them from all directions, ricocheting off boulders and rocks with deadly echoing sounds ringing across the mountains.

Alexantiou realised they were in a hopeless situation, and decided it was time for his friends to give up. His riveting black eyes had turned red from the endless explosions that turned the entire area into a quarry of drifting smoke. The strong stench of gunfire became so pungent that breathing became difficult for the three of them.

Suddenly the firing stopped and a loudhailer blasted out: 'The game is up! Give yourselves up, there is no escape!'

The lads did not dare to poke their heads out to ascertain their predicament, afraid that a sniper would pick them off. Trapped, they needed answers and very quickly at that, before it was too late.

'Let's make a break for it.' Andonis suggested.

'Shall we risk it?' their commander asked, looking his friends straight in the eyes. They agreed to take a chance and escape, realising they were all doomed if they remained inside. Without further discussion, Alexantiou picked up a smoke grenade and tossed it outside.

Immediately, dense smoke covered the entire area, and the three of them grabbed their Kalashnikov machine-guns. They let out a volley of bullets across the entrance, but Alexantiou's gun jammed. Desperately he tried to free it, but his gun was too hot and, by the time he managed to get it working again, the dense smoke had cleared.

The sliver of a chance to escape had vanished like the drifting smoke and there was no way out of the hideout. They were completely trapped and surrounded by hundreds of guns pointing directly towards them.

Unable to move, they knew that their fate had been sealed, and Alexantiou demanded that his two fighters gave themselves up. He ordered them to get out, but they both refused. Without hesitating, he picked up his pistol and fired a bullet at Andros' foot.

'Now get out!' he yelled at him. 'Go and bring up your child! Now! You, too, Andonis, help your brother over the slope.'

Andros stumbled and grabbed at his foot which gushed with blood that quickly stained the earth. Andonis was shocked, but he knew why Alexantiou shot his brother. Reluctantly, he obeyed his orders.

He picked up a white cloth and tightened one end on a stick. Helping his brother with one hand, and carrying the stick with the other, he started to leave their hideout.

'I shall never forget you for the rest of my life!' Andonis said.

Tears flooded his red eyes, as he realised this was the last time he would set eyes on his friend and *Mastro*. He saw Alexantiou standing upright with a proud expression written clearly on his face. Dressed in his combat uniform, beret over his black hair, with machine-gun ready in his hands, Andonis knew that his *Mastro* had already accepted death.

'You are wiser than some and braver than others. You are truly a man to love and admire till death.' Andros said to him, while holding his bleeding leg wound.

He fretfully gazed at Alexantiou and begun to bawl his eyes out knowing the ultimate price their *Mastro* was about to pay for the freedom of the country that he loved so much.

'They may take my body but never my soul.' he stated calmly. 'Go you two go, before it's too late!' he then said to them angrily.

Reluctantly, Andonis raised the white flag out of the entrance and waited for a response. The firing stopped instantly, and he waved the flag about as a sign of submission.

'Come out !' the loudhailer blasted across the hillsides.

Andonis and his brother turned and looked at Alexantiou for one last time. 'Come with us.' pleaded Andonis.

'I shall remain here and I shall die.' he said to them, and urged them to move out.

Slowly, his two comrades stumbled to the outside and disappeared from his sight.

He had already succumbed to his fate, and he psyched himself up to face death bravely and not like a coward. 'God, give me courage to die a free man.' he muttered, and crossed himself a few times.

Alexantiou was left on his own surrounded only by crumbling earth falling from the roof of the hideout. Carefully, he looked around and checked his stock-pile of ammunition. There was plenty of it and he could hold on for a long time, before the enemy got to him.

The two *Andartes* were quickly apprehended. Andros had his foot looked at by a medic and was quickly driven away, while his brother was handcuffed and interrogated by a Greek policeman at the side of the road.

Shattered, Andonis told the policeman that Alexantiou was ready to die rather than be captured alive. The British commander realised that he was dealing with a determined fighter and decided to try for one last time to convince Alexantiou to give up.

He roared into the loudhailer warning him to give up, but for his efforts he received a burst of fire from Alexantiou's machine-gun. Everyone realised this lad was not prepared to see reason and the army immediately began a heavy bombardment of the hideout. They fired thousands of bullets and launched a great number of devastating grenades against their enemy.

The news of the stand-off reached everyone's ears and crowds began to gather in sympathy with the *Andartes*. Newspaper reporters had also arrived in droves. They saw the thousands of troops and could not believe how three lads were able to hold up against such a well-equipped army. As time went by the crowds grew larger, but were kept at a distance by the army in fear they may end up with a riot on their hands.

The battle raged on for two hours and, in the process of cross-firing, a soldier lost his life and many others got wounded. At a loss, the army often paused to plan its next move, but one brave soldier had had enough and decided that one lone fighter against the whole army was utter humiliation.

He carefully slid down the slope without being detected and somehow managed to get close to the entrance of the hideout. He pulled the pin out of a grenade and tossed it inside the small cave. A deafening blast followed, accompanied by Alexantiou's return machine-gun fire. The soldier hurriedly climbed up the slope to escape the oncoming bullets.

The army immediately started shooting and hurling endless number of grenades, creating absolute pandemonium over the entire valley. The sky had turned grey from the explosions and spray of gunfire. A cloud of dark smoke lingered between the hills and drifted across the valley, carrying an overpowering stench for miles.

The British commander finally recognised that no response was coming from inside the hideout and ordered his troops to cease firing. He assumed that the lad had perished and the battle was over.

Devastated, Andonis realised that his friend had stopped shooting back, and angrily shouted at the top of his voice: 'Can't you see he is dead?'

The British commander, flushed with success, grabbed him by the scruff of the neck and dragged him across the narrow street.

'Then you go and get his body out,' he shouted at him. He then un-cuffed his hands and pushed him over the slope.

Andonis stumbled and fell, rolling down the slope. He got up . . . looked around and noticed that hundreds of guns were pointing at him. Carefully, he approached the entrance.

'Alexantiou, it's me Andonis! I am coming in!' he shouted, hoping he would get a response from his *Mastro*.

There was no response, and he entered the dark, smoke-filled crumbling hideout. Alexantiou was sprawled on the ground in agony with one of his legs blown apart, but he was still alive. His face was completely black from smoke and his uniform was ripped in shreds. Seeing him in such a state Andonis got panicked. The pool of blood was quickly accumulating under his leg.

'I am done, but not dead yet.' Alexantiou whispered to him.

Andonis inspected his wounded leg and realised his friend was in bad shape. His leg was severed at the ankle and dangled to one side, held only together by his skin. He knew that no one could survive such an injury without immediate medical attention. Andonis grabbed discarded clothing and bandaged the wound as best as he could to minimise the bleeding.

With both his hands covered in warm blood, he angrily approached the entrance and with determination, he shouted at the soldiers who were expecting him to bring out the last remaining *Andartis*.

'There are two of us now, come and get us!' he yelled and frantically started firing Alexantiou's machine-gun at the enemy, who quickly scurried for cover.

The British response was decisive and immediate. The army began shooting at the two *Andartes* completely embarrassed at being out-foxed by this lad. In complete pandemonium the battle raged on with no chance of apprehending the two persistent fighters. They had decided to die for what they believed was their right to defend what was just.

Drastic decisions had to be taken to stop this continuing humiliation of the army. The commander in charge, a burly looking man, got on his radio to discuss the new development with the Governor.

'Burn them out!' the Governor yelled angrily at his army's inadequacy.

The commander in charge immediately ordered a fuel truck to be brought closer to the hideout. At the same time he instructed two helicopters to hover over the hideout and start dumping petrol fuel over the area.

It had already been decided to burn the two lads alive . . .

When the truck got into position, the commander ordered gallons of gasoline to be pumped directly over the hideout. The driver of the truck grabbed the fuel hose and began to gush out gallons of fuel down the slope. Instantly, the entire area began to stink with the evaporating gasoline that quickly drenched the hillside. Once he had finished, the driver reversed the truck to a safe distance.

The trapped lads realised what the British were up to. The fuel quickly began to seep into their cave and in a matter of minutes they were soaked to the skin with it.

'Don't be afraid brother.' Alexantiou said to Andonis, realising their end was near.

'We shall both die for Cyprus.' Andonis answered, accepting his fate and grabbing Alexantiou's hands.

While seated on the ground, they both prayed briefly for one last time. But above all else, they encouraged each other to meet *Charon* straight in the eye and accept their fate. They had chosen when their time was up and not Him.

They had resisted captivity for nearly eight hours and both knew that they could no longer escape or prolong the inevitable.

The British army had had enough, and they were anxious to put this affair behind them for good. Without any sense of emotion, the commander gave the order to set the hill ablaze . . . With a volley of tracer bullets, they fired at the site and instantly a sheet of flames burst into the air.

Andonis' legs and arms immediately caught fire. While there was still some life left in him, Alexantiou, who was engulfed in flames from head to toe, managed to yell at the top of his voice.

'Get out! Save yourself!'

Confused and scared, Andonis flew out realising there was no hope for his commander; his entire body was already consumed by a raging inferno and flames reached the ceiling of their hideout.

No sooner had Andonis reached the outside, than their stockpile of explosives and ammunition detonated and it seemed as if the whole world had blown up. Andonis managed to roll on the ground and was able to put out the flames on his body, but he was quickly apprehended by soldiers who helped to pull him away from the inferno.

Immediately, an evil choking stench and black smoke drifted across the hills. The fire rose to massive heights, burning everything in sight. In a matter of minutes, the wild conflagration was raging throughout the hillsides fanned by the late-afternoon wind and consuming everything in its path.

The crowd and press reporters were horrified by such a barbaric act, and began to yell abuse and throw rocks at the army. But, they were held back by hundreds of soldiers. The army repelled the angry crowds by shooting above their heads to stop them gaining ground.

The conflagration continued all night and no man, woman or child was prepared to leave this hallowed ground, until the final chapter of this inhuman act was completed. They kept vigil and remained awake and prayed all night keeping company with Alexantiou, who chose to sacrifice his life for his country. In their uncomplicated minds, they could not comprehend that such barbarity was possible at the hand of a civilised nation. They cursed the army between clenched teeth in silence. In support of their hero, they held burning candles all night and stared with grief at the death site.

By mid-morning, the fire died out, but not before the entire mountainside was totally consumed by the furious flames. Choking smoke lingered everywhere from the smouldering thickets and woods, and not a single tree was left standing. Soldiers tried many times to enter the hideout that had transformed itself into a kiln, but were unsuccessful; it was too hot to even go near the place.

By noon the next day, they forced Andonis to go and pull the body out.

He went in and found Alexantiou's hideously charred remains. The stench of burned flesh choked him, and he could not help but cry at the sight of the charred body of his friend. One of his legs had been severed from the rest of his body and lay to one side still smouldering, while half of his once handsome face and head had been ripped apart. Andonis wanted to throw up, but managed not to. He attempted to grip the leg that was still attached to his friend's blackened shrivelled corpse, but the instant he pulled it the leg dislocated at the joint and came away.

In a panic, he burst out of the hideout, unable to remain in sight of his dead friend's charred body. Horror-struck, he sat on the ground, and the revolting stench of burning flesh nauseated him. Suddenly, he burst into loud sobs like a frightened child.

The soldiers put back the handcuffs on him and he sat on a boulder with nowhere to go. He was trapped for good and a morbid depression had overcome him. In total shock, he was not able to utter a single word, except to sob his heart out like a child and mutter over and over again:

'Ola-Skata . . . Ola-Skata . . . Ola-Skata . . .'

Between sobs, he noticed Alexantiou's elderly father led up the hill by two armed soldiers. With his balding head bowed, he dragged his feet like a broken man ready to collapse. Without a

230

word, they directed the obedient, elderly man towards the smouldering hideout and down the slope.

Distraught, the old man entered the collapsed entrance of the hideout when suddenly his legs gave way at the sight of the charred body of his son. He burst into a cry of pain and collapsed to the ground. He fainted and lost all sense of reality.

When the old man came round, in a dignified proud manner, he asked for his son's remains so he could bury them in the family plot. But the army arrogantly refused his request as punishment. They did not want this young lad to become a martyr and a symbol of defiance for the liberation of the small island.

Instead, they would bury him among the other unmarked graves of *Eoka* fighters, in the prison grounds of Lefkosia.

The Governor, thrilled by the success of his troops over at Maheras, removed the name of 'Alexantiou' off his wanted list of *Andartes* . . .

CHAPTER THIRTEEN

ALEXIS OPENED HIS eyes and saw smiling faces over him Humbly dressed, a couple in their fifties, together with their two dark-haired boys, were standing next to his bed watching over him. He glanced at the strange faces confused at how he got there . . . The last thing that he could remember was running for his life and holding his injury with one hand.

He gently let his fingers slide under the bed covers and touched his wound. Instead of feeling torn skin, he felt bandages around his waist.

'Where am I?' he asked, bewildered at seeing the faces staring at him.

'He's alive!' the youngest of the boys yelled in Turkish.

'Thank Allah, you are not dead.' the man said to him in broken Greek.

'Where am I?' Alexis asked again, and tried to sit up.

'No! No!' the Turkish woman insisted, in worse Greek than her husband, and gently put her hand on his shoulder to stop him.

'My son found you half dead!' the man said with pride, and lightly stroked his eldest boy's head.

The boy, tall and skinny, smiled at Alexis, proud at having saving his life.

'Are you *Eoka*?' the youngest lad asked, without mincing his words.

Alexis looked at the curly-haired boy who was anxious for his answer, and smiled at him.

'Yes I am *Eoka*!' he said to him.

'I told you so!' the boy shouted at his brother, excited that he was proven correct, and walked out of the room followed by his brother.

The woman tended to his pillow to make him more comfortable, and then went out of the room. Her husband, a fragile-looking man, stayed behind to have a chat with this lad who had nearly died on them on numerous occasions. He pulled up a chair and sat next to the bed, examining Alexis' face eager to find out what had happened to him.

Alexis noticed that the man was missing a few front teeth, but had masses of thick black hair cropped short at the sides, and a thick moustache. His thin face was weather-beaten and evenly tanned, making his eyes sparkle whenever he spoke.

'My name is Imbrahim you are lucky that my son found you. You were nearly dead but thank Allah my nephew the doctor did a good job at stitching you up.'

'How long have I been here?' Alexis asked curiously.

'About three weeks' the man replied earnestly.

Alexis nodded his head in gratitude, and stared into the man's alert black eyes, overwhelmed by the kindness he and his wife had shown towards him.

'We could not let you die. I knew you were one of them *Andartes* lads but don't worry, you are safe here!' Imbrahim assured him, to put his mind at rest.

Alexis looked around the simple room and realised this family was not well off judging from the way they were dressed, and he felt humbled by their devotion to helping a stranger in need. Above all, he was astounded by their human kindness in not handing him over to the authorities for the reward on his head.

The man's wife brought him a bowl of hot egg-lemon soup with rice and chicken. She was a good-looking woman with an attractive face full of life, and was dressed in a traditional Turkish garment that swept the floor. Her head was wrapped in a white embroidered headscarf and from the fringe, over her forehead, a row of colourful, glittering sequins dangled whenever she moved her head. When she smiled, a gold tooth at the right side of her mouth sparkled brilliantly, accentuating her friendly smile.

Her husband helped him sit up.

He felt very weak. The pain around his waist was excruciating and he found it difficult to remain in the same position for long. There was a strange silence in the room and all he could hear was the dreamlike voices of the man's children, playing outside. Their cries sounded like they were coming from a distant but mystical world of make believe.

Imbrahim's wife handed him the soup and gracefully walked out again to attend to her chores, sweeping the floor with her long dress as she went along.

Alexis took the bowl of soup and slowly sipped the warm broth, careful not to spill it over the bed covers. He could feel that a stubbly beard and a moustache had grown over his face, while his hair had grown below his earlobes. His whole body was weak and he hardly had enough strength even to sip his soup. His arms weighed a ton, and he was unable to focus his sight without feeling his eyelids wanting to close from tiredness. He could tell that he was in a desperate state and only proper convalescing would bring him back to health.

'Are you not scared, harbouring an *Eoka* fugitive?' Alexis asked his saviour, concerned for his safety.

'We live in complete isolation in these parts of the woods, no-one ever comes here.' The man explained. 'I am a shepherd and these mountains are my life. I cannot be cooped up in villages and towns. That's not for me or my family. If you had lived long enough with nature you too would appreciate what life is all about and would then realise that life is most precious and Allah's gift to man. What man does with such a gift is up to him. There are those who cling to life at all costs others squander it and there are those who preserve life in harmony with nature. I am a free man in these forests and I choose to preserve life. You are safe with us!'

Alexis listened to the devout Moslem and, as weak as he was, he realised that this man's attitude to life was well balanced and felt a comforting sense of security from this family. They might be Turks but for him, they were no different from others, irrespective of their creed. They were simply good, honest people with big hearts and he was fortunate they had found him. If poverty has no envy, then this man had no enemies at all and he could live a blissful life of his own choosing without interference from anybody.

Within two weeks, Alexis was able to move about. There was a large scar across the side of his stomach that was still tender and he could hardly touch it without pain. He was beginning to regain his strength and felt totally obliged to the Imbrahim family. He didn't know how he could repay them for the kindness they had shown him. Without them, he would certainly have been found dead in a ravine, or his mangled body ripped to shreds by nocturnal predators.

Examining himself in a mirror, he no longer recognised the Alexis he once knew, the one full of life and vigour, who joked, laughed and sang at the top of his voice with his friends at their *Limery*. He suddenly felt alone, an exposed fugitive with a price on his head. He felt so vulnerable that he began to assume that everyone was his enemy. His face got thinner and he lost weight, while his once vibrant eyes appeared weak and tired. His handsome face lost its youthfulness, which was replaced by a hardened look, one that had seen death straight in the eyes many times over. He began to hate himself for killing others. The only way he could rationalise or justify the killings was that they were necessary—for the freedom of his country!

The sweet bloom of youth had disappeared forever, not only from his face but also from his heart. He was wounded physically and mentally and, with those injuries combined, he could not but feel angry with himself for being so naïve to have chosen to forsake all that was decent and honourable in his life. The price of freedom was high indeed, and he was just beginning to realise how demanding such a price was by the loss of his own soul. He was reconciled to the fact that liberation was a worthy cause and he had to continue to fight the enemy as his friends had done even with the possibility of losing his own life. They called him from beyond the grave to avenge and honour their deaths, if only until liberation.

He constantly thought of his friends, but the news of Alexantiou's death shook him so badly that he did not eat for two days, much to the dismay of Imbrahim's wife, who tried to rejuvenate him by cooking fresh poultry and the best cuts of tender lamb for him.

He often sat alone on a large boulder overlooking the mountain peaks across the isolated valley, totally engrossed in his own thoughts. His memory drifted remembering the life he had enjoyed with his pals. Somehow, he could not believe that he would never see them again. It wasn't long ago since they were walking towards Scara, full of life and determination, believing they were superhuman and everything was within their reach. Yiannis' constant melody haunted him, and Aris' vibrant blue eyes never left his mind once. But it was Alexantiou's death that touched his most sensitive feelings when he thought of him being burned alive. He compared his death with Petros' electrocution on their very first mission, and those terrible memories fused within his mind forever and became an integral part of his young life.

Imbrahim's kids kept him company while their father was out grazing the animals. The youngsters could hardly speak a word of Greek, but that did not stop them from trying to communicate with him by using hand gestures. They took it upon themselves to show him around the area, and each day they dragged him along into the forest and valley that spread for miles. Their quaint two-room house was perched amidst lush, timeless, tall pine and cypress trees that overlooked the most wonderful landscape one could ever wish to see. There was an everlasting hush day and night, except for the noisy cries of crows and occasional owls that echoed across the green valley. The eagles glided gracefully over the massive mountain peaks and were often seen to dive, to capture some unsuspecting prey and make a meal out of it.

The days went by and Alexis felt well enough to travel. He was anxious to leave this isolated place and cease to be a further burden on the impoverished family who had saved him from certain death. He wanted to send word to his people and let them know of his fate, especially to the *Eoka* Leader so that he could decide his next assignment. He was sure everyone would have assumed him dead by now.

Determined to make a move he asked Imbrahim to make contact with Ahmet. But the journey meant a day's bus ride to Varoshia from the nearest village over the other side of the mountain. One bright morning his Turkish saviour rode his mule and trotted down the hillside to make contact with Ahmet.

He was away forever it seemed, and his sons waited impatiently for his return, eager to find out what presents he might have brought back. For two days they pinned their eyes on the valley below, veiled over in wild flowers, hoping to catch sight of him returning.

On the third afternoon, the familiar outline image of their father riding his mule appeared in the distance, with others walking alongside him. Jubilantly, his eldest son galloped like a young stallion along the steep, winding, narrow footpath to greet him. His young brother instantly followed behind, but his legs were too small to catch up and he started calling his brother to slow down.

Alexis heard the boys' chirping voices and gazed at them running towards their father. He noticed that others were walking beside him, but could not distinguish who they were. He had a feeling that one might be Ahmet.

As they approached, he recognised Ahmet's strong physique, and right next to him walked Spyros, tall and upright, surpassing Ahmet's height by at least six inches. At the other side of the mule walked his stocky friend Michalaki, who did not want to miss this opportunity of seeing his pal after so many months.

Full of excitement at being about to meet up with his faithful pals, he began to walk slowly down the stone-strewn footpath, eager to meet them half-way.

The instant they clapped eyes on him, the three of them spontaneously sprinted up the hill, shouting his name and simultaneously bursting into rapturous laughter. They waved their hands in absolute jubilation.

Spyros, with his long legs, was the first to reach his lost friend, and instantly wrapped both his arms around him and gave him a lingering heartfelt embrace. He held him tightly in a strong bear-hug refusing to let go of him, and not uttering a single word, completely overwhelmed.

Ahmet pushed Spyros away, and took hold of his childhood friend and brother, and nearly burst into tears.

'Alexis my dear friend, what have they done to you?' Ahmet said to him, and stared into his tired brown eyes, noticing how much weight he had lost.

'I am fine Ahmet, it's only a *bora* and shall soon pass.' Alexis brushed his concern aside, overjoyed that the group was together again.

As soon as Michalaki put his arms around his friend, he began to bawl his eyes out, so mixed were his emotions.

'I don't care what you think, I can cry if I want to!' he warned the others, and furrowed his brows like two swords crossing each other in anticipation of them making fun of his sensitivity.

'It's alright Michalaki, you are allowed to cry! I shall cry with you from joy!' Alexis said, and gave his buddy a loud kiss on his chubby cheek, tasting the tears with his lips. He put one arm around his shoulder and both started to walk for the house.

Their jovial reunion was the happiest moment in Alexis' life and for a moment he forgot his own predicament. Surrounded by his pals, he felt at peace with himself and a sense of security had overcome him. They slowly trekked up the steep hill laughing and joking with one another. He didn't stop chatting, and talked about anything that came into his mind. These were rare cherished moments, and they all wanted to make the most of this special reunion.

They reached Imbrahim's house and everyone helped to unload the laden mule. Alexis' parents had sent baskets packed with food and many gifts to Imbrahim and his family, in appreciation and deep gratitude for saving their son's life. They had sent word through Ahmet that they would be forever indebted to them, as long as there was any breath left in their lungs.

After a hefty meal, the entire household congregated in the yard under a glorious moonlight to discuss the latest developments and their personal experiences of the last few months.

Alexis listened to his jovial friends and wished these moments would never end. But this was not to be, not at least until the struggle came to an end. Spyros had arranged a safe house for him, until his fate was decided by the Leader. He was sure he would end up in the mountains again, and continue the life of an *Andartis* in some other part of the island.

Alexis craved to see his family and meet up with Xanthia to give her the longest kiss ever, but above all else, he was anxious to wrap his arms around his traumatised mother and comfort her. Ahmet told him that the entire neighbourhood had taken him for dead, and they had even held a church service for him. The prospect of that reality had transformed his mother's life forever, and each day she dragged her heavy feet to the local church to pray and plead with *Panayia* that no harm would come to her other two children.

The lads were eager to make a move, not wanting to waste time. But at the same time they did not want to risk travelling in daylight and had decided to stay up all night. They killed time by reminiscing about the past and *Eoka* exploits until it was time to leave.

At three o'clock in the morning, they bade farewell to Imbrahim's family and the four of them trailed down the steep mountain to reach Spyros' car. Once inside, Spyros headed jubilantly straight for Varoshia.

They drove without incident for two hours through isolated, rural roads, and felt lucky they did not come face to face with the British army or sudden road blocks. At daybreak, they reached the outskirts of the ancient ruins of Salamina. From this point on the journey posed a greater danger of detection by the sudden appearance of military or Turkish patrols, being in such close proximity to the Walls and highly populated areas.

They were turning the final bend of the long asphalt road, and Alexis could feel the salty breeze coming from the nearby sea. He could faintly make out the monastery of Apostolos Varnavas on his right, and recalled the experience he had shared with the three elderly monks. He also remembered Hambi's strong convictions and discussion they shared together on his way to join the *Andartes*.

He looked towards the direction of the monastery and visualised the three pious brothers, dressed in their long white gowns, feeding their flock of hens in complete isolation and talking softly with one another. He recollected the day he knocked at the door of their monastery as a scared, hunted boy, but that was a long time ago. He was now a seasoned fighter and no longer a scared boy, but a man who had learned the art of killing others for an elusive dream. Fate had brought him close to those kind monks again, now no longer a boy or an idealist, but one who began to see things the way they were. For him, even God appeared to be spurious, if there was a God, he would not impel people to be so cruel and selfish, but rather he would have chosen to make people live in harmony and love one another instead, he had created a monster! He didn't know what to believe any more, and gazed at the distant monastery with great respect for the monks' blind faith and dedication to God and His Creation.

Spyros turned into a narrow road overrun by dense, wild acacia bushes adorned with masses of scented flowers that blanketed the roaming sand dunes as far as the eye could see. The profusion of yellow fluffy blooms was blinding against the morning sunlight, and hundreds of bees flew tirelessly from one flower to the other, sucking the sweet nectar.

He parked the car at the very end of the sand-covered driveway, close to the shoreline. They decided that Alexis should remain in hiding until they checked out the road ahead in case there was a roadblock.

Alexis got out of the car and saw his friends drive off at great speed towards the main road.

With time to kill, he walked in complete isolation towards the shoreline and sat on top of a sand dune, watching the morning waves trying to rise and surge against the sandy shore. The crystal clear, blue sea always captured his imagination, and he listened to the swirling, rhythmic sound of crashing waves. He had missed the waterfront and wanted to make the most of it while he could, unsure when he would get another chance to breathe fresh ozone again.

He sat there for a very long time, waiting for the others to show up. But there was no sign of them which made him anxious wondering what was taking them so long. His solitary thoughts were interrupted by the sound of bushes moving, and he looked around to see who was making this noise at such an early hour.

He stood up and gazed across the acacias, but saw nobody. The sound was getting louder and he felt uneasy, thinking that whoever was approaching were not his friends, but strangers. His immediate reaction was to conceal himself in the thicket, and he started to walk up the sand dune when he was spotted by a lone figure carrying a rattan weaved basket.

It was too late, and he decided to change his tactic. 'Yiasou!' he yelled out in greeting to the stranger.

'Yiasou!' replied a small man, returning his gesture. 'What are you doing here?' he asked with curiosity in a high-pitched voice, surprised to see the lad.

'Waiting . . .!' Alexis said to him.

'For a girl?' he asked, and came to where Alexis was standing.

'How did you know?'

'I am here every morning in search of asparagus and believe me I see plenty of hanky-panky going on among them bushes, enough to last me a lifetime.' the dark-haired, haggard man said to the young stranger.

'Yes, this is a lover's den.' Alexis joked with the man, who had two shifty eyes that never let him out of their sight.

He looked at Alexis and frowned, trying to remember something, but could not put his finger on where he met this lad before.

'Do I know you from somewhere?' he asked.

'I don't think so.' Alexis answered, trying to fob him off.

'You lads all look the same, I better leave you before she shows up I will not come back this way' the small man said.

He walked away trying his hardest to remember where he had seen this lad before. He nodded his head, and disappeared into the thick bushes.

Alexis was relieved he had got rid of him before the others showed up. He was getting anxious to reach the safe house, so he could feel secure again among friends, rather than being so exposed. He didn't have much longer to wait; the noise of an oncoming car prompted him to look out. Relief was close at hand.

Spyros' old car was approaching slowly towards him. He went and stood in the middle of the road until the car came to a halt. His pals got out of the car and did not look very happy.

'There is a high security alert and there are blockades everywhere,' Ahmet said to him, with a worried expression on his dark face. His curly hair was wind-swept and half of his shirt was untucked and blowing about by the gusts of wind coming from the sea.

'There are Turkish riots.' Michalaki explained.

'What happened? Alexis asked.

'We don't know exactly but apparently someone put a bomb outside the Turkish Government's information office in Lefkosia and the Turks, using this as a pretext, went on a rampage destroying Greek shops, setting them on fire, looting and attacking civilians across the island. Greek shopkeepers were killed by thugs, while Turkish policemen protected by the British army were inciting the hordes to demand partition. There is mayhem throughout every major city' Spyros explained in detail.

'Stupid idiots they are brainwashed by the English.' Ahmet said, feeling very disturbed by the brutal actions of his Turkish compatriots.

'It can't be *Eoka* that planted the bomb, it's forbidden to do so.' Alexis stated.

'*Volkan* I am sure it was *Volkan*.' said Michalaki sure of his assessment.

'Whatever happens you must stay here until we come for you tomorrow.' Spyros said to Alexis. 'We have brought you food, water and couple of blankets. I think you should hide among the ruins of Salamina, no-one ever goes there, and it's a good hiding place.' he then suggested, anxious about his friend's safety.

'Then I shall hide there, I am used to sleeping rough!' he said to them decisively. He felt devastated at being so close to his family and yet, he was not about to see them.

They all proceeded to the ruins, and with every step forward, their feet sank deep into the soft, golden sand.

Within five minutes, they reached the ancient ruins of Salamina with its tall marble pillars and columns surrounding the *palestra*. A great number of columns were lying on the ground, while other stones were in fact broken down walls encircled by piles of dug-out sand to expose the ruins that had survived for thousands of years.

The lads climbed down the shifting sand and found themselves in the middle of the ruins. At the far end, there was a small covered, ancient bathhouse that offered cover and protection against the elements. They all agreed the niche was a perfect hiding place for him, and one by one they entered the cave-like alcove made up of solid but worn-out blocks of chiselled stones.

The four of them sat around for a while until they decided to make a move in case the unattended car attracted attention. His friends got up and left.

Alexis found himself on his own once again. He looked around the ruins and let his imagination run riot about the people who once roamed freely within this special place that had survived through time, and eons past. He considered these ancient ruins as part of his roots and felt proud of the indubitable evidence of his Hellenic linage. It was proof that, over two thousand years ago, a great number of Achaean Greeks had settled on the island shortly after the Trojan War. With their arrival, they brought the Greek spirit and culture that soon flourished across the land. These silent stone remnants scattered across the heaps of sand, spoke out clearly that Cyprus had always been a Greek nation, irrespective of being colonised by countless rulers. They had come and gone with one purpose in mind; to conquer and plunder the small island.

For fifteen centuries Salamina had been the capital of the island, and had seen glory, power and splendour unsurpassed by all others. It enjoyed respect and became one of the main cities for commerce, intrigue, betrayal and power-struggle of many would-be kings. A defeated Nicocreon, the last king of Salamina, committed suicide together with his entire family here, while the greatest king of all, Evagoras, had united all petty kingdoms on the island. He raised a determined army and liberated the island from the mighty expanding Persian Empire.

In ancient times, this buried city of Salamina was bustling with activity and sprawled for miles across the plains. It also offered one of the greatest harbours for commerce known to man. It enjoyed sanitation and fresh water viaducts, public baths, temples and a great three-sided colonnaded *palestra* for games, complete with porticos and a lively *Agora*, whilst the grand palace of Salamina had become a palace of envy.

Like all empires that sooner or later diminish into oblivion, Salamina had also paid a similar price. Destroyed by earthquakes, a great fire and by seas of shifting sands blown in from the Karpasia plains, had contributed to sealing the capital's fate forever. In due course it was abandoned and left to be claimed by the angry sea through, swelling waves and flooding. Evidence of Salamina's earlier period now rests intact deep below the seabed, protected by the azure waters for future generations to reflect upon.

As always, remembering the past unlocks doorways to the future, and Salamina spoke out clearly to those who care. The present ruins speak of a bygone era for people to ponder and wonder about this city with ample tangible evidence of a glorious past inscribed on marble slabs, mosaics, frescoes, amphora, fallen walls and broken columns. Subterranean crypts and tombs overwhelmed by intricate jewellery, rare precious stones and gold, cram the nearby necropolis at the outskirts of Enkomi. But now, the endless rolling sand-dunes heaving with mimosa have finally claimed the city as their own.

Alexis pondered about this place and its people for a long time, but the scorching mid-afternoon sun made him feel tired and, with nothing better to do, he decided to take a nap. He spread the blankets on the hard stone floor and, after a few twists and turns he soon fell asleep, overcome by tiredness and the pleasant warmth of the stone enclosure.

He didn't know how long he had lain there, but as in a dream he was awoken by the faint sound of a girl's voice calling his name. He jumped up and looked at his watch . . . it was past eight o'clock and he could not believe that he had slept for so long. Cautiously, he tried to listen, but the girl persisted, calling his name softly.

'Alexis, it's me Xanthia.' the girl continued whispering.

Realising Xanthia was outside, he walked out of the dark enclosure and saw his beloved standing at the edge of the *palestra* searching for him and looking in all directions around the ruins.

He could not believe his eyes: there she was . . . wearing her long, white dress that swept the sand, looking like a young Greek goddess in the middle of her temple. Was he dreaming, or was that beautiful slender girl with long flowing hair, the girl he loved and had missed for so many months. He had craved for such a moment, forever it seemed, and now that she had appeared standing there, he was lost for words. The mere sight of her made him feel alive and all he could do was simply to call out her name.

Hearing his voice, Xanthia turned and saw him standing at the top of the sand-dune in his white shirt flapping against the sea breeze. In the background, the ancient walls cast a dark shadow across his face, but Xanthia knew the boy standing there was the love of her life.

'Alexis!' she called at the top of her voice, and started to run towards him.

He rushed in leaps and bounds towards her, overwhelmed with joy. They met halfway across the *palestra* and she instantly flung herself onto him, squeezing him as hard as she could. She joyfully embarked on an endless kissing expedition by smothering his face with her soft lips and crying at the same time in utter bliss. She mumbled unclear words to him between sobs, while he began to kiss her eyes, her forehead, her lips, and her long hair. He held her tight, refusing to let go of her in case he was only dreaming. He had yearned for her kisses for such a long time it was hard to believe that she was not an apparition brought about by his desire for her while he was asleep. It was not an illusion, he was embracing the girl that he loved, and suddenly everything seemed so beautiful, and life really meant something. He held her tighter, feeling her soft body becoming one with his.

Entwined in a tight embrace, they remained standing for a long time in the middle of the *palestra*, refusing to let go of each other. Xanthia never stopped crying, and now that she held the love of her life in her arms she refused to release him from her clutches in case she lost him again.

A sudden dazzling sunset, with brilliant, changing colours was gloriously sinking into the azure waters, making room for nocturnal creatures to rule the night sky. Briefly, they relaxed their hold on one another, and in profound joy stared at the beautiful sight. They exchanged a smile, gazing into each other's starry eyes, overwhelmed with wild passion, and both recognised in unspoken words that this was to be their evening together; one that would be embedded in their memories for all eternity.

Holding hands, they walked slowly towards the hideout and away from prying eyes. Inside, they sat on the blankets, huddled together tightly with their backs resting against the stone-wall, chatting away like two young schoolchildren.

They had so many things to say to each other, but their emotions and desires over-shadowed their words and they continued hugging and kissing passionately, without uttering a word. Their breathing became a sensual battle of desire and both found it impossible to curb their feelings. In the seclusion of their ancient hideaway, they touched each other, oblivious to their surroundings.

Xanthia recognized that this was the night she yearned to lose her virginity, and she had contemplated every detail of such a prospect while riding here to meet him. The moment Ahmet had disclosed Alexis hiding place to her, no power in the world could hold her back from being with him. Now that he held her in his strong arms, she felt powerless and could not wait to become his.

'Let me see your injury.' Xanthia said to him and pulled his white shirt out of his trousers.

She leaned her head close to his stomach, allowing her long hair to fall over her petite face. He felt her shiny mane tickle his belly, and he began to stroke her hair gently while her warm, soft fingers wandered gently over his scars. She looked at his scar and kissed it once with her warm lips.

'God bless the Turkish family that took care of you, my love!' she said, shocked at the size of his scar.

'They were kind people Xanthia and very special.'

'Special? No! They were God's angels, sent from heaven to save you, so we can have a life together.' she said, with sincerity.

She looked up and gazed at him with fire in her doe-like eyes, gave him a kiss on the lips and then lowered her head again over his belly and repeatedly kissed his wound.

He felt her soft lips across his stomach, and a wonderful sensation flashed through his body. He knew precisely what was about to happen.

'We made a vow, remember?' he managed to say, and got hold of her smooth face with both hands. He gently leaned over and kissed her eyes and forehead.

'Sometimes, vows are meant to be broken.' she said to him, breathing heavily. She was not prepared to wait much longer and stood up, leaving Alexis sitting on the floor watching her.

She slowly undid one by one the front buttons of her white dress, unsheathing her delicate, cleavage. In the process of undressing, one of her breasts popped out and bounced gently. Droplets of sweat trickled down her firm breasts, while her eyes gleamed with passion, overwhelmed with desire. Alexis looked at his seductive goddess and felt consumed at the prospect of making love to her.

She was more than ready for what she had dreamed about, and with no inhibitions she gently let her dress fall around her bare feet. Almost naked, in only her underwear she stood in front of Alexis, determined to give herself to him completely. Without uttering a word, she bent down and removed her embroidered underwear and, like a young, naked goddess, with firm tight buttocks and long shapely legs, she totally exposed herself to him in readiness to be ravished by the boy she had chosen to love forever.

Her masses of flowing jet-black hair draped gently over her straight back, and hung loosely down to her slim waist. With one of her customary quick jerks of her head, she thrust back the strands that covered her eyes. She gazed directly into his brown eyes, and sensed that he was as eager as she was to passionately entwine in each other's arms and quench their lust. She was offering him the most precious gift a girl could give to the man she loved; her virginity.

'Release me from my virginity Alexis, for I don't know what may become of us . . .!' she said softly to him.

Overwhelmed by the beautiful, naked sight of Xanthia, he stood up and wrapped both his arms around the contour of her soft body. He squeezed her gently, and his nostrils quivered, intoxicated by the pleasant scent of her smooth skin. He pressed tightly against her firm, jutting breasts. Her dark nipples hardened, and he leaned over and gave them a soft lingering kiss each, as if to say, 'everything will be all right'. His warm lips kissing her nipples had sent her into ecstasy and slowly he removed his clothing.

Suddenly, sunset's last burst of light flooded the alcove, and in a blinding brilliance the sun splashed on their entangled, naked bodies. They remained standing in each other's arms without a stitch of clothing, naked, like the first day they were born. Wrapped in a tight embrace, they were reluctant to let go, and squeezed each other even harder. Alexis felt his erect penis touching her bare skin, and was anxious to let nature take its course.

'*Agapie mou*, be gentle with me.' She whispered softly, and placed her cheek against his, tickling his face with her long eyelashes.

For her, all this was a new experience. She didn't know what to expect or do, but her hormones were in utter turmoil and they dictated her every movement and lustful behaviour. She carefully lay on the blankets while gazing at Alexis' youthful, lean body, overwhelmed by his bulging muscles.

For a high-spirited girl she had suddenly lost the urge to talk, overcome by desire. Like a cooing dove, she lay there on the floor in anticipation of his next move.

He lay beside her and stroked her smooth curved body. His gentle touch caused her to stir like a snake. Carefully, he leaned over her, feeling her warm body and legs becoming one with his. Restlessly, she lolled on the blanket and sensed that her temperature was rising in anticipation of what was about to happen. He could no longer wait and carefully guided his penis towards her private parts.

245

'I shall be gentle.' he whispered in her ear, and kissed her lips passionately.

'Do whatever you wish with me, I am forever yours.' She muttered, and submissively opened her shapely legs wider, feeling his legs between hers gently stroking the smooth skin of her own legs.

With a sensual gaze, she stared straight into his brown eyes in total surrender.

She was transported into a strange world, one full of ecstasy, desire, and lustfulness. All of a sudden, she experienced a completely new sensation the instant Alexis penetrated her. He gently pushed into her with great care so as not to hurt her, and she was utterly lost in a new emotional hurricane.

With eyes wide open, she wrapped both of her arms around his lean body and moved her hips to help him penetrate deeper but at first her hymen remained intact. Overwhelmed by passion, they both moved about in unison when, without warning, she abruptly felt his hard penis thrusting in gentle strokes deeply inside her. Their pelvises fused, bone against bone, and neither wanted to separate from this most wonderful position. Heaven had cast a stupendously beautiful cloud over them, and both were submerged in a world of total bliss, brought about by pure love and innocent desire.

'Hold me tight my love . . .' she mumbled, and let out a soft sound of ecstasy, realising she was no longer a virgin.

She grabbed him and dug her nails into his masculine back and held him tight, as tight as her delicate hands could manage and proceeded to move her soft hips in rhythm with Alexis' thrusts, wanting to feel her lover deeper inside her. With their temperatures rising, they both experienced a wonderful ecstatic feeling and sweat bathed their naked bodies.

Suddenly, she dug her nails into his back, and gave way to a multiple orgasm, murmuring in complete ecstasy and triggering Alexis' penis to explode in spasms and violently erupt deep inside her.

Feeling his precious juices inside her, she pushed harder and grabbed both of his firm buttocks with her hands. With fingers clenched into his skin, she remained motionless, wanting to absorb every drop of him deep within her. That was his gift to her, and no one could deprive her of a single drop of it. Passionately she held him even tighter to make sure he was completely spent.

They remained in that same position for a long time, unwilling to separate from one another, and after a brief pause they instinctively began to make love again. By the time they had finished, they were utterly exhausted and were both bathed in sweat. They lay quietly in each other's arms, in total exhilaration.

For a bubbly, talkative girl, she was suddenly lost for words . . .

'I never knew it could be so wonderful.' she finally said to him, smiling, and stroked his thick hair and moustache.

When she smiled, her face lit up casting a gentle, tempting aura about her, and Alexis touched it to see if it was real or not. Her vivid eyes squinted, and he leaned over and kissed them. His whole world had collapsed in her soft bosom, and for the first time he recognised how much he had missed her. She cooed with profound joy.

Contented, she half-closed her eyes, spread her slender arms out like an eagle and tried to say something to him.

'It was not painful.' She began to say while stoking the dimple at his cheek.

'Hush, my precious one.' Alexis interrupted her, and placed his finger on her lips.

'It didn't hurt as much I thought it would. It was wonderful . . .!' Xanthia repeated again, and bit his finger tenderly. She turned and kissed him as if to say 'thank you, for making me a woman.'

They both lay there in total bliss, but time waits for no man and it was getting quite late. She had to get home, before her parents began to worry about her whereabouts. As their only child, they were always concerned, in case she was captured and sent to a detention camp for some reason.

By ten o'clock she had got on her bicycle, taking with her the bloodstained blanket. She wanted to keep it, and planned never to wash it.

'This is mine.' she said to him. 'I shall keep it forever.'

After more hugs and kisses, she was on her way home, content, and overwhelmed with happiness for sharing those blissful moments with the love of her life.

Following his lonely moon-shadow, Alexis walked back to the hideout and sat himself on the ground by the entrance. In complete isolation, he gazed into the night immersed in wonderful thoughts. He had never felt happier. For the first time in his young life, he came to realise what heaven was all about. Suddenly, life was worth living.

CHAPTER FOURTEEN

ALEXIS BEGAN TO leap in slow motion, intoxicated by the events of the evening. The endless fields ahead appeared as soft as cotton, and were dazzling with a blinding white brilliance which caused him to squint. He took long strides, plunged into the fields facing him and laughed rapturously, while the peculiar whiteness below his feet instantly scattered and floated into the air. Without reason, his laughter suddenly seemed to transform itself into chirping, in harmony with the sound of hundreds of birds that fluttered around this strange, mystical place. At every step forward his feet sank gently into the white fluffy cotton-like substance, and he felt exhilarated. In the far distance, across the pallid emptiness, he detected a small, barren, and remote hill engulfed by the same blinding brilliance and at the very top, a single tree stood out on its own, with its branches adorned by what seemed like glittering tinkling jewels that sparkled in the sun's rays. They tinkled constantly and produced a weird and wonderful magical sound he had never heard before in his life. He could hear the titillating sharp echoes reverberating across the sky, yet they seemed to come from nowhere specifically. The entire area turned blinding white and at the base of the solitary tree, he took a glimpse of his beloved Xanthia. Draped in her white long dress, she was leaning seductively against the trunk of the tree waiting for him. He felt good and began to hasten his pace to reach her. He couldn't help it but smile to himself at meeting up with her so soon after their passionate encounter. A gentle breeze rose out of nowhere, forcing the white fluff to roll gently over the surface of the roaming hill. Like a siren, Xanthia called his name in a mesmerizing voice and he quickened his ascent to reach her. Ecstatically he began to climb the hill. She had both of her arms stretched out, yearning to embrace him. He smiled at her persistence and leaped forward but as soon as he got within touching distance of her slender arms, the strange tree instantly vanished from his sight, taking his loved one with it. All of a sudden, the dazzling white brilliance encompassing the hill disappeared, and in a flash, it was replaced by a dark threatening abyss inundated by millions of slithering snakes. They coiled, looped and twisted trying to climb over one another. The bright sky instantaneously turned into a grim darkness with thick churning clouds. They crashed with one another forcing the loudest thunder and thunderbolts to rumble across the frightening skies.

Feeling at a total loss he jumped over the writhing slimy snakes crushing them with his feet. They hissed and thrust their long tongues out, some trying to dig their fangs into his legs. He screamed in shock and the snakes became frantic and began to slither on top of one another. There was no escape. He hopped over the deadly gliding snakes in search of a clearing, but there was none in sight all he could see was an endless sea of shiny snakes, packed like sardines all the way down the hill forming a massive, slippery carpet. He was surrounded by them and could hardly move, he even tried to fly but it was no use . . .! Standing at the top of the mount encircled by an army of evil creatures, he realised there was no escape. A sudden downpour was released from the heavens above and he found himself plummeting and sliding over the slippery snakes. With no place to hide he was instantly soaked to the bone. Across the dark sky he noticed a helicopter between the gloomy clouds flying low coming fast towards him. A sense of relief had overcome him at the prospect of making his escape from this bizarre place. The loudhailer of the noisy helicopter burst out in a deafening roar; 'You are trapped'.

He woke up in a cold sweat, and wiped his forehead relieved that he was only dreaming and gazed out of the hideout's opening. The blinding morning sun bathed the interior of the small cave. Outside, he observed that the yellow flowers of acacias sparkled in the bright sunshine. Everything seemed calm and peaceful.

'We warn you, come out!' the loudhailer blasted again.

Realising that he was no longer dreaming, and that soldiers were outside, he started to feel weak at the knees sensing that his end was near. He had no weapons and was sure the entire area was teeming with armed soldiers. How had the army learned of his whereabouts? Only his close friends knew his hideout. Perplexed, he wasn't sure what to do, the Devil had many legs and he could not escape his clutches.

'Alexis, this is your last chance, come out. Now!' a Turkish man's voice shouted in broken Greek, 'if not, we shall blast you out.'

Hearing his name, he knew that he was trapped in a snare. After so many months in hiding and on the run, his luck ran out and finally there was no way of escape. Without much further thought, defeated, he placed both hands over his head and walked slowly out of the hideout.

The morning sun blinded his sight temporarily, but he could make out that he was surrounded by hundreds of troops, hidden among the acacias and with guns pointing directly at him. Across the blue waters, he spotted two gunboats blocking a possible escape route. Everywhere he turned, there were troops ready to pounce on him.

He accepted defeat and walked a little further with both hands tightly on his head.

Two burly soldiers walked up the sandy slope pointing their pistols directly at him with fingers on the triggers.

The game was over the hunter had captured its prey. Under gunpoint, they forced him to lie flat on the warm sand. One of the soldiers pressed his face deep into the soft sand with his boot and held it there. Another entered the hideout but found nothing except for one blanket and some food.

'There is nothing here!' the soldier yelled out aloud, prompting the others to come out, one by one, from their hiding places.

Soon the entire area was stormed by troops and he was forced at gunpoint to walk through the thick acacia bushes towards the asphalt road. Once they reached the road, they bundled him in a jeep and forced him to lie flat with his face on the hot metal deck of the vehicle. Four other soldiers climbed up and sat opposite each other with their rifles pointing directly at him. They did not take their eyes off him for a single moment, he was a valued fugitive. The radio operator was talking very fast in a heavy English accent and Alexis could not understand a single word, except for 'Eoka and Andartis.'

Within a few minutes the entire convoy sped towards Varoshia. Passers-by wondered why the convoy was going so fast, but as soon as they took a glimpse of the dark-haired lad at the back of the jeep, they knew what had happened; one of their boys had been captured. They were not surprised! Apprehending the youth had become a daily occurrence and they had got used to such sights. All they could do was to curse the army between their clenched teeth, and hate them even more for incarcerating their boys and girls.

Alexis had noticed the tall eucalyptus trees planted in a straight colonnade alongside the familiar road, forming a long, leafy arcade. He thought of Xanthia who lived close-by, just beyond the dotted line of these trees and felt shattered. From being the happiest day of his life, the day had turned out to be a nightmare and a day of hell.

By ten o'clock in the morning the convoy had dispersed into a military compound that stretched as far as the eyes could see, directly across from the main round-about of the ancient Walls . . .

*   *   *

Two hours earlier, Alexis' house had been in turmoil. The entire family was overwhelmed with excitement at getting the long-awaited chance finally to see Alexis. It was more than a year ago since he became a fugitive, and when Ahmet had told them that he was alive and well, no one could hold them back from seeing him.

Like a busy bee, Kyra-Soteria paced up and down, anxious to get going to see her long lost son. She had often heard of his exploits and regularly received word through his friends that he was well, but since Scara, she had been completely in the dark and went into mourning, wearing black from head to toe. Today, she threw those clothes in a bundle out into the rear yard, and burned her horrid black shawl and long dress. She never wanted to set eyes on them ever again, for they represented nothing but death in the family. Today, she was going to see her Alexis, and she was going to kiss him like never before and stroke his thick hair; she might even burst into a river of tears. For sure she would cry and there was no one to stop her crying from happiness. As a mother she was entitled to shed plump tears to her heart's desire.

Her son's absence had taken its toll on her. Overnight, her hair had practically turned white and endless wrinkles marked her gentle face. Her kind eyes had sunk deeper into their sockets and she had put on weight through depression; worst of all, she had to cope with a constant excruciating pain in her heavy legs. She endured the physical pain, but the pain of a broken heart was harder to bear. That was all over now, happiness and joy was round the corner and she could not wait to put her arms around her son and smile with joy.

Yiorkis had not changed much, maybe a little greyer and less talkative, but he retained his upright posture and put all his effort and energy into his work, as a way of forgetting the loss of his son. He didn't go to work that morning and allowed his helper to open up the store. He wandered in the house like a lost sheep, not knowing what to do to kill time. He fiddled about in his garden, pulling the odd weed out, but he had no enthusiasm for gardening and paced about, waiting for Ahmet to stop messing about with his car so they could take off.

Their daughter was in high spirits and happily rushed about the house humming a well-known tune in a jovial mood at the prospect of seeing her brother. She couldn't wait to confront Marcos and tease him for missing the opportunity to see Alexis. He decided to spend a couple of weeks with his grandparents in the village, and once he finds out that the family had seen his brother, he'd be fuming. He'd blame everyone in sight for ignoring him, but there was no way of contacting him.

Maro had changed her clothes more often in the past half-hour than she usually did in a whole week. She washed and brushed her hair until it was squeaky clean and shimmered in the morning sun.

The older she grew, the more she took on her mother's good looks and had turned out to be a beautiful young woman and the pride of her parents. In the end, she settled on wearing her red skirt and white blouse. She kept singing like a canary, hopping about in happiness and grabbing her mother by the waist and trying to spin her around.

She was happy not only because she was going to see her brother, but also at the news that the Archbishop and all the exiles from the Seychelles had been released and were being flown directly to Athens to serve their exile there.

'Have you lost your mind, child . . .!' her mother would say and laugh whole-heartedly, seeing that her daughter was so excited.

'I love everyone today *mama*!' Maro would yell out in utter exhilaration.

Ahmet had finished washing his car, assisted by a pack of local youngsters who were more than eager to help him out, knowing that he would give them a short ride around the block as a reward. This handsome, dark Turkish lad, with masses of curly hair and riveting jet black eyes had a number of local girls craving his attention. They were always yearning to look at him, and frequently paraded near his house hoping that he would be smitten by one of them. They were not so lucky. He had no intention of getting involved at this stage of his life and often brushed them aside, to the delight of Kyra-Soteria, who knew very well how the female of the species would try anything to trap their prey.

Bored, Yiorkis went out to the street to investigate what was taking Ahmet so long. He found him surrounded by half a dozen jovial youngsters, and smiled at their determination to make the car shine like a sparkling jewel.

'Ahmet, Democratis would be waiting!' he said to him, eager to move on.

'Are the ladies ready?'

By the time he had a chance to reply, his wife and Maro walked down the steps of the veranda and got in the back seat of the shiny car. In a few minutes, Ahmet drove off, leaving their neighbours wondering where they were going at this early hour of the day.

They arrived at Democratis' humble house located in the centre of a sea of dense citrus groves. Ahmet dropped them off and drove at high speed to pick up Alexis. This was to be Alexis' safe-house, and the childless couple in their fifties were more than delighted to offer him a temporary safe place to hide.

Ahmet drove straight for Salamina. But while driving his mind was troubled, fretful that there might still be a chance of coming across a sudden roadblock while Alexis was transported here. Tension was in the air, and he often saw long military convoys on the move in the town. He prayed to Allah that his mission would be a success and with those thoughts in mind, he steadily headed to pick up his long lost friend.

Democratis' wife brought out for her guests orange peel and walnut sweet preserves, water and coffee for everyone. They all sat out in the front yard enjoying the morning sun, to kill time until Ahmet's return. Their stone house was completely obscured from the main road and was well hidden among the tall citrus groves, offering a perfect hiding place for Alexis.

A few yards away, a mother hen marshalled an army of fluffy, yellow chicks in search of seeds. Over the stable door a lone donkey, hearing strange voices, kept popping out his head to see what the commotion was all about. He would gaze at the newcomers, and then give up, enticed back to chewing on dried carobs.

Everyone was thrilled at the prospect of the reunion and they could not wait to hear Ahmet's roaring car. Impatiently, they waited for that blessed moment to take a good look at Alexis and hug him. Kyra-Soteria sat chatting next to her husband, but her thoughts were elsewhere. She was apprehensive and her anxiety would not abate until she wrapped her arms around her son. She looked tired, and often took her husband's hand, squeezed it gently as a sign of encouragement and to be patient.

They were on their third cup of coffee and two hours had passed without a sign of Ahmet. They started to fidget and anxiety set in, all wondering what was taking him so long. Their exhilaration had been transformed into apprehension and Maro was becoming impossible. She started moaning and coming up with all sorts of excuses to justify Ahmet's delay but by one o'clock she had run out of excuses and left to see if she could find out something and put their minds at rest.

She took off like a bullet, and soon disappeared among the lush groves leaving the others to sit it out until her return, or Ahmet's return for that matter.

By three in the afternoon, they took sight of her running along the winding pathway as fast as her tender legs could bear. They all stood up and gazed at this young gazelle running towards them. She looked dishevelled, with her long hair flowing about her face and crying her eyes out. The moment she got nearer she started yelling in panic at the top of her voice.

'I think the army arrested Alexis.' she cried out, panting and gasping for breath.

'What did you say child? What did you say?' her mother screamed at her, and grabbed her by her blouse not prepared to accept her daughter's words.

'They've got him *mama*! They've got him!' she shrieked hysterically.

'Explain, girl, explain!' her father demanded.

Once she had composed herself, Maro began to explain, 'there is a great commotion in town, from yesterday's clashes. I went to the bus depot to take a bus for Salamina and the conductor said to me 'I wouldn't advise it, the army has arrested someone very important among the acacias and even we are not allowed to go near the place.' I didn't want to hear more and I have rushed to let you know'.

Hearing those words, her mother flung her heavy body on the chair and began to weep, not wanting to hear anything more. She knew her son had been arrested and thousands of thoughts flashed through her mind as she feared the worst. She had often heard what the British did to those who were arrested, and she was shattered at the prospect of her son receiving the same brutal treatment.

'It might not have been Alexis.' Democratis said, trying to see a lighter side to this possibly dreadful situation.

'It's possible.' Yiorkis agreed, wanting to calm his wife. He had noticed that her hands had begun to shake and he knew there was no stopping them, unless her anxiety was calmed down.

'I don't think so, the conductor said that the arrested *Andartis* had been on the run for more than a year for the Akrotiri job . . . and had a high price on his head. For me, that's my Alexis.' Maro exclaimed.

She sat next to her mother and both wept piteously.

'What about Ahmet?' Yiorkis asked his daughter.

'I don't know *papa* . . . all I know is that there are soldiers and Turkish police everywhere, especially around the Walls.' Maro answered and put her arm around her distraught mother.

Yiorkis paced up and down the yard, deep in thought. He was traumatized.

Once Kyra-Soteria composed herself, they started the long trek on foot for home. Yiorkis walked ahead of the two sobbing women with his head bowed, anxious to hear word from Ahmet.

Democratis and his wife stood next to each other and saw the distressed family disappear around the bend of his thickly planted grove.

'Poor boy . . . it wasn't meant to be . . .!' he sadly muttered to his wife.

* * *

Alexis was ushered at gun point into a small room. The soldiers locked the door behind him and left him on his own. He looked around the bare room and felt like screaming, but instead he gazed at the solid walls, completely shattered that he had finally been arrested. He could hear echoing footsteps rushing about, and like a captured animal he waited for others to decide his fate.

He didn't have to wait for long when suddenly the door was flung open and a massive Turk with a thick mono-brow accompanied by others burst into the room. A tall Englishman was with them and went straight up to him.

'Stand up.' He bellowed at the top of his voice, trying to intimidate his prisoner. He was carrying a poster in one hand and he carefully compared the photo with his captive. 'That's him all right.' he then added, recognising that they had captured one of the lads that had blown up Akrotiri Air Base.

The Englishman ordered that he should be transported to the Omorphita Interrogation Camp immediately and walked out the room, leaving the Turks behind.

'So Greek, you are the famous Alexis.' The huge Turk said to him and stared into his eyes. 'A special person deserves special treatment; Omorphita is the place for you.'

Alexis was relieved these brutes were not about to start punching him and stared at them with revulsion.

'You have some kind of a blood-brother named Ahmet, do you not?

The moment he heard Ahmet's name, Alexis looked at the Turk wondering how this man knew anything about Ahmet.

'What about Ahmet?' he asked, frowning.

'. . . and you have a younger brother; I have met both of them,' he continued.

'How do you know Ahmet? Alexis insisted one more time.

'He's a Turk is he not?' the man replied indifferently and walked out of the room followed by the others.

The Turk had planted doubts in his mind. He found it hard to believe that Ahmet was acquainted with such a brute. He refused to accept it, and shrugged it off as the man's way of intimidating him and worming divisive thoughts into his mind.

Handcuffed and under armed escort, he was driven to the Omorphita Prison.

By mid-afternoon, he took a glimpse of the notorious and dreaded Interrogation Compound that sprawled across a vast isolated escarpment. He gazed fretfully at the depressing prison and felt scared for the first time in his life, knowing he no longer had control

255

over his life. Trapped, he suddenly recognised how the captured animals felt, ensnared within the tangled nets of the famous dog-catcher of Varoshia.

As soon as the military car entered the prison grounds, he was received by prison officials who threw him in a tiny, sweltering lock-up cell until they were ready to deal with him.

This dreary, oppressive infamous torture complex had spread absolute fear on all captives who had the misfortune to pass through its massive gates. To find oneself within this compound meant one was as good as dead, if not crippled for life. Prisoners incarcerated in this place had no human rights or communication with the outside world. They became nonentities and their lives belonged exclusively to the authorities. Answerable to no one and without accountability, the interrogators' objective was to extract crucial information to help the army put down this uprising that had become such a an embarrassment to the Empire.

Alexis had heard astonishing stories of what went on inside there, and felt that he was about to find out in person what really happens once the interrogators got their hands on him. He was scared, but psyched himself up to be brave and accept the worst. He was not prepared to betray *Eoka*.

Abruptly, his thoughts were interrupted by the sound of loud footsteps that stopped outside his cell. Two soldiers opened the door, and at gunpoint asked him to go with them. Silently, he stood up and followed them across the corridor and they went into another room at the far end of the long noisy hallway.

An elderly officer dressed in a crisp uniform was seated behind a wooden desk and, as soon as they entered, he gazed at the young lad standing in front of him and took a puff on his cigarette. He stared into Alexis' apprehensive eyes and inspected his new prisoner.

'Young man, you don't look that well to me, are you sick?' the officer asked him in fluent Greek.

'No' Alexis answered arrogantly.

'Very well' said the officer, and stood up. 'We know exactly who you are . . . and as the warden of this camp, I can only give one chance to co-operate with us. If you refuse, I have the authority to hang you here and now and there is no power in the world which can stop us or, you can tell us all you know about *Eoka* and its Leader, this man who calls himself *Dighenis*. That's the only way you can save your skin.'

'I fight for the liberation of my country.' Alexis answered flatly.

'You are a terrorist that's what you are!' the officer angrily interrupted him.

'I am a soldier. I will not betray my brothers or *Eoka*.'

'You all speak the same but I can assure you, you shall spill your heart out once my boys have finished with you!

'I shall never talk.' Alexis insisted contemptuously.

'Don't be a fool lad, think of your mother and father. I am giving them a chance not to mourn over your dead body,' the warden stated calmly, attempting to instil fear into the pitiful looking lad who stood motionless. He realised that he was dealing with a stubborn young man and a seasoned fighter.

'I shall never talk.' He answered again, with determination and to show he was not intimidated.

The warden did not like his attitude. He stared at the prisoner, shook his head slightly and beckoned the soldiers to take him away.

'You shall speak or you shall die!' the warden yelled after him.

His armed escorts took him out into a vast, arid yard and headed straight for a long narrow building at the far end of the compound. It was late afternoon and there was hardly anyone about, except for a few soldiers who walked back and forth guarding the complex. He noticed a number of watchtowers and that the interrogation camp was completely enclosed in layers of razor-sharp barbed wire fencing. Not even a dog could escape this place, he thought, and fretfully followed the two soldiers.

They stopped at one of the doors that lined the building and entered a dimly lit room. They locked him up and walked out again leaving him on his own. He overheard the screams of pain of other prisoners, both men and women, and a deep hatred for his captors overcame his senses. No man should have the right to inflict such pain on other humans, he thought to himself realising, his turn would come soon.

He inspected the bare square room and fear set into his spine.

There were strange gadgets everywhere and leather straps hanging from strong metal hooks on the walls, ceiling and floor. An open drain was visible in the middle of the tiled floor and more leather straps were attached to large hooks embedded in the concrete. There were electric cables coming out of a peculiar looking wooden box that had a small winding handle sticking out of its side. He had never seen such a contraption before and wondered what it was meant for. In the corner of the room, a long rubber hose was coiled on the floor with its other end securely attached to a tap. Against the bare wall, a small table was covered with a number of devices he had never seen the likes of.

He knew this was a torture chamber and a shiver flashed throughout his entire body. He felt very scared about how much pain they would inflict on him and mentally prepared himself for the worst. Absolutely petrified, he stood motionless in the middle of the room inspecting the evil contraptions that coldly stared back at him.

His apprehension was interrupted by the sound of hollow echoing footsteps rapidly approaching, when suddenly the door was flung wide open and six large determined looking fellows entered the room.

They immediately encircled their prisoner.

'Are you ready to talk?' one of the Englishmen barked at him harshly.

Alexis shook his head negatively, and felt like a trapped animal being cornered before the onslaught began. The threatening, bulky men showed no sign of emotion. There was a cold stare in their eyes, and they were in no mood to discuss the matter further with their fearful captive.

'Then, let's begin.' said the same man.

Suddenly, Alexis felt a hard blow at the back of his head. He stumbled and fell on the floor but managed to stand up again feeling dizzy.

No sooner had he stood up, than the six men began a concerted punching expedition across his body. Their punches rained down on him in thunderous blows and whenever he leaned to one side another punch straightened him up again. He felt their solid fists, all over his body, stomach and face. There was no way of escaping his torturers.

They kept spinning him around and thrusting their heavy fists into him from every angle as if he were a punch-bag. Their blows smashed his face and blood began to spurt out from above his eyebrows and nose.

Undeterred, his captors continued to do as much damage to their prisoner as possible.

'Speak up fellow, speak up!' he heard one of the interrogators shout at him aggressively.

Seeing that the prisoner did not respond, they continued with their vicious attack. Because of dizziness and pain he had no idea where voices came from, but he tried to compose himself and accept what they threw at him. His knees turned to jelly and he often stumbled and fell on the floor. Their heavy boots and kicks caused him excruciating pain, and he tried hard to stand, fearful that his scalp would crack open like a shell.

After a while he could no longer remain standing. He tumbled to the floor yet again and his torturers finally picked him up and attached both his arms to the two hooks embedded in the ceiling.

They pulled the leather straps tightly and made sure his toes did not touch the ground.

They left him dangling like a carcass on butcher's hooks, while they decided to take a break and smoke a cigarette. They threw abuse at him and threatened him with worst to come if he did not cooperate.

Alexis felt like Jesus on the cross, helpless and trapped, encircled by his brutal tormentors. They could do whatever they wished with him and his body had been transformed into their own private whipping post

The men kept up this punishment for at least a half-hour without a break. Their short-sleeve shirts quickly turned red from the splattering of his blood, but they showed no mercy and continued to inflict as much physical and mental pain as humanly possible.

Alexis groaned in agony and felt like a dangling rag ripped to bits. All he could hear was the constant thumping of fists, and angry shouting. It seemed that the men were in a total frenzy and there was no stopping them from enjoying their brutal behaviour. He didn't know how long he could put up with such torment. Every time they attacked him, he expected their blows to be his last, and he would cross over the river *Styx*.

'Strip him!' one of them ordered.

Immediately, two of the men ripped his clothes apart, and stripped him.

Humiliated and completely naked, Alexis swayed back and forth trying his hardest to remain composed, but he lost all sense of reality. His limp body was held upright by the leather straps around his wrists and the men had decided to change their tactics. This time, not only did they thrust their heavy blows against his body, but they twisted their fists at the same time for greater impact. Feeling their punches, he expected his ribs to crush with every punch.

Realising their blows had not produced results one of them picked up a rough leather whip and relentlessly lashed at his bare back and body as hard as he could. He felt the skin of his back being torn apart and soon he was spitting blood from his mouth.

Unable to restrain himself, Alexis found the strength to scream out at the top of his voice. Suddenly, he lost his vision and a cloud of blackness overcame him. He could no longer feel the whip or their fists. He fainted.

'Bastard!' one of the men bellowed.

'I'll fix him,' said another and turned the hose on him.

259

Alexis stirred and regained consciousness.

'Speak up, you bastard! Tell us what we want to know!' another one shouted at him.

Alexis was covered in blood, and his handsome face had swollen like a balloon. All he could see from his bloodstained, puffy eyes were blurred images. Half conscious, he realised that the men had released his bruised body from the hooks and he dropped off onto the hard floor below unable to move.

The men then proceeded to strap him to the floor with his arms and legs apart.

Half conscious, he lay there strapped, waiting for a new torment to begin. He heard the sound of running water, and one of the men placed a rug over his face and held it tight so he could not brush it aside. Suddenly a gush of cold water flooded his face making it impossible for him to breathe. He moved his head around but it was no use, the man held the rug over his face tighter and while choking and trying to gasp for air, he kept swallowing water down. He tried to pull his wrists apart but the leather straps held them in position. The running water kept coming in bucketfuls, flowing into his stomach. The more he tried to breathe, the more the water flooded inside his wind-pipe and in minutes, he could feel his belly swell up. He drank so much water that it made him nauseous and could feel the skin on his belly being stretched to its limit.

'Tell us what we want to know . . .!' he heard one of the men yell at him.

He just shook his head. The blood from his wounds merged with the running water, stained the entire floor and steadily seeped into the open drain hiding any evidence of mistreatment.

Without warning, one of the men began to stamp with his heavy boot on his bloated stomach forcing the water from inside his belly to burst out of his mouth and arc across the room. The stamping continued, and once his stomach was empty it was refilled with more water and quickly followed by steady blows and stamping that continued for an hour.

The men finally got tired and dragged his limp body into an adjacent cell. They dumped him on the hard floor and walked out leaving him to lie there naked. Alexis curled up and started to shiver with pain and shock. After a while, he felt someone inspecting his wounds, but he was in no position to know what was happening to him; he was oblivious to reality.

The torture was maintained daily for six weeks, but he resisted disclosing any kind of information about the Movement.

His hair and beard grew long and he felt dirty all over. Black and mauve bruises covered his entire body. His nose had swollen up and there were countless open wounds across his face and weak body. The harsh treatment had taken its toll, and as time progressed, his young, agile body had turned into a living skeleton from sleep deprivation, torture and lack of adequate food to the dismay of the doctor in charge of the compound infirmary. He had recognised that the prisoner had had enough, but no one paid any attention to him; his job was to heal the wounds of the prisoners and not make military judgements.

The warden was becoming impatient with Alexis' stubborn attitude. He had a gut feeling that this lad had crucial information and yet would not succumb to the torture. In utter brutality, he authorised the maximum torture to be inflicted on him, in the hope that he would be able to break down this young man.

He had also decided to replace the previous interrogators and called in a different team of inquisitors who specialised in new techniques and were not squeamish about implementing them. If they could not break this lad's spirit, no one would.

A tall ginger-headed Scot was in charge of the new team and he set out to extract information from the pitiful looking lad who had been transformed into the living dead and incapable of thinking clearly. The new officer planned to finish his job in one straight session and he didn't care how many hours his team worked, as long as their methods brought about positive results.

'I advise you to talk before it is too late. If you die on us so much the better. Then we can all go home.' he said to his prisoner as soon as they entered the torture chamber.

Alexis became accustomed to his daily dose of torture and did not care what they did to him any more. He had reached the maximum pain barrier and no one could hurt him any more. He could no longer feel pain. His body and mind had turned into a nonentity and he was more than ready to accept any punishment thrown at him.

'You will be sorry . . . ' the Scot insisted.

'Then I shall die!' Alexis muttered in a whisper between swollen lips.

He succumbed to the fact that he was better off dead than alive and could not care less what they did to him.

The men forced him to remove his clothes and then strapped him to the ground.

Alexis anticipated that the usual water treatment would commence. The mere thought of it caused him to feel the liquid churning inside his stomach before they even turned the tap on. To his surprise, they did not do that. Instead, he heard the smashing of glass bottles against the side table. The men put on black gloves and picked up loose slivers of broken glass.

They knelt next to his feet and hands and began to insert the sharp slivers deeply underneath his fingernails and toenails. To make them more painfully effective, they gave each piece of glass a quick twist as it penetrated.

The excruciating pain was so unbearable Alexis's screams nearly brought the roof down.

He tried to resist, but the leather straps held him securely on the floor. Open wounds quickly formed around his wrists and they began to bleed from his constant attempts to free himself by pulling as hard as he could possibly endure. He yelled at the top of his weak lungs, but there was nobody about to hear him, and his torturers continued to press the broken glass even deeper into his fingers.

He gazed at his rapidly swelling fingers through the slits of his bloated eyes and noticed that a steady flow of blood was running on the tiled floor and down the drain.

One of the men stamped on his fingers and toes to ensure the glass smashed into smithereens so it could penetrate even deeper.

Instantly, his fingers turned red from the swelling and a flow of blood trickled from each one. Each finger and toe instantly swelled up like a small golf ball. He could no longer bend them and he tried to keep them apart so they would not touch each other, but his attempts were, futile. The throbbing pain became impossible to bear and his body started to shake and spasm. He fainted.

He was soon brought back by the splashing of a bucketful of water against his emaciated face. He screamed out but his captors showed no mercy. Two of them released his arms from the floor and forced him to sit on a wooden stool. They mocked and threatened him that there was worse to come.

In his pathetic state he sat on the stool in a daze, groaning, when he noticed that a saucepan was boiling on a table. Steam rose from the bubbling, scorching water and he wondered what was coming next.

'Time to eat,' one of the men said to him sarcastically and lifted two boiling eggs with two tongs. He walked to where he was seated in the middle of the room, and stood in front of him.

From behind, another one lifted both of his limp arms half way up, while the others stood aside watching.

With a smirk on his face, the man facing him placed both tongs under his armpits, and the other one standing from behind immediately pressed both of his arms down, crushing the soft, boiling eggs under his armpits.

Alexis did not expect this and he screamed so loud he thought that his eardrums would burst, but the man held his arms tightly in the same position to ensure the scorching runny egg dribbled down his bare flesh.

They repeated the same torture treatment for a while, and refused to ease up. They yelled at him and slapped him but he wouldn't give in, instead he groaned and stumbled off the stool.

Huge blisters almost immediately covered both sides of his body and he could see his skin bloating like a massive balloon ready to burst. He lay on the floor with both his arms stretched apart and screamed like a wounded animal in agony and excruciating pain.

The men lit a cigarette each and took a brief rest as they watched the pitiful lad who had become no more than shrivelled, bruised skin and bone. They had been torturing him for more than eight hours and got nowhere with him. Time was running out, and they wanted to break this stallion that made a fool of the British authorities.

With arms and legs apart Alexis lay on the floor, unable to stand, anticipating their next session. He knew his tormentors had not finished with him and gave up all hope. He lay there like a discarded rag, waiting until they finished smoking. His life was in their hands.

'This bastard is stubborn, we are not getting anywhere with him,' the man in charge said to the others, and stared with contempt at his prisoner who kept groaning.

'Let's give him a couple of sparks,' another one suggested.

'That would kill him for sure but what the heck, we have a job to do. Lift him up.' The officer in charge agreed.

With difficulty they lifted Alexis' dead weight and fastened both of his arms to the ceiling hooks. Half unconscious, he was left dangling naked in the middle of the room, when unexpectedly the compound doctor dressed in his long white coat walked in unannounced. The instant he set eyes on the naked lad hanging from the ceiling he went livid.

'This boy has had enough put him down!' he yelled.

'We have a job to do.' The ginger-headed Scot said, paying no attention to him.

'You have done more than enough for one day, put him down. Now!' he bellowed.

He immediately began to inspect the injuries and burns on the dangling lad who did not respond in any way.

'What are you? Animals?' he shouted at the officer in charge, distressed by what he saw.

'He is a valuable prisoner' he said, trying to justify their behaviour.

'Have you not heard of the Geneva Convention? This lad is as good as dead!' the elderly doctor angrily screamed at them again, fuming at such barbarity.

'We are nearly done with him.'

'Not nearly; you are done! And that's that!' interrupted the good doctor.

'I think you should take this matter up with the warden.'

'Then I shall!' the doctor said and stormed out of the torture chamber to see the warden.

Not wasting valuable time, the team took advantage of the situation and quickly taped wires around Alexis' testicles, before the doctor had time to return with the warden. One of the men was instructed to stand watch and warn them if he saw them coming.

The officer in charge approached the wooden box and plugged a cable into the wall socket. He rotated the handle of the strange box and a flow of electrical current was instantly sent into the prisoner's testicles.

Alexis screamed and his whole body went into convulsions. Hanging by the leather straps, he jerked and frantically kicked his legs, but the electric shocks kept coming in short intervals, sending him into wild contortions. They kept the electric shocks up for ten minutes without a rest. The stench of burning skin quickly filled the room, but his torturers persisted in a hurry to make him talk, before the warden showed up.

Alexis felt his testicles sizzling and expanding like two balloons packed with warm liquid. The pungent smell of burning skin persisted forever it seemed, and no matter how much he tried to remain composed, he could no longer cope with the pain. Nauseated, he vomited once and passed out.

'He will never talk, take him down quickly before the others return,' ordered the officer, disillusioned that he had failed to make his prisoner disclose information.

His colleagues hurriedly unbound the leather straps from his wrists and let his limp body drop to the floor. They quickly removed the electric cables from Alexis' body, and each lit a cigarette to wait for the warden

The distraught doctor returned without the warden, but instead he brought with him two orderlies carrying a stretcher. As soon as he saw what the interrogators had done to the boy, he shook his head in revulsion.

'You animals, this is not a Nazi concentration camp!' he screamed at them, and his whole body shook with anger.

The men looked at him with total indifference. They continued smoking without any sense of compassion for the lad who lay unconscious on the floor. He might as well be dead as far as they were concerned.

The orderlies carefully put Alexis' naked body on a stretcher and headed for the infirmary. Appalled by the disgraceful conduct of the interrogators, the doctor followed the stretcher, mumbling to himself at such atrocities inflicted on another human being by a group of civilised British army personnel.

He felt totally ashamed . . .

CHAPTER FIFTEEN

ALEXIS HAD SPENT endless agonising days in the small infirmary. He was oblivious to what was happening to him and went into a fretful daze, incapable of shaping any sense of reality. From persistent pain and weakness, he hardly spoke or moved but lay on his bed covered in bandages and accepting without question whatever treatment the doctor prescribed. His muscles had shrunk and he had become a living skeleton from malnutrition and the relentless punishment.

The doctor kept Alexis' legs and arms spread apart until the swelling went down, but it was a slow process and his wounds were not easy to deal with. He treated his burns and his fried testicles with great care, and he assigned a young nurse to watch over him constantly. As far as the bruising was concerned, he was not worried, knowing that in due course the obtrusive black bruises and swelling all over his body would ultimately be healed. The red burn-marks and ugly scar tissue however, would remain forever as a reminder of the mistreatment he had received.

The medic tried his utmost to bring him back to a half normal condition, but he was fighting a losing battle; every time he removed tiny glass splinters lodged between his finger and toenails, he discovered new ones. The treatment was slow, time-consuming and most painful, causing his young patient to scream every time he put his pincers close to his injuries. He had to accept the reality that his patient was going to lose a number of his nails and possibly not be able to use some of his fingers either but, being a kind person dedicated to his profession, he tried his utmost to cure the unfortunate lad.

The matter that troubled the kind doctor most was the condition of Alexis' testicles. He had a suspicion that he would probably end up impotent, and that bothered his deep sense of compassion, realising the lad may have been permanently damaged at such a young age.

'They have ruined this poor boy.' He kept muttering to his assistant, whenever he attended to his injuries.

With the good care and medical attention provided by the doctor and his loyal nurse, Alexis was able to get his senses back and after three weeks he was able to understand what was happening to him. The doctor spoke Greek fluently and could explain the seriousness of his condition to his young patient. He made it clear to him that his testicles may or may not recover from the injuries they received from the electric shocks, but there was a small chance that in time, they may just heal on their own. He could not guarantee it, but with additional medical treatment there was a slim chance of total recovery.

Those encouraging words gave Alexis hope, and reluctantly he accepted his fate that he would probably remain impotent for the rest of his life, unless a miracle happened. This was going to be his most private secret and he felt shattered at the thought of impotence.

When the doctor broke the news to him, he immediately thought of Xanthia and he wished that he were dead. God was cruel. He played games with people's lives and emotions, keeping them alive for his own enjoyment, and then discarding them to the whims of fate and the four winds.

He stayed in the infirmary forever it seemed, but in time he was able to move around with the help of a pair of crutches. He got accustomed to the ward and was able to mingle with other prisoners who had incurred fewer injuries than himself. He got to know most of them and that made life a bit more bearable being surrounded by his own people, and sharing their own personal experiences.

At other times, he would stand by the window and stare outside into the compound inspecting the detested torture buildings that stared back at him.

He would wonder how many others like him would receive the same treatment as he had tolerated. The thought of it made him shiver with fright. He never wanted to go back there again. If they came for him, he would find a way to die rather than endure such brutal treatment again. His body and mind could no longer cope, and he decided to end it all if the same interrogators came for him.

As he got better, he realised that he could no longer walk normally. He walked with his legs slightly apart and with his right foot turned inwards. He had also developed a tic which made him move his head for no reason, from right to left. He was self-conscious of these unbecoming moments and he felt very uncomfortable, not being able to control his head.

Alexis' total character had suddenly changed, from being a joyful lad into one with mood swings and irrational behaviour.

He'd dwell on horrible thoughts and suffered from constant bouts of depression. His mental state of dejection and misery made the doctor worry about the traumatic mental damage the torturers might have done to this lad. There were obvious signs of a degree of mental illness and disturbance in his mind and was likely to worsen if he suffered a sudden mental shock or a traumatic experience in the future.

'With a long period of convalescing, and proper treatment you shall become well again, mentally and physically,' the doctor kept reassuring him to make him feel better, whenever he attended to his many wounds.

Alexis believed in the good doctor, and those words of his gave him hope and optimism that one day he would be as good as new again.

One scorching morning, a military van drove to the infirmary and a pack of armed soldiers jumped out, and entered the small hospital. They spoke with the doctor, and were given a list of patients. The soldiers immediately marched into the ward and one of them called out at the top his voice six names. Alexis' name was among them.

At gunpoint and in handcuffs, the prisoners were escorted to the waiting van and herded in to sit at the back. The van immediately took off like a bullet, not giving the prisoners a chance to even thank the kind doctor and his loyal nurse for taking care of them.

After five months of hell, Alexis recognised that he was finally leaving this place for good. He stared at the drab depressing buildings, and he knew those dehumanising chambers would remain embedded in his memory forever, like a reoccurring nightmare

The detainees became ecstatic when they realised they were being transported to a proper prison camp.

Once the van drove through the dreaded barbed-wire of the compound, they spat simultaneously on the floor to the utter disgust of the soldiers who were guarding them. They all cried out in jubilation that the Omorphita torture chambers had seen the last of them.

The military van headed straight for Kokkinotrimithia concentration camp or Camp K, as everyone called it.

For Alexis, it seemed quite strange being driven across villages and gazing at the faces of bystanders again. People stood and stared at the military van, shook their heads in revulsion, knowing that the lads were being sent to a detention camp. The women crossed themselves in abhorrence, while young boys and girls raised their fists in defiance, encouraging the prisoners to keep on fighting.

Once the van reached the final hill facing Camp K, the prisoners for the first time caught sight of the massive camp. It appeared to be sprawled across arid fields with hardly any vegetation, and the mere sight of it sent fear and apprehension into everyone's beating hearts. Silently, they gazed at the camp, trying to anticipate what was in store for them inside this threatening looking enclave.

They saw endless rows of shiny metal barracks enclosed with rolls of barbed wire, watchtowers and soldiers moving around. From the distance they could detect the movement of hundreds of prisoners inside their own fenced yards. The camp appeared to be sectioned off in compounds and each compound housed four or five corrugated barracks. Surrounding the entire camp, a high fence encased all the compounds together, while a wide clearing encircled the camp, followed by the final perimeter fence.

Armed soldiers and tracker dogs constantly walked within this pulverised clearing, guarding the entire camp.

As they got closer, Alexis had noticed old men, women and young mothers carrying children with scarves over their heads seated at the side of the road, in the hope that the authorities would let them see their loved ones.

As soon as they saw the green military van approaching, they raised their heads and waved at the prisoners, muttering words of sympathy.

There was a persistent cacophany of sound in the air escaping from the camp across the escarpment. As they got nearer, the drawling sounds became clearer; the shouting and muttering of hundreds of prisoners who moved about aimlessly. They moved in groups under the sizzling sun, unable to find shade anywhere within the arid grounds.

At the main gate, the six prisoners were split up and each one was escorted to his assigned compound. Alexis was taken to compound 14. He was received by two soldiers who showed him with indifference, his assigned barrack. Prisoners watched and greeted the new arrival who was destined to be part of their lives from now on.

Once the soldiers had shown him his barrack, they brought him out into the open courtyard and asked him to remain still. They fired a bullet into the air to attract the attention of the other prisoners, then, they turned to their prisoner and shouted into his ear at the top of their voice.

'*Eoka* shall perish!'

'Never!' the prisoners shouted in defiance and raised their fists in the air.

Alexis was confused, remained still and shook his head nervously as if he was trembling. It seemed this was an ongoing private game between the prisoners and the army, who enjoyed herding all these prisoners in one place, knowing they were mere numbers and their lives belonged to them.

One of the soldiers hit Alexis in the back with the bayonet of his rifle.

'Take your clothes off,' he ordered.

Alexis hesitated momentarily, not sure if the soldier was serious or not. But the next blow on his head prompted him to start stripping in front of everyone. He realised they wanted to initiate his arrival by humiliating him in an attempt to break his spirit, underline their authority and make him aware who was the boss in this place.

He removed all his clothing and stood completely naked in front of everyone feeling totally embarrassed and humiliated. As soon as the soldiers saw the ugly burn marks on his sides and scar tissue across his back, they smiled.

'Omorphita is getting much better.' One said to the other.

'Now get moving! You are to walk around the yard until sunset,' the older of the two soldiers bellowed and pushed him hard to get moving.

Alexis stumbled and fell to the ground but he quickly stood up.

A soldier hit him hard with the bayonet of his rifle and then marched off with indifference, leaving their new prisoner behind knowing there was nowhere else for him to go; he was trapped like all the others.

Alexis began his embarrassing torment and walked naked all day in circles.

With nothing to do but pace about, he got the chance to introduce himself and make acquaintance with his other compatriots. Once he got accustomed to his predicament, he no longer felt embarrassed by his nakedness and walked with ease.

Many joked with him and he joked back, while others were shocked at the way his scarred body appeared, realising this lad had gone through hell. He walked with his legs slightly apart, while twitching his head. Self-conscious of his condition, he felt uneasy but, after a while, even that did not matter.

No one paid much attention to his impairment, because most of them had a story of their own to tell of how much suffering they had experienced at the hands of their interrogators. Many had received similar torture, while others were incarcerated for being young or being in the wrong place at the wrong time. The majority of the detainees were innocent and had nothing to do with *Eoka*, but the authorities had arrested them in their attempt to segregate them from society as a means of minimising a possible threat. Their mass incarceration had become a symbol of moral resistance. Being locked up inflamed their spirit of resistance and instead of winning them over, the army had managed to create a giant of absolute defiance.

There must have been at least five thousand men and women herded together in different barracks without trial at this concentration camp alone. Camp K had become synonymous and renowned across the island for the ill treatment of detainees. It had been established upon Nazi lines and everybody within its barbed wire was a mere number and a non-person.

The pride and blossoming flower of Cypriot youth was incarcerated in identical camps elsewhere, in the likes of Pyla, Polemi, and many other concentration camps across the island.

The Governor found it necessary to build new ones in order to house the innocent and the guilty, in his vain attempt to break the spirit of resistance, but he was fighting a losing battle. These people were unbreakable and courageously continued their struggle, to his utter dismay.

He authorised brute force to achieve his objective but failed to recognise that, in retaliation to violence, violence is permissible under international law and these men who were now locked up like herded animals were fighting for what was their inherent right; to combat violence with violence.

Whereas tolerance and understanding could bring about positive results, violence could only escalate violence to a grand scale, and yet the Governor had chosen violence as means to stamp out people's aspiration for freedom.

As far as the prisoners were concerned, the matter was very simple; in the absence of justice there is no remedy for wrong and that alone exonerated them from any actions taken against the British authorities who persisted in maintaining an unjust policy, as a means to solve the issue of freedom for the small island.

The final result was nothing less than bloodshed and misery for all.

The British government had come to realise that the Governor's tactics did not bring about desired results and, without warning, London had decided to remove him and try a new policy.

The Governor was replaced by a seasoned diplomat and former Governor of Jamaica.

*   *   *

Alexis found it difficult to cope with the monotonous confinement of being locked up. He was accustomed to the life of *Andartes* who roamed freely in the mountains and slept under trees in the open countryside under open skies, and now that he was crammed in with so many other detainees, he felt constrained. Being a likeable character, he made many friends, especially with those who shared the same barrack, and in time he began to accept his new life as a prisoner in compound 14.

271

His compound was located at the very edge of the perimeter fence, and he often stood and stared beyond the buffer zone, which the prisoners named Dead Zone; anyone caught within this forbidden area was instantly shot and killed. Guards stood on tall towers overlooking each compound in readiness to kill, while others with tracker dogs circulated inside this deadly buffer zone. Yet, beyond the last rolls of the razor-sharp barbed wire, lay the freedom that everybody aspired to.

Farmers were seen ploughing the surrounding land that stretched far into the horizon, and prisoners often tried to converse with them from a distance by asking for information and news of what was happening on the outside, and in the real world. The daring ones frequently provided news, but others ignored the prisoners in fear of their own lives, worried that they may end up inside and join the dishevelled detainees.

Although a new civilian Governor had been put in charge, the severe harsh conditions inside the camps did not subside and persisted as before.

Detainees were constantly subjected to interrogation by the army who appeared determined to make life a misery for everyone. At sunset, everyone was locked up and the prisoners became sitting targets for the whims of British commanders, guards and army officers. Soldiers often burst into individual barracks in the middle of the night inflicting mass torture and mercilessly beating up prisoners. Without any given reason, they would try to keep the prisoners awake all night by firing their guns in the air and throwing rocks against the corrugated metal structures. Sleep deprivation had become one of their most effective methods of punishing the prisoners, en-masse.

One day in the third week of Alexis' incarceration, three detainees had come up to him discreetly while he was standing on his own looking beyond the wire fence. They approached him from behind and one tapped him lightly on the shoulder.

'Akamantis, welcome to Hell.' One of the men said to him and introduced himself as Soteris.

Startled, Alexis stared at the men's faces. He was puzzled how they knew his secret name. 'I have been in worse places.' He answered.

'You have the evidence all over your body. This place is a different kind of Hell, you'll see, we have been locked up for over a year and our eyes have seen terrible things in these places.'

Recognising that they were *Eoka* members, he felt relaxed and pleased that the Movement had finally made contact with him.

272

They presented themselves as the invisible secret *Eoka* authority within the compound. News had reached their ears that he was a valued *Eoka* member, and they wanted him to be aware of their presence in case he needed assistance in some way. The men opened up to him and explained their role as the secret committee of the Organisation.

Soteris was a large fellow in his mid-thirties and was married with three children, while the other one was a stocky dark looking man with a rounded face and short in stature. The elderly priest reminded him of the three monks at Apostolos Varnavas and spoke with a soft voice but he seemed to have a permanently troubled expression on his sullen face. His long, black dusty robe had turned grey and was in shreds at the hems from sweeping the ground.

They discussed the appalling conditions of Camp K and how the army treated the detainees but, most of all, they wanted to warn the young fellow to remain vigilant and be careful with whom he spoke to inside the camp.

'I always thought that we are all compatriots here.'

'That's where you are wrong. There are moles planted among the detainees who are working for the authorities. Not everyone is an *Eoka* member. We have communists, Anglophiles and those who are against the Organisation,' Soteris explained.

Alexis was shocked and could not believe his ears. He looked around and gazed at the crowd of prisoners lingering around the arid yard, finding it difficult to comprehend that some of those dishevelled looking men could actually be working for the authorities. He nervously jerked his head in amazement and then studied the faces of the other prisoners who appeared so innocent and yet some were likely to pose a serious danger.

'We have information that the British have recruited and brought over three hundred additional collaborators from London—both Turkish and Greek—to spy on *Eoka*. They are highly paid so be very careful. If you are not sure of someone, avoid him,' the priest stated with abhorrence.

The four of them spent all afternoon together, walking in circles and chatting about anything that came to mind. Alexis liked his new friends. They were older than he was but very sincere and he could not ask for anything more. After a long discussion, Alexis plucked the courage and disclosed his feelings.

'I cannot be cooped up I have to break out.' He said firmly.

'Many have tried and failed.' Soteris said, surprised that this young lad had such thoughts at this early stage of his incarceration.

273

'I shall not fail as long as my people are informed. With their help I shall succeed. Can we get word to the outside?'

'It's not impossible,' the priest said to him, impressed by the lad's attitude, wanting to help him.

'The longer I remain here . . . for sure they would hang me,' Alexis said to the men who seemed taken by his daring spirit and determination.

'We shall certainly help.' The stocky man stated and scratched his head thoughtfully.

'All I need is a wire-cutter.' Alexis said to the men and started shaking his head.

The men looked at his thin, handsome face and felt sorry for him, realising that this lad had no control over his impediment and sometimes jerked his head about. His wide eyes sparkled with life, yet they recognised that he had been ruined for life. The men were furious at what the army had done to him, but kept their thoughts to themselves so as not to offend him or cause him additional grief. The three of them were impressed by his soft mannerisms and forthright attitude. He spoke his mind and feared no one and had gained their respect for not revealing any secrets of the Organisation, despite what he had had to endure at the hands of his torturers.

'Wire cutter? That's impossible. You have seen how they strip everyone who enters the compound,' answered Soteris, convinced there was no way a wire-cutter could be smuggled into the compound.

'If you can send word to my family, my friends would find a way,' Alexis said with conviction, believing that nothing was impossible.

He had total faith in Spyros' abilities, and he knew that his loyal friend would turn the world upside down to free him from this deplorable place.

'Easter is coming up, maybe the new Governor will find it in his heart to make conditions easier for us. Go ahead, make your plans and we shall see to it that a letter is smuggled out to your family.' the priest said, convincingly.

From that day on, Alexis developed a close relationship with Soteris and spent most of his free time with him. Soteris, always wearing his white short-sleeved shirt, buttons undone, and rollup sleeves, his exposed hairy chest appeared like the solid rock of mount Troothos. Wide-shouldered, he epitomized legendary strongmen, ready to tackle anything to prove their strength.

Walking side by side, they circled the yard each day, mingling with the other prisoners and strolled aimlessly until nightfall. Soteris had introduced him to a seventeen-year-old lad named Varnavas, an *Eoka* member who was always writing poetry. To Alexis' delight, he also played a harmonica like his old friend Yiannis who had lost his life at Scara.

The three of them became inseparable and the idea of escape persisted in everyone's mind. Knowing that Alexis had been a devoted fighter in the select group of *Andartes*, they showed great respect and blind faith in his determination that escape was possible. Recognising that Varnavas was good at playing the harmonica, he recollected Yiannis' haunting melody that had stuck forever in his mind and, one lazy afternoon Alexis tried to make Varnavas learn it, so he could play it in memory of his old friend.

Seated outside, under the shade of their hut, he hummed the tune to him over and over again, until his young friend had mastered the melody. From that day on, he kept playing it all the time. Soon other prisoners learned the tune and whenever he played it, they joined in, singing it aloud across the compound. Prisoners in the adjacent compounds also learned the tune and in one voice they often sung 'Yiannis' Melody' as a sign of defiance to infuriate the authorities. The women prisoners, holed up in separate huts, sang the tune the loudest and raised their high voices deafeningly across the entire camp.

Prisoners in Camp K soon adopted 'Yiannis' Melody' as their own theme.

It was a simple tune but it meant so much to Alexis and he was thrilled that at last he could hear it again. Every time Varnavas played it, he allowed his mind to drift to those memorable endless hours, days and nights he had shared among his old friends as *Andartes*, crammed in their small hideout. He would frequently hum the tune to himself in remembrance of his good friends who had lost their lives for the cause.

Escape played in Alexis' mind every second of the day and he wandered about the yard studying every detail in his attempt to find breach in the security.

The more he studied the situation the more it became apparent that breaking out of this formidable concentration camp would not be easy. In the evenings while the prisoners were locked up, he spent endless hours gazing at the revolving watch-tower lights going back and forth illuminating the entire compound. He recognised that breaking out of this place was dangerous but also impossible. But, he did not give up and continued his search hoping that a solution would be found.

He studied the situation weeks on end but one evening, while studying the lights' rotation, he realised that on numerous occasions the illumination did not reach the entire length of the buffer zone and failed to flood the yard completely. Only when the beams met

275

simultaneously at precisely the same time did they cover the entire length of the Dead Zone.

He put all his effort into analysing this observation and had come to the conclusion that there was a small dark area about two yards wide that offered a viable prospect of breaking the security. He observed that the lights often did not overlap one another at that specific location and that gave him hope. If only he could cut the wires across that one narrow path, there was a slim chance of avoiding detection and escape was not impossible. To his delight, all guard-dogs were also locked up in their pens at night, and they did not begin to roam the buffer zone until early dawn.

He disclosed his findings to his two friends and they were convinced that escape was close at hand if only they could get their hands on a good pair of wire-cutters. They put their heads together, but the answer to their quest evaded them and there was no way of getting such cutters while inside. Alexis did not give up, and he insisted that if he could get word to his friend Spyros he'd find a way out of their predicament.

He decided to write a letter to his parents, in the hope that the elderly priest may smuggle it out of the compound.

His parents had no idea what had happened to him, and he was always worried about them. A message from him would lift their spirits beyond expectations. He also planned to insert a cryptic message to Spyros, in the hope that he would understand it. He was equally concerned not to jeopardise their plan if the letter was intercepted on its way out, and so wrote an innocent sounding letter.

My dearest mother and father,

This letter might come to you as a surprise, but as you are well aware I must have been betrayed and here I am locked up and no longer a free man. I hope to God, that my letter reaches your hands safely.

My dearest, dearest mother, do not cry for me for I am well in health, body and mind. I have not been mistreated and soon this experience shall become a bad nightmare with happier days ahead.

My dear papa, you have taken a heavy burden as always on your shoulders, and I have caused grief, but it will soon be over and we shall all be together as one family again . . .

To my loving sister and brother I send you my love and plead with you both to watch out and take good care of yourselves. You do not want to end up like me no matter how romantic it may seem. Life is most precious so do not squander it for anything. I pray to God that my eyes shall see you both safe and well.

As for the love of my life, Xanthia, tell her that she is always on my mind, and I can hear church bells toll announcing our wedding as soon as I am free. Tell her that I love her with every breath that I take each day and, we shall soon be in each other's arms forever.

I miss my brother Ahmet and I cannot wait for the day when we shall laugh together like always. The day I am released, we shall all visit Salingari Taverna, smash some plates and get drunk to celebrate my freedom the instant these heavy shackles are cast to the four winds.

To my loyal friends Spyros and Michalaki, please tell them that we must take a break when this struggle finally comes to an end. I cannot wait for that day, and I am most anxious to see them soon.

Give my love and best wishes to all my friends and pray for us all, during the Easter Holiday! God, how I miss you all!

Your beloved son, Alexis
Compound 14, Camp K

Once he had composed the letter, Alexis gave it to the elderly priest to try and smuggle it out of the camp. If anyone could do it, he would be the best person to get it through without the guards' detection. He enjoyed greater freedom than the rest of the detainees and he was permitted to visit prisoners in the various compounds to offer them spiritual guidance and listen to their grievances.

There was nothing more to do but to wait for some kind of sign that Spyros got his message, if at all.

*　　*　　*

Spring was approaching fast. The countryside and fields surrounding the camp turned green and a pleasant, crisp air began to blow from the East. The potato, artichoke and aubergine plants began to sprout through the fertile earth and soon the entire area transformed itself into an endless carpet of lush, green vegetation. A blanket of red poppies and yellow daisies appeared in their thousands dotting over the vast fields in readiness to dominate and merge in a colourful profusion across the land. Without fail every year the countryside transformed and adorned itself in preparation for the week-long Easter festivities.

The letter to his parents was smuggled out without difficulty, and each day Alexis gazed at the open fields in anticipation for some kind of sign from his friend Spyros. He knew that something would happen, but he had no idea how his friend would find a way to contact him. With hope, he kept his ears and eyes wide open.

Four weeks went by without a word or a sign, but in the fifth week, while he was strolling around the camp with his two buddies, they stopped and gazed at a crowd of the farmers crouched on the ground weeding and watering their plantations. The three of them envied their freedom and looked at the men and women in hope for that elusive day when they, too, would be able again to roam the countryside as free men.

A number of the field workers approached close to the fence and tried to converse with them. From a distance, the best they could do was to raise their voices and shout at one another, attempting to make small-talk with the captives. If anyone got too close to the perimeter razor-wire fence, a pack of vicious guard dogs pounced and barked at them, sending fear into their spines and forcing them to quickly withdraw and keep a fair distance away.

Two of the workers moved about at the fringe of the fence and discreetly walked up and down, weeding the nearby field. They kept looking inside the camp and began to sing a child's rhyme. They kept repeating it over and over again, singing the same tune. Wearing red scarves over their heads, they carefully kept walking along the length of the fence to inspect the incarcerated men.

It was the rhyme that first attracted Alexis' attention. He and his childhood friends at *Loukkos* practically sung it on a daily basis and the melody had stuck in their minds. As soon as he heard it, Alexis got excited and looked about to see where the singing was coming from. He and his friends rushed alongside the fence and gazed across the fields, searching for those who kept singing at the top of their voices.

Alexis spotted the two fellows who walked about, weeding and singing. He immediately recognised Spyros' tall stature and next to him stood Michalaki who pinned his stare on the compound. Without hesitation, Alexis began to wave his hands and simultaneously gave out a whistle as loud as he could. He repeated his whistle, and that attracted Spyros' attention. As soon as they spotted Alexis, they responded by waving their hands and carefully walked closer to the fence.

'Thank God he got my message,' Alexis said to his two companions who also got excited, seeing that their friend was thrilled by such unexpected contact.

The lads came as close to the perimeter fence as possible and, once their eyes met, Spyros and Michalaki smiled broadly at their friend. They waved their hands in excitement, but restrained their joy in case the authorities intervened and arrested them for knowing one of the prisoners. They moved along pretending they were weeding and then walked off and mingled with the rest of the workers, before they attracted attention.

'I knew he'd find a way to make contact!' Alexis said to his friends, unable to hide his overwhelming excitement.

'Making contact is one thing, breaking out is another,' Soteris said to him with a serious tone in his voice.

'I have faith in Spyros, he'll get us out of here. Wait and see!' Alexis retorted with conviction that freedom was imminent.

From that day on, Alexis kept a close watch in case Spyros showed up again. Two days went by and then, on the third day in the late afternoon, he saw his friends out in the open fields surrounded by a bunch of screaming youngsters trying to fly their kites. Alexis could not understand what he was trying to do, but he recognised Spyros' masterpiece; a massive kite with a long red, cloth tail, like the one they used to make with bamboo and wax paper.

Many of the prisoners stood by the fence and watched the noisy kids running everywhere, holding their kites as they dipped and dived across the blue sky.

This unusual sight had also attracted the attention of the prison guards, who gazed at the jubilant screaming youngsters in anticipation that some of the erratically flying kites would plunge into the ground and smash to bits. They were not wrong. Some swung and took a deep dive straight to the ground, while others ended up inside the compound with no chance of retrieving them.

As soon as Alexis saw the first one land inside the compound, his eyes lit up and he recognised what Spyros was trying to do. He was planning something with his kite, and from then on, he kept an eye on his kite with its long red tail that was flying at a great height.

The wind was blowing away from his compound and there was no chance of directing his kite towards it. By late afternoon, the wind refused to change direction. Dusk was approaching fast and soon the siren would blast out in a deafening roar for every prisoner to enter their huts and be locked up for the night. With apprehension, he watched the kite and wished that the wind would change in his favour, but time was running out.

It was not meant to be, the siren blasted in a deafening roar and one by one the detainees entered their huts.

Alexis and his friends went to the small window and pinned their eyes on the flying kites. Darkness fell across the camp but the youngsters refused to pull their kites in, and kept them in the air until the tower searchlights were turned on.

By nightfall the wind had changed direction and three kites drifted and flew above the vast compound. That gave them hope

279

that something was going to happen but they had no idea what Spyros was planning. The three of them became vigilant all night, until they could no longer keep their eyes open and fell asleep.

At the first sound of the morning wake up call, Alexis and his two friends ran frantically around the yard for some kind of sign.

Above the main lavatory hut, Soteris had spotted a section of the long red kite tail before anyone else had the chance to see it. He quickly pulled it down and his eyes nearly popped out of their sockets.

At one end of the tail, a spanking brand new wire cutter was attached.

He quickly grabbed it and hid it inside his trousers. He then picked up the tail and began to inspect it, trying to figure out how Spyros had managed to drop the tail down without the kite. He noticed that a long cord was attached to the other end of the tail that disappeared beyond the fence. He stared at it and wondered in puzzlement.

Alexis together with Varnavas came running towards him empty-handed. There was a distressed look on their faces, and both appeared disappointed that they had found no sign of Spyros' intended plans for their escape. As soon as they came closer, Soteris waved the red tail about with a wide smirk on his face and pointed towards his trousers.

'Yes! Yes!' Alexis shouted and spasmodically jerked his head about full of excitement.

'What a lad!' Varnavas stated, amazed at Spyros' ingenious mind.

The three of them had decided there and then that they would attempt to escape the same night knowing that Spyros and Michalaki would be watching out for them every evening.

The day couldn't lapse fast enough, and by late afternoon they went to see the priest and informed him of their escape plans. He was absolutely amazed that someone had managed to smuggle a wire-cutter inside this impregnable concentration camp. With apprehension and concern for their lives, the soft spoken priest blessed them for a successful escape.

Suddenly, freedom for the men was close at hand.

With luck, by tomorrow morning they would be far away from this deplorable, oppressive place so they could resume the fight against the enemy. They spent all day planning every detail of their escape and the more they discussed it the easier it appeared. They could not wait for nightfall to arrive.

Getting out of their hut after lock-up posed no problem at all, because prisoners often sneaked out in the middle of the night to use the lavatory behind their barrack. They had tampered with a corrugated panel beforehand so that it could be removed with ease and without being detected by the night guards on the towers.

While the rest of the prisoners were fast asleep and snoring to their hearts' desire, by two-thirty in the morning, the three men put their escape plan into action.

They climbed off their bunk beds and quietly sneaked out into the open yard behind the lavatories. To their delight, it was a moonless night and the night sky was clouded over by heavy, dark clouds ready to burst into torrential rain.

Soteris was the first one to go out and he quickly ran across the clearing before the tower beam caught him. He entered the smelly lavatory and Alexis with Varnavas immediately followed after him.

There was a strange surreal silence around the vast camp with everyone tucked in their bunk beds being heavily asleep. Only the searchlights of the watch-towers moved in steady rotation flooding the entire area and turning the pitch darkness into daylight.

Inside the toilets, the three lads hurriedly removed their shirts and covered their faces and the upper part of their bodies with mud. Soteris led the way forward, and in complete silence they sneaked to the back of their barrack and walked along the corrugated wall until they reached the designated location for their escape route.

In complete darkness, they briefly glanced around and waited for the searchlight to rotate away from the fence that stood directly in front of them.

Soteris' mission was to cut the single wire-fence that enveloped the entire perimeter of their own compound. The high fence stood about thirty yards away from their hut and, as soon as the tower-light moved away, he ran across the yard and quickly snipped away at the fence-wire.

He maintained this task for five minutes while Alexis and Varnavas watched him running back and forth, until he was finally able to make a breach, big enough for them to crawl through.

With their backs leaning against their hut, the they stood briefly and gazed at the large opening. That was the easy part.

Before reaching the primary barrier of the Dead Zone, there was a twenty-yard clearing to cross that was constantly used by jeep-patrols during the day. Before any other attempts were made, they had to overcome this one barrier first; their gateway to freedom.

This formidable fence encircled the entire Camp K by boxing the endless compounds together. Beyond the first barrier of the Dead Zone, there was a dangerous fifty-yard clearing to crawl across without being noticed. This part of their escape attempt posed the greatest danger.

Soteris carefully evaluated the precise dark spot Alexis had pointed out to them and fell flat on the ground, leaving his friends standing behind to keep an eye on the rotation of beams.

With slow movements he slithered across the yard like a snake, and as soon as he reached the fence he began to cut the wires one by one. It was a slow process and he often had to remain motionless until the lights moved away before he could continue. There were so many intervals they began to get worried that there might not be enough time to complete their mission before the pack of guard dogs started sniffing and making their rounds within the secluded Dead Zone.

His two anxious friends watched him snipping at the double-layer-thick barrier and softly tapped their hands as a warning to stop, whenever a light was heading in at his direction. He would immediately remain still without moving a muscle until the light passed. With persistence, he finally made a large breach. His arms and torso were covered in scratches and some of his wounds began to bleed, but he didn't care. All he wanted was freedom and to get out of this dehumanising prison.

Satisfied with the size of the opening, he tapped his palms once signalling the others to make a move. His hands were aching from cutting the thick wires, and while he was waiting, he rubbed them together to circulate the blood in an attempt to relieve the pain.

Alexis dashed across, fell to the ground and began to slither through the compound fence with Varnavas right behind him. They went through it and slowly started to crawl at a snail's pace to master the common clearing that enveloped the entire camp.

Soteris, as their lookout, kept his eyes wide open watching the rotating lights and after ten minutes they were sprawled flat on the ground next to each other.

Re-grouped again, they remained motionless and stared with apprehension across the vast Dead Zone. Alexis was correct with his observation. The searchlights hardly covered their spot and only once in a while did both tower-lights managed to flood the entire vicinity.

Without wasting time, Soteris crawled through the opening and moved forward about two yards inside the fence. Alexis went next and he grabbed Soteris' foot while Varnavas did the same and held on to Alexis' foot.

The three of them began to slide forward. They moved ahead inch-by-inch at such a slow pace they risked wasting valuable time. But the lights maintained their steady rotation, forcing them to remain still every couple of minutes. One kick meant all was clear, two kicks meant detection, and they all had to freeze to the ground. It took them nearly half an hour to go across fifty yards but, in the end, they managed to reach the final rolls of the barbed-wire.

Alexis took over from Soteris and began to cut the wires.

It seemed there was no end to them. He worked like a beaver and holding the cutters with both hands he clipped away. His aim was to make a tunnel big enough for them to slide through the three-yard-thick final barrier. With hearts pounding from anxiety and foreheads covered in sweat, the men persisted, knowing the dreadful outcome if they were caught. For them it was a certain death by a long rope and they were not prepared to lose their lives yet.

Alexis continued cutting the wires one by one and eventually he began to form a tunnel. Surrounded by razor-sharp wires, not only had he to cut the thick steel, but he also had to push the wires aside and secure them to the rest, so he could devise a beaver's tunnel, big enough for them to pass through. His movements were restricted and soon his back and bare arms began to bleed from hundreds of cuts.

It took him such a long time to cut through the thick fence that the first pallid light of dawn appeared across the horizon. The three of them became anxious, knowing the dogs would be out soon to start their rounds, within the Dead Zone.

'Make it faster!' Soteris kept whispering to him.

With apprehension his friends kept urging him to hurry up, and in the end he was through.

He crawled out of the final perimeter fence and remained flat on the ground while the other two carefully passed through the tunnel. Once they reached the other side of the fence, they proceeded to crawl away from the concentration camp and entered fertile ground.

They smelled freedom at last, and they could hardly restrain their enthusiasm that they had out-foxed the army and had made a successful escape from Camp K.

The sun had not risen yet and, as usual, they had noticed the familiar crowd of workers dispersing across the fields. Immediately they began to crawl straight for them. Once they got nearer, they got off the ground and stooped pretending they were part of the workers.

As soon as the field-workers noticed the lads' faces covered in mud and bleeding scratches, they knew what had happened. Three men quickly took their shirts off and handed them over to them, while a woman poured water from a clay pitcher so they could wash the mud off.

A man with a thick moustache and tanned weather-beaten face raised his thick arms in the air and clapped his palms together.

'Everybody, go home! There is no work today! Go before the army arrests all of us!' he ordered in a harsh voice.

Immediately, the crowd of men and women hurriedly dropped their tools and started to walk away as quickly as possible, knowing the horrible outcome when the authorities discovered the breakout and possible escape route.

The three escapees walked among the workers until they reached the fringes of the vast vegetation fields. Suddenly Alexis noticed Spyros' car parked at the far side of the gravelled road that cut across the grassland.

They headed straight for it and saw his two friends sleeping in the front seat.

Alexis banged on the windscreen and woke both of them up. Half asleep, they looked at him, gave him a wide smile, and got out of the car. They briefly embraced each other and with rapturous laughter they all got inside the car and Spyros drove off at a high speed.

CHAPTER SIXTEEN

KYRA-SOTERIA WAS no different from the rest of the thousands of mothers who suffered the anguish of not knowing the fate of their children being locked up in prisons and concentration camps. The most frightening part was the knowledge of the continued execution of their men. Every time an order for a hanging execution was issued by the Governor, they fretted at the thought that another young life was about to be snuffed out and they lived in constant fear that the next noose was not around their own son's neck. Their only avenue was to plead with God to put a stop to this madness that had persisted for so long with the loss of hundreds of innocent lives.

Every afternoon, like a daily ritual, Kyra-Soteria was on her way home from church.

She had just prayed for her son's safety not knowing how he was being treated in that notorious Camp K. She kept his letter in her bosom close to her heart and would not part with it. Hearing from him gave her hope and she could not thank enough the young girl who brought the letter to them at the risk of her own life. She made her daughter and her son Marcos read it over and over again, analysing his every word and forcing them to read it again in case she missed a word or something.

With a black scarf over her head, and with deep solitary thoughts, she trekked along the narrow cobbled alleyway oblivious to her surroundings and avoiding talking to anyone. She grew older and put on weight and the doctor put her on a special diet, but that hardly made a difference. Worry was slowly killing her.

Dragging her swollen feet she headed for home being at peace with herself for talking to *Panayia*. At the church she prostrated humbly in front of the *iconostasio*, made libations by lighting two large candles and spoke quietly directly to *Panayia*.

'You are a woman Holy one!' she muttered. 'You understand the pain of a distressed mother, please protect my son Alexis. I have not seen him for years. Reach out and protect him and, all those other young lads whose lives are at risk by this catastrophe that had besieged our land. Please hear me this once! If you have to, take my life instead of his! I humbly implore you to grant me this one wish and then I shall die in peace. He is not a bad boy, my holy Mother, I am punished each day for my sins by not setting my tired eyes upon him. Death for me is near I can feel it, but before I reach your blessed kingdom, grant me this one last yearning. Bring him safely home to me. If I am gone before you make your decision, at least save him from evil and have mercy on me. I implore you to hear me this once, for I am your humble servant for life!'

When she finished, she got off the floor and stared into the icon's glowing eyes that seemed to want to speak to her as if to say, 'I hear your pain, go in peace,' she then crossed herself and walked out into the empty alleyway and headed for home.

Maro had decided not to go with her today and, while coming back from the church, she missed her daughter's chirpy chatting that kept her company during the long trek.

Before leaving for the church, they were sitting—mother and daughter—on the sofa having a chat in readiness for both to depart; Maro to visit Xanthia and her mother to visit the church.

'Be careful Maro.' her mother advised her and gazed at her pretty face that overflowed with the sparkle of youth. She lovingly stroked her long black hair and tenderly kissed her on the cheeks

'Don't worry about me *mama*, I can take care of myself.'

'I don't like what I hear about the Turks lately, they seem to have gone mad. Only a few days ago they came out of the Walls and attacked the locals for no reason at all. That area is becoming dangerous!' her mother insisted.

'I am seventeen, *mama*, Kaliopi is coming with me!' her daughter reassured her worried mother.

'Even so, I am worried! I wish Ahmet was with us, he would protect you now that Alexis is not here.'

'There is a rumour that he was the one who betrayed Alexis for the reward.'

'Don't believe in rumours my child, slanderous words are sharper than knives! I don't believe our Ahmet would do such a thing.' her mother interrupted her. She was not interested in hearing bad words about Ahmet. She had a soft spot for him.

'What happened to him, then? He completely disappeared and we've heard nothing from him since they arrested Alexis, that was months ago.' Maro insisted.

'Who knows child, maybe he's locked up by the Turks inside them Walls,' her mother said, and quickly changed the subject. 'Today your father went to see the carpenter to order a crib for the baby,' she added.

'Isn't it nice that Xanthia is having a baby?' Maro said with excitement and her eyes lit up at the prospect of her becoming an aunt.

'The poor girl, I wish Alexis was with her now. She needs him.

Every expectant mother needs her man next to her when that great moment comes.' her mother said, feeling upset for Xanthia.

'*Mama*, when this is over, we are going to have a wonderful wedding!'

'That we shall my child but when?'

'Soon, *mama*, soon! They are talking about a solution.'

'I hope so my child! I hope this madness comes to an end.' She muttered and crossed herself.

'It will soon be over *mama*, you wait and see!' Maro reassured her worried mother who believed no-one.

'Your father and I have been discussing Xanthia. We'd like her to come and stay with us, so she can leave that neighbourhood, it's too dangerous being so close to the Walls,' her mother said to her daughter changing the subject.

'How about her mother?'

'I was talking to her the other day, and she plans to go back to her village to get away from that place. She's terrified of the Turks.'

'I shall tell Xanthia what you said, she'd be thrilled. Wouldn't it be nice to have a baby in the house? I hope it's a baby boy.' Maro said happily, and stood up to leave.

'Whatever God wishes my child.' Her mother said, and she humbly made the sign of the cross with her three fingers from forehead to her waist.

With difficulty, she pulled her weight off the couch to see her daughter depart to pay Xanthia a visit across the town.

Maro put on her white jacket, kissed her mother once and rushed out the front door. Her mother stood by the veranda and saw her run to the bus stop.

'Be careful Maro.' She muttered between her lips.

Maro turned her head and looked at her mother, making her long hair swing in the wind and rapidly waved her hand goodbye.

When she disappeared around the corner, Kyra-Soteria walked inside to get herself ready to visit the church and pray for her son.

*   *   *

That same evening the muezzin was in perfect form. His reverberating voice was as clear as a running spring and he let it drone across the rooftops calling the faithful to come for prayer. He prayed to Allah and asked for his guidance and protection from those Greeks who sought to destroy them.

Standing at the top of his minaret, he turned his head to the East and chanted for a long time until he decided the East had

287

heard enough, and then walked to the other side and faced the West.

He placed his palms around his mouth and called out as loud as he could so everyone would hear his prayer. Once he was satisfied that his call had reached everybody's ears, he turned towards the North and then to the South, not leaving anything to chance. By the time he had finished his call to prayer, his throat started to hurt and he could hardly speak, but he was content with those vibrant words of his, knowing that Allah and all those people inside the Walls had heard his calling.

He straightened up his headdress that flapped in the wind, and slowly climbed down the winding staircase, and headed directly for the interior of his mosque.

Ahmet was sitting on the veranda of his local coffee house sipping coffee and playing backgammon with his friend Hassan and neither of them could not but hear the powerful prayer-call. They did not budge. Instead, they continued their game while watching the activities of the late afternoon. Between his moves he stared across the square and let his eyes wander at the masses of people that roamed around doing their late shopping. He was in a thoughtful mood.

Ever since he was forced to live among his people, he kept to himself. Held at ransom by the *Volkan* hordes, his baby sister's life and those of his relatives were in constant threat if he refused to help out the Turkish side. Without choice, he had given in and joined the nightly patrols on the lookout for any Greek activities that may pose a threat to their community.

Totally devastated with guilt for betraying the people he had loved all his life, he hated himself and had lost his self-esteem. In time, he had lost weight and there was hardly even a smile on his handsome face. Without realising it, he had developed a sad and irritable attitude and he was constantly angry with everyone. Devastated, he hardly ever mixed with the others, except for Hassan, a long-time childhood friend who had become his loyal companion.

In a dilemma, he felt like a fragile mocking bird held in a cage, wilting and dying while being cooped up within the Walls.

At the adjacent table sat Fatin, a well-built brute whom Ahmet had no time for. He hated this overweight slime-ball of a man. He was a well-known member of *Volkan* and his mission was to become his shadow and followed him everywhere, not leaving him out of his sight for a moment.

Sitting arrogantly in his chair, he smoked his hookah and with his deep-set eyes undressed every young girl that happened to pass by.

He made loud derogative comments at each one or gave them a sharp dog-whistle and felt proud of himself for his boldness.

Next to him sat five others who joked with one another and paid no attention to Ahmet and Hassan who were seated at the nearby table. Armed with pistols, as new recruits of the new Auxiliary Police Force, they were conceitedly sure of themselves and talked with loud voices, making sure that everyone could hear them.

It was getting late, and the sun had set a long time ago, bringing out the street merchants trying to flog their goods.

Fatin was getting bored and stood up. He raised both his long arms above his head, and started to stretch himself like a lazy cat. He looked around the square and was not pleased what was going on; most of the girls had disappeared and only men and old women were about.

'I feel like getting my hands on some juicy Greek girl,' he exclaimed and uttered a dirty laugh.

Ahmet gave him a stern angry look, but avoided making a comment. Instead, he got off his chair in readiness to leave.

'Come, let's go,' Ahmet said to his companion and walked down the few steps of the veranda.

With flashlights illuminating the way forward, they headed into the dark night for their post at the western side of the Walls. As soon as they took leave, Fatin and his pals followed after them, but kept behind and at a fair distance away from them.

Within fifteen minutes Ahmet with Hassan had reached the base of the lookout post, and slowly climbed the old dilapidated stone staircase that took them to the top of a wide parapet that encircled the entire fortress.

From such a height, they had a clear view of the Greek neighbourhood on the other side of the Walls. The dim lights beyond flickered into the darkness in clusters, and they were quite aware that a number of Greek outposts were also positioned on the rooftops of those darkly-lit houses looking towards them.

At the top of the parapet, Ahmet and his friend took their posts.

Fatin and his buddies seemed to be in discussion at the base of the Wall. With flashlights lighting up their faces, they stayed put reluctant to climb up the steps. Fatin was whispering to his companions and he was pointing in another direction.

'I am going over the Walls' he said to his friends, with a determined tone in his voice.

'In Allah's name why do you want to do that?' one of his friends asked.

'Are you afraid of them Greeks?' he bellowed with anger at him.

'We could cause a riot, be sensible!' another one objected.

'So what? I am bored to death!' he barked at his worried friends, and walked away from them.

When he had covered a few yards, he looked back and saw that they were reluctant to follow him. 'Are you coming?' he shouted at them.

One by one they walked towards him and, as a group, began to walk away towards a well-known breach of the Walls.

Hassan had noticed their searchlights moving fast away from them and immediately ran after them to find out what they were up to, by refusing to take their posts. He caught up with them and they told him that they were going over to the Greek side.

Fretfully, Hassan, a small lad, ran back and told Ahmet what they were planning to do.

'Idiots! They will cause trouble for us all!' Ahmet said, and ran after them to try and stop them.

But, it was too late! They all vanished into the night.

They both searched for the group, but they had lost them in the narrow dark alleyways. Distraught, Ahmet with Hassan persisted with the search and they quickened their pace to try and catch up with them before they had the chance to leave the Walls. They knew precisely which part of the breach they were heading to and went straight for that area.

Arriving there, they squeezed through the tight crack in the Wall and found themselves outside over a steep rampart. Cautiously they climbed down over the Greek side and started searching for Fatin in the hope that they were not stupid enough to start something that would embroil the entire community in a dangerous situation.

Ahmet knew that it takes only one idiot to brew up a poison stew and both friends desperately searched the entire area.

Unable to find them, they turned their attention towards a sparsely populated sub-division surrounded by unfinished road-works. With every step forward, they became apprehensive in case their movements became suspicious to the Greek civil watch, who would instantly blast out a public warning that the Turks were on the rampage. Such an alarming situation would be devastating for both communities.

Either way, he had to risk that possibility and find Fatin and bring him back at all costs before the trouble could escalate beyond reason.

Fatin and his hordes eluded them and for no reason at all they hid behind a thick cluster of bushes next to a deserted road. They sat on the ground and each lit a Senior Service which they smoked leisurely, while inspecting the sleepy Greek neighbourhood. They were on the lookout for some activity and excitement to alleviate their boredom.

The entire area appeared deserted. At this late hour, people were not prepared to roam around in the open, being frightened of a possible attack by the Turks from within the Walls. Their lookouts gave them some kind of security and they could sleep much easier at night, knowing there were sentinels watching for any sudden Turkish movements.

By the time they had finished their cigarettes, Fatin and his friends began to get fidgety from doing nothing. Then one of his friends noticed the movement of two dark silhouettes approaching them from the top of the slope.

They walked along the gravelled street chatting quietly, oblivious to the time. There was a majestic full moon above that turned the night into day, and the sky was studded with bright twinkling stars that stretched into infinity.

'I see someone coming.' Fatin's friend whispered.

Immediately everybody turned and looked in the direction of the two figures that walked obliviously at the side of the street.

'Allah, they are girls.' Fatin exclaimed in a low voice, thrilled that he had finally found the action he was after.

'Your wish has been granted, you are about to taste the juice of Greek flesh.' Another said, putting ideas into his head.

Unaware of their spectators, the two girls approached closer. One of the girls was slightly on the heavy side while the other one was slim with long flowing hair that swung about with every movement of her head.

Like a pack of wolves scenting their prey, the men remained silent and focused their eyes on them without even blinking an eye. They watched the unsuspecting girls who kept coming closer.

Oblivious of their presence, the girls carried on talking and giggling as they went along.

The men had already decided that the girls were theirs for the taking. They remained motionless until the girls approached the thick bushes.

At the right moment, they pounced from their dark hiding place and encircled the two girls.

Startled by the sudden appearance of the six shadowy men, the girls were at a loss and tried to say something. But, as soon as they realised that the men were Turks, they froze in fright. Terrified, they sensed instantly what was about to happen and turned white, petrified by the prospect of the men's intentions. Trapped between

291

the six of them, they looked across the sleepy neighbourhood but not a soul was about.

Fatin pulled out his pistol from its holster and pointed the gun at both of them.

The moment the girls saw the gun, they shivered from fright and looked at one another in panic. They knew that they could not escape the brutes and attempted to scream at the top of their voices. But the louts quickly grabbed them and placed their hands on their mouths.

There was a brief scuffle, but in the end the men were too strong and maliciously slapped the girls hard on their faces and pulled their hair out in handfuls so that they would submit to their desires.

The teenagers began to cry, but the men showed no mercy on the Greek girls. They were anxious to rape their victims before anyone showed up.

They seized them by the hair and dragged them like two discarded rugs across the rock-strewn surface of the ground. The girls desperately kicked about to free themselves, but it was a losing battle. The rough men threw them among the thick bushes and the terrified girls found themselves, pinned down, held in position by their captors' strong arms.

The men carried on talking with one another in Turkish and the girls had no idea what they were saying, thus adding to their trauma.

Fatin and two of his friends got hold of the slim one while the others tackled her friend and placed her on the ground at a distance away from him. The men ripped the girls' blouses apart exposing their breasts, and placed their clammy hands all over them, feeling their softness, while others started touching their private parts.

Flung onto the hard ground strewn with sharp stone-chippings, the girls were in a helpless situation and cried out pleading for mercy, but the Turks had not a single drop of decency flowing through their veins. This was a price worth the risk, and they had always lusted for Greek girls. Now that they had the opportunity to fulfil their dreams, they were not about to let that good fortune pass them by.

The girls continued to struggle and desperately threw their hand in the air while kicking their legs about like captive animals, sensing they were about to be slaughtered. There was no escape for them! The men were determined to rape them and held them tight to the ground. Their young innocent lives belonged to these barbarians who were about to violate and maliciously deflower them.

Fatin clumsily undid his gun holster and threw it aside on the ground. Then, he unbuttoned his trousers and pulled them halfway down to his knees while instructing the others to hold the girl tight. He ripped off the girl's underwear, forced one of his hands between her tightly squeezed legs and started to feel and stroke her private parts. His other hand was grasping his erect penis that was ready to explode in uncontrollable animal lust.

'Hey Fatin this one is a bit fat what am I going to do with her?' one of his friends whispered to him from the distance.

'Do what you like with her, this one is mine.' Fatin yelled back to him with indifference.

The girl below him struggled, squeezed her legs tight and moved her hips about to stop him, but all her efforts were in vain.

With one powerful pull he spread her legs apart, while his friends held her hands so she could not move them. Clumsily he laid his massive body over her and she begun to smell his breath, when suddenly his slobbery lips fused with hers, dripping with saliva over her face. He tasted her tears and started to lick them with his slimy tongue. She felt sick and turned her head, but her captor persisted while his friends urged him to finish so they could take over. But he was in no hurry and continued to torment the girl who lay helpless under his heavy torso.

Without warning, he thrust his rigid penis into her. Panic stricken, she screamed with pain, but her mouth was covered and no sound came out. He paid no attention to her plight, and began to violently push harder into her, but he was having difficulty. He tried a few times without success and got angry.

'She's a Greek virgin!' he bellowed, while thrusting even harder.

His friends liked what he said, and insisted that he should finish so they too could experience what a Greek virgin is like. Blinded by sexual desire and in frenzy, they started manhandling her exposed breasts.

Fatin thrust violently again into her and finally managed to go deep inside her. Pleased with his achievement, he went into a wild passion and between groans kept thrusting his engorged penis into her as hard as he could, by forcing his prey to have sex with him.

In fear of her life, the young girl succumbed to her ordeal and lay motionless while he kept pumping into her violently. She felt that her legs were about to split apart by his brutal attack, and prayed to God the Almighty to strike him down dead. The pain was so excruciating that she felt sick every time his penis moved inside her.

Suddenly she threw up, causing the man who was holding her mouth to swear aloud in Turkish for getting a handful of her vomit. He gave her a hard slap on the face. She no longer cared what they did to her and lay on the ground like a living corpse. Her rapist kept up his copulation until he finally let his semen spurt out into her. She felt his spasmodic thrusts and realised that he had finished. Satisfied, he pulled out of her, while she began to feel his semen slowly seeping out of her bleeding vagina.

No sooner one had finished, than the others took it in turns to have brutal intercourse with the helpless captives.

One of the Turks had decided that he no longer wanted to copulate with the slim girl with so much semen leaking out of her. He pressed her fragile face hard on the ground, forcing her masses of hair to spread out. With one hand he grabbed a handful of her hair tightly, while the other clutched at her buttocks attempting to sodomize her. After a few tries, he managed to violate her.

Feeling his large, thick penis inside her anus, the terrified girl screamed out in such an intolerable state of pain that she fainted.

Unconcerned, her rapist continued his savage violation of her, and persisted until he had ejaculated.

She came around in total agony for being ripped apart. In a daze, she felt the warm blood dripping between her legs. She was unable to move. Traumatised, terrified and in a complete physical exhaustion she laid on the ground like a wreck waiting for the worst to happen.

Fatin had decided to rape his victim one more time, and he started to touch her exposed firm buttocks. He pulled his trousers down again and he was about to lie on top of her when one his friends called out into the night.

'There is someone coming, I think is Ahmet!' one of the Turks shouted.

Ahmet had finally caught up with them, and headed straight to where the men congregated. They hurriedly tried to pull themselves together so they could run away, realising their secret was out.

Once Ahmet got nearer, they all scattered about like thieves in the night, trying to get away from him and his companion.

'What the devil is going on here?' he stated with shock as soon as he saw the two bodies laying flat on the ground.

He realised what his compatriots had done to the girls.

'You animals!' he bawled out loud unable to restrain himself.

He looked into the night to see if any of the culprits were about. Among the bushes one of them was desperately trying to cover his penis.

Ahmet had noticed the dark shadow and went straight for him. He grabbed him by the neck and thrust him to the ground while the villain desperately attempted to pull his trousers up so he could make a run for it. Ahmet recognised Fatin and a scuffle ensued between the two, but Ahmet had the upper hand. Fatin was unable to move with his trousers halfway down to his knees and he fell on the ground next to his motionless victim.

Ahmet, in a blinding fury, put both of his hands around his neck to strangle him, cursing him at the same time in Turkish.

The girl lying next to them slowly turned her head around and saw what was happening. Dishevelled, confused and in a panic she recognised Ahmet's voice and imploringly raised her head slightly, looked up and stared at him.

'How could you, Ahmet?' she muttered in a low trembling voice.

Hearing those words, a sharp dagger pierced through his heart. He recognised that gentle frightened voice.

'Maro! No! Please no!' he cried out like a wounded animal the moment he realised that the girl next to him was Alexis' sister. His eyes instantly filled with tears and he pressed his hands tighter around Fatin's neck.

Fatin began to choke, but that was not good enough for Ahmet. With his mind clouded by anguish and despair, he pulled out his dagger and plunged it into Fatin's belly. Frantically he continued stabbing him until he made no more sounds and lay motionless on the ground with his trousers between his legs.

Before Ahmet had time to turn to Maro, she slowly and methodically reached out and grabbed hold of her captor's gun that lay nearby at a hand's reach.

Overcome by shame, she raised her bruised arm and in a trance slowly put the gun against her temple. Without uttering a single word she pulled the trigger once. Her blood splattered across Ahmet's face and clothing.

'Maro . . . No . . .!' he wailed at the sight of Maro's limp body that lay still on the ground.

He grabbed Maro's body with both arms and shook her, so he could bring her back to life. It was no use. There was no life left in that limp young body of hers.

Ahmet began to punch his head with both fists in self-punishment and started to cry like a child. He knelt beside her, unable to accept that this wasn't just a nightmare. He started to sway back and forth, holding the lifeless body in his arms while sobbing and bawling his eyes out from helplessness.

His friend Hassan approached him from behind, devastated by the sight of the two girls. Quietly he tapped his distraught friend on the shoulder.

'The other girl is also dead . . .' he muttered sadly, not believing what the Turks had done to these poor girls.

Seeing Ahmet crying and holding the limp body in his arms, Hassan shook his head in astonishment and asked, 'Do you know her?'

'She's my sister!' Ahmet yelled, and burst into loud sobs. 'My baby sister!' he then roared again and punched his head.

Hassan didn't know what to say and looked at his friend in pity. But he was in no position to sooth his anguish. He kept shaking his head in bewilderment and disgust.

'I must take her home . . .' Ahmet muttered to himself between sobs, paying no attention to his friend.

He lifted Maro's naked body up and tenderly covered it with her torn dress. He pressed her warm, lifeless body next to his chest and slowly proceeded to leave.

He stopped briefly and looked at his astounded friend.

'Go away Hassan. Go away and save yourself! We are dealing with beasts and not men!' he said to him and walked off on his own.

Hassan turned and headed for the Walls, in total shock at man's barbarity against his own.

Ahmet walked towards the main road, and once he reached it, stood in the middle of the darkly-lit lanes carrying the limp body closely to his chest.

He saw a car approaching and he did not move. Once it got near, the strong lights flooded over him forcing the driver to come to a sudden stop. The curious driver quickly came out to see what happened and when he learned what had taken place, he helped Ahmet inside his car and both drove off for Maro's home.

On the way there they stopped briefly at the first house they came across and told the inhabitants to call the authorities, so they could pick up the other two bodies that lay among the bushes.

*   *   *

Yiorkis and his wife were sitting in their living room waiting for the return of their daughter. Marcos was out roaming with his friends and the two of them lounged about in the room that hardly ever changed. Alexis' portrait, smiling enigmatically, was hanging on the wall above the settee, with his hair neatly combed to one side. Next to it hung Ahmet's portrait, also full of smiles and showing his well-set white teeth and masses of curly black hair. A smaller picture had both of them holding their bicycles while from behind Marcos contorted a funny face at them both. The humorous snapshot always prompted those who saw it to smile at the boys' arrogant pose. Above the two portraits hung a framed photo of Alexantiou,

296

the young *Eoka* hero who was recently burned alive by the British army.

Now and then, Yiorkis would glance at the wall clock and check the time. A cut-out image of a colourful rooster kept pecking noisily up and down and ticking rhythmically, causing the clock's hands to move on at a steady pace.

'What time did you say Maro was coming back?' he asked his wife when he realised that the time was well past nine thirty.

'She did say about nine.'

'It's nearly ten! She will get it for being late!' Yiorkis interjected with a little bad-temper.

'You know girls, my husband, they have plenty to talk about. I told her to ask Xanthia to come and live with us,' Kyra-Soteria said defending her daughter.

She was thrilled if not ecstatic at the prospect of having Xanthia and the baby staying with them. She was planning to spoil the baby rotten, and knitted a great variety of baby clothes in preparation for that wonderful day.

Yiorkis remained in a sceptical mood, but his wife persisted and lovingly ruffled his grey hair.

'You did right.' her husband finally said to her, but his thoughts were elsewhere.

'Just think about it, we are going to become grandparents! How do you feel about being called *papou*?' his wife asked, trying to tease him, being in a joyous mood.

'I feel fine wife . . . but what's keeping Maro so long?' Yiorkis asked and knitted his thick eyebrows together, not interested in his wife's chitchat.

He was anxious to see his daughter home knowing that the army was always on the rampage, rounding up and arresting the young ones for no reason at all and sending them to detention camps.

Every so often, he would get up and go outside on the lookout in case he caught a glimpse of Maro's return. When there was no sign of her, he would go back inside and sit down again feeling dejected.

Marcos came home from visiting a friend, and the three of them sat around waiting for his sister to show up. They were not going to let her get away with it. Marcos already had his own plan how to deal with his sister for being so late coming home.

By eleven o'clock, a noisy car came to an abrupt stop outside their home. The driver kept pressing hard on its horn, and waking up the neighbourhood.

The deafening sound caused them to leap up off their seats.

297

Yiorkis, followed by his son, went outside to see what was happening. His wife slowly pulled herself off the couch and walked out to the veranda, sensing something was wrong by the sounding urgency of the car's horn. She stood in the dark and locked her gaze ahead at the stationary car.

The back door of the car opened and a dark, shadowy figure appeared trying to take something out of the back seat. Yiorkis recognised Ahmet, and with mixed feelings of joy and apprehension he gave out a smiled.

'Ahmet!' he exclaimed and started to walk down the few steps of their veranda, to put his arms around his other lost son.

Ahmet did not answer. Instead, he carefully picked Maro's body off the back seat and, holding the limp corpse in both arms, he stood paralysed on the spot. With tears in his eyes, he stared at the old man who approached closer. Ahmet immediately burst into loud sobs.

Yiorkis saw his daughter's lifeless body and his knees buckled. His son instantly came to his rescue and helped his elderly father to remain standing.

From above the veranda, Kyra-Soteria did not miss a thing and carefully tried to master the steep steps to get closer. Her husband turned back and tried to stop her, but she pushed him aside with all her strength and rushed to where Ahmet was standing.

Seeing Maro's limp body, she burst into agonising screams and tried to pull the body away from Ahmet, but he held it tightly refusing to let go. He never stopped crying for a moment and he moved a few steps forward towards the house.

Realising that his sister was dead, Marcos had joined his mother and both cried out loud, bringing out the entire neighbourhood. One by one their neighbours quickly came out into the night and began to congregate outside the house, whispering with one another and asking what had happened.

Kyra-Soteria collapsed on the spot. Yiorkis rushed inside the house and returned with a cup full of water and sprinkled it on her wrinkled face. As soon as she came round, she burst into a heart-piercing wail.

Ahmet carefully took the corpse inside the house and laid Maro's body on her bed. Yiorkis could not stop his sobbing and stared at his daughter's smashed, pretty face and knelt next to her, unable to remain on his feet.

His wife threw herself into the room, and the moment she took a good look at Maro's corpse covered in blood-stains and her clothing torn to shreds, she threw herself over her daughter's corpse and wrapped her arms around her. She knew her daughter was gone forever. She banged her fists on her chest and in agony she yelled like a wounded animal and screamed so loud, that she passed out again next to her husband.

Three women who could not control their emotions, but to weep with her, had managed to bring her back with splashes of cold water. Supporting her by both arms, they carefully guided her outside in the back yard so she could get some fresh air.

The entire house was suddenly crammed with neighbours who congregated in each room, while the women let out rivers of tears to flood their eyes. They sobbed and cried while the men shook their heads totally shocked. Stunned by the sudden catastrophe, a throng gathered outside in the street and around Yiorki's house. They arrived in the middle of the night so they could share their neighbour's pain and sudden anguish.

Outside in the yard, Kyra-Soteria knelt on the ground and wailed. She screamed out into the night as loud as her weak lungs could. She raised her hands in the air and bowed to the ground yelling in agonising cries that made everybody's hair stand on end.

Her trauma had no remedy and she pulled her grey hair out in handfuls and thrust her fists against her bosom hitting and punishing herself. She kept a long vigil and cried out at the top of her voice, making other women cry with her. Her high-pitched voice, broken by sobs, echoed into the silent night, causing the next-door neighbour's dog to start howling. It sensed the presence of death in the area.

In shrill cries of woe, she threw herself onto the ground with burning sorrow in her soul. Her bare knees sunk deep into the ground and lamented in despair. Nobody could stop her anguish and trauma at losing her beloved daughter, and she constantly wailed:

> 'Maro . . . where are you my child . . .!
> What have they done to you . . . my precious girl . . .!
> What, am I to do . . . what, am I to do . . .!
> Maro . . . come back to me . . .! Now . . .!
> Let me die with you . . . my precious one . . . Maro . . .!'

She would stop for a brief moment and then start again worse than before.

Her hands and body shook spasmodically, and she could no longer control her shakes. Only a deep grave would release her torment. Weeping women encircled her, but did not interfere and kept their distance by letting her express her anguish and grief the best way she knew how.

Suddenly she was fuelled by fire. She clumsily stood up and rushed inside the house. Seeing her distressed state, everyone stopped their whispering and stared at this distraught old lady. Dead silence had engulfed the entire household in anticipation of her next move. Her body and arms shook worse than an earthquake.

She went and stood in front of Ahmet, who was cornered by men asking him questions.

She speared her stare directly into his tear-wet eyes. She was about ready to explode. Her clothing was torn to shreds, and her sweat-covered bosom was practically hanging out of her dress. Her dishevelled, long grey hair was tossed wildly across her face and she was ready to tear apart anyone who came close to her.

Concerned, her husband tried to give her the medicine the doctor had prescribed for her but with one thrust she threw the bottle across the floor. Instead, she pinned her wild gaze directly on Ahmet, who had brought such a catastrophe in her life.

'Tell me what happened to my daughter!' she screamed at him at the top of her voice.

'The Turks, mother . . . ' he muttered.

'Don't call me mother,' she bellowed at him. 'Just tell me . . .'

'She was raped . . .!' Ahmet had finally managed to say, drawling his words

On hearing those words, she went into a temporary trance while her body shook uncontrollably. In shock, she was unable to utter a single word. Suddenly she lashed out at the lad who stared with sadness at her wrinkled face.

'Get out. Get out of my house murderers!' she screamed, and thrashed out at him, scratching his face with her nails. 'Get out of my house and curse you and all your kind, murderers, murderers! Out . . .!' she yelled again, and attacked Ahmet with all her might.

Her husband tried to hold her back and called for Marcos to take care of his mother. He then turned towards Ahmet, who was standing in the middle of the room surrounded by men, women and children.

'God-damn you and your people, get out!' Yiorkis finally bellowed at him and showed him the door.

> 'Alexis . . . where are you my son?
> Look what they've done to your sister, son . . . '

Kyra-Soteria wailed and screamed not giving her husband a chance to speak to Ahmet.

'Katares! Katares!' she suddenly screamed out curses at Ahmet again, with hate in her trembling voice.

Ahmet appeared traumatised. Kyra-Soteria's curses touched him deeply in his heart and distraught with guilt, he bowed his head and turned around to leave the house.

He reached the door and someone grabbed him by the neck. It was Yiorkis.

'We gave you bread, a home and love! Go to Hell and the Devil, be with you always . . .!' Yiorkis shouted at the top of his voice.

Yiorkis' face was covered in tears that trickled down his unshaven face. Once they reached his chin one by one, the drops kept dripping onto the floor.

Speechless, Ahmet examined the face that he had always loved. He felt the man's pain but no matter what he said, he could not compensate for the loss of this kind man's daughter. Without hesitation, he pulled his shirt wide open exposing his hairy chest.

'Kill me now.' He said in a low voice.

'Go to Hell! I shall not have Turkish blood stain the ground that we walk upon,' Yiorkis bawled at him and pushed him towards the doorway.

The onlookers remained in total silence and furiously exchanged glances as sharp as daggers with one another in readiness to pounce upon the distraught Turkish lad.

'Get out of my sight! *Katares*, till the day you die!' Yiorkis yelled out one more time and pushed him further towards the door.

Those spoken words of curses were deadlier than the sharpest daggers and Ahmet felt his broken heart torn apart. He stumbled and fell on the floor. He lifted himself up and slowly tried to break through the crowd.

Marcos with tears in his eyes came from behind and punched him once, in the back. 'Alexis will kill you!' he shouted angrily.

Feeling his hard punch, Ahmet stumbled again, but was held upright by the onlookers who maintained their silence during the whole encounter.

Simultaneously, the crowd suddenly started shouting curses at him and some punched him on the face. Out of respect, he did not respond and accepted the rain of spit against his face and their constant punching and shoving. Totally humiliated, he understood their feelings and considered himself responsible for Maro's death, being a Turk. He wished the earth would open up to swallow him deep into the ground forever, so the pain would go away. But he was not so lucky.

When he got outside, he noticed his friend Michalaki among the mournful but angry crowd. His faithful old friend looked at him as an enemy with a deep hatred in his eyes. Maro was his favourite and nobody could bring her back, and so he cried and sobbed for the senseless loss of her young life.

There was no place for him here and heartbroken he moved along to depart from this place that had meant so much to him. When he reached a distance away, the furious crowd spontaneously started to throw a volley of rocks at him. Damned, and with tears in his eyes, he disappeared around the corner and headed on foot to reach his own prison and hell within the Walls.

No grown-up slept a wink during the entire night, but kept vigil offering their moral support and condolences to the distraught family. A few streets away the same traumatic scene was repeated, by Kaliopi's family.

Yiorkis, together with his son Marcos, walked over to see the family, pay their respects and mourn for the loss of their own daughter.

Once she composed herself, Kyra-Soteria with the help of the other women stripped the corpse, and tenderly she proceeded to wash her daughter's bloodstained and bruised body. Every time she gazed at Maro's pretty face which had been smashed by the bullet, she would burst into long scream and pull her hair out in agony.

When she composed herself again, she lovingly anointed the body and gently combed her baby's long hair. Then she dressed Maro in her favourite white dress and covered her corpse with a pure white embroidered shroud.

Her soul was in torment and she sat next to Maro's bed refusing to leave the corpse on its own. She talked to Maro all night surrounded by the other women who remained with her until the next day.

By ten o'clock in the morning, a coffin was brought to the house and her father helped by his son carefully put Maro's body inside the long black casket. They rested the coffin on top of a table in the middle of the living room so everyone could pay their last respects.

The news of Maro's and Kaliopi's death quickly spread across the town and people came from every corner of Varoshia to pay their respects. All schools and shops shut for that day in mourning, and hundreds of distraught students showed up in the neighbourhood, furious at what the Turks had done and demanded revenge.

A heavily pregnant Xanthia came and immediately took her position next to Maro's mother, refusing to leave her alone for a moment.

A sad priest wearing his black robe had arrived and visited both houses and blessed the dead girls in readiness to take the long death procession to the cemetery. He gave the families plenty of time so relatives and other mourners could get the chance to see the dead girls for the last time and pay their respects.

Around noon, the church bells began to toll in a steady singular death knell announcing the girls' death. They continued to ring echoing across the locality calling for others to gather for the church service or to show up at the cemetery.

By two in the afternoon, the elderly priest took his position at the forefront of the procession and began to lead the mourners forward, by shaking his incense burner. Aromatic smoke started to ascend into the air. At the cross-roads, Kaliopi's coffin-bearers met up with Maro's and both the families amalgamated their grief and headed towards the church for the final interment.

Hundreds of black banners were raised and fluttered among the crowd, including prohibited Greek flags. Every house that lined the route to the church and cemetery displayed a black sheet on their doors or gates in a gesture of mass mourning. Black clothes were draped everywhere, and as the sad procession moved forward, others joined the crowds wearing black armbands.

Marcos and Michalaki soberly walked in the front, supporting Maro's coffin on their shoulders, while Alexis' friends Adamos, Dimitri and Andreas carried the other end. Vasili, Yiorkis' loyal pudgy friend, walked at the very front hoisting the largest black banner in the air. He was in a terrible emotional state and clamped his mouth, flabbergasted by his friend's calamity.

After the church service, the cortege sombrely trekked to the cemetery located on the outskirts of their local municipality. At the cemetery, hundreds of mourners spilt over the adjacent fields and many were forced to climb the perimeter walls to have a view of the final service.

The emotional turmoil turned to pandemonium with people crying aloud in public grief, while the gravediggers had dug two graves next to each other.

Kyra-Soteria knelt on the freshly dug, soft earth next to her daughter's grave and kept cursing the people that had brought such a catastrophe upon her family. She cursed them aloud and often gazed at Kaliopi's mother who was also kneeling and pulling her hair out. The women screamed and yelled in anguish, while others remained in complete silence, unable to shed any more tears; their eyes had completely dried up.

The bearers eventually lowered the coffins into the graves and the elderly priest proceeded to the final part of the burial service. He sprinkled blessed olive oil over the white shrouds and broke a plate against the edge of the shovel, letting the chippings drop gently inside the opened coffins. Between his muttering of prayers, he picked up a handful of earth and threw it over the bodies prompting others to do the same.

At that moment, Kyra-Soteria went hysterical, realising the end had arrived. Seeing that her daughter's white shroud was gradually being covered with endless handfuls of soil, she passed out, unable to cope. For her, the end was near and she did not want to live any more.

A black crow out of nowhere suddenly flew and perched at the very peak of a tall pine tree, forcing the fragile branch to swing. He looked around and started to crow at the top of his lungs.

CHAPTER SEVENTEEN

ALEXIS, TOGETHER WITH his new friends, was transferred by Spyros to join the *Andartes* at the Pentadactylos mountain range. They were driven to an abandoned, isolated stone house in the middle of the forest, encircled by dense pine and cedar trees. Perched on the side of a steep hill, the house overlooked the magnificent coastal town of Kerynia and the vast sea beyond. The three lads settled in their modest hideout and for months they used it as their main base. Alexis loved this kind of lifestyle and he felt rejuvenated once again for being able to roam freely across the hills.

His traumatic experience at the hands of his torturers had left their mark on him and he found it difficult to run as fast as before, handicapped by his deformed ankle. He could never stop the nervous tic of his head and felt embarrassed by this unsightly stigma. In time, he learned to cope with his problem and he tried his hardest to make these jerking fits stop, but he could not.

Since he left the Omorphita torture chambers, he had never once had an erection no matter how many times he tried. In the privacy of his own bed at the night, he attempted many times to arouse himself but it was a useless exercise. There was no sensation. He kept this, innermost secret to himself in the hope that once this war was over, he may seek out treatment to cure his problem as the good doctor suggested.

He was going through a bad, traumatic psychological experience that left its mark by his often irrational behaviour. Each time he fell asleep, he faced recurring nightmares that haunted him. He'd dream about his friends and others who had lost their lives, but above all, he'd dream about the torture he'd suffered at the hands of those brutal men who sought to break his spirit and transform him into a vegetable. He would yell out and wake up screaming, totally soaked in sweat.

Under such disturbing conditions, Alexis, as a group leader, had the responsibility to show his friends survival tricks and tactics that he had learned during his stay at his *Limery*. Soteris, being the eldest, appeared more seasoned and weighed his words carefully, while young Varnavas had become their protector and they always looked out for him. For a young lad, he quickly learned the art how to be a fighter and looked up to Alexis with great respect.

305

They would spend their evenings by making bombs and explosives in preparation for the next mission, or simply sit around chatting with one another while listening to Varnavas playing his harmonica. They would trek for hours in the rough terrain and by the time they returned back to the safety of their hideout, they would be exhausted and immediately fall onto their mattresses.

Like every other day, Alexis with his two companions had returned from a lookout that had failed to produce positive results and, disillusioned, they sat around a small fire roasting walnuts.

Winter had come down on them with a vengeance, and they found it hard to keep warm inside their dilapidated shelter. They kept a fire burning at all times, but the howling wind always seemed to find its way through the cracks. It was quite late at night and the rain refused to leave them in peace and kept coming down in buckets. They placed a few dishes to catch the raindrops leaking through the roof and settled in for the night.

No sooner had they warmed themselves up than they heard muffled footsteps approaching from outside. It was past ten in the evening and they became suspicious and pulled out their guns in readiness. The stranger knocked lightly and waited for a response.

With caution, Alexis pushed the metal door-bolt aside and opened the door, while Soteris had his Kalashnikov machine-gun pointing directly at the opening.

A shivering young albino boy, no more than twelve years old, was standing at the threshold with chattering teeth.

'I have a message for *Akamantis*,' he said in a trembling voice, and instantly pushed himself inside the warm room and squatted next to the fire.

'Give it to me,' Alexis said to the lad and stared at him, having not seen him before.

'Are you *Akamantis*?' he asked and frowned, while suspiciously inspecting the man who had his hand stretched out.

'Yes I am *Akamantis*. Give it to me' Alexis insisted and slapped the lad slightly on the head as a warning. 'Where is Lefterakis?' he then asked.

'He's not well'

'A shepherd's son, not well?' Soteris stated and looked at the shivering boy.

The lad let his pink eyes inspect the small room and spotted the hot walnuts over the open fire.

'What do I know, he's just not well maybe he's sick or something.' the boy retorted, and unbuttoned his wet coat, while staring at the walnuts.

He put his hand inside the inner pocket of his sheepskin jacket and pulled out an envelope. He handed it to Alexis, then grabbed a handful of roasted walnuts and took off again into the pitch black night and pouring rain.

Alexis ripped open the envelope and sat next to the fire to read it. 'It's from Spyros.' he said to the others, and began to read the hand-written letter.

'He never forgets you, they say that 'a man is truly lucky, if he has one good and sure friend in life,' and you sure have one,' Soteris said to him while unpeeling a burning hot walnut.

No sooner had he read a few lines than Alexis' face turned deadly pale, and his head began to jerk. As he read further, the worse his movements became, causing his friends to stare at him with anxiety as they realised the letter had bad news for him. They dare not ask what the message was, but kept their mouths clamped shut until he spoke.

Without uttering a word, he read it again and suddenly screwed up the piece of paper and threw in into the fire. He stared into the flames and remained motionless for a long time. Then he clenched his fists and banged them loudly on the table, forcing the walnuts to roll and scatter across the wooden floor.

'God, what's happening to us?' he roared at the top of his voice, 'What's happening to us?' he screamed again. He stood up and began pacing up and down nervously and shaking his head.

His two friends stared at him speechlessly with deep anxiety in their eyes. It was not like him to behave in such a manner and, seeing him walking back and forth like a caged animal, they did not know what to say to him.

He flung himself on a chair and put both of his hands over his head.

'What is it Alexis?' Soteris finally asked.

Alexis stared at his friends with eyes brimming with tears, and could not come out with it. He slowly walked up to them and put his arms around their shoulders, seeking comfort, and pulled them close to him. He found the strength to speak to them.

'One of the girls killed was my sister!' he burst out, and sobbed heartbreakingly. He squeezed his long arms tighter around his friends.

Soteris and Varnavas listened with horror.

The shock left them stunned and they did not know what to say to him to console his sudden grief. They wrapped their arms around him and held him for a while, until he finally pulled away from them.

He looked Soteris straight in the eyes like he was searching for something. Standing in the middle of the bare room, he resembled a crumbling leaf, shaking against a fearsome wind.

'Why is the price for freedom so demanding? Why do we behave like animals? Why? Tell me Soteris, why?' he said to his sullen-faced friend.

His friend had no answers to give for such a terrible loss, except to shake his head in abhorrence and disbelief that such a catastrophe had come so close to them. They both felt Alexis' pain and took it personally.

'Fate, Alexis! None of us can control fate!' Soteris finally said to his distraught friend, who kept sobbing.

'I wish this madness had never started. I have lost so many good friends, why now my sister?' Alexis said, and looked imploringly at his silent comrades.

His friends were stunned and felt a deep sense of sympathy for Alexis who had given up so much for liberty and freedom for the country that he loved. Losing his sister was too much a price to pay and their blood boiled to avenge their friend's loss.

'We shall make them pay for it many times over!' Varnavas said with fury in his young dark eyes.

'Yes, they shall pay for it!' Alexis said angrily, and hit both his fists on the table.

He stood motionless in the middle of the small room in a trance within his own dark thoughts. He spoke no more and with his head still jerking he slowly walked outside in the pouring rain. His friends did not stop him, but looked at him with anxiety, concerned for his welfare.

The room was too small for such a heavy burden and he needed space, vast open spaces to handle his emotional turmoil and sorrow. He walked into the dense forest allowing the downpour to soak him to the bone and roamed aimlessly for hours.

Worried about him, his two friends went out into the night to search for him in case something happened to him. They started to call out his name and blew into their whistles in the dark. With flashlights in their hands, they covered a large area, but there was no sign of him. After two hours of searching in vain, they returned back and sat around the fire apprehensively waiting for his return.

Time was moving on when suddenly the front door was flung wide open by a hard kick. It was Alexis.

He stood in the doorway with a wild look on his face, letting a gust of wind inside the warm room. The rain splashed against the threshold and heavy raindrops were blown with the wind halfway across the wooden floor. At the sight of him, his friends became startled. He was not the Alexis they knew before.

In front of them stood a much older lad with staring eyes, breathing heavily with his chest ready to explode. With his arms stretched across the door opening, he gazed at his friends while letting the rain pour down his handsome face and over his lean body. A big puddle quickly formed around his feet as he stood there watching his astounded friends.

Suddenly he burst out laughing, wild and uncontrollable, which made his two friends stir with uneasiness. With large strides he found himself inside the room and let the door behind him close by the force of the howling wind. With a thunderous bang against the doorframe, the door shut itself.

Alexis walked over to Varnavas, placed both his wet hands against his cheeks and gazed straight into his worried eyes. Varnavas was a little scared by the unlikely behaviour of his hero and didn't know what to do or say. Instead, he looked into Alexis' wild eyes and didn't like what he was saw. There was an ocean of despair and a frightening transformation on his handsome face; with glazed eyes and knotted brows Alexis, seemed like stranger to him!

'Varnavas, play 'Yiannis Melody' for me. Play it and don't stop!' Alexis said to him and pinched his cheeks lightly.

Varnavas pulled out his harmonica and started blowing into it. The sweet melody, instantly fill the room and somehow soothed Alexis. Slowly, he went and crouched in the corner of the room with his head gripped between his knees. He let his fingers twirl over his drenched hair and listened to the music. He stared ahead without uttering a word, allowing the rainwater from his drenched clothes to form a puddle around his body. With lugubrious eyes, he gazed at the burning fire. A morbid depression had overcome his senses.

Confused, he sat on his own in the same spot for the entire evening.

From that day forward, Alexis became moody and a troubled lad who had lost all sense of reality. His two friends noticed the dramatic change in his character and how he always sought solitude by wandering on his own around the hills for many hours. They had also noticed that he was taking unnecessary risks and that deeply worried them. During a mission, he would plunge daringly into unthinkable dangers, always risking his own life in order to accomplish their mission. He was frequently careless but, no matter how much they tried, they could no longer control or restrain him from taking life threatening chances.

Their worst fear was the obvious change in his character that made them believe that he was actually losing his mind. He was turning into a manic depressive who no longer had control over his behaviour. While having a conversation with them, his mood would change for no reason at all, and he'd start to laugh aloud and then stop. Whenever they asked him why he laughed, he would not remember. It was this unnatural behaviour of his that made them start to think that he was slowly going crazy.

As time progressed, those strange spells of his had become more frequent and many times he would run like a madman into the deep forest, shouting and screaming at the top of his voice. Whenever those spells occurred, his fragile, disturbed mind would play tricks on him and he could never control himself. Often, he would get into abnormal extremes of mood, but mostly he would sink into a deep depression and seek out isolation from his friends. Other times, he would run like a maniac, tear his clothes off and turn violent, all good reasons to cause his friends to think the unthinkable; their friend needed professional help, but that was nowhere to be found until the war was over.

Yet, at other times he'd be completely normal, talkative, lively, and behave without the slightest sign of irrationality.

Alexis convinced himself that the only way to be free from his traumatic change in character was revenge. His mind was obsessed by the urge to destroy all enemies of *Eoka* and that included the British army and collaborators but especially the Turkish hordes, who had killed his sister. He constantly talked about it, and as far as he was concerned Ahmet above all others had to answer for Maro's death! He held him personally responsible. As time progressed, the idea of revenge grew bigger each day and had manifested itself deeply into his tormented mind.

*   *   *

It had been a very happy day for the small group. They received orders from the Leader that *Eoka* should maintain a ceasefire until further notice.

With nothing to do but to sit around, the lads lounged alongside a steep slope overlooking Kerynia. They gazed across the small horseshoe bay and had noticed that it was jam-packed with small fishing boats, and wishing they were there, munching on fresh seafood rather than bread and olives. At the far end of the crescent-shaped bay, the ancient castle of Kerynia at the edge of the promontory jutted proudly out into the blue sea. The British army had turned the castle into a prison that held hundreds of *Eoka* captives between its solid walls, with little chance of escaping.

The lads watched with envy and imagined the evening crowds strolling along the bay, visiting the outdoor restaurants and enjoying the night's activities. It was a perfect lazy evening and everyone seemed in a joyous mood, especially Alexis, who kept joking with Varnavas and teasing him about playing his harmonica.

The sun was gradually setting beyond the vast horizon, creating the most wonderful sunset anyone could wish for. The calm waters were completely covered by blinding, brilliant colours— magnificent red, yellow and orange hues that skimmed over the blue sea.

The three *Andartes* watched in awe at the beautiful sight ahead, when Soteris spotted their young albino courier, climbing up the steep hill loaded with food and provisions.

'The boy is here,' he said, pleased to see the lad bringing food.

As soon as Alexis saw the boy he started to shake. Immediately his friends knew he was about to go into one of his spells. As the lad approached, the worse his condition became.

Without warning Alexis grabbed his machine-gun and pistol, and began to yell out loud at the top of his voice like a madman. Distraught, he got up and started to run with his awkward limp into the forest in search of solitude realising he could no longer control his actions.

His friends, who were used to his behaviour, let him be, knowing he'd be back soon—as he always did after spending a couple of hours on his own. The courier was stunned at seeing him in such a state and got a little scared.

'What have I done?' he asked with a sense of guilt.

'Nothing, he will be fine,' Soteris said, to put the lad's mind at rest.

'I feel that I am some kind of jinx.' The boy said, and sat next to them. 'There is rumour in the air that there is some kind of agreement being negotiated. Soon the war would be over and you can all go home!' the lad added, changing the subject once he had made himself comfortable.

'We sure hope so.' Soteris said, anxious to see his family again.

'What's wrong with *Akamantis*?' The boy asked, before trekking down the hill. He felt upset for being the cause of Alexis' sudden outburst.

'Don't worry, he'll be back soon, it's not your fault.' Varnavas reassured the boy.

They waited all night for Alexis, but he failed to return. With grave concern, they set out in the middle of the night under torchlight to look for him, but he was nowhere to be seen. They searched all night and continued their hunt the very next day without success. It seemed that he disappeared from the Earth completely and downhearted they returned to their hide to make a report to the Leader.

They were never to set eyes on him again.

CHAPTER EIGHTEEN

SINCE HIS RELEASE from exile, the Archbishop and his entourage had settled in a suite at a grand hotel, off Sintagma Square in Athens. From there, they maintained regular contact with the *Eoka* Leader and were in a better position to ascertain the events in a coherent manner. The new civilian Governor of Cyprus also began to have a regular discussion with him, and living in Athens, has made communication much easier.

The man of God felt that his exile had not as yet been lifted, not while he was prohibited to go back to the island. As the official political leader of the struggle, the British government, through its new Governor and the Colonial Secretary, maintained direct contact with him, trying to convince him that a solution was imminent.

As a churchman, without any conniving thoughts in his trusting mind, he was a perfect ploy for manipulation by all those silver-tongued politicians who filled his mind with empty promises.

The Greek government, on the other hand, exerted great pressure on him to accept a reconciliatory solution based on 'independence' rather than 'self-determination' for the island. To get its way, the pro-British government had forbidden all new arms shipments destined for *Eoka*, to ensure that *Dighenis* maintained the ceasefire until the problem was negotiated and resolved between the governments of Britain, Greece and Turkey.

While these top-secret meetings were being held behind closed doors, the most important participants in the whole affair was completely ignored and side-lined; the *Eoka* Leader was kept in total darkness as to what kind of a solution the three powers were brewing up.

That was their best well-kept secret, and the people of Cyprus, including the *Eoka* fighters, had become pawns in an international manipulative political game.

Perplexed and under extreme pressure, the Archbishop was about to meet up once again with a group of British, Greek and Turkish officials, to iron out their differences, and resolve the Cyprus issue.

By ten o'clock in the morning, a group of politicians, including the new Governor of Cyprus – who had flown directly from London with his government's instructions – congregated in a luxurious hotel suite in readiness to put their cards on the table and resolve the issue once and for all.

Once the formalities were over, the Colonial Secretary took the floor and put forward his government's final instructions.

'It has been decided that 'limited independence' for Cyprus would be acceptable by my government which also guarantees the protection of the Turkish Cypriot minority. A new Republic would be established that allows the presence of Turkish and Greek troops to be stationed on the island – in the capacity as peacekeeping forces – while Britain on the other hand, shall maintain sovereign military bases and other installations there. Greece, Turkey and Britain shall become guarantors of the territorial integrity of the new Republic to ensure its sovereign independence,' explained the Colonial Secretary.

The Archbishop, including the Bishop of Kerynia and other Greek Cypriots present, were completely astounded by what was described.

'My people demand self-determination, that is what they are fighting for and for certain the *Eoka* Leader would not accept anything less!' the Archbishop retorted, realising the peace plan offered would not be acceptable by the Colonel.

'*Eoka* has nothing to do with this agreement.' Interjected the Greek representative.

'Nothing to do with it? *Dighenis* is the only man who has every right to be involved with these negotiations! It is he, and his brave *Eoka* fighters, that made it possible for us to congregate within this room. Don't tell me that he is to be discarded like he does not even exist!' angrily stated the Bishop of Kerynia, who smelled the stench coming out of the politician's mouth.

'My government is not prepared to deal with terrorists,' the Colonial Secretary stated firmly.

'Terrorist? My God! Our boys and girls are not terrorists, they struggle for the freedom of their country! Let me remind you, dear sir, what your great statesman, Sir Winston Churchill, stated publicly—*it is the primary right of men to die and kill for the land they live in and punish with exceptional severity all members of oppression*—that was good enough for Britain to use terrorism against Nazism, and now your government has the audacity to call our boys and girls terrorists because it suits them to do so?' the Bishop yelled, offended by the Secretary's condescending attitude.

'That's exactly what they are! Terrorists!' he insisted.

'Our fighters are people with conscience and honour! They strive for freedom from British subjugation and they have resorted to using violence for liberty, like Britain does to protect its interests.' the Bishop insisted.

314

He was not prepared to accept the man's double talk.

He was in total dismay at what was about to happen. There was nothing anyone could say to make him change his mind. Suspiciously, he saw the traps very clearly. As a proud church-man, he did not trust any of those foreign pen-pushers who sought to destroy his beloved country. He knew their plan; to gain a strong legal foothold on the island for generations.

'This is the deal! It has already been decided,' stated the Colonial Secretary.

'This is a betrayal!' said the Bishop, angrily and went on to add in Latin: '*Vi vin repellere omnes leges omnisque jura permittunt.*'

'Explain!' bellowed the Colonial Secretary, who had turned defensive, because of the Bishop speaking in a language he did not understand.

'*To repel violence by violence is permitted by all laws and by all rights!*' explained the Bishop, by quoting Cicero.

He was totally fuming at what was being brewed in foreign cauldrons, at the expense of the people of Cyprus.

'It's our right as a free nation to repel British colonialism!' he added assertively.

'It is the only viable solution my government would consider if it's to relinquish its rights to the island. Failing this, we shall continue to fight *Eoka* and enforce our next plan, by bringing in a Turkish 'commissioner' from Ankara to help us run the affairs of the country,' the British official expounded categorically.

'This is a political blackmail,' the Archbishop objected.

'Call it what you like, it is your only option on the table. Athens and Ankara had already agreed that, this is the only solution to the Cyprus issue,' the Governor stated, not paying any attention to the Archbishop's objection.

'Greece has no right to negotiate on our behalf, nor does Turkey!' shouted the Bishop. He was very upset by what was said, and he realised that a trap had been set.

In a heated argument the men discussed the overall plan proposed by the big three, and in the end, the Archbishop succumbed and agreed in principle to the solution presented.

The dignified Bishop was infuriated with him and stood up shaking with anger.

'What about our sworn pledge for a plebiscite? Above all else, what about our boys and girls who are fighting for liberation? Do they not have something to say about this? Are we to ignore them?' the elderly Bishop shouted in a harsh voice at the Archbishop and started to tremble in fury.

'Face reality, this is a solution that had already been agreed upon by all governments concerned,' the Greek official said to him with indifference.

'But not by our own people or by *Eoka!*' the Bishop yelled, interrupting the Greek official in disgust, 'they have the right to decide! Not me or, you, you, or, you!' he shouted and pointed his fingers at everyone in the room.

'This is politics . . .!' stated the Colonial Secretary.

'It stinks!' said the Bishop in abhorance and grabbed his long white beard in agitation.

The Archbishop took the Bishop in the adjacent room and tried to calm him down while attempting to persuade him to see things in greater clarity. They were trapped.

They could not possibly maintain the fight without Greek military support, and any efforts without such backing were doomed to failure.

The Bishop emphatically disagreed and had decided to break ranks with the Archbishop. He knew that the *Eoka* Leader would be infuriated by such a 'sell-out' by the Archbishop and his advisors for yielding to political pressure. But above all else, he was livid for failing to consult *Dighenis*, before accepting *fait accompli*.

'A shepherd shall lead his flock to safety and not over treacherous cliffs; *Eoka* should be here' the Bishop insisted angrily.

'We are not in a position to dictate the terms of negotiations.' said the Archbishop attempting to pacify the angry Bishop.

' . . . and why not? *Eoka* had been fighting for four years and could last forever if necessary!' stated the Bishop.

'But, we have achieved independence.'

'If we accept their terms, we shall not wallow in glory but shame.' the Bishop insisted.

'It is not a matter of glory but freedom.'

'Your Eminence, independence and freedom are not the same.' the Bishop interrupted angrily. 'The agreement they are asking us to sign is a stepping-stone for partitioning the island on a permanent basis. Just think about it: the British would be entitled to hundreds of square miles as sovereign military bases including other facilities, Turkey would station on the island hundreds of troops and Greece would also do the same! These foreign troops would have the freedom to roam across our country at will, with no checks or accountability. This is no freedom, it's another form of subjugation. A blind man can see that!'

'My good friend and companion-in-exile, Cyprus shall become a Republic and we would run our own affairs, surely this is a great achievement. We shall no longer be under the British yoke!'

316

the Archbishop insisted, who had already decided to sign the treaty.

'Your Eminence, you and your advisors are wrong. We had one master, and now there are three. We would never get rid of them. Personally, I will have nothing to do with this national betrayal' the graceful Bishop stated firmly, and walked out of the room furious with his Archbishop.

In his absence, the negotiations continued all day, and a draft peace agreement had finally been reached.

In response, the Greek Prime Minister and his Turkish counterpart immediately flew to Zurich. There, they met the British Prime Minister and the three of them initialled the basic declaration for the independence of Cyprus.

Meanwhile, the Cyprus delegation including the Archbishop had flown to London.

The Archbishop, under extreme pressure and unrelenting black-mailing tactics used against him by the Greek government, had signed the agreement on behalf of all Greek Cypriots. The Turkish Cypriot leader signed next to him on behalf of his own community.

Under the terms of the agreement, no *Eoka* representative was present or permitted to partake at the Lancaster House negotiations.

*   *   *

Listening on his small radio in his hideout, the *Eoka* Leader heard the devastating news that a deal was struck and had already been signed in London that had sealed the fate of Cyprus forever.

He was infuriated at the audacity of the Archbishop and his advisors who had decided unilaterally to reach an agreement without first consulting the people or himself, as had been agreed—under oath—beforehand.

He could not believe his ears that such a betrayal was possible, not while there was breath left in them for continuing the battle until they were victorious. His intuition for not trusting politicians had been proven correct once again, and he felt utter revulsion for their cunningness and shamefulness for deceiving their own people. He completely lost respect for the Archbishop, who had forsaken the *Eoka* fighters who had made him a success—and now he was about to become the symbol of liberation and freedom.

The *Eoka* Leader was in a dilemma with his existing arsenal, supporters and fighters, he could maintain the struggle indefinitely, but that meant a civil strife which would probably unleash a monster by setting one Greek against another. That bothered his deep sense of conscience.

He could not be the cause of brotherly bloodletting and reluctantly decided to accept that the struggle for self-determination was over. The small island had been betrayed by its own people and he felt completely shattered by what happened, especially at the loss of those innocent young lives that had paid with their blood in the misguided dream that Cyprus would be permanently liberated from the British yoke.

The Archbishop was planning to return gloriously to the island in a few days time and the Ethnarch was most anxious to receive some kind of public announcement from the *Eoka* Leader, that the deal reached and signed was with the overwhelming approval of *Eoka*.

Dighenis refused to be part of this deception and wanted nothing to do with it. He expressed those misgivings to his *Eoka* commanders to make them understand that *Eoka* had taken no part in this terrible agreement that set the foundation for partitioning the island. After a four-year struggle, the battle as far as he was concerned had come to an inglorious end.

Devastated, the Leader reluctantly gave his final orders for a complete cease-fire in an *Eoka* leaflet:

March 9, 1959.

TO THE GREEK CYPRIOT PEOPLE AND EOKA FIGHTERS

When, on 1 April 1955, I raised the flag of the revolutionary liberation movement I declared that our purpose was the liberation of Cyprus, and I asked for the support of the Greek Cypriot people and the help of the whole nation. This was given completely throughout four years of hard struggle.

Now, after the agreements between the Governments of Greece and Turkey at Zurich, which have been ratified in London by the Ethnarch and by those appointed by him as representatives of the people, I am obliged to order a cease-fire.

Refusal to accept the agreement and the continuation of the struggle would divide not only the Cypriot people, and probably the whole nation. The results of national division would be incomparably more disastrous than those, which some people believe, will flow from the solution of compromise, which undoubtedly does not satisfy our desires.

So, instead of a battle cry, I call today for concord, unity and love, in order that you may build the new structure of the young Republic on the ruins and ashes of the Cypriot epic, which glowed with such glory and national majesty.

In spite of all my efforts, politics has failed to give the complete and untrammelled freedom I wanted. Cyprus is very small in extent and it would be difficult for me to achieve any more alone, faced with an all-powerful Empire.

My conscience is clear, for I know that I have done my duty. It was the politicians' task to exploit the epic struggle of the Cypriot people and they had failed miserably.

From the day the Zurich Agreement was announced I have asked myself whether we should accept an agreement which does not completely fulfil our desires, and whether I should reject it and continue the struggle. I have reached the conclusion that the continuation of the fight would have the following results: It would divide Cyprus and perhaps the whole Greek people, with disastrous results.

I therefore call on you to obey your Leader's last orders to put down your arms and cease fire. We must maintain the unity and iron discipline which aroused the admiration of even our enemies, in the four hard years of struggle. It is the duty of all of us to obey.

Now my thoughts turn to those who are no longer here: those patriots who fell bearing the sacred banner of the Cyprus freedom. I wait for that blessed hour, when I shall hang golden offerings and unfading wreaths on their immortal tombs.

Gather round, all of you, united in support of the Ethnarch, who is today the symbol of unity and strength, and support him in his difficult task. This is my last wish, and I call on everyone to comply.

EOKA

The Leader—Dighenis

*   *   *

Soon after the Treaty Agreement was signed in London, the Archbishop, his political advisors and entourage arrived victorious on the island.

At the airport, he was met with a thunderously joyous reception with thousands of people lining the streets to welcome their long lost Ethnarch. People cried with joy and old ladies fainted, while a sea of Greek flags and banners flew proudly in the air to welcome their Archbishop.

Most *Eoka* sympathisers boycotted his arrival, and those members who decided to attend were there merely to welcome their Ethnarch and not the liberator of the struggle for self-determination.

The *Eoka* Leader remained in hiding for eight days longer, to ensure that all detainees were released from the prisons and concentration camps under the terms of the agreement. He also did not trust the British to honour their word not to apprehend him and he remained hidden in safe houses across the island.

His last wish was to be allowed to pay homage to the graves of his brave men and women who had fallen, but the British would not permit such humane gesture.

Under strict security measures, he met in Lefkosia with a number of his loyal leading comrades for a final get together. More than fifty members attended the secret farewell gathering and emotions ran high. There was a gloomy mood on everyone's faces realising that their struggle for freedom had finally come to an inglorious end.

Speechlessly, they gazed at their Leader, who was practically in tears as he walked around embracing them in turn.

Dighenis felt so proud of his fighters that he wanted to reach out and embrace everyone and hold them forever. He knew these were cherished moments that come once in a lifetime, and they could never be repeated again. He could see the glowing fire of patriotism in everyone's eyes and felt humbled by their loyalty and devotion, but in the end he had to accept Fate's decision.

Most of the young men and women in attendance he had never met before and only knew them by their code names written on scrap of papers. Seeing their determined faces, he could not help himself but shed emotional tears for failing to complete his mission in fulfilling their aspirations for the total liberation of the small troubled island.

The very next day, after a brief meeting with the Archbishop and other prominent men and women who had given valuable services to the struggle, he was quickly ushered onto the Greek Prime Minister's personal aircraft. Escorted by the Royal Hellenic Air Force he was flown directly to Greece and far away from Cyprus.

Cypriots were not given the chance to express their feelings of gratitude, yet a million cheerful people lined the eight-mile route to Athens to receive this mysterious and elusive *Dighenis* who had taken arms against the mighty British Empire. They packed the squares, streets and rooftops of the capital to welcome the heroic Leader of the legendary *Eoka* and Leader of the Cyprus Struggle for Liberation.

CHAPTER NINETEEN

ALEXIS WANDERED INTO the deep forest and rugged valleys aimlessly he was unable to separate reality from illusion. The sudden appearance of the albino boy had triggered within his fragile mind something that he had no control over and had to get away from.

He walked for days and slept under low-branched trees like a wild animal not knowing what to do any more. His mind played tricks on him and he was hardly in a mental state to control the spells that kept occurring on and off with no warning. He realised that he was a lost soul, surrounded by the vast forest with no way of getting out of it. Dressed in combat uniform and beret, he wandered in circles not caring about his life any more.

He would run for no reason, cry and laugh, but was always on the lookout for the enemy in case they trapped him again and sent him to Omorphita. He wanted to die and leave this place behind for good but he still had a mission. His sister's death had not been avenged and that motivated him to carry on, while trying to cope with his pathetic state of mind.

When his senses were calmed, he would think clearly and wonder how he had arrived in the forest on his own, with no sign of Soteris or Varnavas.

His face was covered in scratches, and he grew a beard while his black, thick hair had reached the nape of his neck. Oblivious to his physical condition, he plunged into the endless terrain in search of a way out, or at least to find a road so someone could show him the way home.

Confused, he didn't know what he expected out of life any more, but the thought of a homecoming and of revenge motivated his actions.

When sleep overcame him he would curl up anywhere and stay there until his bloodshot eyes opened again and he would carry on in isolation amidst the labyrinth of pine trees and bushes. He would often travel during the night, not bothered by the darkness, but the mountains were so vast he felt trapped and unable to master the unfolding hills that never seemed to end.

Early one morning he woke up in a cold sweat after his usual nightmare and found himself engulfed by thick bushes.

He heard the sound of dry twigs being broken by someone. He pricked up his ears and stared wildly to see who it was and raised his gun in readiness to shoot. Beyond the slope, he spotted a lone British soldier, moving about among the thicket. Alarmed, he stared and pointed his weapon at him. With steady hands and blind fury in his eyes, he aimed to kill the enemy and fired one loud shot.

The bullet found its target and the soldier stumbled and fell to the ground without making a sound. In total exhilaration, Alexis gave out a deafening cry of triumph and cannoned down the slope to inspect his trophy.

He ran so fast that he fell to the ground and found himself rolling down the hill. His body finally came to a stop alongside the dead soldier. On close inspection, he realised there was a wild long-horned *moufflon* lying on the ground, spasmodically jerking about with blood gushing out of its wound.

At the sight of the red blood he quickly stood up, looked at the dying animal and shook his head with revulsion for killing the rare *moufflon*. Then he realised that there was no hope for him. He flung his machine-gun into a ravine and took off, disgusted with himself for allowing his mind to play such destructive tricks.

Unable to control his actions, he often sang aloud the *Andartes* song and kept repeating it over and over again:

> *Andartes . . . forward, lead the way*
> *With guns in our hands, we shall free this land*
> *Andartes . . . forward, lead the way*
> *Fear no death or pain . . . for tomorrow is freedom day*

Nothing seemed to matter any more. He was engrossed within his own illusionary world and kept remembering those friends of his that had lost their lives. He questioned himself; why was he spared to remain alive and face such trauma in his young life? Many times he had a conversation with death and yelled at him with anger whenever he felt dejected and melancholic.

'*Charon* . . . Take me with you! Look I am here . . . God damn you! Take my soul, so I can rest! Where are you?' he'd shout out in the middle of the forest and raise his arms in the air so *Charon* could see him.

But he would get no answer and move along in isolation.

As the days went by, his appearance had come to represent a living scarecrow. His eyes were constantly bloodshot from exhaustion and his pale face had lost the vitality it once had. His uniform was torn to shreds and hung loosely on his thin, tall body, but he moved on not caring about the state he was in.

For three weeks he spent his days like an animal surrounded by trees.

On a hot sunny day, he finally came across a gravelled road and started walking along the middle of it. He had managed to come out of the thick forest and he could now see the sloping hills below. He felt good that every step forward would bring him closer to his people.

While trekking down the long winding road, he saw a donkey grazing at the edge of a gentle green meadow, dotted with thousands of red poppies and yellow daisies. Trampling over the tall grass, he walked across the field and carefully untied the strap on the donkey's neck.

With one quick jump he mounted the black donkey who obediently brayed once and started to trot down the hill, taking the rider towards the village.

On the outskirts of a quaint hillside village, a farmer dressed in traditional peasant's black cassocks had spotted his donkey with someone on its back. He dropped what he was doing and rushed to salvage his animal. At the sight of the wild looking stranger, he crossed himself at the state of the pitiful rider. He stood in front of the animal forcing it to come to a stop.

'Where are you going?' he asked in bewilderment.

'Home!' Alexis said contemptuously, and looked at the small man.

Alexis kicked the animal with his heels to spur him on.

'Hey, wait!' the man yelled and grabbed the animal's mane trying to stop his donkey from moving forward. 'Come down, you don't look that well,' he added, concerned for the young rider.

'No, I have to keep going!' Alexis insisted.

The man realised that this wild and pathetic looking lad was an *Andartis* who had lost his way and he wanted to help him.

'We are free, there is no war.' the man said to him, trying to persuade him to get off the animal.

'Free? I don't think so!' Alexis said and shook his head suspiciously.

'Yes, Cyprus is free! Let's go and celebrate at my home. I have a wine cellar,' said the man; anxious for the young lad to go with him.

His bloodshot eyes lit up at the mention of wine.

'Is it far from here?' Alexis asked.

'No. It's just a few minutes away. Let's go and drink to Cyprus.'

'Cyprus! Long live Cyprus!' Alexis bellowed, jumped off the obedient donkey and started walking alongside the man.

They reached the farmer's house and as soon as his wife took sight of the undernourished bearded lad with long hair and torn clothes, she let out a cry of fright.

'Bring some wine Despina,' the man ordered, while directing the stranger towards the back of the house, paying no attention to her.

'Wine?' his wife asked, and crossed her bosom a few times, in bewilderment.

'Yes! Wine, wife! Are you deaf? We are celebrating our victory over the British,' he added again and shoved her away.

She went off mumbling to herself, thinking that her husband had gone mad.

The two of them sat at the back of the house. His wife returned carrying a clay pitcher full of red wine and two glasses. She put them on the table and looked at the young fellow with pity, puzzled by his dishevelled state. She shook her head and stared at him, unable to work out why he looked like that.

'Bring some cigarettes and *meze*. We are both famished! Fry some eggs with artichokes and bring out your best cuts of meat,' the man ordered while pouring a glass of wine for his guest.

They both started to drink the wine and the man purposely kept filling Alexis' glass to the brim. After a few glasses, Despina returned and spread on the table a variety of dishes full with hot and cold *meze*.

Immediately, Alexis ate ravenously like he had never tasted food before. The man and his wife looked at the wild-looking lad with empathy and gazed at his every move as he gulped the food down. Every time he took a mouthful he had to push his long moustache and beard aside so the fork could reach his mouth.

'This is good,' he kept muttering, thanking them at the same time for their hospitality.

With his belly full, and after a great number of glasses of wine, he felt drowsy and started to yawn. He could no longer keep his eyes open.

'I feel tired my good man,' he said apologetically. He put his hand over the man's shoulder in gratitude.

'Come and lay down. We shall continue this after you've had a little rest,' the man suggested, anxious to see this wild looking lad pass out.

'No I must get going,' Alexis insisted and tried to get up on his feet.

The moment he stood up, he stumbled and collapsed onto the floor unable to make a move. He instantly passed out from exhaustion.

As soon as the man saw him flat to ground, he quickly grabbed him by the back of his shoulders and pulled him inside the house. His wife helped by carrying the lad's mud-covered legs. They stripped him completely and gave him a wash. Then they dressed him and let him sleep.

Alexis slept for nearly two days. He was awakened at the sound of the first crowing of the cocks and looked around him in amazement at his new surroundings. He looked about the humble room and saw three young children playing quietly on the floor next to his bed.

As soon as they realised he was awake, they ran out, calling with squeaky voices that the wild-man in their bed was alive.

The man and his wife walked into the room and saw him inspecting his clean-shaven face in a wall mirror. Dressed in a white shirt and a black pair of trousers, he stared at his black hair that reached below the nape of his neck.

'*Kalimera*! How do you feel?' the man asked him with a smile.

'Clean.' Alexis answered, and stared at the two unfamiliar faces jerking his head slightly.

'Don't even mention it,' the man said with kindness. 'Where are you from?' he asked.

'Varoshia.'

'That's not far from here, I shall take you there,' the man said, realising that this lad was in bad shape.

'I must leave this place, because I get some kind of bad spells and I don't want your children to see me like that. It would scare them' Alexis said, feeling pleased that he was behaving normally.

'My name is Aris, what do they call you?' said the man.

Alexis looked at the man and remained silent for a brief moment deeply engrossed in his own thoughts.

'I knew someone called Aris once,' he said in a low voice, and let his mind drift into the past. 'I am Alexis.' he added, and shook his head nervously.

The very same afternoon, Aris drove off to take him to Varoshia, but Alexis insisted that he should be dropped off at Salamina instead. By nightfall they arrived there, and after thanking the good man, he started walking over the sand dunes towards the Walls.

Always on the lookout for British troops he entered into the thick acacias, not accepting that the struggle had come to an end. He wanted to enter the Walls, but he knew that there would be Turkish guards about. He had to find a way to get inside them, so he could face Ahmet for one last time. His mind constantly played tricks on him, but like an elephant who never forgets, Alexis knew that he had a mission to accomplish first, before he could be at peace with himself.

He waited until nightfall and then began the long trek to the impenetrable Walls.

There was a full moon and he could see his way around as clear as in daylight. In no time at all, he reached the massive Walls. Standing at the bottom of the fortress, he looked up in search of a way in, but there was no chance of entry from where he was standing. He could not risk trying to enter from the main Gates knowing that they would be well protected by armed Turks, so he walked around the Wall's perimeter towards the waterfront.

The moment he heard the splashing of waves, he remembered *Tripa* as the only possible way in without been detected. He knew it was a dangerous undertaking, as Ahmet had warned them when they were young, but he did not care. He had to get inside . . .

He approached the waterfront and started walking along the sharp reefs. He proceeded towards *Tripa* and felt the force of waves crashing at him from the open sea. But, undettered, he moved on through the roaring waves. He was soon submerged halfway up his body by the cold water and found it hard to move.

The surge of water and big waves crashed with a roar against the side of the formidable stone structure. All he could see was dark water and the massive slippery Walls that posed such a danger to him.

Determined, he plunged into the swelling waters and started swimming towards *Tripa*, not sure if it was completely submerged or not. The only way to find out was to swim around the bend of the Walls and see if there was a way in or not. The tide was up and kept pushing him back and forth but, with perseverance he managed to swim around the bend.

While swimming, he looked about to find the familiar opening. Against the moonlight, he had spotted the top edge of *Tripa*; it was completely submerged by the angry sea and the only way to reach the other side was to dive under water.

He took a deep breath and swam like a fish towards *Tripa*.

In complete darkness, he kept touching the slippery side of the Walls until he was able to feel the rough side of the opening.

With a hard kick, he dove deep and, holding his breath, he swam through the opening of the tunnel. At the other side, he found himself above water-level and was able to swim the distance to solid ground. With tired effort, he walked out of the water and stood briefly at the edge of the swelling sea to catch his breath.

Drenched to the bone, he looked around and inspected the sleepy neighbourhood. Hardly any light escaped from the congested cluster of shabby homes.

He began to walk towards Ahmet's house in the hope that he would meet up with his old friend there. His own life did not matter any more and being inside the enemy camp did not scare him the least. Blinded by dark thoughts of revenge, he walked along the empty narrow alleyways. He rested his hand on his gun-holster and like a thief he proceeded with caution, keeping an eye out for any troop movements.

Within ten minutes, he had reached the familiar stone wall, and carefully climbed over it.

He was overcome with apprehension and could feel his heart pounding from anxiety, ready to burst from its ribcage. He crossed the empty backyard and slowly walked towards the single-room structure, situated about forty yards from the main house. That was Ahmet's private place.

He remembered the endless happy nights they had spent together in that room but, realising what he was about to do, fear and confusion overcame him.

Ahmet had to be at home this late at night. Slowly Alexis peeped through the dirt-stained window-pane. A radio was playing, and a voice sung a Turkish song softly.

He saw Ahmet's lean, shirtless, tanned body sprawled across a single bed. He was smoking and staring at the ceiling deep in thought. The room was dense with smoke and his dishevelled curly hair was tousled over his dark unshaven face.

Alexis felt distraught at what he was planning to do. His emotions were in turmoil and seeing Ahmet again, he began to have second thoughts, but his word was his bond, and he had to complete the job. He owed this much to his sister and there was no way of turning back now.

Alexis walked to the front of the house and knocked lightly on the door.

'Who is it?' Ahmet's familiar soft voice was heard from inside.

'It's me, Alexis!' he answered abruptly. There was an emotional storm brewing up inside him that was ready to explode.

Alexis heard footsteps echoing against the marble floor, then Ahmet hurriedly unbolted the door. He pushed it wide open and saw Alexis standing at the threshold, completely drenched.

Surprised by the sudden visit, Ahmet stood face to face with his long lost brother.

They stared at each other momentarily unable to find the right words to greet each other. Alexis gazed at Ahmet and saw that he too was troubled somewhat. At first glance, his scruffy appearance seemed completely out of character.

A wide genuine smile appeared on Ahmet's unshaven face exposing his strong white teeth. He knew that one day they would meet again. That day was now, and both had so many things to say to each other, and yet, they could not find the proper words to break the ice. Instead, they remained standing at the threshold, gazing at the transformation brought upon each of them by the cruel events of time.

'I knew you'd come.' Ahmet finally said, and stood aside to let him in.

Without a word, Alexis walked inside the room. It reeked of alcohol. At first glance, he noticed a half-empty bottle of *zivania* next to the bed and an ashtray full of cigarette butts. A framed photograph was hanging on the opposite wall, showing both of them smiling when they were teenagers and standing proudly alongside their bicycles. They looked so young, and for a moment Alexis did not recognise himself. The shadowy room seemed gloomy and there were cracks in all four walls from neglect. A noisy old paraffin lamp suspended from a ceiling hook was trying to illuminate the small room.

Alexis dragged his right leg and stood in the middle of the room. Ahmet had noticed the lameness, said nothing and shut the door behind him. He continued to inspect Alexis' transformation under the light. For a brief moment he got a shock seeing the state of his beloved Greek friend, nervously twitching his head about like a sick man, unable to control the spasms. His handsome face had been transformed beyond recognition, and those dark vibrant eyes of his, that he had always remembered him by, seemed to have sunk deeper into their sockets. He wanted to put his arms around him, and give him a warm welcome, but he knew it would not be possible. There was a vast gulf separating their two lives, and there were no bridges long enough to unite the ends.

Ahmet handed him a towel to wipe himself dry. Without a word, Alexis took the towel and began drying his dripping long hair and soaked clothing.

'Sit down, Alexis,' Ahmet said in a low voice.

'You know why I am here,' Alexis answered and refused to take a seat. Instead, he stared into Ahmet's disturbed jet-black eyes.

'I know. I have been waiting for you. Every night I listen to footsteps outside hoping they'd be yours,' Ahmet said to him, filling his own glass with *zivania*. He drunk it down in one quick gulp, and refilled it. 'Please have a drink with me,' he pleaded and threw a shirt over his lean torso.

'Our days of happy reunions are over!' Alexis said to his pathetic looking friend who seemed to have lost the will to live.

'Alexis my friend, look at the state of you! We are both doomed . . . so, do have a drink with me before we part forever,' Ahmet said, and poured Alexis a glass of *zivania*.

Reluctantly, Alexis took the glass and sat down on a chair alongside the small, square, wooden table. He looked at his glass and turned towards Ahmet who remained standing, and noticed that he was staring at him.

'How can I drink with the killers of my sister,' Alexis said. He pushed his glass aside and spasmodically shook his head.

'Never! Never say that! For I deserve to die is true, but, I am not a murderer! How could you ever think that I, Ahmet, who adored Maro like I adore my own baby sister, could commit such a barbaric act I would give my life to protect her . . . how dare you accuse me of such barbarity? If the people that I have loved all my life have now come to hate me, then life for me is not worth living! I have saved my tormented soul for this, our last meeting, my brother. I battle with my conscience with every breath that I take. A morbid shame out of guilt tears my entrails apart each day . . . I see Maro's traumatized eyes and I break into tears. My life is wilting Alexis, and I have to die, so this everlasting mental torture may finally come to an end . . . I am no longer alive, I died the day our Maro died and that dreadful day your mother and father cursed me. They wedged a sharp knife into my heart and it pains my soul, for I cannot take any more torment! Thank you for coming Alexis. After tonight I shall die a happy man,' Ahmet said to his angry friend.

'What the hell happened?' Alexis asked, somewhat perplexed seeing that Ahmet's eyes were full of tears.

He recognised that Ahmet's deep sense of guilt and shame was destroying him mentally and physically. There were emotional distressing signs on his dark face. He seemed to have turned into a lost soul without hope, just like himself.

'I had nothing to do with your arrest, nor with Maro's death,' Ahmet said and took another sip from his glass.

He pulled up a chair and sat opposite Alexis and looked him straight in the eyes, like he was searching for something. He felt happy sitting next to his lost brother and wanted this night to last forever. Ahmet wished that he could turn the clock back, and transport them into those wonderful uncomplicated days of their past. The youthful but everlasting memories of yesterday were deeply embedded into the darkest corners of his mind. Those memories gave him the strength to live, so he could meet up with Alexis for one last time.

'My world has collapsed! Do you expect me to forgive and forget? Our lives can never be the same again!' Alexis yelled at him and banged his fists on the table furiously.

Ahmet looked across the table, picked up a cigarette and lit it. He inhaled deeply, exhaled and let the smoke linger over his unshaven face, while considering what Alexis had just said to him.

'Why did you not keep your promise, damn you? You, of all people! Why?' Alexis burst out, again demanding answers to calm his troubled mind. He twitched his head with anger.

'There was nothing I could do. I was trapped, imprisoned like you by *Volkan* and events' Ahmet said to him in a thoughtful mood, remembering the past.

'Look at me! Look at this face!' Alexis yelled and slapped his cheek once, 'I am not the Alexis we knew before. I am a broken man! They have destroyed my life inside those torture chambers . . . do you know what it means to be impotent, crippled and mentally unstable? People laugh and make fun of me . . . Yes, Ahmet, this is the new Alexis talking to you, a deranged Alexis,' Alexis said, anxious to let everything out for the very first time.

Ahmet was shocked by Alexis's comments, and only then did he realise how high a price his beloved friend had paid for the liberation of his country. There was nothing that he could do to reverse events. He shook his head in abhorance and tried to explain what happened in order to calm his doubts.

'The man who betrayed you, it was that slime-ball, the asparagus-picker . . . Remember? But, when I did find out, it was too late! He was flown to England with his blood money! He escaped my clutches, the bastard,' Ahmet said. He took another gulp by putting his mouth to the bottle and drinking it nearly empty. He grabbed another bottle out from a wall cabinet and opened it up.

'Let's have one last toast to a liberated Cyprus,' Ahmet said trying to ease Alexis' anguish.

Alexis felt sorry for the way his old friend appeared.

He looked a wreck. He turned into a sad-looking fellow who did not care about anything any more and took to the bottle to forget the past. There seemed to be no future or hope for him any more and neither for himself.

Looking at Ahmet's imploring eyes, he finally succumbed and reached out for the glass of *zyvania*. He took a sip, and then put his glass down again.

'To a free Cyprus.' Alexis muttered with indifference.

Ahmet smiled, pleased with his friend for drinking his glass empty in one gulp. He refilled it, and gazed at Alexis with a mixed sense of brotherly love and pity. He was shattered seeing his friend jerking his head about nervously and not being able to control those spasms that seemed to go on forever. He wanted to ask him so many questions to make up for all those lost years but he knew there was no time left. They were both lost in their own dark worlds without a sliver of hope. The youthful aspirations they once shared had turned into nightmares beyond their control. Their bloom of youth had passed its prime and they became troubled lads searching for answers and wondering what went wrong.

He went on to explain in detail what happened from their last meeting at Salamina. Alexis listened to his soft voice without interrupting him once. Gloomy-faced, he paid heed to his every word and the more he explained the gloomier he became. But now, it was far too late. Yesterday's events dictated their destiny, and they were both victims of today's reality. The struggle for liberation had ended, but on its rocky path, it sadly left a great number of broken dreams behind.

When Ahmet finished explaining, Alexis stood up in the middle of the room and gazed at his confused friend who did not move from his seat. Subconsciously, he let his hand touch the butt of his pistol and held it there.

In the absence of conscience, people inflict atrocious acts on others, but he had a conscience and found it hard to pull the gun. His hand seemed to have frozen in the same position and he could not move it, let alone pull the trigger. He was beginning to have second thoughts and realised that he did not have the cold heartedness or brutality within him, to blow Ahmet's brains out so cold bloodedly.

He felt sorry seeing how devastated he was by the whole tragedy and wanted to get out of this room as soon as possible and never to return. Forgiveness and compassion had come into his mind. At least he learned the truth and somehow the dark thoughts for revenge that had built up within his disturbed mind had diminished to some extent.

Ahmet had noticed Alexis' hand resting on his pistol and realised what he was planning. He did not care any more. He had expected this moment for a very long time and he deserved to die.

'Alexis, I will not let you stain your hands with my blood, my friend. We had a happy life together. Now, I curse those who ruined our lives, and we can no longer live together! May Allah strike them scoundrels dead,' Ahmet said, in his deep, soft voice and walked to a side drawer next to his bed.

He opened the drawer and picked a pack of cigarettes. Inside, a pistol with a number of bullets was scattered between papers. He closed the drawer and lit another cigarette, but not before offering one to his angry friend.

'My soul is consumed with hatred and revenge.' Alexis admitted while twitching.

'I would hate as violently as you do if my sister's life was snuffed,' said Ahmet.

'I cannot burn forgiveness on the altar of our own hatred. I have seen too much death not to care, and I must practice compassion instead of hatred.' He said to Ahmet.

He on the other hand remained silent, listening to his friend who appeared confused and not certain what route to take, in order to overcome his tormented mind that sought revenge.

After a short pause Alexis walked and faced Ahmet who remained standing. Slowly he raised his hand up and touched Ahmet on the shoulder.

'Let this be our last goodbye . . . and God forgive us both for what we have done!' he added and twitched his head from nervousness.

Ahmet was taken by surprise by Alexis' gesture of forgiveness and was lost for words. He gazed at his friend, nodded his head and wished the earth would open up to pull him deep into the abyss. It would have been better if he killed him on the spot, rather than allow him to live with the guilt of Maro's death for the rest of his life. But, here they were two lost souls in search of answers to their plight. They should be celebrating the liberation of Cyprus with their friends at *Salingari Taverna* instead here they were, facing each other as enemies.

Since things do not normally happen by themselves, Alexis had decided forgiveness and compassion was purer than revenge. He also realised that he was a lucky man for having such a good friend like Ahmet who was prepared to die because of shame and guilt. It would be shameful to do greater wrong by seeking his blood for a terrible mistake.

'I have just heard the first rooster crow, it's is time for you to go before the Turks find you inside the Walls; for sure they will lynch you. Farewell my beloved friend and forgive me for everything' Ahmet said to him apologetically.

Alexis remained standing on the same spot, gazed at his friend's sad face for one last time and walked out of the door, without uttering another word. The first pallid light of dawn cast its glorious veil across the sleepy neighbourhood to greet another fine day.

Ahmet saw Alexis' dark silhouette walking clumsily away towards the wrought-iron gate. He kept jerking his head about, his right foot twisted and walked with his legs slightly apart like a troubled old man. Seeing his friend under the morning light, Ahmet was horrified observing his pathetic state of walking and broken-down posture. He could not restrain himself and shed fat tears at seeing his friend in such a condition.

As soon as he vanished from his sight, Ahmet walked back into his isolated world and went straight to the drawer. He picked up the pistol, and methodically loaded the gun with two bullets. Without hesitation he placed the gun barrel close to his temple and pulled the trigger once. The piercing sound of the morning gunshot reverberated across the rooftops.

Ahmet instantly tumbled on the bed with blood pouring out of his wound like a flowing tap. Alone, he jerked about for a moment and then stared into the empty ceiling.

The bedclothes were instantly covered in a pool of blood that quickly seeped across the floor. With arms spread apart, Ahmet remained motionless sprawled onto his bed with one of his legs dangling over the side.

There was no soul left in his slumped body. *Charon* wasted no time paying him a visit. He grabbed his soul and hurriedly flew back into his dark abyss, adding another young life to his collection. No matter what, he always wins. Busy as always, he laughs and grins at everyone knowing that life on Earth is temporary and ultimately Death reigns supreme.

Alexis heard the sound of a single gunshot coming from Ahmet's place and he stopped dead in his tracks. He quickly decided to turned back and check on him. He had a bad feeling that he had done something silly. Those black melancholic eyes of his gave him away, and Alexis knew that his friend would try and find everlasting peace. With long strides, he returned to the tiny house and knocked at the door once but received no answer.

He flung the door open and apprehensively entered inside the room.

At the far corner, he saw Ahmet's motionless body sprawled across the bed laying in a pool of blood which formed a puddle around his dangling leg touching the floor.

Seeing Ahmet dead, he wished that he had never entered this room and started to jerk his head nervously. He took a few steps forward and bent over him. Gently, he lifted his blood-covered head up, and held his friend in his arms like a child.

'Forgive me, Ahmet!' he muttered and gazed at his lifeless face. Ahmet's jet-black eyes stared passed him.

Alexis could not accept that his old friend had taken his own life, brought about by morbid guilt and shame for something that he did not do.

Momentarily, he heard the faint sound of movements and voices coming from inside the main house and got to his feet.

Like a wild beast, he burst out a cry of anguish and ran out into the narrow deserted alleyway. Accompanied by the sound of his echoing footsteps stamping against the cobbled alleys, he proceeded towards the main Gate of the Walls. He felt a strange sensation overtaking him. There was a weird pressure throbbing inside his skull and dizziness amalgamated by anxiety suddenly had overcome him.

He placed his hands over his temples, squeezed them hard but there was nothing that he could do to stop those strange feelings of pressure.

His vision was failing him and he began to see a haze of blurry red images wherever he turned. The houses suddenly appeared elongated and shapeless, drenched in a thick blood-red colour. He cannoned towards the main Eastern Gate.

He came across Turks, and they all ran away scared, seeing his stained clothes and pistol in his hand.

The sight of blood and death had triggered the worst nightmare for Alexis; his fragile mind had lost all sense of reality and reason. Unable to control his actions, he entered into the strange world of illusion, and make-believe.

He went through the large Gates and ran out towards the hospital grounds. The morning sun had just shot its brilliant rays across the rooftops, signifying that another hot day was on its way.

Anyone who took sight of the way the deranged long-haired lad behaved stared with pity and muttered. 'He's mad . . . poor boy . . .!'

Alexis ran towards the main town square and *Agora*.

As he got closer, he had noticed that large crowds were heading in the same direction as he was. They all had smiling faces and laughed away as they went along. The men, women and children dressed in their Sunday best carried Greek flags on high poles, and hundreds of banners flapped gracefully with the morning wind. Everyone seemed to be in a jovial mood.

Alexis heard trumpets and drums playing in the distance. He was thrilled by the vivacious activities of the day, and ran even faster to reach the town square. The closer he approached the square the louder the sound of trumpets and drum-playing became. He realised that a lively parade was in progress.

Lured by the marching sounds, he soon found himself standing at the pavement of the main avenue. All the sidewalks were jam-packed with spectators carrying blue and white flags and waving them about jubilantly. Hundreds of children were dressed in pristine clothes and yelled with joy at the sight of the oncoming parade.

As soon as he saw the parade approaching closer, he too got excited and he started to act crazily by skipping and running about, in the middle of the street. People stared at him in shock seeing his dishevelled state, bloodstained clothes and a pistol in one hand. Alexis didn't care and he continued running, oblivious of his own irrational behaviour.

Bystanders roared with laughter at the pathetic looking idiot. Undeterred by the constant cacophony of angry roars, yelling and insults thrown at him Alexis took up position in the middle of the street and with his legs apart, he maintained his skipping and silly hand gestures. He completely lost control of his head that jerked from right to left without hope of ever stopping.

The crowd laughed and whistled at him in amusement, while others shook their heads in pity for the sorry lad. .

'Look at that fool, what an idiot! Get him out of the way!' they yelled, trying to remove this crazy lad who was determined to spoil their parade in celebration of the liberation of Cyprus.

Many began to throw empty cans at him, fruit and watermelon skins. Others spat on his face if he got too close to them. The more daring ones tried to apprehend him and shove him out of the way.

He would point his pistol at them and quickly resume his position in the middle of the road, to continue his imitation of trumpets, drums and cymbal playing. His silly mock of sounds would instantly make people roar with laughter, at the sight of this crazy fool.

As the parade came closer, Alexis ran and positioned himself ahead of the three main flag carriers. He planted his broken down body at the very front and would not budge for anything. People tried to remove him but soon gave up by his determination to remain there. He would laugh at them and move along with the parade.

The deafening sound of the band playing freedom songs gave him a sudden urge to start singing the *Andartes* song. He raised his voice and began to sing out loud his favourite tune:

> '*Andartes . . . forward lead the way . . .*
> *With guns in our hands, we shall free this land*
> *Andartes forward lead the way . . . '*

He would often stop in the middle of his singing and raise his hands in the air and yell with passion: 'I am an *Andartis*! Long live the *Andartes*'. Then he would continue his singing at the top of his voice, and jerk his head spasmodically like a loose leaf cast in the wind.

'*Andartes*? Him? God save us all!' Onlookers would bellow and then burst into uncontrollable laughter.

Seeing the parade moving closer to him and the multitude laughing, he often got confused . . .! His fragile mind constantly played tricks on him. He truly believed the mass were the enemy coming to get him, and he got petrified imagining that *Charon* was there with them. He could clearly see Petros' face pleading to go with him. With the bystanders laughing at him, he imagined their strange contorted faces being stuck against obscure window panes, chanting in a deafening roar:

'What a foolish boy you have been . . . what a silly boy with a dream . . .!'

He could no longer focus on people's faces but rather saw strange images moving in slow-motion.

Suddenly, as he moved forward, he had noticed a marching throng at the rear of the parade wearing blue headbands and carrying the tall banners of Camp K. As they came closer he could hear that they were singing 'Yiannis' melody'. He wasn't sure if his mind was playing a trick on him, or if he was just imagining the whole thing.

He pricked up his ears and listened to the faint audible tune.

Yes! They were playing 'Yiannis Melody'! Alexis raised his arms in the air, jumped and hopped with joy and burst into spontaneous laughter and tears.

He ran towards the ex-detainees and joined them. He began to sing at the top of his voice the familiar melody in remembrance of his good friend Yiannis. The melody rekindled his troubled mind to summon up past memories. Some of the ex-prisoners recognised him and quickly spread the word among each other as they marched forward.

'It's Alexis! *Akamantis* . . . the one who had escaped from Camp K' they muttered and quickly passed the word to one another.

They looked at the pitiful sight, and instantly five hundred fists were raised simultaneously in the air, to show they were behind him all the way and sung out loud:

'Andartes . . . forward lead the way . . . '

His comrades, both men and women, chanted the *Andartes'* song over and over again at the top of their voices, in support of one of their compatriots who had lost his way. Soon others joined in and in no time at all the entire parade sung with them in a deafening chant that nearly brought the roofs down from pure exhilaration and patriotism.

Overfilled by emotion, Alexis raised his arms in the air and let fat tears trickle down his stubby beard. He sung as loud as his lungs could possibly be stretched, realising that he was among friends. He suddenly felt safe and looked around to see if he could recognise any

336

familiar faces but he did not see any, except, for the colourful proud banners of Camp K flapping in the wind.

The parade rhythmically snaked forward and disbursed at the main square of the church. The awaiting crowd made a human corridor for all the banner and flag carriers to enter inside the massive church, where thousands of people congregated to hear the public speakers.

Every rooftop, balcony and window was packed with onlookers, while in the square there was no gap to poke even a stick. People crammed next to each other so they could get a good view of the main speaker; their exiled Archbishop. Nobody wanted to miss the speech of their Ethnarch, on this very important day of Freedom.

Alexis mingled with the crowd and pushed his way towards the church so he too could hear about the liberation struggle that had finally come to an end. He paid no attention to what people said about his appearance or bloodstained clothing. Instead, he jerked his head and forced his long hair to fall over his unshaven face. Determined, he pressed harder so people could make room for him to move forward.

As he pushed forward, suddenly, a hand grabbed him from the back by his shoulder.

He turned round and saw an old wrinkled woman dressed in black. She was holding him tightly with no intention of letting him go. Curiously he looked at the old lady, twitched his dimple on his cheek once and without warning she instantly burst into tears.

He nervously shook his head about, unable to remember who this old woman was. She held him tight, as tight as her old callused hands could, and refused to let him go from her arms.

'Alexis . . . my son . . .!' she yelled out of desperation and tried to put her arms around his shoulders to embrace and give him a long hug.

Suspiciously, he frowned and pushed her back. Being totally at a loss, he stared into her tired fretful eyes unable to ascertain what this old woman wanted from him. Perplexed he noticed that for no reason at all she suddenly begun to tremble in spasms.

Next to her stood a pretty girl dressed in a white short-sleeved dress carrying a wide-eyed child in her arms. The girl looked at Alexis and gave out a smile of joy. Her raven black eyes sparkled and for a brief moment she was lost for words.

'Alexis, *agapie mou*, you are alive!' she managed to say.

'We are free! Cyprus is free!' he yelled at them both with indifference and shook his head at them.

'Don't you recognise us?' the old man standing next to them shouted at him in desperation. He grabbed him by the arm and started shaking him.

Alexis looked at the elderly gentleman dressed in his Sunday best, and shook his head nervously not having the faintest idea who these people were, who kept shouting and grabbing him. The old lady would not let go of him, while the man held him tightly by the arm and trying to talk to him. But the deafening buzzing cacophony of the crowd made it impossible to hear one another.

'Thank God you are alive, this is our son!' the slim girl shouted again, and looked into Alexis's confused eyes. She immediately burst into tears and hastily handed the child over to the elderly man.

She reached out and tried to put her arms around him but Alexis pushed her away.

'My mother? Son? Hah . . . Hah . . . Hah . . .!' he laughed crazily and pinched the cheeks of the child gently.

He turned and gazed at the pretty dark-haired girl and saw that her eyes were flooded with tears. He gazed into her eyes for a brief second and then gave her a short smile.

At that moment, Spyros and Michalaki dressed in their crisp parade uniforms appeared in the distance. They kept popping their heads above the crowds and desperately shoved the swarm aside, rushing in their direction. They had spotted Alexis!

The crowd surged forward dragging the pitiful figure of Alexis with them. Puzzled and confused, he turned his head and transfixed his stare directly on the three anxious faces.

The END . . . of the BEGINNING

If ever in Cyprus . . . a fool crosses your path,
Do not condemn him . . . praise and understand him.
For he may have been the one . . . who had paid the
Penalty for Freedom . . .
So you may live, and he should die . . .

GLOSSARY

Aetos	Eagle	*Limery*	Den/Hideout/Lair
Agora	Market		
Andartes	Guerrillas	*Mastro*	Master
Aspris	White	*Meze*	Small dishes of food
Autocephalous	Independent	*Moufflon*	Indigenous horned sheep
Ayia	Saint (female)		
Ayios	Saint (male)		
Akamantis	Mythological King	*Ola Kala*	Everything's okay
Apostolos	Apostle	*Ola Skata*	Everything's shit
Agapie mou	My love	*Ouzo*	Alcoholic spirit
Bora	Hurricane/Catastrophe	*Palestra*	Ancient games arena
		Panayia	Virgin Mary
Caique	Narrow boat/Bosporus type	*Papa*	Father
		Petres	Stones
Charon	Death personified	*Pappou*	Grand-dad
Commandaria	Cyprus sherry		
		Salingari	Snail
Effendi	Master	*Scimitar*	Short Arab sword
Eoka	Nat/Org. of Cypriot Fighters	*Souvla*	Morsels on large skewer
Endaxi	Okay	*Styx*	Mythological River of the Dead
Enosis	Union with Greece		
		Tripa	Hole, Opening, Breach
Fait-accompli	Accomplished fact		
Glossa	Tongue	*Volkan*	Underground Turkish Organisation
Gymnasium	Secondary School		
Hallumi	Cypriot Cheese	*Xhi*	Anti-communist movement in Greece
Hanum	Turkish woman		
Hodja	Muslim teacher	*Xenomania*	Obsessive attachment to foreign things
Iconostasio	Icon-stand		
Iman	Head of Muslim law		
Kalimera	Good-morning	*Yiasou*	Hello or Goodbye
Kalinikta	Good-night		
Kalispera	Good-afternoon	*Zivania*	Cypriot alcoholic spirit
Katares	Curses		
Kyria	Madam	*Zenon*	Cypriot stoic

Yiannis' Melody

Hear--- my voi-ce my bro-ther--- Hear--- my ca-ll and rise Life--- is not -- for ev-er---------

------ on - ly a speck in time We have-a-dream-to-share-to free-this-land-of-mine To-gether-we-shall-fight To------

---gether-we-shall-cry but-never-ask-why--For we-must-free-this-land-of mine For we-must-free-this-land-of mine

When I shall call---- your name Reach out and lead---- the way For--- I will be

there--- Hear--- my voi--ce my mo-ther--- Hear--my cri-es and sigh--- Li-fe is not--- for

ev-er---------------- on - ly a speck in time----

340

Printed in the United Kingdom
by Lightning Source UK Ltd.
105634UKS00001B/120